Regulatory Takings

Regulatory Takings: Law, Economics, and Politics

William A. Fischel

Harvard University Press

Cambridge, Massachusetts
London, England
1995

Library of Congress Cataloging-in-Publication Data

Fischel, William A.
    Regulatory takings : law, economics, and politics / William A. Fischel.
        p.   cm.
    Includes bibliographical references and index.
    ISBN 0-674-75388-7 (acid-free paper)
    1. Land use—Law and legislation—United States.   2. Right of property—United
States.   3. Eminent domain—Economic aspects—United States.   4. Police power—Economic aspects—United States.   5. Land use—Law and legislation—California.   6. Eminent domain—California.   I. Title.
KF5698.F573   1995
343.73′0252—dc20
[347.303252]   95-1361
                    CIP

To Janice and Josh

Contents

Preface

This book explores the regulatory takings issue through an eclectic selection of economics, legal scholarship, history, political science, quantitative evidence, and personal experience. The book has two primary audiences. I speak at times especially to my fellow economists and kindred social scientists. Economists are often puzzled by the takings issue. It looks simple at one level, but the legal talk is so complex and arcane that it is hard to penetrate the scholarship. My book thus contains a few more explanations of legal issues and scholarly concepts than a book written solely for lawyers would.

The other and (I hope) larger audience is made up of lawyers who are familiar with the takings issue and who want to hear what an economist has to say about it. If legal scholarship is arcane to economists, much economic writing on takings is for lawyers inaccessibly mathematical and vague about legal institutions. To help the lawyers out, I describe the economics literature in an entirely nontechnical fashion and apply its lessons to real cases. This does not mean that the analysis is conducted on an elementary level. The book explores several issues at the frontiers of applied economics, such as the applicability of the Coase theorem, the effects of land use controls on housing prices, and the relevance of the Tiebout hypothesis.

I came to write this book as a result of my interest in the economics of land use controls. Most of the famous regulatory takings cases involve land use disputes. My 1985 book devoted a couple of chapters to the takings issue. Despite what seemed like generous treatment of an obscure issue, takings remained a persistent enigma to me, and some-time around 1988 I resolved to write a book about it.

I prepared for this undertaking in several ways. The more conventional one was to write articles about economic aspects of the takings issue and local government regulation. During a year-long stay at the University of California at Santa Barbara in 1985–86, Perry Shapiro and I collaborated on two articles that explored the takings issue from an economics perspective. These form the core of Chapters 4 and 5. Richard Brooks, who was then director of the Environmental Law Center at Vermont Law School, and I organized a conference of lawyers and economists in 1988 to discuss three major Supreme Court takings decisions. I wrote the introduction for the conference volume that appeared in the *Columbia Law Review* (1988). To broaden my background on legal issues, I audited courses in constitutional law, property, contracts, and local government at Vermont Law School in 1989–90.

My less conventional preparation was to observe the regulatory process first hand. I have been on the Hanover Zoning Board of Adjustment since 1987 and its chair since 1993. Zoning boards deal with exceptions to regulations that are often the objects of takings litigation, and I have had the experience of having to balance private property rights against community police-power regulations. An important lesson of my zoning board experience is how informative it can be to visit the site at issue. This inspired me to visit a number of locations in which famous regulatory takings cases have arisen to help bridge the gap between theory and practice. The most obvious fruit of my site visits is Chapter 1, which explains how Scranton, Pennsylvania, dealt with the adverse decision in Pennsylvania Coal v. Mahon (1922).

Finally, I spent a year at Boalt Hall Law School in Berkeley during a sabbatical in 1991–92. Most of my law library research was done there, and I absorbed some of the culture of academic law from my friendly and stimulating colleagues. Living in California also gave me another opportunity to observe that state's land use regulations in action. In Berkeley I was able to observe how an activist zoning board and stringent rent controls operate under a court system noted for encouraging regulation.

The preceding preparations alone have left me with a large institutional debt. My sabbatical leave was provided by Dartmouth College, and its Rockefeller Center for the Social Sciences funded a grant to the

Economics Department to enable me to extend my leave for an entire year. The University of California at Berkeley gave me comfortable office space at Boalt Hall, and its Law and Economics Program named me a John Olin Foundation Fellow in 1991–92. I am particularly grateful to Dan Rubinfeld and Robert Cooter for facilitating the visit. I also wish to thank the instructors of Vermont Law School courses, Gil Kujovic, Steve Dycus, and Linda Smiddy, for furthering my knowledge of the substance and culture of law school. Although I have written this book from front to back, some of it draws on parts of previous articles in the *Chicago-Kent Law Review* (Fischel 1991c), *Journal of Legal Studies* (Fischel and Shapiro 1988), *Journal of Economic Literature* (Fischel 1992), and *International Review of Law and Economics* (Fischel and Shapiro 1989; Fischel 1995).

Listing the names of those who commented on draft chapters of my manuscript is apt to suggest their endorsement of the end product, which would often be unwarranted in this controversial area of legal policy. Thus let me carefully note that the following people have provided constructive, though often critical, comments on one or more chapters: David Callies, Robert Ellickson, James Ely, John Hart Ely, Richard Epstein, Charles Haar, Gideon Kanner, Michael Klarman, Douglas Kmiec, Alex Kozinski, Sumner LaCroix, Marc Poirier, Robert Post, Raymond Reinhard, Louis Rose, Susan Rose-Ackerman, Michael Schill, Perry Shapiro, Stewart Sterk, and James Wooten.

Finally, I wish to honor my wife, Janice, and my son, Josh, by dedicating this book to them. As a one-time real estate salesperson and as a current member of the Hanover Planning Board, Janice has given me insights into land use issues as well as uxorial support. Josh has patiently endured my research journeys to California, an itinerary that looks inviting to an adult but is difficult for a youth who is also active in his hometown affairs. I love you both.

Hanover, New Hampshire
December 1994

Regulatory Takings

Introduction

The Fifth Amendment of the U.S. Constitution concludes, "nor shall private property be taken for public use, without just compensation." This is referred to as the Eminent Domain Clause and the Just Compensation Clause as well as the Takings Clause. The regulatory takings issue asks under what circumstances judges should hold that a regulation has sufficiently infringed upon property rights that it amounts to a taking for which just compensation should be paid. The purpose of this book is to seek a viable middle ground between judicial deference to the often unfair regulations that burden property owners and judicial imposition of compensation for every legislative infringement on private rights.

More than any other law and economics issue I have encountered, the regulatory takings issue seems subject to scholarly corner solutions. One "solution," which loosely describes the practical law in most courts, is to regard the Fifth Amendment's command of just compensation as applying only when the government takes title to or physically invades property, as in highway construction or dam building. A new zoning classification that restricts a property's use in such a way that causes losses as great as a partial taking by the highway department is held to be "mere" regulation, with no compensation due. (When "mere" precedes "regulation" in a court opinion, you don't have to read further to know the result.) The regulatory takings doctrine enunciated in the landmark decision in Pennsylvania Coal v. Mahon (1922) is usually held to apply only to those extreme

1

and unusual situations in which the owner is left with no use whatsoever of his property.

I cannot see how law professors who teach property can, at the end of the course (where eminent domain is usually placed), deal with the "mere regulation" doctrine with a straight face. Everything the law student has been taught up to that point indicates that legal "property" is not a clod of earth but a bundle of legal entitlements. Property rights can be sliced up in any number of ways. A private individual who interferes with another's lease, easement, sale, or testamentary disposition of property is liable for monetary damages and subject to injunctive relief. How can the government get away without paying for the many restrictions that it unilaterally imposes? Even the supposed virtue of having a "bright-line" distinction between physical takings and "mere" regulation does not hold up. Governments have occasionally adopted severe regulations that devalued property they coveted and then tried to purchase it by eminent domain at the newly reduced price. If one accepted the bright-line distinction, such a scam would be beyond judicial review.

One response to the embarrassing corner solution of fully compensable physical invasion versus hardly-ever-compensable regulation is to apply private property law's constraints to the government. This requires an exception to permit something that private owners cannot do, namely, to force sales upon payment of "just compensation," but it otherwise puts the government on the same footing as a private individual. Zoning regulations, if allowed at all, would be fully compensable for the loss in value they impose. Of course the regulations may confer benefits from which losses may be deducted, but this rule would put regulations on the same ground as regular eminent domain, in which special benefits conferred by a new road on remaining property are sometimes deducted from compensation paid when only part of the land is expropriated.

The theory of what's sauce for the private goose is sauce for the public gander has received its fullest treatment in a 1985 book by a prolific and influential legal scholar, Richard Epstein. But Epstein's, too, is a corner solution, or nearly so. The corner here is that unelected judges get to call almost all the shots about the economic powers of the state. The Fifth Amendment's Takings Clause would eliminate most of the regulatory initiatives of the twentieth century and quite a few of the nineteenth's, as well. This isn't the conclusion of a critical alarmist. Epstein points it out, and he regards it as a virtue of his analysis.

The problem with Epstein's corner solution is not its internal logic but its view of the functions of courts in a constitutional democracy. By what license are courts of law, presided over by people who are at best indirectly accountable to the electorate, to tell duly elected legislators how to conduct their business?

The question of the legitimacy and efficacy of judicial review informs much of this book. I had originally planned to write a book that dealt with the contributions of economic theory to the takings issue, dressed up with applications to actual cases. Most of the cases involved land use regulations, whose economic effects I had devoted the larger part of my career to examining. But as I proceeded, it occurred to me that there was a tension in my scholarship that would not allow a simple review of court decisions.

I had become impressed with the underappreciated efficacy of local government in delivering local public goods. American localism is not an atavistic structure inherited from fur-trapping forebears, but a widely preferred and generally more efficient way of providing public goods. This sanguine view of local government creates a tension with property rights. One of the necessary conditions for local-government efficiency is the operation of the same local land use regulations that often come under attack in the takings issue.

My sympathy for local government was one reason I had been so curious about a major event that has undermined it, California's famous Proposition 13. This tax-limitation initiative was adopted by two-thirds of the voters in California in 1978. Proposition 13 reduced all local property taxes to less than half their previous level, and, more important, the constraint has not been effectively evaded. Local school districts in particular are now almost completely dependent on the California legislature for their revenues. The sense of self-governance in school districts is nearly gone.

I remained curious about this populist rejection of local government for several years, and in 1989 I finally published an explanation: I submitted that the California Supreme Court decision Serrano v. Priest, which in 1976 effectively insisted on equal spending per pupil across school districts, induced the voters to vote for Proposition 13. California voters had on two occasions prior to 1978 resoundingly rejected statewide initiatives that promised to cut property taxes and leave the state to fund local schools. After the 1976 *Serrano* ruling, however, there was no longer any reason for voters to keep that half of the property tax that funded schools, so they voted to cut their property taxes in half. I later found that the state legislature had realized how angry the voters were about rising property-tax burdens in 1977, but they were unable to provide local property-tax relief because of the court-imposed responsibility to equalize school spending (Fischel 1994a).

I presented an early version of "Did *Serrano* Cause Proposition 13?" to a faculty seminar at Vermont Law School. People found it interesting, but one member of the audience had a question for me. Here I was excoriating judicial activism in economic affairs in my *Serrano* paper, but elsewhere I had criticized the same judges for insufficient activism in the protection of property rights. Where did I stand on judicial review, anyway?

I do think there is a role for judges in the protection of property, but it is more circumscribed than I once thought desirable. Thus the other side of the inquiry, local self-governance, raises the issue of why property needs extra protection in a world in which property is generally well thought of by a majority of people. This book explores that issue on several fronts. My conclusion is that "just compensation" persists because democratic bodies continue to insist on it. They insist on it for political reasons, wanting to spread out concentrated burdens. Thus the real issue for judges is to ask which types of regulatory bodies are apt to impose unfairly concentrated burdens. The nature of politics, rather than the law of property, is the more fruitful line of inquiry.

The advantage of this formulation is that it breaks out of the corner solutions. The normative focus of the judge is a self-conscious question: Why do the litigants need me to decide this? My view is that often they don't need the judges. The litigants in school finance and most regulatory issues need meaningful access to political bodies, and they need some means of mitigating the full brunt of regulatory burdens. Most property owners have both options at higher levels of government. They form interest groups with owners in a similar situation and lobby and logroll in the halls of Congress and state legislatures. These bodies are also aware that owners of property that is elastic in supply may withdraw it if it is overregulated, to the detriment of many of their citizens. This threat of exit is taken seriously at the state and national level. I advance these propositions as theories, and I also explore numerous examples in which legislatures have responded to such concerns.

Things don't work out for property owners when the government structure is loaded against them and they possess an asset that is physically immobile or otherwise inelastic in supply. Local zoning regulations sometimes raise this problem. Much of zoning involves what I regard as an arguably efficient arbitration function. Residents and businesses in already-developed areas often propose changes in established buildings to which their neighbors object. Zoning boards resolve such disputes in ways that seem more or less equitable.

Disputes between owners of undeveloped land and existing residents are another matter, particularly in suburban jurisdictions. The politics in this case often pits a large and well-organized group of existing homeowners against a single prodevelopment landowner, who may not even be a resident. The landowner represents the economic interests of would-be residents of the community, but the political process is skewed against her. In such cases, I submit that increased judicial scrutiny is appropriate. Apartment owners in cities with stringent rent controls would also fit this description. Being an outvoted minority does not, of course, mean that all land use regulations and rent controls should be pilloried by judges under the Takings Clause. It does imply that judges should take a closer look to see that owners subject to regulation are being treated fairly in those situations.

Plan of the Book

The book starts with traditional jurisprudential issues and then proceeds in later chapters to economic issues that have not usually been central to takings scholarship. The overriding theme is that the comparative advantage of constitutional courts in protecting property rights is to intervene when the economic protections of "exit" and the political protections of "voice" are attenuated. The issues of fairness and efficiency that I show underlie the takings issue should otherwise be left to the political branches of the state and federal governments.

Chapter 1 describes in detail the most famous regulatory takings case, Pennsylvania Coal v. Mahon (1922). Using materials that have not previously been applied to the case, I explore the gulf between legal doctrine and practical result. The Kohler Act, whose uncompensated transfer of the right of surface support from mine owners to surface owners was held by Justice Holmes to have gone "too far," in fact was never intended to be enforced. Its primary purpose was to force mine owners to pay a tax and be subject to a regulatory structure that would most likely have passed constitutional review if it had been presented on its own.

More surprising was that the owners of coal mines acted as if they had lost the case instead of winning it. They were not eager to remove coal in such a way as to despoil surface owners, and they agreed to repair the damage that they caused. I submit that the owners did so because of a combination of political, economic, and social pressures from within the community in which most of their managers and employees lived. This example suggests that lower courts and nonjudicial remedies should largely be allowed to determine the course of the takings issue when the impact of regulation is internalized by local residents. In other situations, judges should ask, when a taking is alleged, what standards voters would impose if the economic effects fell on themselves. Such an inquiry should largely be taken up by state courts, which are closer to the action. As I conclude after a review of recent cases in Chapter 1, the proper (and arguably actual) role of the U.S. Supreme Court is to supervise state courts whose political inclinations have been to read the regulatory side of the Just Compensation Clause out of the Constitution.

Chapter 2 reviews the legal and economic principles of eminent domain and the history of its application. I describe American takings law as the product of democratic constitution-making in which citizens wanted to promote development without unfairly distributing its burdens. As an example of the dynamism of takings law, I point to the continual tension over the "public use" doctrine. Constitution writers were vitally concerned that taking be for public use, not just private use. What they meant by public use, however, has always encompassed projects that seem to go well beyond the classic "public goods" of economics.

Historical examples from American railroad building and other public works issues demonstrate that takings have always been a point of contention for people who wanted both an effective government and secure property rights. Fair apportionment of the burdens and benefits created under the power of eminent domain occupied the courts, legislatures, and constitution makers throughout the nineteenth and early twentieth centuries. Concern with fair apportionment should, I submit, be the basis for modern regulatory takings as well.

Chapter 3 places the Takings Clause in a broader theory of constitutional jurisprudence. The Constitution is primarily a document that facilitates self-government of a people spread over the breadth of a continent. I show that the history of the U.S. Constitution demonstrates a concern about majoritarian exploitation of property owners. This concern was most acute in what James Madison characterized as the "small republics" of the states. Judicial anxiety about state infringements on private economic arrangements flowered early in the twentieth century in a doctrine now labeled "economic due process." Judges acting under its authority reversed a great deal of state and some national regulation because they disagreed with the economic policy behind it. I submit that such review was by then inappropriate, because the states were no longer the "small republics" that motivated Madison's concern.

The excesses of economic due process induced a reaction in the 1930s that has gone too far in the other direction, with judges unwilling to apply obvious constitutional doctrines when property interests are concerned. To counter this reaction, I reexamine in Chapter 3 the classic "Footnote Four" of United States v. Carolene Products (1937), which telegraphed the Court's abandonment of economic due process and the rise of the equal protection doctrine and favored rights. I find in Footnote Four a limited but significant role for judges in the protection of property interests. In doing so, I embrace John Hart Ely's "political process" theory of the Constitution, which discourages judges from taking an active role in reviewing the products of properly apportioned, pluralistic legislatures. Judges have a limited capacity to evaluate regulatory regimes and an undemocratic hold on their office. They should normally respect the substitute methods—economic exit and political voice—by which property can be protected by its owners and their allies.

But Chapter 3 also points out situations in which judicial review is required because the assets in question are immobilized and the political process is inexorably majoritarian or highly attenuated by the political isolation of the regulators. The paradigmatic instance of the majoritarian problem is local government land use regulation. Local governments are the modern equivalent of Madison's "small republics." Judicial review in such cases is not undemocratic, but a means of facilitating the power of democracies to commit themselves over time when other disciplines are attenuated.

In Chapter 4, I review the economically oriented theories of the takings issue expounded by Frank Michelman and by Richard Epstein. Michelman's theory provides an indispensable vocabulary for evaluating the question of just compensation. His utilitarian comparison of "demoralization" costs, which arise when compensation is not forthcoming, with "settlement" costs, which arise when it is, provides a general framework that nests the efficiency and equity issues that have historically informed constitutional concerns about takings.

Economists have suggested that Michelman's framework is insufficient because it does not consider the "moral hazard" of property owners subject to takings. Law and economics scholars have emphasized the reciprocal hazards of any rule that makes only one party liable. If landowners are always compensated, some economists say, landowners will carelessly build in front of the highway department's bulldozers. I show in Chapter 4 that Michelman's framework requires only modest modification to accommodate the valid moral hazard problems. I demonstrate that Michelman's theory and the moral hazard modification can provide a coherent justification of such perplexing cases as Miller v. Schoene (1928) and Andrus v. Allard (1979).

Richard Epstein's theory emphasizes property-law applications to takings, and his analogy of the government's obligations to those of private individuals resolves several puzzles in eminent domain law. My conclusion in Chapter 4 is that Epstein's work is flawed by its excessive reliance on judicial review. Most other critics of Epstein are loathe to point this out, since they are in other ways enthusiasts of judicial policy-making. Epstein's work is useful to show the inconsistencies between takings law and property law, but it resolves those inconsistencies in ways that seem irreconcilable with the spirit of democratic self-government that pervades the rest of the Constitution.

Chapter 5 continues the examination of modern economic theories of takings. My judgment on them is mixed. The theory of rational expectations holds that landowners should have seen the taking coming and so should not expect compensation. This is shown by logic and history to be an unsatisfactory extension of a useful positive theory onto thoroughly normative terrain. The insurance rationale for compensation is also rejected as missing the point. Even if just compensation were like insurance, the unaddressed question is, who pays for the insurance?

Somewhat more consistent with takings law are attempts to model the Rawlsian notion of deciding about compensation behind a "veil of ignorance." I describe in Chapter 5 a model that Perry Shapiro and I developed that shows that the type of government that is anticipated by constitution makers makes a difference in the compensation rule they would adopt. This not-too-surprising result indicates that economic theory does not have to lead to recommendations that are completely at odds with long-standing jurisprudential principles of just compensation. Chapter 5 also points out, as have many other works, that compensation at market value for losses is usually less than full compensation. Unlike others, however, I point out that this shortfall has been known throughout American history, yet state constitution makers have nearly always declined to offer more than market value for eminent domain.

Chapters 6, 7, and 8 turn away from constitutions, case law, and economic theories of jurisprudence and ask the economists' nagging question: Does any of this stuff really matter? My later chapters review, without much technical apparatus, evidence for three empirical propositions that are central to my view of takings: (1) takings law does matter, insofar as derogating it induces inefficient and unfair land use regulations (Chapter 6); (2) local government, whose land use regulations often verge on takings, is an important means of democratic self-government that is preferred by Americans for good economic reasons (Chapter 7); and (3) economic exit and political voice are effective means of protecting property rights against the depredations of pluralistic state and national legislatures, but their efficacy is more limited at the local level because of the very characteristics that make local government more efficient (Chapter 8).

Chapter 6 begins with evidence from economic studies of land use controls, especially the literature on capitalization. Many studies show that local regulations can transfer economic value from one class of property owners to another, typically from owners of land with development potential to owners of already-developed properties. This is the classic insider-outsider problem that local governments are especially subject to and that makes them more appropriate objects for judicial review than larger governments.

The more controversial part of Chapter 6 is my detailed review of the handiwork of the California Supreme Court in the 1970s. This was a negative experiment in takings jurisprudence, in that the court systematically suppressed the constitutional protections of private property from regulation. I argue that the California court created a "regulatory commons," in which local governments and even private parties imposed regulations that were undesirable from a regional or statewide point of view. The most visible result of the suppression of the rights of development-minded landowners has been the amazing rise in California housing prices that began in the early 1970s and persists to this day. The extraordinary housing price differential has national efficiency implications, which warrants federal court supervision of the state courts.

Chapter 7 reviews the economic literature on the efficiency of local government and joins it with some of the legal literature on localism's virtues and drawbacks. Local government in the United States has long been an activist in economic affairs within its borders. The tension here is that the Tiebout model, the touchstone of the efficiency of local government, requires land use regulations for it to work well. Both lawyers and economists have long been thoroughly ambivalent about localism. I make a case for accepting much of this regulation as part of a historical evolution in understandings about property. Because I think that property regimes are the product of democratic understandings, I have come to accept much of local zoning—at least that which acts as a substitute for private covenants—as constitutionally valid as well as economically efficient.

Chapter 8 advances the idea that state and national legislatures actually behave differently from local governments. The same regulatory issues are shown to be treated differently by local as opposed to state government. This is the empirical underpinning of my theory of why courts of law must pay more attention to the regulatory takings doctrine at the local level than at the state level. It is not that the states can do no wrong; it is that state politics affords a richer opportunity for owners of property to protect themselves from unreasonable regulations. I use plant-closing laws, billboard regulations, farmland preservation laws, and rent control as actual examples to illustrate the differences between state and local regulation. The rent-control issue is used as a fine-grained example to explore how the threat of capital mobility may or may not discipline local government regulatory excesses.

Chapter 9 combines the empirical propositions advanced in Chapters 6–8 and the theoretical considerations from Chapters 1–5 into a doctrine of regulatory takings. The doctrine focuses largely on local government, where the majoritarian anxiety has been historically most acute, and on the regulation of land, an asset for which the threat of exit or withholding supply is not a viable discipline against unfair regulation. Before developing the apparatus to balance local self-governance with fair treatment of landowners, I gingerly foray into administrative law. If pluralistic politics is the balm that protects landowners from state and national legislative excesses, what if the legislature creates a body that is deliberately insulated from political pressures? I argue, though with less evidence than in the local government case, that regulations adopted by independent agencies ought also to be subject to a higher level of judicial scrutiny than ordinary legislation.

Turning to the more familiar and ubiquitous territory of local government land use regulation, Chapter 9 examines in detail the question of land use exactions. The U.S. Supreme Court has taken an unusual interest in them of late. I show that its recent decision in Dolan v. Tigard (1994) offers a more coherent remedy to takings issues than did Nollan v. California Coastal Commission (1987). I nonetheless think that the rationale for the decision misses the root of the takings problem. Takings law is about the fairness of initial entitlements. Supervising their exchange, as the exactions cases do, does little to cure the burden of the original regulation.

The approach to regulatory takings that makes more sense is a "normal behavior" standard. My rule for balancing local self-governance with regulatory fairness is borrowed from Robert Ellickson's examination of suburban growth controls (1977). He argued for a self-regarding historical standard. If a community has been developed as a mixture of single-family homes on quarter-acre to one-acre lots, then a developer who proposes to do more of the same is presumed to have the right to do so. Downzoning his otherwise similar property to a minimum lot size of three acres should constitute a taking for which compensation should be made.

"Normal behavior" is a variant on the old harm-prevention/benefit-extraction rule. I defend the harm/benefit rule as being consistent with historical takings practice, but I also show why normal behavior is an improvement. It holds that a developer who is denied permission to build something inconsistent with preexisting norms, such as an industrial park or high-rise apartments, should be granted no more than the traditional and deferential "rational basis" review. Reasonable exactions and other developer-community deals should be sufficient to grease the regulatory wheels for such projects. Landowners who are burdened by "supernormal" standards, especially those recently applied, should be compensated for the devaluation caused by downzonings. My chief variation of Ellickson's normal-behavior standard is to apply it to my own experience as a member of a zoning board. I use my own ambivalence about regulatory takings (my board has been sued under the doctrine) to wish the ship of regulatory takings on a cautious but purposive voyage into the twenty-first century.

1

Of Coase and Coal: Regulatory Takings in the U.S. Supreme Court

Pennsylvania Coal v. Mahon (1922) is the original and most-cited Supreme Court decision on regulatory takings. It is known to almost every student of property law. Underground coal mining in the Scranton, Pennsylvania, area was causing homes and other structures on the surface to sink into the earth, sometimes with disastrous consequences. In 1921, the Pennsylvania legislature passed a law that forbade the removal of coal in such a way as to cause surface damage in built-up areas, which effectively prevented the mining of coal in urban areas. The constitutional problem with this law was that most surface owners had purchased their land with explicit notice in their deeds that the coal mining companies were not liable for any above-ground damage they caused. The U.S. Supreme Court held that the legislation was a taking of the coal owners' property for which just compensation was required if the state wanted to enforce the law.

This chapter explores both the legal and the institutional background of *Pennsylvania Coal* that I gathered from research in local sources in Scranton. As the reader already knows from the Introduction, things were quite different from what one would expect from reading the opinion in isolation. The Court's decision was not so much wrong as irrelevant to the long-standing dispute between mine owners and homeowners. The mutual economic dependence of the mine owners and surface dwellers, most of whom worked in the coal industry, led to a resolution of the problem that relied little on formal laws.

The latter part of the chapter briefly reviews several recent regulatory takings cases. The U.S. Supreme Court has revived interest in the doctrine by occasionally allowing the landowner to prevail. I comment on these cases to explain why the Court should not be expected to articulate a well-developed doctrine on regulatory takings. Instead, its mission on regulatory takings can be read as implying two principles. First, individual state courts may not depart so far from the federal takings doctrine as to read it out of their constitutions. Second, the regulatory takings doctrine is most useful as a supplement to eminent domain doctrines when the regulations are adopted by local governments and applied to immovable assets.

1.1 Pennsylvania Coal *Is a Minor Classic*

In order to emphasize the limitations of judicial review, this section reproduces the short majority opinion in the Court's famous regulatory takings case, Pennsylvania Coal v. Mahon (1922), along with my running commentary. It is unusual to reprint widely available opinions in a work of this sort. However, this one is short (unlike most modern opinions), and even seasoned property lawyers may want to compare its version of the facts with the material that I present in my commentary and in subsequent sections. I urge lawyers who are familiar with the decision at least to read my comments. They point out facts that other commentaries have overlooked and that are important for my later story about Scranton.

Pennsylvania Coal is famous partly because the author of the opinion, Oliver Wendell Holmes, Jr., was one of the most highly regarded jurists in history. The opinion is especially compelling because Holmes was prominently opposed to using the Constitution as a shield against business regulation. (His most famous statement of this was his dissent in Lochner v. New York [1905], discussed in section 3.6.) Perhaps because of this seeming inconsistency, *Pennsylvania Coal* is not one of Holmes's most famous opinions among biographers who dwell on his liberal credentials. Sheldon Novick (1989), the author of the first book-length biography of Holmes, did not even mention it. Nor did Holmes's popular hagiographer, Catherine Drinker Bowen (1944), even though her brother, Howard Drinker, was a lawyer for the Pennsylvania Coal Company on the case.

Pennsylvania Coal Co. v. Mahon, 260 U.S. 393 (1922)

Mr. Justice Holmes delivered the opinion of the Court.

This is a bill in equity[1] brought by the defendants in error [the appellees, the Mahons] to prevent the Pennsylvania Coal Company from mining under their property in such as way as to remove the supports and cause a subsidence of the surface and of their house. The bill sets out a deed executed by the Coal Company in 1878, under which the plaintiffs claim. The deed conveys the surface, but in express terms reserves the right to remove all the coal under the same, and the grantee takes the premises with the risk, and waives all claim for damages that may arise from mining out the coal. But the plaintiffs say that whatever may have been the Coal Company's rights, they were taken away by an Act of Pennsylvania, approved May 27, 1921, P.L. 1198, commonly known there as the Kohler Act. The Court of Common Pleas [the state trial court] found that if not restrained the defendant would cause the damage to prevent which the bill was brought, but denied an injunction, holding that the statute if applied to this case would be unconstitutional. On appeal the Supreme Court of the State agreed that the defendant [the coal company] had contract and property rights protected by the Constitution of the United States, but held that the statute was a legitimate exercise of the police power and directed a decree for the plaintiffs.[2] A writ of error was granted bringing the case to this Court.

[1] Although law courts have long been united with equity courts in the United States, terminology such as "equitable relief" sought by a "bill in equity" is used to conjure up requests for injunctions. Monetary damages, the usual remedy for a taking, could not have been sought by the coal company because it had originally been sued by a private party. The Commonwealth of Pennsylvania was not a party to the lawsuit.

[2] The coal company won in the trial court but lost when the case was reviewed by the Pennsylvania Supreme Court. It is significant that the Pennsylvania Supreme Court acknowledged that the coal company had contract and property rights, but such rights were nonetheless trumped by the police power, which economists might call "regulatory authority."

The statute [the Kohler Act] forbids the mining of anthracite[3] coal in such way as to cause the subsidence of, among other things, any structure used as a human habitation, with certain exceptions, including among them land where the surface is owned by the owner of the underlying coal and is distant more than one hundred and fifty feet from any improved property belonging to any other person. As applied to this case the statute is admitted [by the Pennsylvania Supreme Court] to destroy previously existing rights of property and contract. The question is whether the police power can be stretched so far.

[3] Anthracite or hard coal, the object of the Kohler Act, is the clean-burning fuel that was extensively used for home heating before World War II. Most deposits are in the Scranton vicinity, and Pennsylvania was the only supplier in the eastern United States. Bituminous or soft coal, which was not regulated by the Kohler Act or any parallel act at the time, is ubiquitous in western Pennsylvania and in other nearby states. Bituminous coal was largely used as blast-furnace fuel by the steel industry. Because it polluted the air, the use of bituminous was banned in most large cities. In 1915, anthracite sold for about four times the price of bituminous (Richard Mead 1935, p. 14).

> Government hardly could go on if to some extent values incident to property could not be diminished without paying for every such change in the general law. As long recognized, some values are enjoyed under an implied limitation and must yield to the police power. But obviously the implied limitation must have its limits, or the contract and due process clauses are gone. One fact for consideration in determining such limits is the extent of the diminution.[4] When it reaches a certain magnitude, in most if not in all cases there must be an exercise of eminent domain and compensation to sustain the act. So the question depends upon the particular facts. The greatest weight is given to the judgment of the legislature, but it always is open to interested parties to contend that the legislature has gone beyond its constitutional power.

[4] Holmes was willing to cut the government a lot of slack. The diminution in value of the asset affected by a new regulation had to be sizable before the Court would be interested. This off-hand qualification is the source of the "diminution in value test," one of several unweighted criteria by which an attorney can supposedly determine when a regulation becomes a taking.

Far more significant was that Holmes disallowed the argument that *all* property is held under the "implied limitation" of police-power regulations. If this were the case, the police power could be used as a substitute for eminent domain as well as an evasion of the contract clause. Article I, Section 10, of the Constitution lists actions that the states may not commit, which include passing any "Law impairing the Obligation of Contracts." The Due Process Clause of the Fourteenth Amendment says "nor shall any State deprive any person of life, liberty or property, without due process of law. . . ." These limitations on the powers of the states would be empty if the police power were never subject to judicial review.

> This is the case of a single private house. No doubt there is a public interest even in this, as there is in every purchase and sale and in all that happens within the commonwealth. Some existing rights may be modified even in such a case. Rideout v. Knox, 148 Mass. 368. But usually in ordinary private affairs the public interest does not warrant much of this kind of interference. A source of damage to such a house is not a public nuisance even if similar damage is inflicted on others in different places. The damage is not common or public. Wesson v. Washburn Iron Co., 13 Allen 95, 103. The extent of the public interest is shown by the statute to be limited, since the statute ordinarily does not apply to land when the surface is owned by the owner of the coal. Furthermore, it is not justified as a protection of personal safety. That could be provided for by notice. Indeed the very foundation of this bill is that the defendant gave timely notice of its intent to mine under the house. On the other hand the extent of the taking is great. It purports to abolish what is recognized in Pennsylvania as an estate in land—a very valuable estate—and what is declared by the Court below to be a contract hitherto binding the plaintiffs.[5] If we were called upon to deal with the plaintiffs' position alone, we should think it clear that the statute does not disclose a public interest sufficient to warrant so extensive a destruction of the defendant's constitutionally protected rights.

[5] To give further support to his contention that the legislature had gone too far, Holmes also pointed out that Pennsylvania's common law (created by its courts) recognized the obligation of support as a separate estate in land. The relevant estates were the surface estate (owned by Mahon), the subsurface estate (the coal owned by the company), and the support estate (the one the Kohler Act effectively took from the company and gave to Mahon). Each estate was transferable, so in principle a third party could own the right of support.

The "third estate"—the right of surface support—was in fact new. It was first recognized in Penman v. Jones (1917) and was the brainchild of Philip V. Mattes, who wrote the influential briefs for the city of Scranton in *Pennsylvania Coal*. (More on Mattes and *Penman* in section 1.9.) That the right of support is an estate in land was, however, only a matter of rhetorical emphasis for Holmes's opinion. Contract rights were long ago recognized by the Court as property rights that could not be taken without just compensation.

> But the case has been treated as one in which the general validity of the act should be discussed. The Attorney General of the State, the City of Scranton, and the representatives of other extensive interests were allowed to take part in the argument below and have submitted their contentions here. It seems, therefore, to be our duty to go farther in the statement of our opinion, in order that it may be known at once, and that further suits should not be brought in vain.[6]

[6] Working out the broad implications of the case, as Holmes announced he would do here, verges on an advisory opinion, which courts in the Anglo-American tradition are loathe to do. This was why Holmes went out of his way to indicate that broader interests had been represented by attorneys for cities and the state in all the legal proceedings. Mr. Mahon was an attorney who participated on the brief in the Pennsylvania court arguments, and the case was viewed by contemporary Scranton newspaper accounts as a deliberate test of the constitutionality of the law. (The state court brief mentioned that Mahon had purchased the house from his father-in-law, who was an executive of the Pennsylvania Coal Company.) Philip Mattes, who fashioned the legal strategy for the city, said in his autobiography that Mahon had brought the suit at the behest of the company to have the trial located in a favorable jurisdiction (1974, p. 27). Mattes complained that Mahon's allegiance to the coal company complicated the city's legal strategy, but Holmes apparently recognized that the sincere arguments favoring the Kohler Act were briefed by the city and allied parties.

One of the more remarkable readings of this opinion was that of Justice Stevens in the 1987 *Keystone* case (section 1.17). Stevens distinguished the similar issue in *Keystone* from that of *Pennsylvania Coal* by asserting that Holmes was not considering anything more than the Mahons' private home and that the rest of the opinion was "advisory" (480 U.S. at 483–484). Frank Michelman (1988, p. 1600), the doyen of liberal property law, called Stevens's view of Holmes's opinion "amazing," and, more predictably, Richard Epstein (1987, p. 19), leader of the libertarian-conservatives, called it "incredible." I mention this because Justice Stevens seems oblivious to the criticism. He repeated without qualification that *Pennsylvania Coal* was merely advisory in his dissent in a 1994 takings case, Dolan v. Tigard (62 L.W. at 4585; discussed in section 9.14).

> It is our opinion that the act cannot be sustained as an exercise of the police power, so far as it affects the mining of coal under streets or cities in places where the right to mine such coal has been reserved. As said in a Pennsylvania case, "For practical purposes, the right to coal consists in the right to mine it." Commonwealth v. Clearview Coal Co., 256 Pa. St. 328, 331. What makes the right to mine coal valuable is that it can be exercised with profit. To make it commercially impracticable to mine certain coal has very nearly the same effect for constitutional purposes as appropriating or destroying it. This we think that we are warranted in assuming that the statute does.
>
> It is true that in Plymouth Coal Co. v. Pennsylvania, 232 U.S. 531, it was held competent for the legislature to require a pillar of coal to be left along the line of adjoining property, that, with the pillar on the other side of the line, would be a barrier sufficient for the safety of the employees of either mine in case the other should be abandoned and allowed to fill with water. But that was a requirement for the safety of employees invited into the mine, and secured an average reciprocity of advantage that has been recognized as a justification of various laws.[7]

[7] "Average reciprocity of advantage" is another of Holmes's remarks which, along with the previously mentioned "diminution of value," has been invoked in later cases. The law upheld in *Plymouth Coal* (1914) is an unusually tidy example. It required owners of adjacent mines to leave extra pillars of coal in place to assist in protecting the employees in the neighboring mine. Coal was mined underground by the "room and pillar" method. "Pillars" referred to the coal left in place to prevent the mine roof from collapsing as "rooms" were excavated. A pillar could be a column or a wall of coal. Don't think of Greek temples; the volume of pillars was about a third of the coal in the vein.

One coal mining technique involved removing the pillars to get the remaining coal after the rooms were hollowed out. Removing pillars caused more surface subsidence than leaving them in place (hence the

Mahons' complaint), and it also meant that a nearby mine would get less protection from underground flooding (hence the problem in *Plymouth Coal*). Flooding would occur naturally after mine abandonment because most mines required pumps to reduce the water table. Because all coal mine owners got some advantage—safer mines—in return for costly restrictions, there was an average reciprocity of advantage to coal mine owners from the Barrier Pillar Act at issue in *Plymouth Coal* that Holmes thought was absent in the Kohler Act at issue in *Pennsylvania Coal.*

> The rights of the public in a street purchased or laid out by eminent domain are those that it has paid for. If in any case its representatives have been so short sighted as to acquire only surface rights without the right of support, we see no more authority for supplying the latter without compensation than there was for taking the right of way in the first place and refusing to pay for it because the public wanted it very much. The protection of private property in the Fifth Amendment presupposes that it is wanted for public use, but provides that it shall not be taken for such use without compensation. A similar assumption is made in the decisions upon the Fourteenth Amendment. Hairston v. Danville & Western Ry. Co., 208 U.S. 598, 605. When this seemingly absolute protection is found to be qualified by the police power, the natural tendency of human nature is to extend the qualification more and more until at last private property disappears.[8] But that cannot be accomplished in this way under the Constitution of the United States.

[8] The "natural tendency of human nature" is familiar enough to economists. It is the principle of substitution of a cheaper means of accomplishing a goal for the more expensive one. Holmes assumed that legislatures are economically rational. If property can be acquired by police-power regulations, for which no compensation is due, then the legislature is apt to expand the scope of the police power to avoid the expense of acquiring it by eminent domain.

> The general rule at least is, that while property may be regulated to a certain extent, if regulation goes too far it will be recognized as a taking.[9] It may be doubted how far exceptional cases, like the blowing up of a house to stop a conflagration, go—and if they go beyond the general rule, whether they do not stand as much upon tradition as upon principle. Bowditch v. Boston, 101 U.S. 16.

[9] The phrase "goes too far" is also famous, but, like "diminution of value," it gives no guide to how far is too far. Holmes's resort to this

language ought to suggest how difficult it is to formulate a precise policy with respect to regulatory takings. His main purpose was to show that there is *some* limit to police power. (The economic basis for the conflagration rule will be discussed in section 9.19.)

> In general it is not plain that a man's misfortunes or necessities will justify his shifting the damages to his neighbor's shoulders. Spade v. Lynn & Boston R.R. Co., 172 Mass 488, 489. We are in danger of forgetting that a strong public desire to improve the public condition is not enough to warrant achieving the desire by a shorter cut than the constitutional way of paying for the change. As we already have said, this is a question of degree—and therefore cannot be disposed of by general propositions. But we regard this as going beyond any of the cases decided by this Court. The late decisions upon laws dealing with the congestion of Washington and New York, caused by the war, dealt with laws intended to meet a temporary emergency and providing for compensation determined to be reasonable by an impartial board. They went to the verge of the law but fell far short of the present Act.[10] Block v. Hirsh, 256 U.S. 135. Marcus Brown Holding Co. v. Feldman, 256 U.S. 170. Levy Leasing Co. v. Siegel, 258 U.S. 242.

[10] The cases that "went to the verge of the law" upheld rent control and price control during World War I. Holmes wrote the opinion in the Washington, D.C., rent-control case, Block v. Hirsh (1921). He made it clear that the balancing of public interest against private loss favored the public interest when there was a war going on. Most commentators who pounce upon *Hirsh* either to praise or criticize Holmes fail to note that in a case subsequent to *Pennsylvania Coal,* Holmes wrote an opinion remanding a similar Washington, D.C., rent-control ordinance because the war emergency no longer applied (Chastleton v. Sinclair 1924).

> We assume, of course, that the statute was passed upon the conviction that an exigency existed that would warrant it, and we assume that an exigency exists that would warrant the exercise of eminent domain. But the question at bottom is upon whom the loss of the changes desired should fall. So far as private persons or communities have seen fit to take the risk of acquiring only surface rights, we cannot see that the fact that their risk has become a danger warrants the giving to them greater rights than they bought.[11]
>
> Decree reversed.

[11] The phrase from the previous paragraph about "shifting the damages to his neighbor's shoulders" and from this paragraph, "upon

whom the loss of the changes desired should fall," are keys to this opinion. Holmes was not saying that the Kohler Act was irrational. He conceded that where the streets themselves start to cave in, there is a public cost that justifies the use of eminent domain. But merely passing a rationality test, or even a full-scale benefit-cost analysis, does not relieve the government of an obligation to pay in a proper trial. The obligation does not flow from judicial skepticism about a law's rationality, but from a sense that it is unfair to redistribute ownership rights long after their initial establishment.

Holmes's final remark disposed of an issue that some commentators have seized upon, that danger of subsidence unexpectedly increased over time because new technology facilitated removing coal pillars (Carol Rose 1984; brief for Mahons, 260 U.S. at 406). "Pillar robbing" was not a novelty, however. Peter Roberts (1901) reported that it had become a common practice in the early 1890s. It was more likely economics than technology that induced coal companies to "rob out" more pillars. The price of anthracite had doubled between 1911 and 1921 (Mead 1935, p. 14). Whatever the cause of new mining, Justice Holmes dismissed it with a wave of the hand: ". . . we cannot see that the fact that their risk has become a danger warrants the giving to them greater rights than they bought." I discuss in section 1.15 why clear-eyed Scrantonites would have assumed such a risk.

1.2   Brandeis Pointed to the "Nuisance Exception"

The lone dissent in *Pennsylvania Coal,* by Justice Louis Brandeis, is almost as famous as Holmes's majority opinion. Brandeis chiefly argued for what is now called the nuisance exception: if a land use is itself noxious, dangerous, or causes a public nuisance, the legislature is free to regulate its use without compensation, even though the police power may cause great loss to the property owner. Holmes and Brandeis appear to have differed on whether the subsidence regulated by the Kohler Act actually amounted to a public nuisance. Holmes seems to have blithely assumed that there were no spillover effects from the Mahons' prospective damage or the damage to roads and streets, while Brandeis just as blithely assumed that if the legislature said it was a nuisance, it must be so.

Brandeis cited as an example of the Court's deference to legislative autonomy a prohibition case, Mugler v. Kansas (1887). Kansas had adopted, by amendment to its constitution, statewide prohibition of liquor. To make it stick, the state legislature also passed legislation requiring the uncompensated destruction of existing stocks of liquor. The owner of a brewery sought compensation for the destruction of his stock and the devaluation of his property as a result of prohibition. The U.S. Supreme Court held for the state, using language that implied that no exercise of the police power could result in a taking that called for compensation (Catherine Connors 1990; for background on *Mugler*, see section 8.1).

In one sense, *Mugler* was not exceptional. Although from the 1890s to the 1930s the Court was famous for overruling business regulation, even the most conservative of the justices accepted the primacy of the police power to regulate against "public bads," as economists might put it. The Court often upheld laws that caused great devaluation of property if the statutes seemed reasonable to them in this light. For example, in Hadacheck v. Los Angeles (1915), the Court sustained the uncompensated discontinuance of a long-established brick-making factory, a large and acute loss to its owner, who went to jail rather than comply. The formerly isolated brick factory had been engulfed by the sprawling city of Los Angeles, which then rezoned it out of existence. The Court took note of the nuisances of the factory and blandly declared "there must be progress" to discount the notion that new residents could have avoided the nuisance. (Despite this precedent—or perhaps because of Mr. Hadacheck's pathetic stubbornness—modern zoning typically exempts previously established uses from new standards.)

The Holmesian diminution of value standard also did not help a property owner in a later case. In Euclid v. Ambler Realty (1926), decided four years after *Pennsylvania Coal*, the Court upheld a newly adopted zoning law that was alleged to have eliminated three-quarters of the value of Ambler's vacant industrial site by zoning most of it for residential use. Again the Court invoked nuisance analogies, likening nonconforming uses in residential areas to "a pig in a parlor." *Euclid* is chiefly famous as the case in which the Supreme Court approved of the then novel institution of comprehensive zoning. Planners who draw lines between residential and industrial districts have ever since had to put up with the pun of "Euclidean zoning."

How could *Pennsylvania Coal* fit into this pattern of decisions, in which other large losses went uncompensated? Carol Rose (1984,

p. 581) concluded in her reevaluation of the legal materials that the case "turned not on the question of 'too much' taking, but on the fact that the statute transferred rights from one finite class of property owners to another." I think it at least as likely that the Court was influenced by the crisis caused by the shortage of coal for home heating, which the Kohler Act was thought to exacerbate. In any event, I will presently show that the Court's decision in *Pennsylvania Coal* itself probably had no effect on coal mining or the subsidence problem.

1.3   Of Coase and Coal

This section evokes Robert Ellickson's "Of Coase and Cattle" (1986). Ronald Coase, in his famous article (1960), used a hypothetical controversy between an owner of cattle and his neighbors. Coase showed that whether cattle were permitted by law to stray on what cattlemen would call an "open range" or were required by law to be fenced in a "closed range" did not matter for the ultimate allocation of resources if transaction costs were low. If cattle-straying were efficient, the rancher would pay his neighbors to allow his animals to trespass in the closed-range regime, and his neighbors would be unable to pay him to desist if the range were legally open.

Ellickson undertook fieldwork in Shasta County, California, a ranching area in which legal rules had actually been changed from open range to closed, to see if Coase's hypothetical stood up. Ellickson found instead that the legal rules had hardly any bearing on the conduct of the ranchers or their neighbors. Ranchers were expected by unwritten but well-known norms to take care of their animals on open and closed range. Their neighbors used extralegal but carefully measured self-help to discipline ranchers who violated the norms. The variation in legal rules that is the subject of countless scholarly papers in fact controlled no one's behavior.

Inspired by Ellickson's inquiry, I wanted to find out what happened before and after the Kohler Act and *Pennsylvania Coal*. My early thoughts about the outcome were that Scranton and the other anthracite coal cities just had to bear the damage of subsidence. The Mattes brief for the city of Scranton painted a picture of disaster, which has been accepted as the likely outcome of the decision in the legal literature (Bosselman, Callies, and Banta 1973, chap. 8). Indeed, I had often told students that the apparent mayhem wreaked by *Pennsylva-*

nia Coal might explain why the doctrine of regulatory takings was so sparingly applied after the case. I subscribed to this view because I assumed that, as a result of *Pennsylvania Coal,* the companies proceeded as before to mine without regard for surface structures except when the owners had retained the right of support or, even more unlikely, surface owners subsequently purchased the rights of support from the coal owner. I thought the latter option especially unlikely because it seemed highly impractical to acquire pillars of coal beneath buildings at risk, even if the value of the building exceeded the value of the coal in place. What follows is an account of how I discovered that nearly all of my assumptions were wrong.

1.4   Subsidence Was a Problem but Not an Epidemic

In search of an answer to the Ellickson-style questions about *Pennsylvania Coal,* I read several historical accounts of the anthracite coal mining era in Pennsylvania. I was struck by how little was written about the subsidence problem, which was in stark contrast to the picture painted for the Court in the briefs of the city of Scranton. In their study of the anthracite saga, *The Kingdom of Coal* (1985), the historians Donald Miller and Richard Sharpless did not even mention subsidence in the 360 pages of their interesting book. (Professor Sharpless, in a conversation of September 18, 1993, said subsidence was not mentioned because it was not much of an issue.) The issue that occupied them, as well as contemporary accounts in the 1920s, was industrial relations.

Anthracite mining was dominated by seven companies, each vertically integrated with railroad or canal shippers, and anthracite miners were by 1920 one hundred percent unionized. Struggles over the resulting economic surplus resulted in numerous strikes, the longest of which (163 days) ended in September 1922, shortly before *Pennsylvania Coal* was argued before the U.S. Supreme Court. The strike's effect on the supply of anthracite coal made national news, which the Supreme Court must surely have been aware of. The labor strife generated several popular books with titles like *Coal's Worst Year,* by Helen Wright (1924), and *The Anthracite Question,* by Hilmer Raushenbush (1924). The former work mentioned that the federal government began rationing of coal in 1922 as a result of the strike, and the latter leaned toward nationalization of the mines. Neither book mentioned subsidence or the court decision in *Pennsylvania Coal.*

When I visited the Anthracite Heritage Museum near Scranton in December of 1992 and asked the librarian to help me locate works on subsidence, all that was available were technical pamphlets and a few relatively recent (post-1950) newspaper clippings that illustrated some damage. The damage was often dramatic. Pictures show whole houses swallowed up, and reports indicated that lives were sometimes lost, which seemed to belie Holmes's suggestion that notice alone was enough to provide for personal safety. Surface damage nonetheless seems to have been episodic and limited; cities were not literally falling into the earth. Nor did any of the newspaper stories raise the question of legal liability for surface support. The men who worked in the mines experienced far greater disasters, on which there was a vast literature. Anthracite coal mining in its heyday claimed more than five hundred lives a year.

1.5 New Technology Facilitated Coal Remining

The lack of attention to subsidence raised the question of whether the decision in *Pennsylvania Coal* had the effect that the Kohler Act's advocates said it would. The Scranton brief (1922, pp. 25–26) by the city attorney, Philip Mattes, warned, "if the law is destroyed, we are returned once more into the feudal ages. . . . The Kohler Act is our sole protection against a new campaign of ruthless mining . . ." But the Mattes brief is by an attorney who in fact drafted the Kohler Act and its companion, the Fowler Act. (The Scranton *Times* of April 27, 1921, referred to the two acts as "the Mattes bills.")

I found a different perspective in a work in the Lehigh University library, *Reflections of an Anthracite Engineer,* by George E. Stevenson. The book was privately published in 1931, but most parts had previously appeared in a Scranton newspaper (the *Republican*) in the late 1920s. Stevenson worked as a consulting engineer in Scranton from 1897 to 1930, and he described in detail many of the problems at issue in *Pennsylvania Coal*. He knew the case well, but he did not serve as a consultant to either side, for reasons that will become apparent.

Stevenson's account and several other sources showed that much more could be done about subsidence than I had once supposed. When anthracite coal was initially extracted on a large scale in the mid-1800s, only large chunks of it were sold. Smaller pieces ended up in refuse dumps that became vast, artificial mountains called culm banks. Around 1891, a new "wet preparation" technology made it practicable to reclaim the leftover, smaller pieces of coal. Smaller coal sizes had become valued in the home-heating trade, and many of the great culm banks were reprocessed.

The remaining refuse from the culm-bank recycling as well as from wet-preparation processing of newly mined coal was combined with water and pumped back into the mines, a process misleadingly called "flushing." The purpose of flushing old mines was to provide roof support (Peter Roberts 1901, p. 221). The water would drain off, and the dry refuse would fill up the vacant "rooms" beneath the surface. The added support allowed much of the remaining pillars of coal to be extracted (Stevenson 1931, p. 30; U.S. Bureau of Mines 1912). Thus it appears that well before the 1920s it was both possible and economical to reduce the threat of surface subsidence by reinserting waste material into mines. This also casts doubt on the idea that a new technology that allowed old mines to have their pillars taken out was in fact responsible for more subsidence. The support from the coal pillars was often replaced by the detritus put in place by flushing and sometimes by more labor-intensive constructions.

Stevenson gave an account of the events that led to the Kohler Act. The initial impetus for mine-subsidence legislation was the extensive damage done by subsidence to a schoolhouse in West Scranton on August 28, 1909, barely a week before school was to begin. The near-catastrophe galvanized local citizens to form the Surface Protective Association.

Stevenson was a consultant in the investigation of the schoolhouse subsidence. His recollection illustrates the complexity of the problem. The school district had assembled the school lot from several parcels, most of which did not have the right of support. Most of the building, however, was positioned over land whose deed required that miners leave one-third of the coal in place. Beneath the property were eleven separate veins of coal, a situation common in Scranton. ("Vein" is a misleading term; coal was deposited in broad layers of various thicknesses beneath the entire city, rather like the icing in a sloppily made torte.) Several of the veins beneath the schoolhouse had been mined. Inspectors were unable to determine whether the terms of the deed had been violated by the Peoples Coal Company, which had done the most recent mining. Stevenson said that no legal action was brought against Peoples Coal.

1.6 *Surfaces Could Be Protected by Coasian Bargaining*

The new Surface Protective Association began to agitate on several fronts to forestall subsidence. As a result of its efforts, a state commission was formed to investigate the issue, including the legal rights of support. George Stevenson testified before the commission that "continued mining of anthracite in Scranton is vital to Scranton's growth and prosperity" (1931, p. 49), a sentiment widely shared, according to newspaper stories. To reassign liability for damages without compensation would be, according to Stevenson, a "gross injustice to the owner of the coal."

Then Stevenson (1931, pp. 49–50) went on to state a close approximation of the Coase theorem in his testimony:

> As an economical proposition it seems to me that where the present value of the surface and improvements is less than the present value of the coal beneath the surface, and it is necessary to sacrifice the surface and improvements in order to win the coal, or sacrifice the coal and cease mining it in order to save the surface and improvements, that the matter of which shall be sacrificed resolves itself into a question of value only.

So far, of course, this was only a statement about the conditions for economic efficiency. But Stevenson immediately showed how efficiency could be obtained by bargaining:

> The area overlying the anthracite coal fields in which the surface and improvements are of greater value than the mineral yet to be won beneath the surface is comparatively small as compared to the area where the coal is of greater value than the surface and improvements, and it does seem that the owners of the surface, and the owners of the mineral, and the municipality might, by agreement, in these restricted localities, work out a system of artificial support of the surface that would insure protection at a cost that would warrant such a plan to be put into operation.
>
> It is self-evident that where the surface values and improvement would not equal the cost of artificial support, that it is idle to talk of sacrificing the more valuable mineral beneath the surface to save the less valuable surface and improvements. (1931, p. 50)

This was only half of the Coase theorem. Stevenson had asserted that it was possible for surface owners to purchase the support estate when the value of their buildings exceeded the value of coal. He did not point out, since it was not at issue and was perhaps self-evident to him, the other half: mineral owners could purchase support rights from surface owners in the event that mineral owners did not already possess the support rights (an uncommon situation) and the value of coal exceeded the value of surface improvements. That addition would have made the full Coase theorem. The initial owner of the right of support (Pennsylvania's "support estate") was irrelevant to the final use of the land.

In true Coasian spirit, however, Stevenson did point out in the passage just quoted that transaction costs were apt to be low, insofar as the area on which surface improvement exceeded the value of coal was relatively small. (Scranton was built over layers of coal, but the coalfields were far larger than the city.) A few paragraphs later, he implicitly recognized that holdouts might be a problem in purchasing support rights beneath a system of public streets, so he allowed that this might be facilitated by "an extension or broadening of the right of eminent domain, bearing in mind always that the owner of private property cannot be deprived of that ownership for public use without due compensation" (Stevenson 1931, pp. 50–51).

1.7 Nonlegislative Agreements Protected Surface Structures

Two years later, in 1911, the Pennsylvania Mine-Cave Commission issued a report that offered a compromise concerning rights. It recommended legislation that surface-support disputes be subject to arbitration prior to appeal to the courts and that companies be required to give sixty days' notice prior to mining beneath surface land they did not own. It also provided that maps of mines be made public.

More remarkable were the nonlegislative agreements that the commission obtained. As long as the state or municipality refrained from legislation restricting company rights, the companies agreed to protect all public highways and streets. In addition, Stevenson reported (p. 52) a condition seemingly contrary to his hard-line Coasian position that value alone was to determine use: "The companies were to pay the cost of repairing all dwellings damaged by mining having a value of $5,000.00 or less." (This happened only after 1917; the original agreement called for paying only 50 percent of the cost up to $5,000, according to the Scranton *Republican,* May 28, 1921, p. 19.) "Whenever the danger of surface subsidence is imminent," Stevenson said, "the companies agreed . . . to sell for a fair consideration to owners of structures exceeding $5,000.00, such pillar coal as they may reasonably desire to purchase for the support of said structures. The price of this coal was later fixed at 35¢ a ton." (Coal in place at the time was selling at nearly $1.00 a ton, so even the populist Scranton *Times* conceded that it was a bargain [March 1, 1913, p. 6].)

To show that the latter solution was workable, Stevenson described a transaction made under it. He assisted in the purchase of coal in place beneath land "occupied by large industrial and public utility concerns" for "more than $100,000." Along with some flushing and backfilling of mines that had already been opened up beneath the surface, Stevenson claimed that these precautions prevented all future subsidence at the site.

The foregoing account puts the Kohler Act in a much different light than most scholars seem to have regarded it. By a combination of threats of legislation and, I will demonstrate, some degree of mutual interest, almost all of the apparent goals of the Kohler Act seem to have been accomplished prior to its passage. Few homes in Scranton were valued at more than $5,000, so most owners got their protection for free. (The U.S. Coal Commission [1925, p. 14], said that a good-quality house in the Scranton area rented for $20 per month, a rent that would justify a purchase price on the order of $2,000.) Besides appealing to popular sentiment, the companies' donation to small-holders kept transaction costs down, since providing support for one small lot also provided support for its neighbor. For the more valuable properties, Stevenson made it clear that purchasing or repurchasing support rights was perfectly feasible.

The example that Justice Holmes used to illustrate public shortsightedness, municipal failure to purchase support rights for streets, seems to have been effectively donated by the coal companies. Although some of this donation must have been conciliation in the face of legislation, it seems likely that part of the agreement resulted from a desire to promote community safety that worked indirectly to the companies' advantage. One might even call it an "average reciprocity of advantage."

1.8 Peoples Coal Defaulted on the Agreements

Why, then, did the "extremists," as Stevenson called the members of the Surface Protective Association, continue to press for mine-subsidence legislation, and eventually prevail in passing the Kohler Act?

Here we have to turn from Stevenson to accounts by John Beck (1986), Philip Mattes (1928), and contemporary newspapers. Both Beck and Mattes were considerably less sympathetic to the companies than Stevenson, but they acknowledged that voluntary agreements had been reached as a result of the efforts of the Surface Protective Association, largely confirming Stevenson's account. The voluntary agreements did not forestall opportunistic activity, however. On February 3, 1919, a major subsidence occurred without warning. "Whole rows of buildings in the heart of Hyde Park [a section of Scranton] collapsed; sidewalks were upended; sewer, gas, and water lines burst" (Beck 1986, p. 98).

The Peoples Coal Company, which had probably caused the school-house collapse in 1909, was found, after a year's detective work, to be deliberately robbing pillars of coal in its Oxford Colliery beneath Hyde Park. The company's mining was contrary to the 1917 voluntary agreements and, more important, contrary to a court injunction. At least some surface deeds in Hyde Park had legal support rights (*New York Times,* March 12, 1920, p. 1). Dramatic police work in what is locally called the "Battle of Oxford" finally uncovered the company's subterranean larceny. Several people connected with Peoples Coal, including a consulting engineer named George E. Stevenson, were arrested, the last for "disorderly conduct and making threats" (*New York Times,* March 11, 1920). According to the Scranton *Times,* Stevenson roughed up the mayor of Scranton, who had entered the Oxford mine along with the police and a band of reporters (March 10, 1920). Stevenson, a Quaker by birth, made no reference to the event in his *Reflections.*

A year later, three officers of the Peoples Coal Company (not including Stevenson, who was a consultant) were fined $250,000, an amount determined by the cost of repairing surface damage and replacing sub-surface pillars (*New York Times,* May 10, 1921, p. 19). Unfortunately, Peoples Coal, which leased rather than owned coal rights, seems to have been judgment proof. One of the company officers fled the state and the other two went to jail because they could not pay the damages. According to Beck, "the more significant result of the battle was the Kohler and Fowler acts, passed in 1921 amidst legislative disruptions almost as dramatic as the battle itself" (1986, p. 98).

To supplement accounts that were sometimes colored by partisanship, I spent three days examining the (unindexed) Scranton *Times* of this period. (The *Times* was an advocate of the Surface Protective

Association, but its major stories jibed with those of the rival *Republican,* which editorially favored the more moderate antisubsidence measures of the Scranton Board of Trade.) From this perusal, I found that mine subsidence was a long-standing issue in the Scranton area, and that the Surface Protective Association had more or less continuously urged state legislation to do something about it.

The voluntary agreements of 1911 were initially greeted as a great breakthrough, but the surface owners constantly lobbied for more concessions and more legislation. Both the state legislature and the mine owners responded positively but grudgingly. In 1913 the governor approved a bill (the Davis Act) protecting public highways from subsidence, a condition already conceded by the coal companies under the continuing negotiations with surface protection groups. The governor vetoed a bill that would have extended the same protection for private homes, however. Another round of voluntary agreements in 1917 established the previously mentioned promise of repairs to homes valued at $5,000 or less (Mattes 1928, p. 374).

The other point I gleaned from newspaper accounts was that the Peoples Coal Company was responsible for most of the major subsidence damage (Scranton *Times,* April 27, 1920; July 30, 1909). It was truly a rogue company. Not only did Peoples violate the informal agreements; it also violated the law by taking coal that was specifically reserved for support. The catastrophic damage that virtually every account of the Kohler Act points to was largely caused by a single, outlaw company. I do not mean to say that no other companies caused subsidence damage. But damage by others appears to have been much less frequent, and the companies involved appear to have honored the informal agreements to repair damaged property.

1.9   The "Mattes Bills" Involved Taxes as Well as Regulation

The Kohler Act was not an isolated piece of legislation. It was passed at the same time and in tandem with a tax measure called the Fowler Act. The Scranton newspapers indicate that both bills were written in Scranton by the city solicitor, Philip Mattes.

Mattes was clearly the right man for the job. He had previously secured the right of support for much of the downtown area in Scranton using a legal argument that would have been worthy of his Philadelphia brethren. A coal company had in 1873 sold to developers the surface rights to what later became Scranton's downtown, but it expressly reserved the coal and the right of support. The company later transferred its mineral rights to a subsidiary company. But in the transfer, the conveyancer forgot to mention specifically the right of support that went with the mineral rights.

By inventing the theory of a severable "third estate" (the right of support), Philip Mattes argued that the right of support had remained with the original company, since support was not mentioned in the transfer to its subsidiary, and it was specifically withheld from surface owners. When the original company that had supposedly forgotten to transfer the right of support went bankrupt, its assets were transferred to a bankruptcy trustee. The trustee, a Scranton bank, was willing to sell for a small price the support rights to surface owners of the downtown area, which thus was protected. The Pennsylvania Supreme Court upheld this creative theory in Penman v. Jones (1917). (The dubious logic of the decision was criticized in a famous article by Wesley Hohfeld [1917], who did not consider that the Pennsylvania Supreme Court may have eagerly swallowed a theory that extricated much of the state's third-largest city from the hazard of subsidence.)

Mattes's more ambitious task in 1922 was to protect other Scranton surface owners whose deeds clearly surrendered the right of support. His invention of the "third estate" in *Penman* actually made the task more difficult by highlighting the state's recognition of the right of support. The Kohler Act's injunctions against causing urban subsidence stood out clearly as transferring the third estate from mine owners to surface owners. However, there was a peculiar exception to the act's provisions that, among modern scholars, only Lawrence Friedman (1986) noticed from reading Pennsylvania Justice Kephart's dissent in Mahon v. Pennsylvania Coal (1922). The Fowler Act, adopted on the same day as the Kohler Act, enacted a tax on anthracite coal. It was not an ordinary tax, though. Coal mining companies did not have to pay it *unless they wanted relief from the obligations of the Kohler Act.*

The Fowler Act's tax applied to all anthracite mined by a company in the state. The tax revenue was earmarked by the Fowler Act to set up a "mine-cave commission." The commission would regulate mining and compensate surface owners and municipalities in the anthracite mining area of Pennsylvania (nine counties around Scranton) who were damaged by mining operations. At a rate of 2 percent on all sales of coal, the tax would generate a considerable amount of revenue.

The reader may find it peculiar that the Fowler Act's "tax" should really amount to a payment for an exception to the newly imposed regulatory burdens of the Kohler Act. But that is exactly what it was. We regard this as peculiar today because we now think of the state government as being able to tax almost anything it wants. Before the 1930s, however, many courts were less deferential to legislative classification. The 1921 Pennsylvania legislature apparently felt compelled to make the Fowler Act's tax optional, that is, payable only if the mining company sought an exception to the Kohler Act, because of a state constitutional issue.

The state legislature had in 1913 passed a tax on anthracite coal (and not on bituminous coal) to obtain money to fix subsidence damage. The tax was struck down by the Pennsylvania Supreme Court in Commonwealth v. Alden Coal (1915). The Pennsylvania court in *Alden Coal* said that the tax was contrary to provisions in the 1873 state constitution requiring uniform taxation and banning special legislation. Similar constitutional limitations were adopted by almost all states in the nineteenth century (Lynn Baker 1994).

In order to induce the coal companies to pay the Fowler Act's "optional" tax, the Kohler Act had to involve obligations that were more extreme than those informally agreed to by the coal companies (Scranton *Times,* Dec. 11, 1922). The feature of the Kohler Act that seems to have done this was its remedy of private injunction, the source of the controversy in *Pennsylvania Coal.* Mr. Mahon sought an injunction against the coal company to prevent mining beneath his house. If the company wanted to lift the injunction, it would have to agree to pay the tax, not just on coal it mined beneath Mahon's land, but on all coal it mined in Pennsylvania. By this method the drafters of both acts apparently hoped that the Pennsylvania courts would regard the Fowler Act taxes as not amounting to an unconstitutional special tax. (Aficionados of modern land use cases might thus characterize *Pennsylvania Coal* as an exactions case involving unconstitutional conditions, as discussed in section 9.13.)

1.10 The Legislature Wanted to Tax Anthracite but Not Bituminous Coal

The Pennsylvania legislature could have avoided judicial review of anthracite taxes simply by taxing both anthracite and bituminous coal at the same rate. It did not want to do this. It was not that bituminous mining caused less surface damage than anthracite mining, although there appears to have been no large city underlain with bituminous coal in the same way that Scranton was underlain with anthracite. The main reason for discriminating was that Pennsylvania enjoyed a monopoly on anthracite production, so that out-of-state buyers could not switch to other sources of supply, while bituminous coal was mined extensively in nearby states.

Because many cities banned the burning of the smoky bituminous coal, demand for anthracite was inelastic. Much of the burden of the regulation and tax would thus be shifted forward to consumers in other states. This inference is supplemented by the candor of the Pennsylvania governor at the time the Fowler and Kohler Acts were passed. As the U.S. Supreme Court noted in *Heisler* (discussed in section 1.11), the governor urged passage of the anthracite tax because the burden would largely fall outside the state (260 U.S. at 258). This view was widely shared (Scranton *Times,* April 21, 1921).

The possibilities of tax exporting were not lost on the rest of the state, either. In April 1921, the same month that the Kohler and Fowler Acts were passed, the legislature passed a separate tax on anthracite to be used as a general source of state revenue. Just why they passed a tax that had been previously declared unconstitutional in *Alden Coal* is not clear. Perhaps they thought that changes in the makeup of the state supreme court would yield a different decision. (If so, they were right.) The state tax, instituted by the Williams Act, collected 1½ percent of the value of all anthracite coal shipments.

When the Williams Act was being considered, the "Anthracite Block"—the legislators from the nine anthracite-producing counties around Scranton—tried to divert half the act's revenues to their counties to pay for subsidence damage. (They had been successful in this previously, but the entire tax had been struck down in the 1915 *Alden Coal* decision.) When the group's efforts failed to give any but vague assurances of future consideration of its needs, the Anthracite Block tried unsuccessfully to defeat the 1921 Williams bill. The Scranton-area legislators were sensitive to the fact that demand for coal was not perfectly inelastic. They also worried that the Williams bill, which was adopted, would make it more difficult to pass the Kohler and Fowler Acts.

It was a close call. The lobbying for the Kohler and Fowler bills was intense, and the depredations of the Peoples Coal Company were widely (and erroneously) publicized as being the norm for all companies. Still, the bills were bottled up in committees by chairmen who were favorable to the coal companies. Then a political miracle happened: the Speaker of the House was ousted near the end of the session for reasons unrelated to the coal mine bills. The Anthracite Block seized the lapse of legislative discipline to push its bills to the floor and had them passed.

Governor Sproul then took his time before signing the Kohler and Fowler Acts. He was constantly lobbied by both sides, and the coal companies came up with their largest concession yet: they would agree to be responsible for all surface subsidence that they caused, with no limit on financial liability. Given this concession, the mine owners' resistance to the bills can only be attributed to the size of the Fowler Act taxes and the prospect of having to deal with the proposed mine-cave commission.

1.11   Mine Companies Fought the Tax and the Regulation

The coal mining companies contested the Williams Act (statewide taxes) and the Kohler Act (and by implication, the Fowler Act's earmarked taxes) separately in the courts. In Mahon v. Pennsylvania Coal (1922), the Pennsylvania Supreme Court upheld the Kohler Act. This was a victory for the surface owners, but it turned out not to be critical. What the surface owners had hoped was that the Fowler Act would be distinguished from the previously unconstitutional anthracite taxes by its "voluntary" nature. Instead, the Pennsylvania court gave the surface owners an even bigger victory. In Heisler v. Thomas Colliery (Pa. 1922), the Pennsylvania Supreme Court simply ignored the contrary precedent of *Alden Coal* and upheld the Williams Act's taxes in language that appeared to make the Kohler Act unnecessary to get the companies to pay the Fowler Act's taxes.

Both decisions were appealed to the U.S. Supreme Court. The challenge to the Williams Act's anthracite tax in *Heisler* involved equal protection and the Commerce Clause. Several states that were importers of Pennsylvania anthracite sided with the coal companies in opposing the Williams Act tax. The U.S. Court unanimously sustained the tax. The only reversal for the surface owners was *Pennsylvania Coal*. This decision brought down the Fowler Act along with it, since the only reason coal companies had to pay the Fowler Act taxes was to escape the Kohler Act.

The sustaining of the Williams Act's anthracite tax in *Heisler*, however, altered the legal landscape. The Scranton *Times* noted a few days after the U.S. Supreme Court decision in *Pennsylvania Coal* that all was not lost. Because the courts would now sustain an anthracite tax, all the city needed to fund the Fowler Act was to go back to the state legislature and seek a new tax. They did not need the Kohler Act to force the coal companies to pay it, since the state constitution was no longer a bar to an anthracite tax.

Within a year, the Anthracite Block had in fact persuaded the state legislature to earmark half of the taxes collected under the Williams Act for the anthracite region. But now they encountered a different roadblock. Gifford Pinchot, the new Republican governor of Pennsylvania, decided that the state could not afford to forgo the tax revenues for general state expenditures, and he was unwilling to raise the rate of taxes on anthracite (Scranton *Times,* July 13, 1923). He therefore vetoed the bill. A later attempt to revive the Fowler Act with another tax was also vetoed. (Readers familiar with the history of the conservation movement will recognize Governor Pinchot as one of its leaders.) The coal companies did pay the Williams Act's taxes, their constitutional attacks on it having been again rebuffed by the Pennsylvania Supreme Court in Commonwealth v. Hudson Coal (1926).

1.12 *Mine Owners' Behavior Was Not Affected by* Pennsylvania Coal

The coal companies' victory over the Kohler Act was hollow because they had lost big on the tax issue in *Heisler*. The reader might suppose that the companies would turn their victory in *Pennsylvania Coal* to their advantage by taking more coal than had been allowed under the former voluntary agreements. The Kohler Act, after all, represented a defection from the terms of at least one of the voluntary agreements, which was predicated on the Surface Protective Association's foregoing agitation for legislation. Most coal companies had shut down operations during its test, although it is not clear whether this was a political strategy or simply tax avoidance. Yet apparently the companies did not press their victory in *Pennsylvania Coal.*

In a brief *New York Times* article immediately following its story about the U.S. Supreme Court decision, the president of the Lehigh Valley Coal Company declared: "The company has always repaired the property so damaged or recompensed the owner, and despite today's decision, that policy will be continued" (Dec. 12, 1922, p. 29). It appeared that at least one major company was willing to return to the agreements. The Scranton *Times* of December 11 reported this concession by virtually every coal mine company, including the Pennsylvania Coal Company itself. Mr. Mahon's house was apparently not in jeopardy, even if his had not been a friendly suit.

Yet one might wonder whether the coal companies' statements were sincere. Did profit-making companies really go back to supporting the surface owners after Justice Holmes had said they had no obligation to do so? After all, Philip Mattes had said that "Scranton bid fair to become a second Verdun, her buildings razed to the ground by shots from below" (Mattes brief 1922, p. 5). Would companies described as "ruthless" forswear their "pound of flesh," to invoke the metaphor Mattes used more than once in his brief?

I obtained my first evidence on this from a telephone interview on June 28, 1993, and a visit on October 2, 1993, with Mr. E. Stewart Milner of Scranton. His continuous career with the Pennsylvania Coal Company began in 1926, and he worked his way up to chief engineer in 1961. He became its vice-president in charge of Pennsylvania properties in 1975, after the company had moved to Ohio, and he has been a consultant and the keeper of the company's anthracite property records since the company dissolved in 1977. (Michael Miller, a Vermont Law School student from Scranton, gave me Mr. Milner's name after I wondered aloud in class what had happened after *Pennsylvania Coal.*)

Mr. Milner responded with a clarity that belied his eighty-four years to my questions of how the Pennsylvania Coal Company had treated the problem of surface subsidence in the period after *Pennsylvania Coal.* He said that if the company caused subsidence to any surface structure, it sent a crew up to fix the damage, at company expense. It did not matter to whom the right of support belonged, although it typically belonged to the company. When I asked why the company repaired properties that it had no legal obligation to support, he explained that it was just good public relations.

Mr. Milner went on to say that subsidence prevention measures, which were part of his job in planning new mines, were the same regardless of surface support liability. He volunteered that this practice had gone on at least since his earliest employment with the company, up to the 1960s, when the company quit mining in the region. The formal disclaimer of liability for subsidence, which is spelled out in capital letters in each of the company's deeds issued to surface owners, apparently did not matter in the company's precautionary measures. These measures were taken not because of the Kohler Act or *Pennsylvania Coal* (neither of which Mr. Milner was familiar with), but because the company simply assumed liability. Thus the informal practices that predated *Pennsylvania Coal* seem to have continued, at least by the company whose name now stands for the constitutional right to do the exact opposite of what it actually did.

1.13 *Philip Mattes Agreed that* Pennsylvania Coal *Had Little Impact*

Scholars with whom I initially shared the foregoing intelligence were impressed with Mr. Milner's recollection but still a little skeptical. Shouldn't I have asked someone not connected with the coal companies how they behaved? On a return trip to Scranton in March of 1994, I happened to see a law office near the library on which one of the partners was listed as Philip V. Mattes III. I went in and introduced myself to Roger Mattes and Roger Mattes, Jr., the son and the grandson of the author of the Fowler and Kohler Acts. (Philip III was not there.) Both Rogers are attorneys, and they took in good humor my ironic remark about the pictures of coal breakers—huge structures in which coal was processed—on their office walls. They showed me a privately printed autobiography (1974) by their illustrious ancestor, who had died on December 23, 1979, at age ninety-two. Here is what the senior Philip Mattes wrote of his 1922 loss:

> It might be supposed that the victors would cash in on their expensive victory by mining out their pillar coal in all areas covered by the decision. But the absentee management of the mines had gradually been shifted into local hands who were not insensitive to an aroused public opinion. The statement of Governor Sproul [who signed the Kohler and Fowler Acts], the opinion of Chief Justice Moschzisker [who upheld the acts in the state court], the elections of public officials [the founder of the Surface Protection Association had been elected mayor in 1922], the delegations to Harrisburg, the editorials in the press, all played their part in convincing management that the time had come to forego reaping the last gleanings from the rich fields that had paid them so handsomely in the past.

A policy of repairs and compensation to surface owners that had been gradually taking shape to a limited extent was widened and made more acceptable. More important, surface damage was minimized, large sections of the mine workings were abandoned, the pumps were stopped, the gangways were flooded, mining titles were taken over by the public authorities through tax sales and the mine-cave issue largely faded from the scene. (1974, pp. 27–28)

Mattes had also reviewed the mine-subsidence issue in an earlier article for a local-history book (1928). Perhaps still smarting from his 1922 loss, he gave a somewhat disingenuous account of the Fowler Act, saying that coal companies were to finance it by "voluntarily contributing" to a fund, rather than admitting that they were practically forced to do so by the Kohler Act. Nonetheless, at the end of his article, Mattes concluded that by the late 1920s all of the companies "left little or nothing to be desired in their handling of the problem. . . . Even the 'scavenger operators' recognizing the new situation [of local cooperation] and, with only an occasional flare-back into the old 'public be damned' attitude, followed the lead of the larger companies" (1928, p. 380).

The decline in mine subsidence as an issue was also recorded in the annual reports of the Scranton Public Works Department, within which was located the Bureau of Mine Inspection and Surface Support. The 1923 report indicated that mining companies were now cooperating with the city, and that flushing and packing had been undertaken to prevent subsidence in certain areas. (It did not say who paid for it.) The 1926 report indicated that there had been 125 instances of subsidence, most of them of a "mild character," such as potholes. The 1927 report was not so optimistic. It criticized an uncooperative and opportunistic operator called the "Fair Coal Company." By 1928, however, the bureau noted a "sharp and distinct decline in mine caves" despite normal production of coal. It also concluded, as had almost all other observers, that some subsidence was inevitable, since mining beneath Scranton was still essential to the city's prosperity.

Subsidence became less important as the anthracite industry faded after World War II. It had peaked during World War I and was already declining perceptibly in the late 1920s. Demand for anthracite was not as inelastic as the proponents of anthracite taxes had supposed. Petroleum, natural gas, and other innovations gained market shares for domestic heating, particularly after the lengthy anthracite strikes of

1922 and 1925 (Mead 1935, p. 91). Concern about demand was such that in 1930 the state repealed the special anthracite tax (the Williams Act) that had been adopted in 1922, with Representative Henry Fowler (of the ill-fated Fowler Act) leading the fight for repeal.

Fowler, who was also a United Mine Workers official, did not attempt in 1930 to divert any of the tax revenue for subsidence relief as he had earlier. By then he may have been more worried about preserving jobs than obtaining local tax revenue. Not that it did much good. Total anthracite production in 1950 was half of its 1920 peak, and by 1970 anthracite production was one-fifth of 1950's. Today most of the existing supply is taken from a few strip mines. There are no underground mines now operating in the Scranton area.

1.14 Pennsylvania Coal *Probably Made Little Difference*

My research does not give a comprehensive picture of the subsidence issue in Pennsylvania. That it continued to be a problem is suggested by the many laws passed by the state legislature after the 1920s and upheld by the courts without much concern for *Pennsylvania Coal* (Klein v. Republic Steel 1970; Wright v. Buckeye Coal 1981). What I do maintain is that the decision in *Pennsylvania Coal* made much less of a difference for Scranton's problems than one would think from reading the case.

If the Kohler Act had been upheld, the anthracite communities would have gotten earmarked taxes from the Fowler Act, and the commission that it set up would have supervised further mining under the city. The taxes would not, however, have been a net addition to the status quo. With tax money available to provide support, the mining companies themselves would have reduced their own repair and compensation practices. Indeed, this response was anticipated by Mattes's Scranton brief (1922, p. 28) in favor of the Kohler and Fowler Acts.

What would have been different was the availability of funds to repair damage done by the Peoples Coal Company, which was bankrupt. Other coal companies were not willing to cover for Peoples. A representative of the largest mining company in Scranton mentioned after the U.S. Supreme Court's *Pennsylvania Coal* decision that it had always been willing to pay for damages that it caused. Its major opposition had been to the requirement to pay for another company's misdeeds via the Fowler Act's taxes (Scranton *Republican,* Dec. 12, 1922).

The other difference is that the mine-cave commission created by the Fowler Act would have been able to impose prior regulation on the coal companies. Under the informal agreements, the companies agreed only to repair or pay compensation for damages that actually occurred. They also did not pay (as far as I can tell) for personal injuries or loss of life except where negligence was proved. By setting the terms for mining, the commission might have been able to reduce incidents of subsidence and accidents.

But not by much. Few people in Scranton wanted mining beneath the city to stop, so it is likely that some risk of subsidence would have been accepted by the commission. The commission might have become industry dominated or corrupt, so that even less protection would have been afforded. And shifting responsibility for subsidence to the Fowler commission would have created an agency problem. By limiting the liability of the companies that complied with their rules, the Fowler commission might have encouraged companies to undertake subsidence-causing mining about which the commission was ill informed. Hence it is not obvious that the actual incidence of subsidence would have been less if the Kohler Act had been upheld. The major difference that *Pennsylvania Coal* made was probably that past damages by the Peoples Coal Company went uncompensated. And even that would have been undone if Governor Pinchot had not vetoed the subsequent earmarking of the Williams Act's taxes.

1.15 *The Court Overlooked Economic, Political, and Social Internalization*

The conclusion of the previous section makes *Pennsylvania Coal* look like the change in cattle-trespass rules in Shasta County that Robert Ellickson examined. He found that the rule changes did not change the allocation of resources. This was not because people bargained around the legal rules, as the Coase theorem would suggest, but because the legal rules about cattle trespass were not the binding rules. I have shown that the legal rules apparently at issue in *Pennsylvania Coal* also turned out not to be the binding rules. The Supreme Court's decision to sustain the waiver of liability for surface damage against the Kohler Act was not decisive. The coal companies behaved almost as if they had lost the case. They were willing to assume liability for damage to surface structures, and they apparently made good on it as long as they operated.

This sanguine story is, I believe, the result of circumstances that married together the fortunes of coal companies and those of surface owners. Up until the 1940s, Scranton did depend on coal for its prosperity, so undue interference with mining would have been harmful to its economy. In none of the local accounts that I read was it seriously contended that mining beneath the city should simply cease. Coal employed tens of thousands directly, and most other workers owed an indirect debt to the industry.

The coal companies, for their part, must have been at least a little sensitive to the issue insofar as a caved-in city would make it difficult to hire workers and managers. One reason for the coal companies' desire to maintain "good public relations," as Mr. Milner put it, was simple economic rationality. This hunch was confirmed by my talk in March 1994 with Sal Nardozzi, who had been a mining engineer for the state of Pennsylvania in the 1960s.

Mr. Nardozzi had no love for the now-defunct companies, but he did relate a story from the early 1930s about his parents' home in Dunmore, a city adjacent to Scranton. The Nardozzi house was slightly damaged by surface subsidence caused by none other than the Pennsylvania Coal Company. The company promptly repaired the damage to the house, and even replaced the basement's dirt floor with concrete to ensure its future stability. When I asked Mr. Nardozzi why the company repaired the house when it had no legal obligation to do so (he confirmed that the deed had the same waiver that the Mahons' house had), he observed that "ninety-five percent" (which I took to be hyperbole) of the residents in the area worked for the coal company. If the companies did not repair damages, he said, they would have no workers.

When one considers the geography of Scranton and its environs, it is difficult to imagine the companies behaving much differently. Scranton developed on top of some of the richest, most easily mined deposits of anthracite coal in the world. Even if mine owners had anticipated the problems of subsidence legislation, it is hard to see how they could have forestalled it with different legal arrangements. If they had not sold the surface rights to housing developers, their workers would not have been able to get to the mines, as was also noted by

Philip Mattes (1928, 1974). Most miners walked to work at the time. To live "beyond the measure," a Scranton term for living in territory not underlain by coal, was to live many miles from the mines and thus to be unemployed. (Employers could have built and rented housing to their workers, which would also have provided companies with incentives to support it, but such arrangements were economical only in isolated mining towns [Price Fishback 1992].)

On the other hand, if the mine companies had sold the surface rights *with* the right of support, they might have been so swamped in litigation that little coal could have been extracted. If one takes coal out of a mine near the surface, some subsidence is going to occur even under the most careful conditions. Philip Mattes explained that people originally accepted the waiver of liability because they did not anticipate more than minor damage (1974). But even if home buyers had anticipated the future problem, the coal companies would have been reluctant to sell the right of support because of the threat of liability. The threat of subsidence in smaller cities in the coal region did make companies reluctant to sell surface land, and it did restrict home building (Peter Roberts 1904, p. 135; U.S. Coal Commission 1925, p. 536). Scranton, however, was so large that buyers had to accept the risk or be unemployed. They saw that everyone else did, too, and they all worked for the coal companies.

The commonality of interest between mine owners and surface dwellers still left a large obstacle to their cooperation. The subsidence that one mine owner might cause did not necessarily harm the homes of his own workers. Hence some form of collective action to coordinate mining seemed necessary. The agitation by the Surface Protective Association and subsequent commissions served as the basis for agreement among coal mine owners to overcome this free-rider problem. The outcry from the victims of the Peoples Coal Company as well as the complaints of those harmed by lesser incidents of subsidence also made the idea of "letting down the surface"—the mine owners' euphemism for causing subsidence—less acceptable. It cannot, therefore, be said that the Kohler Act and Fowler Act had no effect, because they were part of an ongoing reevaluation of social norms of the use of property.

One other relationship must have contributed to the gradual change in behavior by the mine companies. In trying to locate Mr. Nardozzi, the mine-flushing engineer, I spoke to his son, who is an attorney, in

March 1994. I mentioned that I had previously spoken to Stewart Milner, the Pennsylvania Coal engineer, and that I wanted to talk to someone who had worked for the state. The younger Nardozzi volunteered that he knew Mr. Milner well; they were both members of the same Masonic Lodge.

Scranton isn't such a big place that mine company executives could have a social life that was entirely isolated from that of surface owners. Indeed, many executives of the mining companies may also have lacked the right of support. Philip Mattes mentioned in his autobiography that his father and grandfather worked for the coal companies and that their properties lacked the right of support. As the right of support became crucial for many people in the city, the social pressure to respect surface property must have become immense. After the 1920 Battle of Oxford, virtually all of the civic organizations in the city, to which many mine executives belonged, came out in favor of some type of subsidence legislation (Scranton *Times,* March 3, 1920). To favor a literal interpretation of the subsidence waiver had become so far from the acceptable social norm that the mining companies had no choice. (For those who prefer quantitative estimates of the changed norm, recall from section 1.7 that as early as 1913, the coal companies had agreed to sell pillar coal to support homes for only about a third of the coal's market price.)

1.16 Social Norms Need More Attention than Court Opinions

The near-irrelevance of *Pennsylvania Coal* supplies support for Robert Ellickson's (1991) contention that legal rules take a back seat to social norms when the parties are locked in ongoing relationships. The predominance of norms casts doubt on the utility of the bargaining approach commended by the Coase theorem. Recall that George Stevenson pointed to repurchase of support rights as a solution to the subsidence problem. There was indeed some repurchase of rights, but the dominant form of surface protection seemed to have come from the norm that mining companies were liable for the cost of repairs. Political pressure undoubtedly contributed to the enforcement of this norm, but, in the end, it seems more likely that concern for reputation on other fronts restrained the coal companies from asserting their legal rights to withdraw surface support.

The other lesson I take from the coal story is the limitation on the capacity of the U.S. Supreme Court to resolve regulatory takings. It is difficult to present complex issues for resolution before a court of law, especially one that is much removed from the controversy. It seems more likely that the Pennsylvania Supreme Court knew what was really behind the Kohler and Fowler Acts, and its justices may have decided to reverse their previous positions for that reason. Consider also how little time the U.S. Supreme Court could spend on this or any other case. It was one of many on the docket. The justices read a few briefs, consulted with their clerks, who had spent at most a few days doing research, and then they decided. There is a hint of the "fatal conceit," which Friedrich Hayek derided in socialist planning, in the idea that a court sitting in Washington, D.C., could acquire enough knowledge to control events.

I nonetheless do not think that *Pennsylvania Coal* was wrongly decided. Given that the Court had taken the dispute, it could not look the other way when the Pennsylvania Supreme Court blandly acknowledged that the support estate was recognized as a property right, but that the police power simply trumped it. The U.S. Supreme Court has not been eager to set forth a law of property, but it does have to insist that the Bill of Rights, including the Takings Clause, applies to the states and their state courts. Given that the case was accepted for review, *Pennsylvania Coal* was correctly decided. Moreover, given Holmes's understanding of the facts, his opinion is a paradigm of judicial reasoning. If anything, I hope that clearing up the facts of the case can allow more attention to the reasoning itself.

It is fairly debatable, however, whether the U.S. Court should have taken *Pennsylvania Coal* for review. The Kohler Act was passed by a representative body responsive to those in a good position to reap the benefits and bear the costs of the regulation. Coal was important to the general prosperity of the state and to the Scranton area in particular. The idea that the state, at the urging of the city, would pass a regulation that would foul its own economic nest seems paternalistic, though perhaps understandable in light of the lengthy coal strike of 1922 that caused hardship in many cities. There is little evidence for the idea that coal mine owners lacked sympathizers in the legislature. The U.S. Supreme Court's decision to review *Pennsylvania Coal* was questionable because it imposed a judicial discipline in a place where political calculation might be expected to work to protect each party's interests.

Pennsylvania Coal has been famous for seventy years, and articles about it still appear (E. F. Roberts 1986). I have seen none by anyone who has bothered to go to Scranton. The few articles that go beyond the opinion itself recite facts from the briefs. Even after *Pennsylvania Coal* was seemingly reversed in *Keystone* in 1987, no one interested in takings (including myself) troubled to pull aside the veil.

I take the neglect of the easily obtained facts of *Pennsylvania Coal* as evidence that legal centralism, as described by Robert Ellickson (1991), is the prevailing norm in law schools as well as among the law and economics crowd. The legal centralist is so sure that law matters, and especially that constitutional law matters, that it is hard to even conceive of asking whether a famous Supreme Court opinion actually governed anyone's behavior. It is taken as an article of faith that big court decisions have big consequences.

1.17 Was Pennsylvania Coal *Reversed by* Keystone?

In the spring and summer of 1987, sixty-five years after *Pennsylvania Coal*, the U.S. Supreme Court decided three takings cases that dealt with land use regulation. Even more unusual, in two of them the Court sided with the landowner. Except for Loretto v. Teleprompter (1982) (a hybrid of regulation and physical invasion that will be discussed in section 8.20), modern regulatory takings doctrine had been constructed from opinions in which the government regulation has almost always been sustained.

The first of the 1987 takings decisions concerned, amazingly enough, Pennsylvania coal mining subsidence. The facts of Keystone Bituminous Coal Association v. DeBenedictis (1987) are strikingly similar to those of *Pennsylvania Coal*. In 1966, Pennsylvania's legislature enacted a statute that sounded very much like the Kohler Act adopted in 1921. Underground mining of bituminous coal was restricted in areas in which it might cause damage to surface structures or roadways, despite any contractual obligations or easements that explicitly absolved the mining company of any liability for surface damage. Coal companies that did undertake mining in such areas were required to leave extensive amounts of coal in the ground to provide support for the surface, and, in the event that such support failed, to pay to repair surface damage.

Sixty-five years later, the modern version of the Kohler Act was upheld by the U.S. Supreme Court. It is a tribute to the enduring influence of Justice Holmes and *Pennsylvania Coal* that *Keystone* was decided by a 5–4 vote. Most environmental regulations, even of the seemingly ex post facto variety, are upheld without much trouble these days (Hodel v. Virginia Surface Mining 1981). The dissenters in *Keystone* said the case looked almost exactly like *Pennsylvania Coal*.

The switch of the Court from *Pennsylvania Coal* to *Keystone* is consistent with a thesis that I will advance in Chapter 2. Eminent domain responds to a recurring cycle of economic valuations. In 1922, anthracite coal was immensely valuable, all the more because of the shortages caused by the strike that had just been settled and the lack of nonpolluting substitutes for it. The value of surface real estate was not so high, and, in any case, its owners had reason to discount its value because of explicit notice of the risks of subsidence. Thus the Court would favor coal mining in the 1920s. By the 1960s, general growth in personal incomes had driven up the demand for housing and a pleasant environment. Technological changes over the same period had reduced concern over the extraction of coal, because many substitutes for it had been developed.

I do not want the reader to assume that this is straightforward economic determinism. The switch from *Pennsylvania Coal* to *Keystone* occurred over a period of years in which the Supreme Court withdrew almost entirely from the constitutional review of business regulation. (The withdrawal will be put in context in section 3.7.) Nonetheless, the *Keystone* reversal of *Pennsylvania Coal* is consistent with the influence of economic values on judicial decisions.

My suggestion that the *Keystone* Court was balancing the value of surface to subsurface interests is not easily supported by Justice Stevens's opinion for the Court in *Keystone*. He relied mainly on the "nuisance exception," which Justice Brandeis had invoked in his dissent in *Pennsylvania Coal*. But the *Keystone* Court seemed to do an implicit balancing when it noted that only 2 percent of otherwise extractable coal had to be left in the ground under the ordinance (480 U.S. at 196). If the nuisance exception were absolute, why wouldn't it apply even if *all* coal had become unminable? (Gus Bauman, who attended the oral arguments on behalf of the coal operators, said at my February 1988 conference that the "mere 2 percent" figure seemed decisive.)

1.18   Lead Us Not into Penn Station

The more specific balancing test for takings had been articulated in
Penn Central Transportation v. New York (1978). To describe *Penn
Central*, it is best to consider first a quote from the Brandeis dissent in
Pennsylvania Coal. Brandeis was attacking Holmes's alleged focus on
a single stick in the bundle of property rights, the right to mine with-
out having to support the surface. Brandeis said instead:

> The rights of an owner as against the public are not increased by
> dividing the interests in his property into surface and subsoil. The
> sum of the rights in the parts can not be greater than the rights in the
> whole. The estate of an owner in land is grandiloquently described as
> extending *ab orco usque ad coelum* [from the center of the earth to the
> heavens]. But I suppose no one would contend that by selling his
> interest above one hundred feet from the surface he could prevent the
> State from limiting, by the police power, the height of structures in
> a city.

Before showing the application of Brandeis's hypothetical in *Penn
Central,* I want to point out that Brandeis was swinging pretty wildly
at Holmes here. Holmes was not anywhere in his opinion arguing that
if one stick in the bundle of property is extinguished that fact alone
makes it a taking. It did happen in this case that the "support estate"
was extinguished for certain properties, but that was only a contributing factor in Holmes's overall evaluation of the severity of the regulation. Legal scholars like Karl Manheim (1989, p. 968), who claimed
that Holmes was engaging in "conceptual severance," have let the
urgency of their causes (in Manheim's case, rent control) get in the
way of a fair reading of the opinion.

Brandeis's 1922 hypothetical formed the basis in the 1970s for the
claim of the Penn Central Transportation Company against the city of
New York. The city's Landmarks Preservation Commission had designated the company's aptly named Grand Central Terminal to be a
landmark, not subject to destruction or exterior modification without
review by the commission. (The city's law had been prompted by the
1967 destruction of another city landmark, Penn Station.) The commission was not a rubber stamp; it often turned down proposals for
even minor modifications. Grand Central Terminal is a relatively low
structure set amidst skyscrapers in midtown Manhattan. In 1968, the
financially pressed Penn Central Transportation Company tried to raise

cash by selling the right to erect a skyscraper cantilevered above the terminal. That is, it proposed to sell the same property interest that Brandeis had used to criticize the *Pennsylvania Coal* majority. (This was not the first time anyone had sold air rights, of course.)

The Landmarks Preservation Commission ruled that Penn Central's proposal did not comport with its regulations, and the sale fell through. Penn Central then sued the city for the commission's alleged taking of its property without just compensation. Presumably Penn Central had in mind the possibility that the city would purchase the development rights (or redevelopment rights) on properties designated as historic treasures. It was not such a far-fetched idea. It was first assumed that some compensation would be required for historic preservation. A barterlike system of transferable development rights was developed and defended as adequate compensation by John Costonis (1974). New York had in fact adopted some elements of the Costonis plan.

The Penn Central Company lost on appeal. The New York Court of Appeals (*Penn Central* 1977) held for the city with an opinion redolent of the spirit of Henry George, which his ghost surely appreciated. (George had once run for mayor of New York.) The company was only entitled to the value that it created absent the existence of the city, intoned Judge Breitel, as if the Landmarks Preservation Commission were entitled to appropriate to itself all of the advantages of civilization. The U.S. Supreme Court affirmed, but Justice William Brennan's opinion ignored Judge Breitel's rhetoric. Brennan instead proposed a three-part balancing test to determine when a regulation would go so far as to amount to being a taking. The three criteria are:

(a) The character of the government action. Does it, for example, cause usually compensable physical invasions, or does it abate noncompensable nuisances? (There was little guidance to navigate the ocean of regulation that falls between these extremes.)

(b) Interference with "investment-backed expectations." Is the loss entirely prospective, or has the property owner sunk a lot of irretrievable investment in the project? (The "investment backed" criterion can only be for emphasis, since all property values are prospective and thus expectations.)

(c) The extent of the diminution of value. Is there a reasonable residual of profitability left? Both the New York and U.S. Courts mentioned that the city permitted Penn Central to exceed zoning height limitations on nearby properties, on exception that turned out to be valuable. The U.S. Court did not specifically hold that this scheme amounted to just compensation, and Justice Rehnquist in dissent would have remanded the case to the lower courts for determination of the constitutional adequacy of this swap.

There are two directions one could take, faced with Justice Brennan's list. One is to show, as Andrea Peterson (1989) has done so well, that they are vague and have been applied so inconsistently as to be of little use for lawyers to advise clients. To paraphrase a less sympathetic critic, Gideon Kanner, the Court has always been suspected of basing regulatory takings decisions on ad hoc factors, and *Penn Central* was a signed confession that the justices do not care to do better.

The other direction is to show that the three factors do not make much economic sense, either. I will address the "investment-backed expectations" criterion in Chapter 5. It sounds something like rational expectations, and many economists are attracted to it for that reason. But for the most part, a lengthy economic criticism of the three factors (or the two factors enunciated in Agins v. Tiburon, to be discussed shortly) would belabor the obvious. The fundamental flaw is that the Court gave no indication of the weight that each criterion is to be given by a trial judge or jury. Attorneys with clients need rules better than "the character of the government action" and "the extent of the diminution of value." Such criteria are like saying that aggregate consumption is a function of income, wealth, and the interest rate, and then telling someone to use that information alone to forecast the consumption component of GNP next year.

As for the effects of the actual decision in Penn Central on the city's behavior, the results suggest that the Court's decision did boost the cause of historic preservation. Joseph Rose (1984) indicated that New York's Landmarks Preservation Commission went on a designation binge after *Penn Central*. Uncompensated designation seems especially unfair when the landmark is an isolated building, so that there is none of the reciprocal advantage that accrues to individual owners when whole neighborhoods are preserved. Evidence from Philadelphia's housing market shows that large-district federal designation does little harm to individual owners, but selective city designation causes losses on the order of a quarter of the building's value (Asabere, Huffman, and Mehdian 1994).

1.19   Tiburon Substituted Regulation for Eminent Domain

Open-ended balancing tests are not much help to lawyers, and they run the risk of balancing the Just Compensation Clause out of the Constitution entirely. An egregious example is Agins v. Tiburon (1980), a case that originated in California. The city of Tiburon is a suburb of six thousand people about seven miles directly north of San Francisco. Situated on a hilly peninsula that juts into San Francisco Bay, many Tiburon residents enjoy an excellent view of the city and the nearby Golden Gate Bridge. One indication of Tiburon's amenability and convenience is that its median household income in 1980 was about twice the median for the state, making it one of the wealthiest communities in the San Francisco metropolitan area. The median value of its owner-occupied housing in 1980 was more than twice the state average. It also had (and still has) an unusually large amount of privately owned open space for a suburb situated conveniently close to the center of a major metropolitan area.

Donald Agins, a dentist who lived elsewhere, had purchased undeveloped land on the summit of a ridge in Tiburon in 1968 on which he wanted to build homes for himself and others. The pattern of development in Tiburon historically had been to build up from the end of the peninsula facing San Francisco, covering both the flatlands and the ridge. The ridge runs the length of the peninsula. The part of the ridge beginning about a hundred yards southeast of Agins's tract was already covered with what to this visiting easterner looked like high-density, single-family development. If previous development was any guide, Agins had reason to expect to be able to develop at least twenty homes on the five acres that he had purchased.

Tiburon had other plans for the ridge. It hired a consultant in 1972 to explore options for preserving open space. The consultant recommended purchasing much of the land along the ridge, including the Agins tract. The city council authorized the sale of $1.25 million in bonds to purchase the ridge, and voters later approved this.

The problem with the 1972 bond issue was that the city had underestimated the cost of acquiring property. Property values everywhere were beginning to rise more rapidly than inflation. The city opened negotiations with Dr. Agins, as was required by eminent domain statutes, but the bargaining went nowhere. An eminent domain trial was scheduled but was then dismissed when the city withdrew.

Frustrated by its inability to purchase land, the city council in 1973 rezoned the Agins and other ridge properties to lower densities. Its justification for doing this was a new law passed by the state legislature requiring that all communities provide for open space. The law also specified that private property rights were to be respected in all cases, but Tiburon overlooked that requirement. It is hard to pull up a more obvious sequence in which noncompensable regulatory powers were substituted for otherwise compensable eminent domain actions.

The rezoning of the Agins property and other ridge land permitted single-family homes, but at densities lower than previously allowed in the area and in most other developed parts of the community. Just how great a density could be permitted depended on discretionary findings by the planning commission. Strictly speaking, Agins had not clearly been deprived of the right to put up one house per acre, but it was unlikely that Agins would be able to develop at anything like that density. (Gideon Kanner, who was Agins's lawyer on appeal, told me that he offered in oral argument to drop the case if Tiburon would allow Agins to develop one house per acre, an offer the city declined.) Agins was correct in assuming that the city would block as much development as possible in order to keep his land in open space. A later building moratorium for a time prevented any construction at all. Agins did not have a house on the site by 1987 (*Los Angeles Times,* August 3, 1987, I, 3).

Agins's challenge to the zoning law failed at the level of both the California and the U.S. Supreme Courts. The trial court, noting the California Supreme Court's dicta in HFH v. Superior Court (1975), said that inverse condemnation damages for regulation simply were not available in California. *HFH* was an important step in the California Supreme Court's campaign to insulate governments from regulatory takings damages. The issue had not, however, been heard by the U.S. Supreme Court, which might not take kindly to a state's attempt to limit the remedial powers of the Fifth Amendment. *Agins* looked like the perfect test. However, the California Supreme Court used a number of maneuvers too complicated to describe here to avoid review of its new interpretation of the Just Compensation Clause (Ellickson and Tarlock 1981, p. 168).

After reviewing the facts of the case, the California Supreme Court decided that there was no taking. It went on to point out the supposed evils of paying damages in regulatory cases, among which were that governments might be induced to be too cautious. One might point out that such caution is an important purpose of the Takings Clause, but the California court's holding was not based on that point. It held that there was no taking because there was some value left in Agins's property, and this residuum of value was sufficient to satisfy a balancing test.

Agins was probably the outer limit of the U.S. Supreme Court's balancing attempts. It was decided 9–0, mainly on the grounds that the California Supreme Court had held that Agins had some value left. Tiburon's blatant substitution of regulation for condemnation was studiously ignored. The conservatives on the U.S. Court appeared to have given up on the idea that they could use a balancing test to decide when regulation had gone "too far." The *Agins* affirmation, however, gave rise to other problems relating to federalism and the supremacy of the U.S. Constitution.

1.20 California Tried to Rule Out Damages for Regulatory Takings

The problem that *Agins* raised for the U.S. Supreme Court was how to keep the state courts from eliminating the compensatory requirements of the Fifth Amendment. The ruses the California court used in *Agins* to avoid review of its rule did not long fool the U.S. Supreme Court. Within a year, it took another California regulatory takings case, San Diego Gas and Electric v. San Diego (1981). After a bond issue to purchase the utility's property by eminent domain failed, San Diego had rezoned the property from industrial to agricultural and open space. (It invoked the same state open-space law that Tiburon had used, and likewise ignored the law's property-rights guarantee.) The real reason for the rezoning was apparently to block the utility's proposal to construct a nuclear power plant on the site. The California Supreme Court, citing its *Agins* decision, now boldly held that the rezoning was not compensable even if it was a taking. A five-justice majority of the U.S. Supreme Court declined to reverse the state supreme court, holding that the case was not yet ripe for federal review (Douglas Kmiec 1981–82).

Support for the San Diego Gas and Electric Company came from a seemingly unexpected source. Justice William Brennan, one of the most liberal members of the Court and no enemy of land use controls, issued a strong dissent. He argued for reversal of the California doctrine, and his would have been the majority position had Justice Rehnquist not voted with the majority on procedural grounds. (Justice Rehnquist indicated in a concurrence that he thought the California court's decision should have been reversed but was not ripe for judgment.) Justice Brennan was concerned that the absence of any financial penalty would encourage deliberate legal delays by municipalities. He quoted a California municipal attorney who advised fellow city attorneys faced with judicial reversal of a regulation, "If all else fails, merely amend the regulation and start over again" (*San Diego Gas,* p. 656).

Justice Brennan's position perplexed and outraged many liberal land use lawyers, who wanted to keep the regulatory takings doctrine in the toothless condition to which *Penn Central* and *Agins* had relegated it (Norman Williams et al. 1984). But Justice Brennan regarded the most important accomplishment of the Supreme Court as bringing the states within the ambit of the federal Bill of Rights (Brennan 1986). His concern might have been that if the California Supreme Court could evade the Fifth Amendment's clear command that compensation is the remedy to be offered when a taking is found, this would open the door to, say, the Alabama Supreme Court's holding that the equal protection clause of the Fourteenth Amendment did not apply to it, either.

It was expected by most land use professionals that a case without any procedural difficulties would soon be considered by the U.S. Supreme Court. It took longer than most people thought. Williamson County v. Hamilton Bank (1985) seemed to clearly present the question of compensation for regulation, but it was found wanting on newly manufactured procedural grounds. State remedies had to be pursued to some indefinite end, ruled the Court, before a regulatory takings case could be brought into federal courts. (It does not work that way for other civil rights claims under the Fourteenth Amendment.)

The U.S. Court seemed to be drawing a line and daring the state courts to cross it. The California Court seemed to have unambiguously crossed it in MacDonald v. Yolo County (1986), in which it refused to consider damages for the farmland-preservation designation of an unfarmable suburban plot. (The plot was adjacent to an existing subdivision in Davis, California.) The U.S. Court, however, in yet another exercise of deference to state courts, stepped back from the line again.

It held that all administrative remedies, such as requests for variances, had to be exhausted before MacDonald could get off the farm.

1.21   *The U.S. Court Ran Out of Patience in* First English

Line-drawing finally stopped in First English Evangelical Lutheran Church v. County of Los Angeles (1987). In 1977, a flood destroyed the buildings of a camp owned by the church. After the flood but before the church could rebuild, the county rezoned the area to prevent reconstruction of any building in the flood plain. (A coincidental account of the flood and its damage to the camp can be found in John McPhee, *The Control of Nature* [1989, p. 215].) The county declared its regulation to be temporary, but it set no date for its termination. The church sued for compensation on the grounds that the regulation was a taking.

The California courts held, as expected, that compensation was not due for the supposed taking. All that the church could ask for was to have the ordinance rescinded, as the California *Agins* decision had held. Any loss in the use of the camp during the years the regulation was in effect was not to be compensated. The church appealed this straightforward stonewalling of the Fifth Amendment's Just Compensation Clause to the U.S. Supreme Court.

Since the church had exhausted all state remedies, and since the compensation question was not complicated by a prior finding that no taking had occurred, the U.S. Court finally had to face up to California's evasion of the Fifth Amendment. The Court held, by a 6–3 vote, that if a taking had occurred, the church was owed monetary compensation from the moment the illegal regulation took effect. (Two of the minority dissented because they believed that state remedies had not been exhausted; only Justice Stevens defended the California noncompensation rule.)

Had a trial court ruled that a taking had occurred, the church would have been compensated for its losses as a result of *First English*. Compensation should have been for the losses imposed by the regulation, not by the flood. In any event, however, the California trial and appeals courts subsequently held that no taking had occurred, so no compensation was necessary. The appeals court judge in First English v. Los Angeles (1989) compared the flood-plain zoning to the "harm-prevention" purposes of *Mugler* and *Hadacheck*. Judge Johnson also asserted that the church enjoyed some reciprocal advantage because the same regulation applied to its neighbors. This reciprocity would seem to be nothing more than saying that misery loves company, but it was not even true. When I visited the ruins of the camp in the chaparral-covered hills in 1989, it appeared that the upstream residential neighbor had in fact rebuilt his home.

1.22   Nollan *Required California to Take Takings Seriously*

Another 1987 case was Nollan v. California Coastal Commission. Patrick Nollan, a Los Angeles lawyer, had an option to buy a run-down beach house in Faria Beach, an isolated colony just up the coast from Ventura, California. Nollan wanted to build a larger house. The California Coastal Zone Commission, a statewide body created by a 1972 initiative, said he could do so only if he would grant to the state a public-access easement between his house and the ocean. This would enable people to walk along the beach in front of Nollan's house above the usual high-tide line that marks public ownership. The commission was using its authority to regulate redevelopment as a lever to provide greater public access along the beach. Nollan preferred not to look out his window at the ocean and watch strangers walking by.

The regulations by which the commission had originally restricted beachfront houses from becoming larger were based on the theory that a bigger structure would block the view of the coast by passersby. It was only a theory. Highway 101 passes well above the houses, and none of the view is blocked. (I visited the site in December 1991.) What does block the view of the ocean from the Faria Beach access road, which is below Highway 101, are the apparently legal six-foot fences between the houses and the access road.

The California appellate courts upheld the coastal commission's condition (reversing the trial court), but the U.S. Supreme Court held for Nollan. Justice Scalia found (correctly) that the beachfront easement demanded by the commission would not mitigate the supposed view-blockage at all. For this reason, the beach-access condition lacked "nexus" with the original regulation's purpose. As a result, the easement would be a taking for public use for which compensation was required.

That there would have been a physical invasion of property by beach-combers in *Nollan* was not disputed. The Court ruled, in effect, that

compensation could not be in the form of an exception to another
regulation unless there was a nexus between the regulation excepted
and the purpose of the easement. On this rule, a community could give
an exception to a leash law to dog owners who contributed to a
clean-up fund, but it could not give an exception to dog owners who
promised to paint their houses white.

Nollan is the most problematical of the recent takings cases in terms
of fitting into the rule books that lawyers need to advise their clients.
There is no doubt that many ordinary land use regulations are routinely bargained for cash and goods in kind. Planning commissions are
often asked by developers to grant an exception to regulations, for
which the developer agrees to donate land. Exchanging exceptions to
regulation for transfers of physical property has long been common
practice, and curtailing it could harm developers as well as community
interests (Fischel 1988). I shall deal with this issue in more detail in
section 9.12, which reviews land use exactions in the context of the
recent Supreme Court takings decision Dolan v. Tigard (1994).

I nonetheless think that *Nollan* was properly decided on fairness
grounds. The fairness problem with the condition imposed in *Nollan*
was with the terms of trade. The "bargain" between the coastal commission and Nollan was so one-sided as to be unconscionable, and the
"extortion" metaphor invoked by Justice Scalia surely alluded to that.
But the remedy to that evil is either to recalculate the compensation
along fairer terms (which the Court has now urged in *Dolan*) or to ask
whether the regulations being traded were reasonable in the first place.
Whether some citizens should be denied the right to rebuild their
homes in a manner that seems perfectly consistent with normal California beachfront housing (as Nollan's illegally rebuilt house was)
seems to have evaded the dialogue between Justice Scalia for the majority and Justice Brennan in dissent. (I will expand on the virtues of a
"normal behavior" standard in section 9.17.)

Nollan also fits into my view of the U.S. Supreme Court's takings
behavior in that the decision represented the second barrel of the
Court's response to California's extreme position on regulatory takings. The most blatant challenge of the California Supreme Court to
federal supremacy was its attempt to rule out damages entirely in *Agins*.
First English eventually took care of that, though the California Supreme Court seems nonetheless dedicated to eliminating the remedy
by imposing other jurisprudential roadblocks, as shown by Hensler v.

Glendale (1994). But California had also been an outlier among the states in refusing to find that regulations would amount to takings, whether compensable or only enjoinable. (Chapter 6 describes the California court's more general war against development.)

Nollan might simply represent the U.S. Supreme Court's attempt to show that there are some regulatory schemes so close in spirit to eminent domain that they must be regarded as takings. This reading is consistent with the U.S. Court's reluctance since then to beat further on the California judicial system. Once the U.S. Court got the point across that the Bill of Rights is paramount and does require that states take seriously the possibility of substituting regulation for eminent domain, it has seemed willing to let the state courts go their own way. The Court's continuing concern with California was suggested during oral arguments in the South Carolina *Lucas* case (discussed in the next section). Justice White inadvertently referred to the South Carolina Supreme Court as "the California court" (Richard Lazarus 1993, p. 1417).

1.23 Lucas *Questioned the Nuisance Exception*

Lucas v. South Carolina Coastal Council (1992) presented another beachfront development controversy in which the U.S. Supreme Court sided with the landowner. Like many other states, South Carolina had in the 1970s adopted statewide regulations to control development along its coast, in part because beachfront development was especially subject to erosion and damage from storms (Mark Poirier 1993). South Carolina tightened its regulations in 1988 to prevent any development in a "dead zone" consisting of an area seaward of barrier dunes all along the coast. The hotly contested 1988 legislation deliberately withheld any provision for variances for landowners, who could not develop previously platted lots (Charleston *Post and Courier*, May 27, 1988, p. 1B).

David Lucas had in 1986 purchased for $975,000 two of the last undeveloped lots in a gated resort community called "Wild Dunes" on Isle of Palms, S.C. Both of Mr. Lucas's building lots, each less than half an acre, were entirely within the dead zone. Scores of large, modern houses had already been built in the dead zone on either side of Lucas's lots. His lots appear from the beach like two missing pickets in a long fence of development that included condominiums as well as five-thousand-square-foot houses. The existing beachside homes were not affected by the legislation, except that they might not be allowed to rebuild if they were destroyed by a hurricane. (If they were damaged by Hurricane Hugo in September 1989, they nonetheless appear to have been restored.) Lucas did not have to wait for the hurricane. The value of his property had been wiped out by the 1988 regulations, while his numerous neighbors bore little if any of the burden.

A South Carolina trial court held in August 1989 that the state had taken Lucas's property insofar as he had not even a scintilla of residual value. The court required just compensation paid to Mr. Lucas on the order of $1,200,000. The trial court's finding that Lucas's parcels had no value was treated with skepticism by the dissenters on the U.S. Supreme Court, as well as by academic commentators (Fischel 1991c, p. 909). Justice Blackmun opined that even though Lucas could not erect a building of any sort, he retained some value because he could still "picnic, swim, camp in a tent or live on the property in a movable trailer" (112 S. Ct. at 2908, cited with approval by William Fisher 1993, p. 1409).

My November 1994 visit to Wild Dunes revealed that such options were either impossible or valueless to Lucas. The director of the Wild Dunes Architectural Review Board informed me that covenants explicitly forbade trailers and tents. She said that picnicking would be permitted—provided one stayed off the dunes, as official Coastal Council signs exhort one to do—as would swimming. But such activities would be valueless to Lucas, given that his lots fronted on a wide public beach, on which picnicking and swimming are permitted to anyone without charge. (Automobile access to the lots is restricted, but one can easily walk to them along the beach, which is open to the public.) The trial judge's conclusion seems correct.

As a result of the trial judge's award of damages, "even some of the law's staunchest defenders began to recognize a mistake had been made," as a Charleston *Post and Courier* editorial delicately put it (June 20, 1990, p. 8A). The state legislature amended the law to allow variances for people in Lucas's position, but by then the case had been taken by the South Carolina Supreme Court. That court's ruling for the state made it appear that the legislature had acted too hastily. It accepted the trial court's finding of a complete economic wipeout, but it held that there was no compensation due, anyway. The legislature had carefully couched its coastal zone regulations in the language of "harm prevention," thereby raising the U.S. Supreme Court's old "nuisance exception" of Mugler v. Kansas (1887) and most recently invoked in *Keystone* (1987): if the law is intended to prevent a nuisancelike harm to the public, then compensation for the owner's loss is never made, even though the loss may be total. The South Carolina Supreme Court accepted the state legislature's invocation of the nuisance exception at face value.

The "nuisance exception" may be a sensible rule, but it begs the question of who is to decide what constitutes a nuisance. If the findings of a legislative body trump every other source, then it will not take long for legislatures to learn that they can dispense with payment for the acquisition of open space by declaring its private development to be a nuisance. In reversing the South Carolina Supreme Court, Justice Scalia's opinion alluded to just such a possibility. Scalia insisted that a total elimination of value without compensation had to be supported by something more than a legislative declaration of harm. When even harm-preventing regulation leaves an owner without any economic value, the case-by-case balancing of *Penn Central* is to be discarded, and judges must make an inquiry into alternative sources of law, such as the state's common law of nuisance, to sustain the legislation.

A subsequent trial in South Carolina resulted in a settlement in which the state purchased the land from Mr. Lucas. The state's plans for the newly purchased land raise the possibility that its original designation might have been a little arbitrary. According to Mike Berger (*Los Angeles Daily Journal,* August 11, 1993), the state planned to sell the land to a housing developer to recoup the cost of the settlement. It was later reported that the owner of a house next to one of Lucas's parcels offered the state $315,000 for one of them, promising to keep it undeveloped to protect his view (Charleston *Post and Courier* editorial, Oct. 10, 1993). The state spurned the private preservationist's offer, selling the two nearly identical lots to a developer for $785,000 (*id.,* Nov. 11, 1993). That works out to $392,500 per lot, which means that, when its own money was on the table, the state was unwilling to forgo $77,500 to preserve one of the lots whose previous value of $600,000 to the owner it had denied was a compensable loss.

1.24   *Conclusion: Activism Must Be Tempered by Modesty*

I have found that pointing out that *Nollan* might actually harm development interests (section 1.22) does not go over well in prodevelopment circles. I thought initially that those I spoke with did not understand the logic of the argument, but later it dawned on me what the importance of *Nollan* was. Development-minded landowners had at last won their case in the U.S. Supreme Court. Having been told for years by the Court that there was such a thing as a regulatory taking, but that it simply had not appeared in this particular case, property owners had begun to think it was a phantom doctrine. It was hard for academics like myself to appreciate how important simply winning one is to people who feel they've been abandoned by the courts.

Aside from the psychological importance of the recent landowner victories, none of them leads me to believe that the U.S. Supreme Court is about to embark on a campaign to federalize property law by way of the Takings Clause. Dolan v. Tigard does leave that door open, but, if historical experience is any guide, the Court will find that the flood of litigation will force it to retreat (see section 9.16). On the one hand, given the Court's incomplete grasp of local circumstances in *Pennsylvania Coal,* I do not regard such reticence as a bad idea. On the other hand, the Supremes (as a federal judge of my acquaintance sometimes refers to them) are not about to let a state court evade their understanding of the application of the Bill of Rights to the states, nor should they. It is possible to read more than that into the handful of prolandowner holdings, but it is hard to read any less than that.

This conclusion is not nihilistic. There is a role for a coherent regulatory takings doctrine by the U.S. Supreme Court. Supervision of state courts on Bill of Rights matters is important. Some guidance concerning the substance of a regulatory takings doctrine is consistent with principles of federalism because of interstate spillovers, the effects of which chapter 6 will demonstrate. I will propose in Chapter 9 that the substance of a regulatory takings doctrine should be built less on formal property law and justifications of regulation and more on judicial notice of what people actually do.

The behavioral standard would ask what kinds of regulations people would willingly impose on themselves if they were outsiders to their own community. This version of the golden rule needs judicial enforcement mainly when the outsiders are not a meaningful part of the political process that adopts the regulations and have immobile assets that the insiders can easily grab. Even if the Supreme Court's attention to local land use regulation in *First English, Dolan,* and (arguably) *Nollan,* was accidental, it does point to the special burdens that such regulation imposes. (*Nollan* is more arguable because the Coastal

Commission was set up as a statewide body, though only for a small fraction of the state,) *Agins* seems to have been the nadir in the U.S. Supreme Court's regulatory takings doctrine, although I will submit in Chapter 8 that its reflexive acceptance of rent controls seems almost as bad.

The outcome in *Lucas* is more problematical for my program. There a state legislature had done the work, and I am willing to cut states more slack in modifying property regimes than a local government. But more slack does not mean infinite tolerance, and the South Carolina Coastal Council was selected by coastal-county legislators. The outcome in *Lucas* is justified largely by the uncompromising extremity of the regulation's application. The settlement in the case, in which the state bought the property and then resold it for the very use that Lucas had proposed, revealed the arbitrariness of the regulation. The "total loss" rule that, for the time being, is necessary to obtain compensation in federal court is itself arbitrary, but it does have the virtue of urging state governments to think about the consequences of their actions.

2

Eminent Domain's Democratic Origins and Economic Cycles

This chapter explores three issues of traditional eminent domain law in order to throw indirect light on regulatory takings. The first issue is whether eminent domain is needed at all. I argue that it is, private substitutes notwithstanding. This point is related to the "public use" doctrine, which forbids the government from using eminent domain for purposes that are not public. The public use doctrine has been declared dead by many commentators. In the spirit of looking for alternatives to judicial review, I point to several examples in which politics and mobility dampened the enthusiasm for eminent domain.

The second topic concerns the origins of the just compensation doctrine. Although American takings law has common-law origins, it was taken up by state constitution makers early in the nineteenth century. I emphasize this to point out the democratic origins of eminent domain. It is not solely a matter of U.S. constitutional doctrine. Eminent domain practices were modified in response to changing economic conditions by legislators and constitution makers as well as by judges.

The pattern of modifications of eminent domain law is the third general topic of this chapter. I submit that just compensation has always been a balancing act between efficiency and fairness. In modern regulatory takings, the issue weighs the desire of the private owner to develop real estate against the collective desire of the public to be left in peace. In nineteenth-century eminent domain, the issue often weighed the collective desire of the public to develop transportation infrastructure against the private owner's desire to be left in peace.

This switch in the roles of the public agency and the private owners has been noticed before. The novelty that I suggest is that there seems to have been a regular pattern in transportation issues. When a transportation innovation was proposed, it promised (sometimes overpromised) immense benefits to all. In order to promote it, eminent domain law was modified in ways that shoved aside fairness to the private landowner. The modification that I focus on was called the "benefit-offset" doctrine. But after either reality or the law of diminishing returns set in and the additional benefits of another mile of railroad track seemed much smaller, fairness issues again came to the fore. I propose that this cycle explains the renewed attention to regulatory takings in the waning years of the twentieth century.

2.1 Takings Clauses Are in U.S. and States' Constitutions

The Fifth Amendment of the U.S. Constitution mentions property twice. Americans may not "be deprived of life, liberty, or property, without due process of law." This is the federal Due Process Clause, limiting the reach of the U.S. government. It was echoed seventy-seven years later in the Fourteenth Amendment, which similarly limited the states. The other mention is the conclusion of the Fifth Amendment, "nor shall private property be taken for public use, without just compensation."

The U.S. Constitution is the supreme law of the land, but it is not the only source of law for the takings issue. All of the states except North Carolina and New Hampshire have similar clauses in their constitutions. The apparent redundancy exists because for most of the nineteenth century, the federal courts applied the U.S. Bill of Rights only against the federal government, not the states. If citizens wanted to prevent state legislative infringements on property, they had to word their own constitutions accordingly. Most states did so. It was not a case of reflexive imitation by the states, for, as Lawrence Friedman pointed out (1988), the federal Bill of Rights was influenced by those originally adopted by several of the states during the Revolutionary War and the Articles of Confederation period.

The Fourteenth Amendment of 1868 held that the states could not deprive U.S. citizens of "life, liberty, or property without due process of law." The U.S. Supreme Court has fitfully held that these words "incorporated" most of the federal Bill of Rights so that the first ten amendments are applied to state governments. Persons deprived of U.S. constitutional rights by state or local governments can now vindicate them in federal court. The Fifth Amendment's Takings Clause was in fact the first to be held incorporated. An 1897 case, Chicago, Burlington and Quincy Railroad v. Chicago, reversed an Illinois court decision that declined to compensate for taking a railroad right of way.

Incorporation did not, however, make the state takings clauses redundant. The U.S. Supreme Court has typically insisted that owners of property seek remedies in the state courts before coming to federal court, as shown by Williamson County v. Hamilton Bank (1985). It has also usually deferred to state court interpretations of what constitutes a taking (Agins v. Tiburon 1980). The U.S. Supreme Court's deference is warranted in part because there is little U.S. constitutional property law. The Constitution mentions property but does not define it or grant Congress authority to do so, except for copyrights and patents. What constitutes property for the purposes of the Takings Clause must be established mainly by state sources of law, including common law, statutes, and state constitutions.

The other reason that state takings clauses continue to be important is that many of them contain language stronger than that of the Fifth Amendment. Some insist that the compensation be paid in money and in advance of the taking, some say compensation is owed when property is "damaged" as well as taken, and a few proscribe the use of offsetting benefits in calculating compensation (William Stoebuck 1972). The U.S. Takings Clause might be said to be a floor on the protection of property, with the states entitled to offer it more protection in their courts.

"Inverse" condemnation arises when legal proceedings are initiated by the property owner seeking compensation rather than by the government, which does not seek to acquire legal title. Regulatory takings are often classified under inverse condemnation, because the government rarely offers formal compensation for regulatory devaluations. Most inverse condemnation cases do not allege regulatory excess, however. Landowners adjacent to a newly built public dump or a noisy highway might initiate inverse condemnation proceedings against a government agency for the devaluation of their property by the nuisance spillovers. Despite the frequent use of "taking or damaging" language in state constitutions, many state courts are reluctant to grant compensation for such claims, often sweeping them into the box of noncompensable "consequential" damages (Gideon Kanner 1980, 1989).

2.2 Property Rules, Liability Rules, and Efficiency Definitions

Terminology not heard in the courtroom but heard often in the law and economics literature is the distinction between "property rules" and "liability rules." The paired terms were introduced in a famous article by Guido Calabresi and A. Douglas Melamed (1972). The right to "just say no" to a prospective purchaser is called a *property rule,* while the rule that the owner must give up her property if market value (or some other amount approved by a third party) is offered is called a *liability rule.* Property rules are more protective of initial distributions of entitlements than liability rules, but they do permit trade on the owner's terms, contrary to the third protective rule considered by Calabresi and Melamed, inalienability.

The term "property rule" comes from the usual private rule for property. You do not have to sell your home, car, copyright, or labor services to another private party just because someone offers you a price that equals or exceeds its market value. The term "liability rule" comes from the remedial rule in torts, in which a tortfeasor is liable for the market costs of his misbehavior, but generally not for more than that. Since the torteous event has typically passed, the rule of damages (dollar payment for the loss) is usually all that the law can produce.

The foregoing terminology can get confusing. A homeowner has *property-rule protection* against the demands of other private parties, but only *liability-rule protection* against the demands of the government or others endowed with the power of eminent domain. One does not say that the government has a liability rule, for that might erroneously imply that one could make the government surrender its property if a private party was willing to pay for it. For legal remedies, a person seeking to vindicate property-rule protection would want an injunction that could be lifted only by her consent; a party seeking only liability-rule protection would ask for damages. Most victims of trespass, of course, want damages for past injuries and injunctions against future invasions.

The property rule/liability rule distinction shows that the Takings Clause is less protective of private property than it is sometimes made out to be. The Takings Clause dictates that private property is protected only by a liability rule with respect to the government or some other party granted the power of eminent domain. It allows property to be taken without consent, unlike the Third Amendment, which prohibits the peacetime quartering of troops in private houses "without the consent of the owner."

Lawyers are often familiar with the property/liability distinction, but they are less versed in the nuances of "efficiency." Economists use it in three ways. An action is *Pareto superior* if its result leaves at least one party better off and no one else worse off. Voluntary exchange is normally assumed to be a Pareto superior action. An action meets the *Kaldor/Hicks* efficiency test if the people who are better off *could* compensate those who are worse off and still come out ahead. Kaldor/Hicks does not require that compensation be made, so it is sometimes called the potential Pareto superiority criterion. (The reason for having two tests for "more efficient" is explained in section 4.4.) A stationary condition (as opposed to an action) is called *Pareto efficient*, or sometimes "Pareto optimal," if there is no exchange that can make one party better off without making another worse off. In other words, one is in a Pareto efficient state when no more Pareto superior actions are available. (For a more extended treatment, see Jules Coleman [1980].)

2.3   The Holdout Problem Requires Forced Sales

The major advantage of liability rules is that they cut through the holdout problem. Holdouts are endemic in public projects such as road building, in which many different properties must be acquired and alternative routes are limited. Preventing time-consuming strategic bargaining is an important justification for eminent domain.

The holdout problem also vexes private planners and architects, who blame it for some of the amusing (to a nonarchitect) contortions of modern buildings (Alpern and Durst 1984). A local example that has long fascinated me is the assemblage of nearly forty square miles of contiguous New Hampshire uplands for a private wild-animal preserve in the 1890s. Austin Corbin, a railroad baron who retired to his childhood home in Newport, New Hampshire, acquired 375 separate titles for his park without the use of eminent domain (G. T. Ferris 1897).

I had always wondered how Corbin avoided the holdout problem, and I eventually found that he had not. After he had acquired most of his land and put up a ten-foot fence around its thirty-mile perimeter to contain his animals, Corbin's organization was hauled into court by a landowner named Reuben Ellis. Ellis had bought an old farm within the park while Corbin's agents had been negotiating with its former owner. Ellis paid about $500 for it, but he turned around and asked Corbin to pay him $3,000 for the same land. Corbin resisted, and Ellis got an injunction from the New Hampshire courts against the invasion of his land by Corbin's imported wild animals, which included wild boar (Ellis v. Blue Mountain Forest Association 1898). Corbin's organization could have complied with the injunction by erecting a fence around Ellis's land. The cost of the fence within the fence? The defendant's brief involving settlement of the same case in 1905 put the cost at $3,000, the amount that Ellis demanded for his land.

Despite the holdout problem, most real and personal property acquired by the government is purchased on the open market and through negotiation (Thomas Merrill 1986a, p. 94). Sometimes agencies are required by statute to try voluntary purchases first, but mainly they do so out of simple rationality. Governments that seek to acquire a property by eminent domain must follow elaborate statutory procedures to condemn it. Most states provide for impartial assessors to resolve stalled negotiations, but these can be appealed to a court of law, and a jury trial may ensue. Such procedures are costly for both sides.

A few economists have suggested that eminent domain may actually be less efficient in acquiring property than voluntary transfers (Mitchell Polinsky 1979). An empirical study of the use of eminent domain by Patricia Munch (1976) supported this contention. She found that eminent domain condemnation for a Chicago urban renewal project overcompensated owners of high-value property, because they had better lawyers to contest government appraisals, while it undervalued owners of low-value property.

Munch's study is often cited, but it has not been replicated. It remains isolated, I think, because it is hard to know what to make of her findings as a general policy. The government does not have to use its power of eminent domain. It can use private means of property assemblage. But these are likely to be problematical, too. The controversial acquisition of Owens Valley water rights for Los Angeles in 1905 was done privately and covertly in order to avoid the cost of eminent domain trials (William Kahrl 1981). Los Angeles has been bitterly criticized for its bypass of eminent domain. The bypass allowed the city to escape public scrutiny of its plans.

Because of the public's anxiety about secrecy, modern governments almost always have to operate in the open, and the holdout problem surely remains. Munch showed that eminent domain valuations are easily second-guessed, but she did not address how the holdout problem might otherwise be dealt with. Although economists have made theoretical progress on methods to induce people to reveal their preferences with rather complicated voting rules (Tideman and Tullock 1976), compulsory sale still seems to be the best that can be done as a practical matter.

2.4 Eminent Domain Is Sometimes Overlooked

The larger utility of eminent domain was brought home to me in a 1990 conversation with a Russian city planner named Igor Portyansky. He had taken advantage of Gorbachev's *glasnost* and the accompanying *perestroyka* movement to open up contacts with the West. As a city planner, Portyansky had developed computerized allocation models for urban areas, and he wanted to sell them in the West.

After he demonstrated his program for me, I suggested that the programming problem he was undertaking required more information than anyone could expect to possess. I pointed out that in the United States, the task he was attempting was undertaken by a decentralized system of property ownership guided by hundreds of thousands of entrepreneurial types in the real estate business. Why, I asked him, didn't he advocate selling state land to individuals and cultivate a similar market mechanism? (This was before the 1991 coup attempt and the breakup of the USSR.)

Portyansky patiently explained his opposition to the privatization of land. If the government sold the land to private individuals, it might want to buy it back sometime in the future. The government might need the land for a hospital or a park, but the owner might not want to sell or might sell only at what Portyansky then regarded as a ridiculously high price, "billions of rubles." Private ownership, therefore, was out of the question.

I was puzzled by his response for a few seconds, and then it dawned on me: he'd never heard of eminent domain. One of the casualties of seventy years of communism appears to have been knowledge of basic property law.

Citizens of the former Soviet Union were not the only victims of inattention to property law. Kenneth Arrow, who won the Nobel Memorial Prize in economics in 1972, wrote a paper in 1977 in which he offered a critique of the law and economics approach to resource allocation for such public goods as air quality. He patiently explained the fundamental problem. The numerous owners of entitlements to clean air might strategically conceal their inclination to sell it in order to garner a large amount of the economic surplus from those proposing some productive but polluting activity. He offered an illustration: "Indeed, precisely this situation actually occurs in land assembly, where a large plot of contiguous land is needed, and the odd shapes of some department stores and office buildings testify mutely to failures to achieve efficient resource allocation."

Professor Arrow, meet Dr. Portyansky. Arrow cast his example in terms of private holdouts, but the policy problem he used to criticize the law and economics approach, air pollution, is clearly within the right of the government to address by eminent domain. It can deal with the holdout problem by forcing the sale.

Just compensation under eminent domain does not, however, solve the efficiency problem. The nearly invariable measure of just compensation is the market value of what is given up. Market values are not necessarily the true reservation prices of the owners. Owners may have personal attachments to the property for which market-value monetary compensation cannot purchase an adequate substitute, so that forcing a sale cannot guarantee Pareto efficiency (Jack Knetsch 1983, chap. 4).

Ignorance of reservation prices applies to Arrow's example of oddly shaped department stores. Maybe the holdout owner really does value possession of her little house more than it would contribute to the value of the shopping center, so that the odd-looking shapes "testify mutely" to Pareto efficiency rather than market failure. In any event, I submit that if the public becomes sufficiently upset about the occasional odd shape of shopping centers or loses its sense of humor about a few architectural contortions of office buildings, governments can grant the developers the power of eminent domain, and the grant will most probably pass judicial review. (The nonmarket-valuation issue is explored more in section 5.16.)

2.5 *"Public Use" Is a Minor Limitation on Takings*

Largely because of the holdout problem, private enterprises have often sought the power of eminent domain from legislatures. The constitutional limitation on this is the phrase "public use" from the Takings

Clause: "nor shall private property be taken *for public use* without just compensation." The public use limitation at one time was held by many courts to limit both what the government could acquire and to whom it could delegate the authority to acquire private property.

Antidelegation doctrines were modified as the demand for internal improvements expanded in the nineteenth century. Private railroad builders were routinely given the right of eminent domain. Experimentation indicated the utility of doing so. In response to dissatisfied landowners, the New Hampshire legislature in 1840 prohibited the practice for new railroads. The nearly complete, though perhaps coincidental, cessation of all railroad construction in the state for the next four years apparently induced the state to rescind the prohibition in 1844 (Harry Scheiber 1989, p. 229). The experience probably served as a caution to other states as well, for it appears that no other state undertook this experiment.

As for the "public use" to which acquired property may be put, the U.S. Supreme Court has become extremely permissive. In Hawaii Housing Authority v. Midkiff (1984), for example, it permitted a public housing authority to condemn private land and immediately transfer it to homeowners who had held the land as a long-term leasehold. The "public use" was said to be the antimonopolistic purpose of the plan. Much of Hawaii's developable land is owned by a few landowners who have been willing to lease but not to sell it. The concentrated ownership, it was argued, had resulted in excessively high housing prices. (Don't think of plutocratic owners here; the largest owner is a trust whose income is dedicated to the education of the descendants of aboriginal Hawaiians.)

The connection between Hawaii's condemnation plan and the housing price problem seems tenuous. The source of the monopoly, if there was one, was the landowner's ability to withhold *undeveloped* land from use in the housing market. By transferring only *developed* land from one owner to another (with compensation, the amount of which was also controversial), Hawaii's plan did nothing to encourage the supposedly monopolistic landowners to increase the supply of sites for housing. (For a criticism of *Midkiff* that argued that the monopoly-landowner theory is wrong, see LaCroix and Rose [1993].)

I am nonetheless inclined to agree with the U.S. Court's deferential position with regard to *Midkiff*. The state's or nation's ability to alter its economic institutions is an important public good. James Ely

(1992a) has convinced me that there is little doubt that the U.S. Constitution was written and adopted by people who believed in private property. The Constitution is nonetheless primarily a document that facilitates political action, and its authors expected political forces to modify the economic system. The second-kindest compliment to late twentieth-century capitalism is that it has persisted despite the ability of democratic governments to choose another system.

Just compensation is a means of smoothing out transformations in the economy, whether they be for internal improvements or for institutional change. The Takings Clause serves both as a check to excessive public enthusiasm (since money must be paid) and as a facilitator (since property must be surrendered). But it does not prohibit change. Thus if Hawaii wants to reject some of its anachronistic landholding system, there should be no bar to its doing so if compensation is made. It isn't just roads and post offices that qualify as public goods; economic institutions do, too.

Imagine an American ambassador to some developing country phoning up the U.S. State Department. He tells the Secretary that the country has just decided to take some of the large land holdings of a small group of owners and transfer it to the peasants.

Secretary: "And are American interests among those subject to expropriation?"
Ambassador: "Yes, sir. Don't you think we need a contingent of Marines?"
Sec.: "Well, is the government offering the landowners anything in exchange?"
Amb.: "Of course, but it's still forcing the sale."
Sec.: "The compensation; is it trivial, like five cents on the dollar?"
Amb.: "Oh, no, sir. It's full market value, as determined by an independent court of law."
Sec.: "Mr. Ambassador, have you been spending a lot of time in the sun lately?"

2.6 *Public Use Is Largely Self-Limiting*

Some state courts have become almost as permissive as the federal courts with respect to the public use doctrine, as two famous cases indicate. In City of Oakland v. Oakland Raiders (1982), the California Supreme Court upheld the city's right in principle to condemn the football team to prevent its departure to Los Angeles, although the subsequent suit ultimately failed. Michigan's supreme court upheld condemnation of an old ethnic neighborhood to make way for a new General Motors automobile assembly plant, the public use being to save GM jobs in Detroit (Poletown Neighborhood Council v. Detroit 1981).

One should not conclude from *Poletown* and *Oakland Raiders* that the states have all abandoned review of public use. Thomas Merrill (1986a, p. 96) found that a surprising number of state appellate cases hold for private owners who wish not to have their property condemned when the publicness of the use seems dubious. That many state courts continue to scrutinize for public use long after the federal courts have ceased any serious inquiry indicates again the importance of state law.

Merrill's influential article explains that judges should not worry much about the public use doctrine, because it is largely self-limiting. Eminent domain may be expansive, but it is also expensive. (For some estimates of the expense, see section 2.19.) In markets lacking the holdout problem, in which eminent domain would be inappropriate, the transaction costs of using the market are typically less than that of using eminent domain. Thus the budget-preserving instincts of government agencies may usually be depended upon to limit eminent domain where there are no holdouts.

My own view is that judicial inquiry into public use should continue to be permissive. Having to pay compensation and enduring the transaction costs that eminent domain entails are sufficient to deter legislatures from using eminent domain to accomplish unprincipled redistributions of wealth. To put it cynically, there are so many cheaper ways to accomplish unprincipled redistribution that there is little reason for judges to worry about this particular issue.

There is a deterrent to excesses of eminent domain that may be more important than the financial penalty. The cases that flirt with the borderlines of public use, such as *Poletown,* are also limited by popular revulsion at the government's action. *Poletown* became a *cause célèbre* in Michigan and among urban activists (Jeanie Wylie 1989). *Poletown* provides common ground for the left and right among American scholars of eminent domain (David Schultz 1992 and Richard Epstein 1985, respectively). Although it is small comfort for the Poletown residents who were actually displaced (with compensation), in the future Detroit or any other city will think hard before it razes an established neighborhood for the benefit of a large corporation. (The Michigan Supreme Court also modified its deferential position in Lansing v. Edward Rose Realty [1993], an opinion that seems defensive about *Poletown.*)

Such forbearance may not be an entirely good thing. Keeping General Motors in Detroit qualifies as a public good insofar as the neighborhood attachments of their workers and others dependent on the plant would be broken by its removal. Although not necessary for the argument, community attachments are quantifiable in terms of wage premiums (L. F. Dunn 1979). The city of Detroit seems better qualified than a court of law to decide whose neighborhood attachments, those of the Poletowners or those of the Detroiters who work for GM, should prevail in the political marketplace. Judges cannot tell whether Detroit could have kept GM in town without taking the land in Poletown under the terms that were generous to the company.

Another limitation on the excessive use of eminent domain became apparent after *Oakland Raiders* was decided. It illustrates to local governments the merits of forswearing eminent domain even when there is much room for bilateral bargaining. When the Baltimore Colts began considering a move to Indianapolis, the city of Baltimore sought to induce the football franchise to stay with various financial incentives. Once the city began open discussion of acquiring the football team by eminent domain, however, the Colts literally removed all their assets in a midnight dash for the state border (Mayor and City Council v. Baltimore Football Club 1985).

The move foreclosed the possibility of eminent domain. The team's premature departure scuttled negotiations that might have kept the Colts in the barn. The lesson of the Colts appears to have persuaded Baltimore and other cities to negotiate with sports franchises rather than trying to condemn them (Charles Euchner 1993).

2.7 *Private Eminent Domain Shows Its General Utility*

The famous New York tort case of Boomer v. Atlantic Cement (1970) invoked what looks like eminent domain. *Boomer* is a leading case in nuisance law because it changed the remedial right of a victim of a nuisance from a property rule to a liability rule in certain circumstances.

The Atlantic Cement Company opened a quarry and built a large plant nearby in a small town about twenty miles south of Albany.

Blasting from the quarry shook the homes of nearby rural residents, and dust from the quarry also annoyed them. About a dozen neighbors brought an action to enjoin the cement company. The injunction would have, it was assumed by the court, stopped the entire operation unless and until some settlement was reached with the neighbors. Mr. Boomer was the lead plaintiff.

The trial court, ignoring a good deal of precedent indicating that an injunction (and thus property-rule protection for Mr. Boomer and his neighbors) was the appropriate remedy, ordered the cement company instead to pay monetary damages to the neighbors for the nuisance it created. The New York Court of Appeals affirmed this approach, modifying it by making the damages permanent. In effect, as the dissent pointed out, the court had approved the use of eminent domain by the cement company to acquire the right to blast and create dust.

This case is treated in the excellent law and economics text of Robert Cooter and Thomas Ulen (1988) as an instance of overcoming the holdout problem because of the multiplicity of nearby owners. Under property-rule protection for the homeowners, each one must give her consent to forgo the right to enjoin the nuisance. This creates a strong incentive for the owners to hold out for a price that might be much higher than their reservation price. That in itself is not a bad thing— many people are paid more than their reservation price for their property in ordinary transactions—except that it might take a long time to negotiate, during which the plant would have to shut down and layoff many workers.

In *Boomer*, it was the prospect that the plant's employees would be thrown out of work that was emphasized by the New York Court of Appeals majority. Local employment has long been a matter of public policy. Concern about it would seem to justify the court's decision in the case. Moreover, as Daniel Farber (1987) pointed out in a paper that was otherwise critical of the decision, the financial award to the neighbors did seem larger than usual, reflecting the feeling that their sacrifice should receive extra compensation. (For what it is worth, a lawyer whose firm has worked for Atlantic Cement assured me in 1985 that the company did not take its victory as a license to acquire property without negotiation.)

Let me sum up this and the previous two sections with a negative endorsement: the public use issue is not dead. (A novel attempt to resuscitate it as a central principle is Jed Rubenfeld [1993], as discussed in section 9.6.) Whether there is a justification for forcing a sale will always be an issue. What I hope to have shown is that public use standards are necessarily elastic, because the issue of holdouts is ubiquitous. I also submit that the public use limitation is not solely a matter for judges to decide under constitutional standards. Rational democratic bodies are capable of responding to the potential for inefficiency and unfairness in using eminent domain. The legal burden of proving that a democratic body is insensitive to unfair exercises of eminent domain should not be insuperable, but there are reasons to defer to the government.

2.8 Just Compensation Has Statutory and Common-Law Origins

The presence of the takings clause in state constitutions as well as in the federal Fifth Amendment encourages the belief that just compensation has always been a constitutional idea. This implies that takings would have occurred without just compensation but for constitutional limitations. This is not the case, however, as William Stoebuck's (1972) fine history has documented. American states that lacked a takings clause in the early days of the Republic nonetheless usually paid for property that they took. It was done on a case-by-case basis. Legislation authorizing a taking for, say, a road typically included provision for compensation.

Compensation was not, however, just a matter of legislative benevolence. Several scholars have pointed to decisions in which early American courts found the obligation to pay just compensation in common law and ordered it to be paid when legislatures had not authorized it. Among these decisions was that of the eminent jurist Chancellor James Kent of New York. Kent held that the state could not prevent the damming of a stream without compensation to the owner who sought to do so, despite the absence at the time of a just compensation clause in the state constitution (Gardner v. Newburgh 1816). It is worth a brief excursion into English eminent domain history (guided mainly by Stoebuck) to see why the common law arrived at just compensation.

Legal history often emphasizes the difference between the right of eminent domain and the obligation of just compensation. Eminent domain is said to be an inherent characteristic of sovereignty. Sovereignty is a monopoly on the use of force within a given territory, so it is hardly surprising that, regardless of the legal tradition, the law of every sovereign nation recognizes that the state is able to take private property.

The source of the obligation to pay for property is less obvious. Under the principle of royal prerogative, early English kings were not required to compensate for taking most interests in land. They often built coastal fortifications on land for which they did not pay, and compensation was not initially forthcoming for land on which sewers and dikes were constructed. The king was required by Magna Carta to pay for grain, however, and by later statutes to pay for the use of transportation equipment (Stoebuck 1972, p. 563).

A moment's reflection about supply elasticity suggests an economic hypothesis about the origins of compensation. You are a farmer with a store of corn, and the king's agents come knocking. If you don't expect to be paid for your grain, there is a good chance that you will try to conceal it. If you cannot, you might think about going into some other line of work the next year. Some royal genius is apt to notice that the time and trouble wasted in having to scrounge for corn, when it can be found at all, costs considerably more than the corn itself. After a while, it becomes common practice to pay for corn, and this becomes enshrined in statutes or in that code of common practice called the common law.

Stoebuck has pointed out that as eminent domain shifted from the Crown to Parliament, compensation began to be offered for land as well as for more portable assets. This was natural enough, since Parliament represented the interests of landowners. The British voting franchise was limited to property owners well into the nineteenth century. Hence our tradition of compensation for land may have had its origins in the actions of the first large-scale legislature.

2.9   Democratic Constitutions Required Just Compensation

The English common-law tradition of compensation was embraced by Americans both before and after the Revolutionary War (James Ely 1992a, p. 32). When state constitutions were written after Independence, several of the original states simply assumed that the common-law right of compensation would continue, and they did not enshrine this particular right in their bills of rights. In most cases, legislatures in states without takings clauses authorized compensation for property owners when land was taken.

The apparently discretionary authorization of compensation may have emerged from a reluctance by states to entertain compensation suits by Loyalists whose property was taken without compensation when they fled during the Revolutionary War. (Loyalists were, however, compensated by the British, according to Wallace Brown [1969].) James Ely tells me that most confiscations were made under bills of attainder, which took property from traitors, rather than under eminent domain. Revulsion at this practice contributed to the U.S. Constitution's prohibition on bills of attainder and its narrow definition of treason.

The need for state-constitutional mention of just compensation eventually became apparent, despite the common-law precedents. In the post–Revolutionary War period, state legislatures were eager to develop public works but were often short of cash. Some of them would authorize road construction without paying for the land or, in a few instances, the raw materials. Where the land taken was virtually valueless without the roads, the landowners did not greatly object to such practices, and some state constitutions and legislative compensation provisions explicitly distinguished between unenclosed (and presumably less valuable) land and enclosed land.

In other states, however, uncompensated takings caused political uproars that resulted in the adoption of takings clauses in the state constitutions. Even in Pennsylvania, whose legislature could plausibly point to a "reserved powers" doctrine because William Penn had granted land with the express provision that 6 percent was to be reserved for roads, a takings clause was added in response to dissatisfaction with uncompensated exercises of eminent domain. (Penn was apparently alone in such foresight among the grantors of colonial land, and he deserves the rational-expectations prize, as I discuss in section 5.2.)

State history enters the modern debate about the takings issue because some lawyers regard the original intent of those who adopted the federal Takings Clause as determining what it ought to be today. The original intent issue revolves around what kinds of activities were compensable around 1790, when the U.S. Bill of Rights was adopted (Douglas Kmiec 1988; Robert Bork 1990).

Scholars opposed to the originalist view point to the absence of state takings clauses and the occasional uncompensated takings during the late 1700s as evidence that originalism does not support a vigorous application of the just compensation principle (William Treanor 1985; Laurence Tribe 1988, p. 608). There were instances in which property

was physically taken without just compensation. Regulations that infringed on property rights were also common during the late colonial
and early national period (Forrest McDonald 1985, chap. 2). Only
later did almost all states adopt takings clauses, and judicial review of
regulation under them developed fitfully and incompletely. Critics of
originalism take this record to undermine the case for a vigorous application of takings clauses. Ely (1992b), however, has marshaled substantial evidence that colonial and early state instances of failure to
compensate were rare and usually explicable by the principle of implicit, in-kind compensation.

The lesson I take from the states' early experience is evolutionary.
The historical record is useful in revealing how the evolving republics
responded to reliance on the common law and the discretion of legislators. The record shows that the absence of a just compensation
clause was sufficiently vexing that democratic bodies of the day—state
constitutional conventions and elected legislatures—found it necessary
to insert takings clauses in their constitutions. The adoption of takings
clauses and their persistence for nearly two centuries make a powerful
argument that they should be taken seriously, even if their boundaries
are imprecise. That such additions were adopted by an increasingly
broad electorate (since property-holding requirements for voting were
gradually dropped) also suggests that just compensation is not merely
a response to aristocratic concerns, as its English Magna Carta and
Parliamentary origins might otherwise suggest.

2.10 Railroad Construction Raised the Benefit-Offset Problem

I begin to address the broader aspects of the efficiency and fairness
issues by examining controversial compensation practices by railroad
builders in the nineteenth century. This controversy is often overlooked in works that are primarily concerned with regulatory takings.
In building a railroad or a highway, the question of whether to pay at
all does not arise. The landowner who surrenders property to the
railroad company is always paid, unlike the landowner subject to a
restrictive zoning regulation.

The railroad cases are nonetheless similar to the regulatory takings
question in some respects. The Takings Clause requires compensation.
Compensation remedies are as important as compensation principles,

because the Takings Clause is actually a right to a remedy. The possibility that compensation might not be paid for physical invasions is explored here under the rubric of the benefit-offset issue.

The benefit-offset issue first came to my attention in several articles by the legal historian Harry Scheiber, beginning with what is now a classic study of state court rulings on eminent domain, "The Road to *Munn*" (1971). According to Scheiber, state courts in the early 1800s developed several "expediting doctrines" to assist public agencies and private corporations endowed by state legislatures with eminent domain (1973, p. 233; see also Stephen Siegel 1986). Among the expediters was the benefit-offset principle. Here is how it worked.

If a public agency took only part of an individual's land, it had to pay him for the part it took. The agency could deduct from this payment, however, some or all of the increase in value that accrued to the remainder of the parcel. Thus a railroad, to which states usually gave eminent domain powers, might take 20 acres of McDonald's 160-acre farm. Suppose the 20 acres were valued at $1,000. The appraisers might find that the remaining 140 acres of the farm increased in value by $800 because of improved access to markets, so that on balance the railroad owed McDonald only $200. Thus the benefit of the $800 gain partly offset the $1,000 loss.

As a result of the aggressive use of the benefit offset, Scheiber reported, "in Illinois, railroad takings frequently resulted in assessment of damages of one dollar." The situation was similar, if not always so dramatic, in several other states during the period of early (pre–Civil War) railroad construction. The rule was not symmetrical, though. If the remaining land was devalued rather than enhanced in value by the railroad, another of the expediting doctrines held that there was no taking without a physical touching. (The benefit-offset doctrine was not extended to the logical extreme of having the landowner pay the railroad in the event that benefits to his remaining land exceeded the value of the land taken.)

2.11 Benefit Offsets May Have Been Efficient Subsidies

Scheiber regarded the benefit offset as an important subsidy to the railroad. In this respect, he agreed with one article of the thesis of the Marxist legal historian Morton Horwitz (1977), which viewed legal decisions on eminent domain in the nineteenth century as promoting the interests of the railroads at the expense of yeoman landowners. Horwitz's thesis was contested by the historian Tony Freyer (1981), who found evidence in compensation awards which indicated that the power of property owners in local trial courts exceeded the persuasiveness of railroad lawyers in appellate courts. (Freyer demonstrated the hazards of inferring actual practices from a review of appellate court opinions.) And Scheiber did not agree with Horwitz's general inference that this subsidy resulted in the rich gaining at the expense of the poor. Horwitz neglected the economic benefits that flowed to the poor from more rapid and extensive construction of railroads, and the fact that most farmers "were pathetically eager for railroads" (Lawrence Friedman 1986, p. 19).

Their different perspectives notwithstanding, historians seem to agree with Scheiber that the benefit-offset principle was "a potentially large involuntary subsidy for the projects being undertaken" (1973, p. 134). An economist might take such a statement to imply that railroads were being overproduced. I submit that this was not necessarily the case.

If a railroad in southern Illinois in 1840 were able to appropriate the economic advantages of every mile of new track that it laid, the surrounding land would neither rise nor fall in value, and the railroad would have sufficient incentive to expand the road to a socially efficient extent. To be more precise, the land would rise in value by virtue of expected services from the railroad, but it would fall by the foreknowledge that the railroad would, as a perfectly discriminating monopolist, adopt a price structure that would extract all the benefit for itself.

We know that railroads, even the most gouging, unregulated of them, could not appropriate all of the benefits their construction entailed. Railroads created substantial agglomeration economies that are reflected at least in part by increased land values. Modern urban economics confirms that internal transportation improvements will usually cause increased land values.

Because of the value enhancement, landowners had some incentive to induce the railroads to extend their reach beyond what might have been financially feasible without this subsidy. And despite the free-rider problem—if one landowner succeeds, others benefit as well—American history is replete with stories of towns and land companies that spent a lot of money to induce the railroad to come. It is no more inefficient to have done this than it is for a modern county to agree to provide land for an airport to stimulate economic development. Or, dare I say, for the city of Detroit to want to induce its major employer, General Motors, to stay in town by lending it the power of eminent domain. Hence we could think of the benefit offset rule as an inducement to achieve the efficient level of railroad building.

There are many reasons why the previous theoretical arguments in favor of the efficiency of the benefit offset may prove unworkable in practice. The benefit-offset existed only if the railroad took part of a property. This might induce railroads to select routes that would ensure many partial takings, so that it would pay less, and it could induce landowners to spend resources manipulating the political process to steer the railroad to the parcel next door. Furthermore, the benefit-offset subsidy was on top of numerous other subsidies that railroads were granted, such as outright gifts of public land and exemption from taxes. These qualifications notwithstanding, the benefit-offset principle probably facilitated a more efficient provision of transportation in a land that eagerly sought access to markets.

2.12 The Problem with Benefit Offset Was Its Unfairness

The major problem with benefit-offset financing was not that it provided a subsidy, but that it did not provide enough of a subsidy. Farmer A has forty acres taken but is offered only a dollar in compensation because his remaining land has sufficiently increased in value. His neighbor, Farmer B, gets the same increase in value but has to sacrifice nothing. The problem could have been cured by having a general assessment on all land value increments. The case law recognizes the selectivity of the benefit offset as the reason that the general benefit offset was constitutionally eliminated in Nebraska, for example.

Prudential Insurance v. Central Nebraska Public Power and Irrigation District (1941) involved farmland owned by Prudential (via foreclosure, presumably) that was taken for an irrigation project that served 200,000 acres of land. Of Prudential's 160-acre tract, 106 acres were not formally taken by the project. The 106 acres were considerably more valuable after the project was completed than they had been before. The condemning authority wanted to use the general benefit (general since it accrued to all owners in the district) to reduce compensation to Prudential. The Nebraska Supreme Court held that it could not, because "it is unjust that one person should be obliged to pay for them [the benefits of irrigation] by a contribution of property while his neighbor whose property is not taken enjoys the same advantage" (145 ALR at 4).

The intriguing implication of this proposition is that the Pareto principle is not enough. A public project involves a "Pareto improvement" if some members of the public are better off, and the rest are no worse off. Here was a project that met that criterion: other owners of land were better off, and Prudential was no worse off without the compensation, since the remainder of its land increased in value. Nonetheless, the state constitution required that there be compensation. If this requirement was not simply an unstable anomaly, one not anticipated by voters and constitution makers, then it follows that "just compensation" means something more than providing the correct incentives for public investment.

The reader might ask whether allowing the benefit offset at issue in *Prudential* would have improved efficiency. One would need more detailed data about financing vehicles, but general economic principles suggest that it would have. Public investment theory says that user charges for projects with scale economies should normally cover only variable costs. The fixed costs (such as land acquisition at issue here) should be spread more generally. The fixed costs were in all likelihood paid by general taxpayers, with the usual deadweight loss and administrative costs from taxation. It would seem better to substitute a tax on increased land value, because, as Henry George (1879) taught, land value taxation involves little deadweight loss (Nicolaus Tideman 1982). Even if not all land is taxed, any reduction in general taxation by substituting selective land taxes would probably increase fiscal efficiency.

2.13   State Constitution Framers Balanced Efficiency and Equity

The benefit-offset principle was attacked and greatly modified over time. Scheiber noted that by 1910, new state constitutions had sharply restricted the benefit offset (1973, p. 237). In its place is a distinction between special and general benefits. Property owners who get benefits above and beyond the ordinary benefit from a road or other public project may have their compensation reduced to the amount of those special benefits. But the government may not offset the payment to an owner whose property is partially taken by pointing to the increase in value to the remainder if other property owners in the area generally benefit as well. If the rule sounds fuzzy, it is because it is (ALR 1967). The distinctions between general and special often seem arbitrary and unstable, but the benefit-offset principle was sharply constricted as a means of subsidizing large-scale public projects.

The limitations that state constitutions placed on the use of the benefit offset was part of a broader public debate about limitations on the use of eminent domain to facilitate economic development. Sometimes the issues were brought up explicitly in state constitutional conventions. Scheiber (1989) described evidence from debates in several nineteenth-century state constitutional conventions. In the constitutional conventions of New Jersey in 1843 and of New York in 1867 and 1894, proposals were made to boost compensation for takings by railroads and other public enterprises. As Scheiber noted, in many cases such proposals were adopted. In the aforementioned conventions, however, there was some evidence that additional compensation was opposed by members who thought it would reduce economic development. They were conscious of the trade-off between protection of private owners and economic development by public projects.

The section on eminent domain in *Rocky Mountain Constitution Making, 1850–1912,* by Gordon Bakken (1987), added to Scheiber's suggestion that fairness and efficiency issues were internalized and balanced by democratically chosen conventions. All of the Rocky Mountain states favored some form of private eminent domain to facilitate water development and mining. Water was an important issue in the development of the arid West. The new states were willing to let aggressive developers prevail over the rights of passive landowners, a fact that still colors water law in the region.

There was variation among the states, according to Bakken's account. In Colorado, the farmer-oriented Granger organizations influenced conventions to adopt more limited eminent domain provisions to prevent railroads from undercompensating farmers. The importance of mining interests in Idaho, by contrast, caused the state to adopt rules allowing private mining interests to take water and access routes. The Utah debates were especially telling. Many delegates worried that urban railroad construction would be hampered by takings clauses that included "taking or damaging" language and that required that money be paid in advance.

2.14   Ohio Delegates Worried about Both Sides of Compensation

To supplement the aforementioned secondary sources, I looked at the record of a mid-nineteenth-century constitutional convention in which the sufficiency of compensation was at issue. The Ohio Constitution of 1802 said in Article XIII, Section 4: "Private property ought and shall ever be held inviolate, but always subservient to the public welfare: provided a compensation in money be made to the owner." By 1850 this clause was deemed an insufficient protection of the rights of property owners. A constitutional convention met in 1850, and the issue of compensation for eminent domain was actively debated (Ohio 1851, pp. 257–260, 883–893).

The result was a strengthened eminent domain provision in Ohio's Article I (bill of rights), Section 19, which read: "Private property shall ever be held inviolate, but subservient to the public welfare. When taken in time of war, or other public exigency, imperatively requiring its immediate seizure, or for the purpose of making or repairing roads, which *shall be open to the public, without charge,* a compensation shall be made to the owner, in money, and in all other cases where private property shall be taken for public use, a compensation therefor shall *first* be made in money, or first secured by a deposit of money, and such compensation shall be assessed by a jury, *without deduction for benefits* to any property of the owner" (my emphasis).

The practices to be guarded against by this language were clear in the debates. Private companies would sometimes be authorized by the legislature to acquire public roadways. Some would then erect a tollgate, which was not contemplated by the original authorization, much to the dismay of the original owners of the property. The "open to the public without charge" provision was clearly aimed at correcting that problem. Compensation was often late in coming, and sometimes judgment could not be enforced because the railroad had gone bankrupt. Hence compensation was *first* to be made in money or secured by a bond, except when a "public exigency, imperatively requiring its immediate seizure" was present.

The other hazard addressed by the 1851 language was that railroad companies would, as Scheiber described, take part of a piece of property and deduct from the obligation to compensate the increase in value of the remaining property. The Ohio convention delegate H. S.

Manon explained the objection: "As a farmer, I am not willing that a Railroad Company should take off a strip from my farm, and pay me for it in 'supposed benefits,' while my neighbor, by the side of whose farm the road runs, without touching it, receives equal 'benefits' with me, and yet loses none of his land" (Ohio 1851, p. 884). This sentiment carried the convention.

Yet other proposed restrictions did not. The delegate M. H. Mitchell had submitted a clause that property "shall never be taken for private use but with the *consent* of the owner" (id., p. 257, my emphasis). This was intended to restrict delegation of eminent domain to railroad companies, but it was met with charges that it would eliminate desirable progress. Mitchell's amendment was tabled, and when it and similar restrictions were raised later, they were voted down. The sentiment of a delegate named L. Case was apparently widely shared: "In the county which I represent, there are some fifty or sixty miles of railroad finished or about to be finished. The improvement is popular with our people, and while they demand a change in the rule of damages in taking private property for public use, and ample provisions for its prompt payment when ascertained, they want no provision which would enable one man from mere caprice to delay a public improvement for years by litigation" (p. 890).

Ohio's measured enhancement of the rights of owners against quasi-public entrepreneurs was echoed in other states. The benefit-offset principle was not the only target. A frequent change, apparently initiated by the famous 1870 Illinois constitution, was to add the words "or damaged." The typical takings clause then read "property shall not be taken or damaged without just compensation." The phrase is found in twenty-six state constitutions (Stoebuck 1969, p. 734).

These sources show that eminent domain was regarded as a prodevelopment tool, but one whose provisions often required more compensation than that of the Fifth Amendment. The modern view has it that the more expansive state constitutional language did not make a practical difference (Bruce Ackerman 1977, p. 191). Stoebuck (1969, p. 758), however, who had examined eminent domain practices in detail, concluded that it did, as did the U.S. Supreme Court in Gibson v. United States (1897, p. 274).

This history is relevant to modern takings jurisprudence because the contours of takings law, including both public use and just compensation, have been the object of continuing democratic scrutiny. State constitutional conventions, particularly those of the West, were highly democratic in their selection of delegates and in their ratification of the constitutions and their amendments. The history suggests that modern democratic bodies consciously affirmed the principle of just compensation for takings, but at the same time shaped it to reflect the anxieties of people whose land would be taken and the hopes of those whose property would be enhanced by both public and private eminent domain. The Takings Clause serves several masters.

2.15   Eminent Domain Has Historical Cycles of Compensation

Sections 2.13 and 2.14 show that inequality of sacrifice was the reason that benefit-offset financing was curtailed late in the nineteenth and early in the twentieth centuries. But this begs the question of why the problem had not been dealt with much earlier. Failure to recognize the problem is hard to credit in a country in which land had always been an important and widely held asset and in which lawyers have been plentiful.

I propose that inequality of treatment was suppressed in the early railroad and canal era because the general benefits of such projects were at first so large. No responsible public official, judge, or body of voters wanted to discourage construction of such projects by providing compensation that appeared to be too generous to landowners. To put it concretely, using Scheiber's example, I submit that railroad construction in Illinois in 1840 was popularly regarded as having such a high social payoff for the region that some degree of horizontal inequity was thought to be tolerable. That made the benefit-offset principle acceptable. By 1870, say, enough railroad construction had been completed that the marginal social value of another railroad, even where clearly positive, was not large enough to warrant inequality of treatment of landowners.

The foregoing hypothesis can be summarized with the following diagram (see Figure 2.1). When there is little railroad development, the marginal benefit of laying track greatly exceeds its cost. There are very large social benefits to doing this. But after, say, 100,000 miles have been laid, the net benefits of laying another thousand miles becomes smaller, either because the new tracks are parallel to the old or because the additional locations served by them are less valuable. This

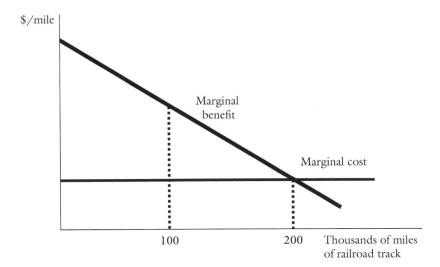

Figure 2.1 Railroad Benefits and Costs

is not to deny the scale economies of completing an entire system; it says only that once one system is complete, additional miles of track are less valuable.

At some point shy of the maximum total net benefit point (200,000 miles in the diagram), the issue of fairness bulks larger, and compensation principles begin to be adopted that attempt to even out burdens. Unevenness of sacrifice is suppressed in earlier stages of development (at 0 to 100,000 miles in my simplistic diagram) because the total social benefits are so large. The public enthusiasm for the gain is such that inequality of gain is easy to suppress. When a person's land value is doubling, it is hard to credit his complaint that he should be compensated because it is not trebling like his neighbor's.

Some readers will recognize in this hypothesis elements of the thesis of the legal historian J. Willard Hurst (1956). He interpreted the development of nineteenth-century American property doctrines as an attempt to promote entrepreneurial activity: "Dynamic rather than static property, property in motion or at risk rather than property secure and at rest, engaged our principal interest" (p. 24). Joel Brenner (1974) has found that a similarly deliberate preference for industrial development pushed aside nuisance law in England during the industrial revolution.

There are numerous other examples of the preference for active uses.

Sometimes it was the U.S. Supreme Court that promoted them. Stanley Kutler's (1971) account of the 1837 *Charles River Bridge* decision supports Hurst's position. The U.S. Supreme Court held that a previously granted charter to the bridge company did not create a vested right for which compensation would have to be paid when the Massachusetts legislature chartered a competitor, unless such an obligation had been explicitly stated in the charter. *Charles River Bridge* was emblematic of a national political change, in which Andrew Jackson's appointees eroded the vested rights doctrines of the Federalist Court.

State courts have even better reason to follow democratic preferences. When the California Supreme Court attempted in 1926 to impose a riparian rights doctrine on the state, voters reacted with an initiative redefining water rights that amended the state constitution in 1928. Voters made it clear that they wanted to promote irrigation by granting water rights to active users, not passive streamside (riparian) owners (Norris Hundley 1992, p. 241).

The practice of limiting payment for property taken by eminent domain by the benefit-offset principle fits nicely into Hurst's general account of eagerness to develop. But Hurst's hypothesis does not explain why the prodevelopment tide turned later in the century. My hypothesis—which is just a generalization of the principle of diminishing marginal utility—suggests an explanation for both the rise *and* the decline of at least one prodevelopment legal rule, the benefit-offset principle.

2.16 The Elevated Railway Raised the Benefit-Offset Issue Again

An explanation for the use of the benefit-offset in the early nineteenth century might be that the cost of raising taxes or private capital for compensation was higher (Friedman 1986, p. 18). Public money was harder to come by then because of poorly developed financial institutions, so subsidies in the form of land made cheaper by the benefit-offset principle would induce railroads to build more. The financial constraint explanation is, however, undermined by the periodic reappearance of the general benefit-offset principle at times when financial institutions were well developed. My first illustration of this is found in New York City.

Extensive intracity railroads developed later in the nineteenth century than intercity railroads because the cities were more crowded. A rail line on the ground would take up the whole street and impose great danger on those nearby. But the development of low-cost steel manufacturing in the 1870s made it possible within a decade to build urban elevated railroad structures that left most of the street open. Low-cost structural steel also made the skyscraper possible, which in turn stimulated demand for speedy transport of workers from the sub-urbs to the employment centers of the city.

In a series of cases between 1890 and 1895, the New York Court of Appeals, the state's highest court, dealt with the question of compen-sation for owners of property along streets in New York City on which the new elevated railroads had been built. The el was a mixed blessing for property owners. The historian Charles Cheape (1980) has de-scribed how the elevated railroads made the rest of the city more accessible and thus increased urban land values generally. Being near an el stop also increased local traffic and made business property more valuable. The el made a lot of noise, though, and some of the traffic it generated was not appreciated by the residents. Moreover, at least until 1906 the New York trains were powered by steam locomotives, which spewed smoke and cinders on nearby property.

The benefit-offset problem can be seen in Newman v. Metropolitan Elevated Railway (N.Y. 1890). An el station built in lower Manhattan, presumably in a neighborhood that was already built up, reduced the residential rents that the owner of an adjacent building could get for the upper stories of his property. Under New York law, he was entitled to compensation for the loss of the light, air, and access easements that led to the reduced rents.

The light and air easements were not specific to his deed. They were legal constructions created by the state court to deal with just such an issue. The question on appeal to the state's highest court was whether the jury could be instructed to offset (that is, reduce) the compensa-tion for losses in the upper (residential) stories by the benefit of in-creased rents that the owner could obtain for commercial use on the first floor. The increased lower-story rents were attributable to the building of the station as well. In other words, if the upper stories' rents declined by $100, and the ground-floor commercial rents in-creased by $75, should the owner receive only $25 in compensation, or should the increase be ignored, so that the owner would get $100? (The figures are mine, not the court's.) The issue of benefit offset was clearly on the table.

The New York Court of Appeals held that the owner was only entitled to the net increase (the $25 in my example). That is, the benefit from the railroad could offset the loss. This was controversial because New York laws specifically forbade use of the benefit offset for partial takings of property.

Why were the New York courts in *Newman* trying to wriggle out of this constraint? I think it was because they felt that the origin of the law was inspired by rural takings, and in those cases the initially huge gains to rural landowners from rail construction had long since passed. In the urban railroads, however, the innovation of elevated railroads promised very large social benefits—tying the city together, making previously unusable sites valuable—much as the earlier rural railroads made remote areas more valuable for agriculture and settlement.

2.17 Benefit-Offset Was Limited Once Again

The benefit-offset question arose again in Bohm v. Metropolitan Elevated Railway (N.Y. 1892). The decision was written by Rufus Peckham, later to achieve notoriety as the author of the U.S. Supreme Court opinion in Lochner v. New York (1904). The lawyer for the railway was none other than the celebrated John Dillon, author of a still-influential treatise on municipal corporations. (Dillon's Rule will be discussed in section 7.12.) Plaintiff Bohm's uptown land on Second Avenue between 116th and 117th Streets was apparently undeveloped prior to the construction of the elevated railway. His property greatly increased in value as the railroad was built up Second Avenue, but Bohm asked for damages in the amount of the difference between his gain and those of properties on side streets and parallel avenues. His claim was apparently that he would have gained even more had the railroad been routed up some other avenue.

Judge Peckham in *Bohm* was nearly beside himself with impatience with a rule that allowed an owner whose property was greatly benefited by the railroad to sue for damages. He called the judge-made rule about air and light easements "imaginary." Peckham denigrated the distinction between general and special benefits, the former not to be used to reduce compensation. It nonetheless seems to me that Bohm was the beneficiary of general benefits, since many other people's property had risen in value as well.

The situation arose again in Bookman v. New York Elevated Railroad (N.Y. 1895). Mr. Bookman asked for damages to his undeveloped uptown (Harlem) property even though his property had increased in value by 138 percent. Bookman claimed that the gain would have been even higher had he not been immediately adjacent to the elevated railroad. The court denied his claim. Judge Finch, with the concurrence of Peckham, acidly wrote of this gain: "It must have been difficult to persuade the owner who took the gain that nevertheless he had been damaged" (41 N.E. at 707).

In later cases, the court attempted to rationalize its readoption of the discredited (and seemingly illegal) general benefit-offset principle by saying that the undeveloped land held by Bohm and Bookman was different from developed land. For undeveloped land, the court ruled that it could be assumed that the railroad caused the value increase, whereas for developed properties, the court assumed that general urban conditions caused the increase in property values. Thus for properties on which buildings had been erected prior to the construction of the railroad, the benefit offset was not to be used. *Newman,* which had allowed the use of benefit offset for a previously developed building, was effectively overruled. (The New York court's subsequent readoption of the benefit offset—it *was* an unstable rule—was overruled by the U.S. Supreme Court in Muhlker v. New York and Harlem Railroad [1905].)

The New York court's distinction between undeveloped and developed land was specious. It was not in accord with the common-law rule of nuisance, in which developing a nuisance (in this case, the elevated railroad) before other development is held not to be a defense against a subsequent claim. The court's distinction also begged the question of whether owners of developed properties had built precisely because they anticipated the railroad's coming. Sam Bass Warner's (1962) description of Boston's suburban development in the 1890s has indicated that builders did indeed anticipate the railroad's growth. Cheape's history of New York City's transit development concurs (1980).

The railroad benefit-offset cases, rural and urban, illustrate again the importance of the size and wide distribution of economic gains in shaping just compensation laws. When economic gains seemed so large that nearly everyone gained, as in cases in which elevated railroads moved into undeveloped areas, the New York court sought to undermine the general/special benefit distinction that had become well established by then. But when the elevated railroads arrived in areas already developed, where additional gains seemed lower than before, the benefit-offset principle was again limited, this time by the specious distinction of causation.

2.18 The Cycle Resurfaced on Interstate Highways

The interstate highway system was in many ways like the development of the railroads. Its arrival, particularly in rural areas, portended greatly increased land values. Public enthusiasm for the project was reflected in a law review article by Charles Haar and Barbara Hering (1963). This scholarly brief urged the use of the general benefit-offset principle to help finance highway construction. Haar and Hering cited numerous instances in which benefit-offset financing was used, and they concluded that federal rules of eminent domain tend to facilitate its use more than the rules of most states. The states are hung up on the distinction between special and general benefits.

A leading federal example employed by Haar and Hering was United States v. River Rouge Improvement (1926). It involved the construction of port facilities in Detroit in which the Court permitted the government to reduce its compensation to dockside landowners by the increase in the value of their remaining property. The case seemed different from the usual taking, however. The owners of the portside property had actually requested that the government undertake the project, and they reaped large benefits from it. Thus the benefit offset looked in this instance more like the quid pro quo of a special assessment, and the U.S. Supreme Court had little difficulty upholding its use.

Haar and Hering specifically approved of the aforementioned New York elevated railroad decisions, which denied, at least initially, that there was an important distinction between general and special benefits. They noted that it would be better to assess all property benefited by the interstate highways, and they conceded in passing that assessing only those whose property was partially taken seemed unfair, but they were not overly concerned about it.

I attribute the authors' downplaying of fairness to the fact that in the 1950s and into the early 1960s, the interstate highway system was regarded with considerable public enthusiasm, although Professor Haar has assured me in a communication that the enthusiasm was not shared by the academic community. The benefits to most people of completing the highway system seemed far greater than the localized costs. It was easy to suppress distributional considerations in such a situation, especially if attention to them threatened the viability of the project.

Although the Haar and Hering proposal did not resurrect the general benefit-offset principle, the actual practice of eminent domain in road construction at the time left property owners and other interests less than fully compensated. This can be distilled from a special publication of the American Association of State Highway Officials, *Acquisition for Right-of-Way* (1962), which contained articles by lawyers and engineers on the practical aspects of eminent domain. (A similar list can be gleaned from Stoebuck's [1969] account of highway access issues.) The following is a rough summary.

- A business whose property was taken received compensation for the value of the land and buildings, but almost never for relocation costs or for the reduced value of the business, which often could not be set up elsewhere because customers were lost. Loss of business goodwill was not compensable.
- Compensation for noise and other inconveniences to residents adjacent to roads was seldom made unless there were extraordinary circumstances.
- Reduction in access to roads that were converted into limited-access highways was seldom compensable unless the substitute access was nonexistent or unreasonably distant. Even a complete loss of access would not be compensated if the blockage by new construction was only temporary and the government was proceeding with reasonable speed.
- Residential tenants displaced by construction were seldom compensated or assisted in finding other accommodations.
- Precondemnation activities that caused losses were seldom paid for. For example, announcements that an area was to be taken would deter tenants from entering into leases. This was often the case with urban renewal projects in the 1960s. The most egregious cases of precondemnation blight were those in which the government then abandoned the project, leaving the private owners with run-down properties and without any offsetting benefits from the project (Gideon Kanner 1973).

Many of these practices were mitigated if not eliminated by legislation and court decisions after the interstate highway system was largely completed. (By 1970, 32,000 miles of interstate highway were open;

the 1990 mileage was 45,000.) For example, the federal Uniform Relocation Assistance and Real Property Acquisition Policies Act of 1970 required that relocation costs be paid to tenants and businesses displaced by eminent domain (Dukeminier and Krier 1988, p. 1025). The initial act in 1968 applied only to highway construction; the later act applied to all federal projects and considerably increased the amount of compensation (Cordes and Weisbrod 1979, p. 51).

In addition to the somewhat more generous federal laws, state courts and legislatures reigned in some of the eminent domain expediters. Precondemnation blight has been ruled compensable in many states, thanks in part to the scholarly criticism of the meanness of the courts (Kanner 1973). Renters now get what Joseph Cordes (1979) regards as adequate financial compensation. State laws have also required compensation for some business relocation costs, in effect reversing court decisions that held them noncompensable. There is also a trend toward compensation for loss of intangible business property, such as goodwill (Newton and Slattery 1983).

2.19 Greater Compensation Does Deter Government Action

The swing toward compensation has its costs, however. Joseph Cordes and Burton Weisbrod (1979, 1985) are among the few economists who have attempted serious studies of the additional costs of providing compensation for relocation from highway construction. After the Uniform Relocation Assistance Act had been in effect for four years, they found "a reduction in real highway construction outlays of 2.2 dollars for each dollar of compensation paid" (1979, p. 55). A related regression on the same sample of fifty states "implies a reduction in federal-aid miles completed of roughly 53 miles per million dollars of compensation paid" (p. 56).

In their 1985 article, Cordes and Weisbrod pointed out that the administrative costs of making compensation were nearly a quarter of the amounts actually paid. Add to this the deadweight loss of increasing taxes, which may be as high as the additional revenue (Edgar Browning 1987), and one can see why enhanced compensation would deter governments from undertaking projects. Although Cordes and Weisbrod regard the increased costs as "unanticipated" by Congress, my historical view of a compensation cycle suggests that public sentiment may have wanted to make it harder to build new highways.

The experience in California presaged that of the United States. A pioneering article by the economist Daniel McFadden (1976) developed a method for inferring the criteria by which the California highway department made its decisions. Using detailed data from 1958–1966 projects, McFadden found that road building decisions were determined largely by benefit/cost criteria, which in those days were enormously favorable to the construction of freeways. In general, the department built where there was the greatest need for roads. (This behavior incidentally explains why new urban freeways immediately became congested; if they did not, the highway department had built them in the wrong place.)

Despite the evidence of substantial net benefit as well as evidence that the highway builders were not insensitive to local opposition and environmental effects, McFadden noted that the criteria he had examined passed from the scene in 1966. In California, "ecological and public transportation concerns led to substantial changes in the organizational purpose and structure of the Division" (1976, p. 56). Once the freeways with the largest net benefits were built, California politicians and the courts became more responsive to distributional issues as well as ecological ones. (I argue in Chapter 6 that the California Supreme Court went overboard in this direction.)

2.20 *Airport Promotion Harmed Property on the Ground*

The airplane invades the sky of many people, and it disturbs the peace of people who live near airports. The rule in federal court is that people near airports can claim that jet noise is a taking of their property only if the noise is caused by flights directly overhead, within the ancient default rule of *ad coelum* ("to the heavens," referring to the extension of ownership of land to the air space above it). Hence one householder kept awake by night takeoffs over her roof can collect damages in federal court, but her next-door neighbor, equally sleepless but not directly beneath the planes, collects nothing.

This is a rule that is rightfully described as perplexing if not silly by law review articles seeking to demonstrate how confused the takings issue is. When one looks beyond federal courts, however, the reality of the paradox diminishes. Michael Berger (1987), a Los Angeles lawyer who specializes in eminent domain, has shown that most state courts have rejected the federal *ad coelum* rule and adopted a general nuisance standard for compensation for airport noise. The only people for whom the federal rule applies are those who live on a federal reservation (and hence are most likely federal employees) and those who live near military airports, which are not subject to state rules.

All of this is not to say that takings from airport noise is a happily settled area of law. Indeed, a major problem arising from the expanded rights of neighbors to airports is that it makes new airport facilities very difficult to develop (Baxter and Altree 1972). Berger's brief suggests to me, though, that state law has again cycled from facilitating a new and apparently beneficial technology to promoting individual fairness and protecting settled enjoyment of on-the-ground property. When airports were new and flight unusual, the value of an additional airport was high. Since airplanes and airports have become as common as buses and bus terminals, the marginal value of flight is lower, and the public inclination to tolerate the nuisances created by them is less. The widening circle of airport liability for takings in state courts is consistent with the notion that the evolution of economic values influences judicial decisions.

2.21   Conclusion: Lessons for Regulatory Takings

My account of principles of eminent domain that constantly respond to political and economic pressures challenges some conventional wisdom. It was argued by Jennifer Nedelsky (1990), whose view was largely accepted by Frank Michelman (1988), that property formed the original model for constitutional jurisprudence that kept a neat boundary between the private and the public. Michelman concluded: "Property could bear such a heavy and crucial ideological load because it was itself such a natural part of normative political imagination— transparent, unproblematic, and visually arresting in the mind's eye" (p. 1627). Michelman did note the work of Forrest McDonald (1985), whose history of the intellectual climate of the Constitution's adoption proves that property was regarded as highly complex, subject to (mostly local) regulation, and qualified in many ways by the common law. Michelman nonetheless used Nedelsky's account of an Eden lost to explain why the regulatory takings cases of 1987 (discussed in sections 1.17 and 1.21) were apt to be stillborn.

The Nedelsky-Michelman vision of property, however, runs contrary to the cycles of eminent domain. The battles over the benefit-offset principle and special assessments demonstrate that property was anything but unproblematic in the nineteenth century. If it were, it would be hard to understand why there was such controversy over what constituted just compensation for the taking of property. The historical controversies as I read them offer a more optimistic reason for the increased attention to regulatory takings in the last ten years.

We may be in the midst of another economic cycle in eminent domain. In the early stages of the cycle, courts favor the state's exercise of takings when the objectives seem to offer unusually high returns. Extremely large and widely distributed benefits seem to justify reducing the compensation to private owners. Judicial review eventually swings toward the side of the private owner when the state's objective has largely been realized and the marginal gains from supporting it seem small compared with the concentrated or unfairly apportioned burdens of less than full compensation.

It is possible that regulatory takings are now going through a cycle similar to those involving transportation improvements. The government "project" here is environmental protection, and the courts have been eager proponents of it, sweeping away nearly all constitutional objections to regulations that promote it. But just as in building railroads, highways, and airports, protecting the environment is subject to the law of diminishing returns.

The first wave of regulations bought large increments to environmental quality. The Clean Air Act and the Clean Water Act initially made major improvements at relatively modest cost (Myrick Freeman 1982). Subsequent legislation inevitably had smaller incremental benefits and larger costs. In this situation, landowners especially burdened by regulations cannot be told, as Justice Peckham told landowners adjoining new elevated railroads, that they share in substantial public gains. This is not to say that there are no public gains. I only argue that the incremental gains are smaller, so that concentrated burdens loom larger.

There is an opposing trend, however, to the modern cycle that was absent in the nineteenth century. Environmental benefits are, by most accounts, highly income elastic in demand. Thus as incomes rise, the amount we are willing to pay for environmental quality rises as well. (This assumes that we do not become so infatuated with a pure environment that real incomes actually fall, although my theory suggests that this should be self-limiting.) Thus it could be that the value of environmental benefits will keep rising despite the diminishing returns to specific regulations. Advocates for regulatory takings can only hope that a concern with fairness in the distribution of regulatory burdens is also income elastic in demand.

3

Constitutional Law, Process Theory, and Democratic Commitment

A standing joke among law professors is that there should be two courses in constitutional law offered in law school: one for students who have studied constitutional law as undergraduates, and another, more advanced course for those who have not. Constitutional lawyers are jealous of their turf.

This chapter nonetheless advances a theory of the Constitution. My trespassing is necessary because one cannot understand the purposes of the Takings Clause without examining the rest of the Constitution. The core of this book's advice to courts is to examine more carefully the alternative means—exit and voice—by which property owners can protect their assets from burdensome government regulation. But the words of the Constitution do not make any such distinction. Instead, I shall attempt to advance the distinction first by examination of Madisonian concerns about property and then by a more familiar account of the rise and fall of property protection under the Fourteenth Amendment's Due Process Clause. Third, I shall invoke the authority of John Hart Ely's theory of constitutional interpretation in support of a selective enforcement of the regulatory takings doctrine. This is important because it establishes that judicial protection of property interests is congruent with a comprehensive theory of modern civil rights jurisprudence.

A further objective of this chapter is to dissuade social scientists from adopting an unthinking judicial centralism on constitutional issues, a centralism that has already been undermined by the discussion of Pennsylvania Coal v. Mahon in Chapter 1. Economists often regard the Constitution as a credible commitment to an institutional structure of property rights, and they assume that courts of law are the best enforcers of that commitment. This chapter shows that both propositions need to be taken with a grain of salt. The Constitution's commands with respect to the economy are seldom unambiguous, and, even when they are, judges are not reliable redactors of its provisions. But I don't want to fall into the opposite trap, which holds that neither the document nor judicial review really makes any difference. Rather, I want to persuade the reader that the Constitution and its life-tenured interpreters are sometimes as much the rocks and the Sirens as they are the ropes of Ulysses.

My narrower theme—that local regulation of immobile assets should receive more judicial solicitude than other regulations—fits into the larger theme. Anxieties about local majoritarianism were an important historical motivation for much of the Constitution. Judicial supervision of local governments facilitates federalism in the same way that enforcement of promises permits governments to confer benefits on future generations. A larger license for judges to change what they regard as inefficient laws adopted by higher levels of government is unwarranted, however.

3.1 Historical Understandings Are Useful but Not Dispositive

Looked at by itself, the Takings Clause seems like an imperative whose interpretation can begin by parsing it: "nor shall private property be taken for public use without just compensation." Scholars such as Robert Bork (1990) argue for an "original understanding" of the Constitution. On this theory, one should find out what "We the People" originally had in mind for the terms "property," "public use," and "just compensation" and adapt the understanding to today's conditions, so that property can be had in radio waves and computer programs.

Among the problems with this approach is that we do not know who should be regarded as the authors of the Constitution. The group most commonly nominated are the "framers," formerly referred to as the founding fathers. But who were the framers? Those who drafted the document in 1787 are the implicit choice, but that hardly comports with democratic theory or the "We the People" with which the document begins. A better choice would be the 160,000 adult, white, mostly property-owning men who voted for representatives to the state conventions that ratified the Constitution in 1787–1789 (Forrest McDonald 1958, p. 14).

But the Constitution is a changing document. As will presently be described, the Fourteenth Amendment was one of the most important changes. Thus the "framers" should also include those who drafted and voted in the 1860s for the Fourteenth Amendment. Perhaps one should include in this survey the people who at various times caused all of the states to adopt or amend the takings clauses and property-defining parts of their state constitutions.

Identification is not the only difficulty with an originalist approach to the Constitution, but it indicates the scope of the problem. I do not rely on an "originalist" approach to the Takings Clause, but not because the history of the Constitution is unimportant. That history informs views of the function of the clause. Before one theorizes about the functions of the doctrine in a thought experiment (as I shall in sections 5.9–5.15), it helps to know whether the hypothetical has not already been confronted by people in real life.

3.2 Federal Power Promoted Economic Development

Constitutional history is usually divided into three major periods. The two events that dramatically changed the Constitution's content and interpretation were the Civil War and the Great Depression. The Constitution of the pre–Civil War period was the one written in 1787 and to which what we now call the Bill of Rights—the first ten amendments—was appended in 1790.

The original Constitution was in large part an economic document (James Ely 1992a, chap. 3). Under the Articles of Confederation, the American common market was retarded by an inability of the central government to perform important tasks, such as levy direct taxes (it had to ask the states for revenue) and have exclusive control over the money supply. Individual states often got in the way of mutually beneficial exchange by retarding interstate commerce for the usual prisoners' dilemma reasons. Capital formation was also retarded within the states by populist laws that devalued debts by specifying that they could be paid in "legal tender" scrip that was freely issued by the state.

The 1787 Constitution was aimed at fixing such problems. It established the fiscal powers of the central government, notably the ability to raise funds by direct taxation and to regulate interstate and international commerce. The body of the Constitution specifically forbade the states from issuing paper money, rewriting private contracts, and imposing interstate tariffs. In this way the Constitution created the common-market framework that is being consciously imitated in Europe and elsewhere.

The 1790 Bill of Rights was less obviously economic in its intentions. The only apparent economic protection, the Takings and the federal Due Process Clauses, are in the Fifth Amendment along with rules about legal procedures, double jeopardy, and self-incrimination. The Fifth itself is sandwiched between the Fourth's assurances against warrantless searches and the Sixth's right to a jury trial. All of these rights promote a stable society that most people regard as necessary for a productive economy, but to modern eyes, they do not obviously channel economic arrangements in any particular way.

It is also important that the entire Bill of Rights was originally directed at the federal government, not the states. Its adoption was part of the Federalists' effort to persuade wavering states, fearful of national power, to adopt the new Constitution. Prior to the Civil War, the U.S. Supreme Court declined to interpret the Bill of Rights as applying to the states. The decision that first established this limitation was in fact a takings claim that had arisen when Baltimore declined to compensate for the obstruction of a private wharf by debris from a city improvement (Barron v. Baltimore 1833).

The Takings Clause could thus be employed only to rein in the economic reach of the national government. Before the Civil War, the federal government undertook remarkably few projects on its own. The issue of whether the federal government had a power of eminent domain independent of the states did not even get to the Supreme Court until Kohl v. United States (1875). It is for this reason difficult to find early cases in federal courts involving regulatory takings, a difficulty that some scholars have said limits the relevance of the Takings Clause to regulations (Bosselman, Callies, and Banta 1973). When the U.S. Supreme Court weighed in against state regulation, it most often employed the Contract Clause, which explicitly applies to the states, and the Commerce Clause, which empowers the federal government and constrains the states (Stephen Siegel 1986). The state courts, however, sometimes did invoke their own takings and contract clauses to strike down excessive regulation (Catherine Connors 1990; J. A. C. Grant 1931; Mark Pulliam 1983).

The pre–Civil War Court held only two acts of Congress to be unconstitutional. In the famous case of Marbury v. Madison (1803), Chief Justice John Marshall established the principle that the Supreme Court *could* find an act of Congress invalid under the Constitution. Having established the principle of judicial supremacy over Congress in a case involving trivial facts, the Marshall Court spent most of its time reining in state laws that threatened to balkanize the Republic or to undermine the institutions that promoted economic development (James Ely 1992a, chap. 4).

The other notable pre–Civil War case that overruled an act of Congress was Dred Scott v. Sandford (1857). Chief Justice Roger Brooke Taney's infamous opinion invalidated the Missouri Compromise that had tenuously bound the slave states to the free states. Dred Scott was held to be the property of his master despite their joint sojourn in free territory, and slavery was held to be a form of property protected by the United States Constitution. *Dred Scott* can thus be read as the first U.S. Supreme Court regulatory takings case (Kermit Hall 1993, p. 195). Taney's decision was widely denounced in the North, and it greatly reduced the prestige of the Supreme Court among the prevailing side in the Civil War. This may help one understand the Court's reluctance, described in section 1.24, to develop a vigorous and detailed doctrine of regulatory takings.

3.3 Madison Worried about Small-Time Majorities

James Madison was the most influential delegate at the 1787 constitutional convention in Philadelphia, and his draft of the Bill of Rights presented in the first Congress was adopted without important changes. Constitutional scholars have for years analyzed his political thought because most of the Constitution is congruent with his thinking (Forrest McDonald 1985). This is not just the opinion of conservative historians. Jennifer Nedelsky, who has deplored what she regards as the pervasive influence of property on modern constitutional thought, sees Madison as a paradigm of his age's thinking (1990). (Laura Underkuffler [1990] has shown that Madison's vision of property encompassed a broad set of rights, so that his anxieties about its protection should not be read as arising solely from financial concerns.)

Madison did not originally like the idea of a Bill of Rights (Paul Finkelman 1990). He was a structuralist in his outlook. In Federalist No. 57 he wrote contemptuously of "parchment barriers" to unjust government. Madison regarded most of the evils of state governments, which were largely unrestricted under the Articles of Confederation, as arising from a government that was excessively populist. The civics-class account of Madison's response, correct as far as it goes, is that he wanted to create a tripartite national government that would filter popular will through the two houses of Congress, an executive, and an independent judiciary.

What the traditional account overlooks is that Madison saw at least as much merit in size itself (Thomas Merrill 1986b). A large national government would be less subject to the evils of "faction" that fed the populist laws of the states under the Articles of Confederation. By making government more complex, deliberative, and remote from popular majorities, the U.S. Constitution was intended to thwart the unmitigated majoritarianism that Madison and others regarded as endemic in state governments.

Because the distinction plays a role in my normative view of takings, it is worth an inquiry into what Madison meant by faction and to whom it applied. The Federalist Papers were written by Alexander Hamilton, Madison, and John Jay (all under the pseudonym "Publius") as tracts to help get the pre–Bill of Rights Constitution accepted by New York. The most famous, Madison's tenth essay, deals with the evils of "faction" in a small republic, and how the evils would be mitigated in a "large republic," meaning the proposed federal government.

Our view of Madison's "small republics," by which he meant the states, is distorted by the present size of the states. In 1790 the median size of the fourteen states was just over 100,000, about the size of Ann Arbor, Berkeley, or Cambridge in 1990. I invoke this comparison in support of my idea that municipalities are the current repositories of the majoritarian excesses about which Madison worried.

3.4 In Federalist No. 10, "Faction" Meant "Majoritarian"

Modern constitutional scholars have often interpreted Madison's reference to "faction" to mean the kind of special-interest politics that we see today in national politics (Peter Aronson 1991; Alexander Bickel

1962, p. 18). Lobbies for the dairy industry, domestic automobile producers, building trades, and teachers' unions come to mind. As such, it would seem that Madison's solution backfired, since modern scholars now complain that special-interest groups feed at the public trough of the state and federal legislatures at the expense of the majority of taxpayers and consumers (Richard Stewart 1990). For this reason, some scholars have suggested use of the Takings Clause to protect the *majority* from the oppression of concentrated minority interests (Glynn Lunney 1992).

I believe that it is an anachronism to read the Tenth Federalist as applying to special-interest legislation. Logrolling, vote trading, and other trappings of pluralistic politics were not what Madison criticized the states for. He was instead worried about unvarnished majority rule, in which one group takes advantage of another purely because of its greater numbers. But he dared not say this too clearly.

The Federalist Papers were not scholarly essays. They were tracts designed to convince a majority of New York voters to adopt the Constitution. It would have been impolitic, even if not necessarily illogical, for Madison to say that he was against majority rule when he needed the vote of a majority of New Yorkers. Hence "faction" in his most famous essay is more likely a code for what we would in the twentieth century call "majoritarianism," unfiltered rule by the majority. (Carol Rose [1989, p. 102] equated Madison's term faction with special interest, but she made what I regard as the correct distinction between national, pluralistic politics and local majoritarianism.)

My view is supported by a close reading of the Tenth Federalist (Clinton Rossiter, ed. 1961). Madison was initially a little shifty about what he meant by faction. He at first defined it as "a number of citizens, *whether amounting to a majority or minority* of the whole, who are united and actuated by some common impulse of passion, or of interest, adverse to the rights of other citizens, or to the permanent and aggregate interests of the community" (p. 78, my emphasis).

That definition would seem to cover all political bases, and it is seldom elaborated upon by modern commentators on the Tenth Federalist. But a few paragraphs later, Madison pared down his broad definition to say what really worried him: "If a faction consists of less than a majority, relief is supplied by the republican principle, which enables the majority to defeat its [the faction's] sinister views by regular vote" (p. 80). Al-

though minorities sometimes "may convulse the society," the damage
is therefore normally remediable. He immediately went on to point to
the true danger: "When a majority is included in a faction, the form of
popular government, on the other hand, enables it to sacrifice to its ruling passion or interest both the public good and the rights of other citizens. To secure the public good and private rights against the danger
of such a faction, and at the same time to preserve the spirit and the form
of popular government, is then the great object to which our inquiries
are directed." His subsequent declaration that pure democracies "ever
have been found incompatible with personal security or the rights of
property" (p. 81) reinforces the conclusion that the real problem of faction in Madison's mind is not minority interests but the majoritarianism
rampant in the small republics.

Madison's cure for the majoritarian problem was not a specific constitutional provision protecting property and other rights. He instead
believed that a system of representation, as opposed to direct democracy, and, more important in his mind, the very size of the electorate
would be sufficient to prevent oppression. The reason that size was
important was that the transaction costs, as we would put it, of orga-
nizing a despoiling majority in a nation as geographically large and
diverse as the United States would usually be prohibitive.

After describing the problems of a small-area, small-population legislature, Madison went on (p. 83): "Extend the sphere and you take in
a greater variety of parties and interests; you make it less probable that
a majority of the whole will have a common motive to invade the rights
of other citizens; or if such a common motive exists, it will be more
difficult for all who feel it to discover their own strength and to act in
unison with each other." If special interests do characterize present-
day national politics, it is in part because of the success of Madison's
vision, not its failure.

The anxiety about the excesses of direct democracy also arose in the
states themselves. The "radical" Pennsylvania constitution of 1776,
which had a unicameral legislature and lacked an independent executive and judiciary, soon lost favor among state constitution makers
(Robert Williams 1988). The model for other states was instead the
1780 Massachusetts constitution, whose bill of rights and separately
elected executive and legislature influenced the federal document. Distrust of majoritarian state legislatures was not confined to the U.S.
Constitution writers at Philadelphia.

3.5   The Civil War Transformed State-Federal Relationships

Madison and other Federalists, notably Chief Justice Marshall, were most interested in creating a strong central government. An equally strong current worried that the central government would consume the states and local governments. For this reason, much of the original Constitution, including the Bill of Rights, was devoted to limiting the power of the central government. Law students even today are told that the federal government is one of enumerated powers. This helps one appreciate why constitutional law is so difficult, since the course then goes on to prove that, since the late 1930s, the national government's authority to regulate and tax a state's citizens has presented few constitutional difficulties.

The post–Civil War amendments were the first to move formally against states' rights. In 1865, the Thirteenth Amendment outlawed slavery without compensation to owners. Slavery was a form of property sanctioned, like other property rights, by individual states. The Fifteenth Amendment, adopted in 1870, forbade the states from keeping former slaves from voting.

The most open-ended source of federal power was the Fourteenth Amendment, ratified in 1868. Its first section nullified one aspect of the *Dred Scott* decision by declaring that U.S. and state citizenship were coterminous. It also tried to ensure that states would not otherwise abuse their own or other states' citizens: "No State shall make or enforce any law which shall abridge the privileges or immunities of citizens of the United States; nor shall any State deprive any person of life, liberty, or property, without due process of law; nor deny to any person within its jurisdiction the equal protection of the laws."

Several scholars have shown that those who drafted and voted for the amendment in Congress were either actively opposed to or would have opposed doing many of the things that the U.S. Supreme Court has since ruled are required by its reading of its Due Process and Equal Protection Clauses. The one-person, one-vote rule of the 1960s is the most dramatic example, and it has occasioned the most criticism from legal historians who pay attention to the intentions of the drafters of the amendment (Raoul Berger 1977; Lino Graglia 1990).

Originalism's greatest virtue is to provide a contextual guide to interpret the Constitution. And the great context of the Fourteenth Amendment was the Civil War, in which more Americans died than in any other, including World War II, when the U.S. population was four times larger. The Civil War marked the culmination of a long conflict about states' rights, with the national government prevailing.

Regardless of what the debates about the Fourteenth Amendment said, the words on the paper do not reflect any intention to limit its scope to, say, newly freed slaves (as the Fifteenth did), or to forbid judicial review that might interpret it one way or the other. In view of the widely unpopular *Dred Scott* decision, it surely would have occurred to the northern congressmen who drafted the amendment to forbid expansive judicial review if they had wanted to keep the Supreme Court from reading its vague words in any particular way.

Armed with the post–Civil War amendments that trimmed states' rights, the U.S. Supreme Court gradually gave voice to the claims of citizens against the activities of their states under the Fourteenth Amendment's due process provisions. Among the litigants with grievances and money to pursue them were businesses subjected to the novel state regulations of the Gilded Age. Although the Supreme Court first reacted with incredulity to the proposition that the Due Process Clause was violated when a business was inconveniently regulated, by the turn of the century a doctrine of "substantive" due process had developed that was to a large degree protective of economic rights.

3.6 Lochner v. New York *Epitomized Economic Due Process*

Among the liberties that could not be removed without due process of law, which in practice meant without the Court's review of the statute's reasonableness under common-law principles, were the liberty to *make* a contract without interference by the state. (The old Contract Clause of Article I, Section 10, protected only previously established contracts, which was problematical enough.) The most famous manifestation of the "liberty of contract" doctrine was the case of Lochner v. New York (1905).

New York had passed a law declaring that bakery workers could work no more than sixty hours per week. The maximum hours provision was part of a larger bill to improve working conditions and sanitation in the highly decentralized baking industry. The bill was passed unanimously by both houses of the New York legislature, and its maximum hours provision had been upheld by a 4–3 vote of the New York Court of Appeals. (Paul Kens [1990] and Howard Gillman [1993] place *Lochner* in its political and constitutional context, respectively.)

Writing for a divided U.S. Supreme Court, Justice Peckham held that such legislation interfered with the liberty of employers and employees to make their own contracts and that the legislation was not otherwise justified as promoting health and safety under the state's police power. Police powers were to be respected, but they were not, on Justice Peckham's view, beyond the reach of judicial review. *Lochner* thus became a synecdoche for an era of judicial hostility to democratic regulation of economic affairs. It remains an epithet by which modern constitutional scholars can with a word condemn proposals for the Court to supervise almost any aspect of business regulation. (To protect my economics credentials, I hasten to add that limiting hours of work seems more likely to harm bakery employees than benefit them, especially given the highly competitive nature of the industry.)

The *Lochner* Court's construction of the Due Process Clause did not invariably doom regulation. The Court in numerous cases upheld business regulations when it appeared to the justices that health and safety issues warranted regulation. The police power was construed as a defense for state interference, but the Court took it upon itself to interpret that power more narrowly than it does today (Kens 1991). The real purpose of substantive due process was to inhibit redistribution of wealth, which is what judges of the era meant by "class legislation." When legislation appeared to clothe redistributive actions in police-power garb, the justices applied what we would today call "heightened scrutiny" of the police-power rationale for the legislation, and this meant that the legislation would often be overturned.

The era of substantive due process to protect property and contractual interests passed away in the mid-1930s, but not all of the decisions decided under the doctrine have lost favor or been overruled (Bernard Siegan 1980). An example that survives as good law is a 1917 case, Buchanan v. Warley, which struck down a Louisville law that attempted to racially segregate city blocks by the then-new technique of zoning. Blacks were not allowed to buy on blocks that were mostly inhabited by whites, and, in a bow to equal protection, whites could not buy housing in black blocks. The Court reasoned not on the grounds that the zoning law violated equal protection of the laws, but on the grounds that it interfered with the liberty of the white plaintiff (Buchanan) to sell to the black defendant (Warley). Buchanan v. Warley nipped in the bud the American experiment in a legalized system of residential apartheid, which had been spreading quickly to other Southern cities (Garrett Power 1983).

The reason the Court could not hold for Warley on equal protection grounds was because it had shot itself in the constitutional foot in Plessy v. Ferguson (1896). *Plessy* held that state requirements of separate public facilities for the races were acceptable as long as the facilities were equal. This doctrine was abandoned, as most schoolchildren now know from their history books if not from looking around their classrooms, in 1954 in Brown v. Board of Education.

I invoke Buchanan v. Warley here to suggest that protection of property interests, even under the now-discredited liberty of contract doctrine, is consistent with the purpose of the famous *Brown* case. My rejection of the *Lochner* approach is based not on its supposed regressiveness but, as I shall argue, on its inconsistency with principles of judicial comparative advantage.

3.7 The Great Depression Routed Judicial Review of Regulation

Lochner had waned as precedent until after World War I. In the 1920s, the fear of imported Bolshevism and the period's militant labor agitation induced the Court to revive the *Lochner* doctrine to suppress all manner of "class legislation" (Michael Klarman 1991a). Until the early 1930s, most such legislation emerged from the states.

Franklin Roosevelt's New Deal presented an agenda not before seen in America, one in which the federal government's role in the economy expanded enormously. The Supreme Court reacted no more kindly to the federal government's regulatory initiatives than it had to novel state business legislation in the previous decade. Unlike the state governors and legislators, though, the President and the Congress could do something about the Court's decisions, chiefly by appointing more favorable justices. President Roosevelt's 1937 "court-packing" plan to accelerate change by enlarging the Court was emblematic of the anti-Court mood. The plan may have accomplished by threat what it failed to do in deed. The change in the Court's direction soon after the announcement of the court-packing plan gave rise to wordplay that has become a staple in constitutional law: "the switch in time that saved nine."

With the switch in time and the addition of new members more to the President's liking after 1937, the Court abandoned almost all review of business regulation at any level of government. The subsequent validation of New Deal regulatory legislation is regarded by Bruce Ackerman as "one of the two great successes of constitutional politics in the modern era" (Ackerman 1992, p. 322). (The other was the civil rights activity of the Warren Court.)

If by success Ackerman meant that lifting the constitutional objections to regulations enabled the Roosevelt administration better to solve the Great Depression, the assessment seems incorrect. Economists of both Keynesian and monetarist stripe agree that both the cause and the cure for the Depression lay in the management of economic aggregates—taxes, spending, and monetary policy (Karl Brunner 1981). The Supreme Court did almost nothing to block such policies. The economists' consensus, as I read it, is that the regulatory initiatives of the New Deal were at best redistributive ameliorations of the consequences of the Depression. At worst, according to Michael Weinstein (1981), the New Deal's price regulations were quantifiably counterproductive to recovery.

Hindsight should not blind us to the extent to which the Great Depression shaped economic thinking as well as legal scholarship. With a quarter of the labor force out of work in 1932, the notion that a decentralized system of exchange would regulate itself became an embarrassment. The economics profession succeeded in preserving a role for markets in subsequent intellectual developments, but it was a role that was decidedly subservient to the obligation of the state to correct the market's misdeeds. The touchstone of the entire field of macroeconomics can still be said to be the Great Depression and how to prevent its recurrence.

3.8   The Commerce and Contract Clauses Were Transformed

After the switch in time, the Court left the field of economic regulation to whatever the legislatures—federal, state, and local—wanted to do. The Court's major positive economic shift was to permit a sweeping preemptive power by the national government over the states. The Commerce Clause had once been a limit on what the federal government could regulate by virtue of the Court-made distinction between "commerce" and "manufacture." Its most notorious application to national legislation was the Court's decision that federal laws to regulate child labor were unconstitutional infringements on state authority insofar as they pertained to "manufacture" rather than "commerce."

The New Deal Court eradicated the manufacture/commerce distinction and its constraint on national authority. The Court in fact reversed its effect. After Wickard v. Filburn (1942), which found that wheat grown for on-farm consumption could be subject to federal crop regulations, the Commerce Clause became the constitutional vehicle by which Congress could regulate almost any private activity and any level of government. The Commerce Clause became, in effect, the basis for a federal police power. (On the Court's continuing use of the "dormant" Commerce Clause, see section 3.20.)

The Great Depression also undermined the utility of the Contract Clause in reining in state regulation. The Contract Clause has a distinct intellectual advantage over the Lochnerian liberty of contract doctrine in that it is actually written in the Constitution. In 1934 (even before the switch in time), the Supreme Court in Home Building and Loan Association v. Blaisdell upheld a Minnesota statute that delayed foreclosures of mortgages, a small but clear infringement on prior contractual obligations. The reason given for upholding the law was the Depression and its obvious hardships, but infringing on contracts during hard times was apparently exactly what the 1787 Philadelphia convention delegates wanted to prevent the states from doing. Justice George Sutherland's dissent recited the history, which should remove any doubt that the Court was aware of it.

The vote in *Blaisdell* was a bare 5–4, but nonetheless it strongly suggests the influence of events on the judges. The near-lynching of a judge by farmers displeased with Depression-era foreclosures was described by Arthur Schlesinger in *The Coming of the New Deal*. Schlesinger's account was quoted to dramatic effect (at least on me) by Paul Brest and Sanford Levinson (1983) in their casebook's discussion of *Blaisdell*. The opinion of Chief Justice Charles Evans Hughes in *Blaisdell* alluded to a necessary flexibility in the face of economic emergencies: "the question is no longer merely that of one party to a contract as against another, but of the use of reasonable means to safeguard the economic structure upon which the good of all depends" (290 U.S. at 442).

The Contract Clause has never been the same since *Blaisdell,* and its disuse may have inspired the employment of the Takings Clause as a means of protecting against ex post facto laws. The Court in Calder v.

Bull (1798) had held that the Constitution's prohibition of ex post facto laws applied only to criminal law, so the freight of dealing with other retroactive legislation was transferred to other parts of the Constitution (Kmiec and McGinnis 1987).

3.9 "Footnote Four" Mapped the Court's Direction after 1937

Having cleared its docket of business regulation, the Court needed some rationale so as not to wipe out its review of all legislation. In the fourth footnote of United States v. Carolene Products (1938), Justice Harlan Fisk Stone outlined the intellectual apparatus. The note is so famous that one can refer solely to "Footnote Four" and lawyers not too far out of law school will understand the reference. If it strikes nonlawyers as odd for an intellectual thesis to appear in a footnote, consider that the Court must decide live controversies, not give advisory opinions. The new New Deal majority on the Court had to issue a subtle manifesto.

After announcing that it was not going to give close scrutiny to business regulation, the three-paragraph footnote indicated two directions for constitutional review. The first paragraph indicated that the Court would take a closer look "when legislation appears on its face to be within a specific prohibition of the Constitution, such as those of the first ten amendments." This statement was presumably designed to ensure that the Court could review censorship and other intrusions on the Bill of Rights, but it did not on its face remove the basis for the review of business regulation. The textual basis of that review, after all, was the "due process of law," words that indelibly appear in the Fifth as well as the Fourteenth Amendments. To deal with that, the Court later changed the interpretation of "due process of law" to a more natural interpretation, that legislative and judicial regularities must be observed in passing and enforcing laws. A modern court can convulse much legislation even with that limited warrant, but the message of withdrawal from review of business regulation in the spirit of *Lochner* remains intact.

The second paragraph of Footnote Four offered the basis for what is now called "process" theory. One reason for deference to legislation is that the political process works like a messy market (as most markets are), with competing interests all shouting for attention and making bargains with one another. This does not guarantee that good legislation will prevail—though the Chicago economist Gary Becker (1983) thinks it works well enough—but it does permit the losers to say, "Wait 'til next year." Legislation whose effects are undesirable can be reversed.

The iterative process of correction does not work if the prevailing faction in one year disables the losers from coming back next year to try again with another coalition. For this reason (which Justice Stone did not supply, though he made it clear in other cases that this is what he meant), Footnote Four said that "legislation which restricts those political processes which can ordinarily be expected to bring about repeal of undesirable legislation, is to be subjected to more exacting judicial scrutiny . . ." Examples given were infringements on the right to vote, restraints on political information (hence raising the Court's attention to the First Amendment above other amendments), and interference with political organization.

3.10 *"Discrete and Insular Minorities" Could Be Property Owners*

The third paragraph of Footnote Four described another, more controversial path of judicial inquiry, but it is related to process theory as well. It invited courts to ask "whether prejudice against discrete and insular minorities may be a special condition, which tends seriously to curtail the operation of those political processes ordinarily to be relied upon to protect minorities. . . ." The note is most definitely not saying that the court must simply protect minorities; otherwise all losers in the political process could claim protection. It points to "discrete and insular" minorities, which I interpret as those so easily identified and carved out from coalitions with potential sympathizers that they are ripe for political exploitation. The examples Justice Stone gave via citations to previous decisions were religious, national, and racial minorities, but there is no indication that this was to be an exclusive list.

The cited decisions in Footnote Four suggest at least an indirect solicitude for property rights. The religious and national minorities cases were Meyer v. Nebraska (1923), which struck down a World War I–era law that forbade the teaching of German, and Pierce v. Society of Sisters (1925), which struck down Oregon's anti–private school law. (Oregon's law had been adopted by a voter initiative fed by anti-Catholic sentiment [David Tyack 1968].) Both cases had been decided on contract and property-protection grounds—the Oregon law devalued the assets of private schools—by a conservative Court. As Brest and Levinson noted in commenting on these cases in their text (1983, p. 648), both decisions show that the *Lochner*-era Court did not draw a sharp line between economic and personal rights. One could equally note that the political process rights given higher stature by Footnote Four did not exclude attention to property owners.

The controversy in *Carolene Products* itself involved federal legislation hostile to the shipment of "filled milk," which was milk with the cream removed and vegetable oil substituted. The federal legislation proclaimed that the stuff was "injurious" and that its sale as a milk substitute was a "fraud." In gratuitous support of this, the opinion cited congressional hearings and the works of experts who praised the health virtues of butterfat, the ingredient lacking in filled milk. (The legislation actually seems to have been designed to protect the incomes of dairy interests more than the welfare of the public [Geoffrey Miller 1987].)

The Court's rationalization of the law in *Carolene* seems at odds with the interpretation of Footnote Four as a total retreat from the review of business regulation. If it had meant to preclude such review, the Court would not have mentioned any rationale for the filled-milk restrictions; it could have said, Congress has spoken. Judges to this day usually add some public interest rationale when they sustain business regulation. Several scholars, including Louis Lusky (1982), who was Justice Stone's clerk in 1937 and who drafted Footnote Four, have argued that Stone's note did not preclude the protection of property from excess regulation, and the nearly automatic upholding of such laws came later and was at odds with it. As Geoffrey Miller's (1987) account of the case showed, the law at issue in *Carolene Products* was overturned a few decades later by a combination of political and legal maneuvers.

Footnote Four nonetheless signaled the demise of the Due Process Clause and the rise of the Equal Protection Clause of the Fourteenth Amendment. As with the post–Civil War rise of substantive due process, the post–New Deal Court did not immediately use the Equal Protection Clause to strike down racial discrimination laws. It chipped away at them, with the high point being Brown v. Board of Education, which in 1954 struck down state laws requiring segregated schools.

3.11 Equal Protection Replaced Economic Due Process

Although not obvious from its text, Footnote Four is generally given as the source of the "strict scrutiny" standard by which judges review legislation. If the legislation impairs some "fundamental interest" (such as free speech and voting, as suggested by its second paragraph) or makes a distinction on a "suspect classification" (such as race, national origin, or religion, as in its third paragraph), then only if the legislation or classification is justified by a "compelling state interest" will it survive strict scrutiny. Few statutes have survived strict scrutiny; the fundamental interest and suspect class classifications are for practical purposes nearly conclusive (Klarman 1991a).

The difficulty with the new standards is not hard to see in retrospect. Having withdrawn one license—the Due Process Clause—for judges to substitute their preferences for those of the legislature, a different license emerged. Making distinctions as to which classifications are "suspect" invites political judgment, even when guided by the "discrete and insular minority" dictum. Even more difficult to contain have been notions of fundamental interests.

From a political process viewpoint, the most fundamental interests are those that promote political participation. Over the years, however, the Court has discovered many more fundamental interests than Justice Stone's Footnote Four might warrant. Procreative and nonprocreative sex between men and women has made it onto the list, but sex between consenting adults of the same sex has barely missed, and sex between consenting adult brothers and sisters cannot even get a hearing. I insert these categories in this order because I was impressed at how the instructor's raising them in succession in the constitutional law class that I audited subdued the urgency of arguments on behalf of a constitutional right to privacy as one of the "fundamental interests" not to be disturbed by legislation.

Despite some pruning of the fundamental-interest doctrine by the U.S. Supreme Court, its use has continued to flourish in the states, particularly in the area of school finance (Serrano v. Priest 1976; Lewis Kaden 1983; Stanley Mosk 1988). As I noted in the Introduction, one of the events that fueled my skepticism about the utility of judicial review was the disastrous effect of California's ruling on school-finance issues (Fischel 1989, 1994a). Even if one does not accept my hypothesis that the *Serrano II* court's order to equalize spending induced

California voters to vote for Proposition 13, evidence from other states suggests that such remedies reduce rather than increase public support for schools (Paul Rothstein 1992; Theobald and Picus 1991). In any event, the use of the Equal Protection Clause by courts to strike down state school-finance systems is indistinguishable from the *Lochner* Court's use of the Due Process Clause to strike down other economic arrangements. Professor (now Judge) Ralph Winter has characterized the economic equal protection decisions as the "partial rule of a junta" consisting of a Supreme Court majority (1972, p. 43).

3.12 Judicial Review Presents the Countermajoritarian Problem

A task of this chapter is to integrate a theory of takings with theories of the constitutional role of judges. The starting point is the difficulty of squaring the concept of judicial review with the idea of democratic government. Why should unelected federal judges, or electorally in-sulated state judges, be authorized to tell duly elected legislatures that what they are doing is wrong? The "countermajoritarian problem," as Alexander Bickel (1962) called it, is at the heart of the problem of judicial review. (James Buchanan [1991], the best-known economist to explore constitutional constraints on legislative control of economic policy, seems unconcerned by problems of judicial competence or le-gitimacy.)

Bickel's phrase actually loaded the dice in favor of judicial review by characterizing democratic processes as "majoritarian," even though Bickel favored, on balance, a comparatively limited role for judges. His phrase has this effect because "majoritarian" sounds like "totalitar-ian," and hence subtly deprecates the democratic process. Yet Bickel's words are also insightful, provided that we recall Madison's observa-tion that all democratic processes are not the same. Some democratic processes deserve the term "majoritarian," and others are more in line with the reasons that people value a liberal democracy over alternative forms of government.

When the theoretical difficulties of democracy are raised, economists are apt to think of the potential applicability of the work of Kenneth Arrow (1951). Arrow's proof that one cannot not generate a consis-tent rule out of seemingly reasonable postulates about how democracy should behave casts a note of pessimism on the merits of democracy

(Farber and Frickey 1991). One might ask whether judicial review is less problematical.

It is not. Most obvious is the fact that the U.S. Supreme Court and most other appellate courts operate on majority voting rules as well, and decisions are often closely split. The voting paradox, which is but one of the problems Arrow raised, is just as likely to arise among nine judges as among hundreds of legislators or millions of voters. And even if this could be dispensed with by the (doubtful) assumption that judicial preferences are single peaked, one would have to ask whether deference to the Supreme Court on every issue does not violate Arrow's nondictatorship requirement. The problem Arrow presented was to find democratic means of solving public problems. It was not intended to justify antidemocratic options.

The rationale for judicial reversal of legislation that seems most popular in law school is the idea that judges should confine themselves to discovering "fundamental interests or values" that are protected by the Fourteenth Amendment. John Hart Ely (1980) and Michael Klarman (1991b) have criticized this approach with wit and scholarly insight that I do not hope to match. Let me add only one concurrence.

Consider the scenario in which a popular Mexican-American candidate for President is belatedly but unambiguously found to have been born on the Mexican side of the border, a fact entirely hidden from her by her deceased parents. Her long and distinguished career as governor of Texas and as U.S. secretary of labor in a previous administration make it obvious that she is the best candidate for the major national party that has nominated her. If the question were litigated, as it certainly would be if the party did not rescind her nomination, it seems possible that a majority of judges who feel themselves guided by the "fundamental values" implied by the Constitution would hold that she should be permitted to run for President and serve if elected.

Even "original intent" might contribute to the campaign. Its adherents could note that the Constitution's unambiguous ban on foreign-born Presidents was probably intended as a check against importing a monarchy, a threat that holds no terrors for Americans now. But, of course, there is no Constitution at all if its most explicit commands can be trumped by fundamental values. The judge who opens himself to such arguments can choose almost any outcome. It is functionally no different than the frank admission that it all depends on the judge's politics.

The last notion trips off the lips of beginning students of law (both graduate and undergraduate) with unsurprising regularity. It's a bit like the appeal of conspiracy theories: they can cover any contingency and are utterly irrefutable. What is slightly more surprising is that "it's all just politics" is the view of Critical Legal Studies, the leftish body of scholarship whose view is largely in opposition to the process theory adumbrated by John Hart Ely.

3.13 John Hart Ely's Process Theory Promotes Democracy

One answer to the countermajoritarian dilemma is to urge judicial review not to reverse the decisions of legislators except when the legislators themselves are acting undemocratically. Turnabout is the theme of John Hart Ely's (1980) approach to judicial review under the Constitution, which is an expansion of the ideas in Footnote Four. Ely summarized his 1980 thesis in a retrospective of his work in a 1991 issue of the *Virginia Law Review*. The following is excerpted from, naturally, footnote 4 of his 1991 article:

> Approached philosophically—I have previously [in his 1980 book] approached it more through an analysis of the Constitution—the general theory is that a group of equals in the "original position" attempting to frame a government would start from the presumption that no sane adult's values are to count for more or less than any other's, which would lead rapidly to the conclusion that public issues generally should be settled by a majority vote of such persons or their representatives—with two, perhaps three exceptions: (1) where a majority of such persons votes to exclude other such persons from the process or otherwise to dilute their influence on it; (2) where such a majority enacts one regulatory regime for itself and another, less favorable one, for one or another minority; or (3) where other side constraints seem sufficiently important (and vulnerable to majority sentiment) that the framers decide by supermajority vote to designate them in a constitutional document and thereby render them immune to displacement by anything short of a similar supermajority vote in the future. The third exception seems to me more problematic than the first two for a liberal theorist. In the context of the American Constitution, however, that is an observation that is somewhat beside the point, as all three exceptions plainly characterize that document to a degree.
>
> It seems to me to follow further—here comes the "legal process"

part—that precisely because of their tenure, courts are the appropriate guardians of at least exceptions (1) and (2) [quoting now from his *Democracy and Distrust*, 1980, p. 103]:

> Obviously our elected representatives are the last persons we should trust with identification of either of these situations. Appointed judges, however, are comparative outsiders in our governmental system, and need worry about continuance in office only very obliquely. This does not give them some special pipeline to the genuine values of the American people: in fact it goes far to ensure that they won't have one. It does, however, put them in a position objectively to assess claims—though no one could suppose the evaluation won't be full of judgment calls—that either by clogging the channels of change or by acting as accessories to majority tyranny, our elected representatives in fact are not representing the interests of those whom the system presupposes they are.

Ely strongly endorsed the reapportionment decisions, which started with Baker v. Carr (1962) and Reynolds v. Sims (1964). State legislators' own interests would work against efforts to adopt a one person, one vote system of representation. The Warren Court decisions that facilitated participation by blacks in the electoral process are seen not simply in the sense of protecting specific minorities but in a more fundamental sense of making sure that democracy does not systematically exclude people from the process.

Ely's emphasis on the judiciary's role in policing the political process rather than in interpreting particular substantive commands led to a chorus of criticism by constitutional law professors. Among the more influential critics of Ely's 1980 book was Harvard Law School's best-known constitutional lawyer, Laurence Tribe (1980). He pointed out that the Constitution has many substantive commands—the Takings Clause was his prime example—that license constitutional judges. Tribe's article was titled "The Puzzling Persistence of Process-Based Constitutional Theories."

And it *is* puzzling, given that a process-based theory mostly urges judges to leave legislation alone. Such a stance reduces the influence of law professors on political life. Constitutional law professors influence judges chiefly by training their future law clerks, who nowadays draft most of the opinions. The scheme leads to some circularity. As Judge and former law professor Richard Posner (1991) cracked, "What professors of constitutional law teach and study is, to an extent I should

think they would find embarrassing, the work of their recently grad-
uated students." It does therefore seem puzzling that Ely, a constitutional law professor, would argue for a system that reduces the
importance of constitutional law professors. (Posner's assertion [1991]
that modern public choice theory undermines Ely's reliance on old-
fashioned, democratic pluralism is examined in section 8.19. I argue
that rent-seeking, which modern public choice theorists both cherish
and deplore, also leads to Ely's position on the role of constitutional
courts.)

3.14 Process Theory Comports with Judges' Comparative Advantage

Constitutional scholarship aside, the more important question is why
judges should pay any attention to Ely's process theory or, for that
matter, to any theory of constitutional law at all. Any answer first has
to address the objectives of judges, a subject on which there is surprisingly little scholarship. (A recent exception is Posner [1993].) My
insight on the question is something Henry Manne, currently dean of
George Mason University School of Law, told me. Manne founded
and has operated for many years an institute that provides, in separate
sessions, legal education for economists and economics education for
law professors and federal judges. On more than one occasion, Henry
remarked to me that he was impressed by how the judges hate to be
reversed by a higher court—they just hate it.

I take the corollary of that sentiment to be that judges like it very
much when their decisions are upheld and last for a long time. Thus I
take as the distinctive objective of life-tenured judges with irreducible
nominal salaries that they want their decisions to last. I extrapolate this
to all appellate judges, including the Supreme Court, and infer that
they do not want future generations of judges to reverse them. The
higher the bench on which the judges sit, the more the vision shifts to
the future, since only in the future can they be reversed. (Courts may
also worry about constitutional amendments to limit their authority,
but William Ross's [1994] history of such efforts in the 1890–1937 era
showed that politicians who embraced this cause seldom got anywhere
with it.)

Think about how a super-rational judge, one on the order of Learned
Hand or Oliver Wendell Holmes, Jr., might calculate how to guaran-

tee her irreversible place in history. First of all, she will be sure to give great credit to historical experience and the value of precedent. If future generations of judges see that you have no respect for the decisions of your ancestors, they are not apt to respect yours. This is simple teleological induction from the commandment concerning one's parents. (A formal theory supporting this approach is Eric Rasmusen [1992].)

Second, the wise justice will be aware of the principle of comparative advantage. What can a judge acting under the vague mandates of the Constitution do better than legislators? The temptation for the short-sighted is to make legislation that elected legislators cannot or did not pass. This is undesirable insofar as the supposed advantage of judges—their insulation from popular politics and their action under a document that is hard to reverse—is in fact the greatest disadvantage to passing desirable legislation. Legislators' concern with reelection is the best means of ensuring that they pass laws that the majority in fact desires. The reversibility of legislation is a crucial means of ensuring that bad laws have short lives. (Section 8.8 discusses examples.)

Ely's process theory shows that the comparative advantage of judges is to guard against *legislators'* assuming the position that some constitutional activists would have *judges* assume: the ability to pass laws that are not in fact desired by the majority, and the ability to ensure that present-day laws are held as a dead hand over the future. Thus Ely's limited but crucial function for the judiciary is to be sure that legislators are in fact acting democratically. This justifies the one-person, one-vote decisions and the close scrutiny of infringements on free speech. Because such decisions promote democracy, they are not likely to be reversed in the future by any democratic bodies subject to their discipline. The best road to judicial immortality is to help prevent democratic decisions from falling into institutional traps that prevent democracies from getting what they want. Judges such as Holmes, Hand, and Stone became famous as coordinators of democracy, not as substitutes for it.

The insistence on the reversibility of legislation presents the problem of future commitments by the legislature. This points to the promise-keeping function of the Constitution. It has two dimensions. One insists that the only "irreversible" laws are those found in the Constitution. A few substantive values (for example, noninterference with religious belief) are obviously intended not to be infringed by later legislation. The other dimension is a mechanism to promote legislative promise-keeping and thus overcome what economists call the "time consistency" problem. This dimension gets more attention in sections 3.16–3.19, because it is not obvious that constitutional review by courts is the only means of deterring legislative promise-breaking.

3.15 The Supreme Court Can Be an Anti-Educator

A desire for judicial immortality might not seem to lead inevitably to John Hart Ely's representation-reinforcing stance. Judges might try to convince future generations of judges and voters that their ideas are really what the democracy wants, even if the people or their elected representatives did not come up with them. But such an approach assumes that judges have a great deal more educational power than they do. I am not saying they have no such power—there *are* almost a million lawyers among us—but the comparative advantage in political education still lies with people in public life outside the courtroom.

Judges might alternatively build on the immortality theme by simply trying to anticipate what the members of the public actually want and giving it to them by breaking legislative gridlock. To the extent that the gridlock is caused by self-dealing malapportionment or the exclusion of some groups from the political process, who, once admitted, are able to protect their interests, this approach comports with Ely's theory. But to the extent that breaking legislative gridlock simply means choosing the side that looks like it's going to win, the idea is a disaster for two reasons.

One is that judges cannot hope to choose objectively between political sides. Their own preferences regarding who should win will invariably color their alleged forecasts. The current example of this is surely the abortion cases, beginning with Roe v. Wade (1973). The Court noticed a groundswell for abortion reform and in *Roe* enacted a statute for the nation to follow (John Hart Ely 1973). This should have settled the issue without the messy process of legislative decision making. Obviously, it was not settled.

The more important reason for not leapfrogging the legislative process is that by doing so the court also short-circuits public debate and public learning about an issue. Without widespread debate and politicking, the abortion issue fell out of the general public's mind and into the hands of what I would estimate is a minority coalition of anti-abortion people. With no general organizations to oppose them, since the pro-abortion forces had been given a free pass by the U.S. Supreme Court, the anti-abortion forces made an effective special-interest coalition. (This conclusion is now the conventional wisdom at many law schools, I am told.)

Let me gingerly invoke another controversial decision, or, actually, nondecision. During World War II, American citizens of Japanese descent on the West Coast were rounded up and put in prison camps for the duration of the war. (Nothing like this happened in Hawaii, whose population contained a majority of Americans of Japanese descent.) Although it never actually ruled on the imprisonment itself, the U.S. Supreme Court validated the laws that led to it in Korematsu v. United States (1944). I do not want to make an argument about the decision or the law it upheld. I want to focus on the subsequent failure of the Court to award compensation for the victims. Instead, in 1988, Congress authorized compensation of $20,000 per survivor and issued an apology for the injustice. (A compelling history from the viewpoint of a Japanese-American family is Lauren Kessler [1993].)

My question is this. What would have happened had the Supreme Court authorized compensation as the result of a lawsuit shortly after the war? (Kessler noted that the government did compensate for some losses after the war, but at a rate that was less than 10 percent of the apparent financial loss with nothing awarded for the time of detention.) My guess is that public reaction to a judicial award to Japanese-Americans would have been much different than the contrition that accompanied the long process of obtaining congressional action. A court order is just that: an order from a distant authority that has to be obeyed. Moreover, the lawyers for the U.S. government, whose purse would pay the bill, would have had to argue that such compensation was not called for.

Court-ordered compensation might even have engendered further resentment of Japanese-Americans rather than, as I read it, the widespread sympathy with their plight that subsequently developed. Equally important is that the guilt that Americans feel about having perpetrated such an injustice makes future injustices less likely to occur. I was impressed that during the Gulf War of 1991, sporadic expressions of hostility toward Arab-Americans were met with reminders of the shameful story of the results of hostility to Japanese-Americans a generation before. (It also helped that 1990s radar and

satellite communications forestalled the public panic over military un-
certainties that in the 1940s may have induced Earl Warren, then
attorney general of California, to support vigorously the laws at issue
in *Korematsu.*)

3.16   Should We Tie Our Descendants to the Mast?

John Hart Ely did concede, with some misgivings, a role for the courts
in upholding constitutional provisions that restrain current political
majorities from reversing rules set up in the past. These rules are the
substantive commands about freedom of religion, trial by jury, compensation for taking of property, and the right to bear arms that populate the Bill of Rights. To concede such a role for the court bothers
Ely and other liberal theorists, however, because to do so gives no
account of why current generations should be bound by rules set up in
the past.

An answer to that problem has been suggested by Michael Klarman
(1992, p. 795) and Stephen Holmes (1988) as well as by writers about
specific items such as the Takings Clause. Their solution involves interpreting such provisions as voluntary constraints that permit those
submitting to them to engage in activities they would otherwise be
unable to do because of the anticipation that promises might be broken. The metaphor is that of Ulysses having himself tied to the mast in
order to listen to the songs of the Sirens.

The problem with the Ulysses metaphor for constitutional issues
arises when the ropes are applied to people who did not vote to constrain
themselves. It is one thing for the generation of the 1790s to agree that
property would not be taken without compensation, knowing that they
themselves might be tempted later in the day to take it. It is quite another for the same rule to apply to people two centuries down the line.
(The objection that they can amend the U.S. Constitution overlooks
the fact that it normally requires a supermajority to do so.)

There is another approach to the problem of consent by current
generations, though. An alternative to the every-generation federal
constitutional convention that Thomas Jefferson favored is loosely
mimicked by state constitutions. States often amend their constitutions, most by a process far more populist than Article V of the U.S.
document. There have also been numerous state constitutional conventions in which the whole document has been rewritten from scratch.

Popular assent to these constitutions' provisions gives us some insight into what would occur in the Jeffersonian model.

The evidence is that the Bill of Rights would do quite well in any generation. Almost all state constitutions throw in all of the provisions of the Bill of Rights, including the right for compensation when property is taken. If anything, the historical tendency is to expand the list and rhetorically reinforce the Bill of Rights. Recall from section 2.9 that almost half of the states added to their takings clauses prohibitions against damaging as well as taking property. (In anticipation of the objection that state amenders might not have thought to drop the takings clause, I note that the National Municipal League dropped any mention of compensation for takings, which was inconvenient for its members, from its 1963 "Model State Constitution," a guarantee that had been in its 1941 edition.)

Moreover, the American example of constitutional declarations of rights is imitated in many other countries, even though none relies as much on judicial review as the United States. Even the former Communist regimes apparently felt that international public opinion required a constitutional recitation of rights. Hence, while I share Ely's doubts about inexplicit consent, the evidence from the states and international experience suggests that we would indeed consent to the substantive rules if the question were posed.

The international experience on economic due process is reasonably clear, also, but it cuts the other way. Anthony Ogus (1990) showed that no other country's courts have attempted anything like the *Lochner* era, even though almost all insist on compensation for takings of property. An interesting comparison is between the constitutions of the United States and Switzerland, which both allow for the possibility of regulatory takings. Enrico Riva (1984) indicated that the Swiss regulatory takings doctrine, which was adopted by constitutional referendum in 1969, is no more coherent and consistent than that of the U.S. Supreme Court. (See also David Currie [1989], who found that the postwar German courts have been similarly flaccid.)

Another Swiss-American comparison by Peter Moser (1994) found similarities in both constitutions' protection of general economic interests. Both countries' protections, however, were eroded over time, especially during times of war and economic crisis. Those of the United States were derogated by the courts, while the Swiss guarantees were reduced more often by popular referenda that changed the constitution to allow expanded regulatory authority. Moser concluded that constitutions provide only a limited means of "credible commitment" (p. 76) to economic orders.

3.17 Independent Central Banks Are More Time Consistent

It might help to approach the problem of intergenerational constraints as an economic policy problem for politics rather than as a constitutional problem for judges. The economic implications of the difficulty that governments have in keeping promises were famously described by Finn Kydland and Edward Prescott (1977). "Time consistency" is a restatement of the problem of enforcing constitutional commitments. It will appear optimal for the government to establish property rights in something to encourage investment, but at a later time it may appear more desirable to take away such property without compensation.

For monetary policy, the context for much of the time-consistency literature, the problem is similar: it appears optimal to establish a non-inflationary monetary rule in the beginning, but at a later time conditions may change so that some inflationary policies will appear optimal. Because investors know this temptation will exist, the desirable credibility of the original policy (price stability) will be undercut if inconsistent policies are not foreclosed. Indeed, the whole issue of "rules versus discretion" that arises in economics is identical to that of constitutionalism versus democracy, except that economists usually consider it cheating to solve the problem with a *deus ex machina* like an independent judiciary.

An example that probes the parallel further is the independence of a central bank. The Constitution authorizes Congress to control the money supply, but Congress has delegated most of the policy-making to the Federal Reserve Board. The Federal Reserve is by statute independent of legislative and executive control. If the Fed wants to slow the growth of the money supply, thus (usually) raising interest rates and reducing inflation, it can do so without the permission of elected officials. The Fed is not immune from politics, of course. Its officers are appointed by the President and approved by Congress, and it must account for its activities to Congress. But in general the independence of the Federal Reserve seems as great as that of most state judges, whose tenure is subject to loose democratic disciplines.

I make this analogy because other nations of the world also have central banks, and many of them are given some degree of independence from elected officials. This is a useful comparison, since American-style judicial review is rare among other nations, including, as Robert Dahl pointedly mentioned, those we consider free (1989, p. 188). There is empirical evidence about the effects of independence on the effectiveness of central banks in controlling inflation, and that evidence may give us a clue as to whether an independent judiciary makes any difference to the time-consistency problem.

The evidence of which I am aware is described in a book by Alex Cukierman (1992), who studied a worldwide range of banks. He found that the independence of a central bank from legislative tinkering does indeed result in less inflation. Cukierman concluded that independence from the political process has considerable utility in overcoming the temptation to take short-run employment gains at the expense of long-run price stability. This looks like a vote for an independent judiciary to enforce prior legislative promises on the future.

The problem with the monetary-policy evidence for the efficacy of constitutionalism is that central bank independence itself may depend on democratic preferences. Nations which desire a lower rate of inflation will implement that desire by choosing an independent central bank. Cukierman presented evidence that the actual degree of central bank independence does depend on endogenous factors such as how costly inflation is to the electorate (1992, chap. 23). As an article in *The Economist* said about the most independent and anti-inflationary of all central banks, "the Bundesbank depends on Germany's anti-inflation culture," a culture forged by the two hyperinflations of the 1920s (Oct. 3, 1992, p. 95). Without that background, the article concluded, neither the political independence of the bank nor the price stability it promotes would last long.

3.18 Sovereigns Need Commitment Devices

Another manifestation of the utility of a constitutional-commitment rule emerges from a more distant history. Economic historians tell us that one of the problems that kings had in a nation-state was how to raise money to conduct their wars (North and Weingast 1989). International financiers were reluctant to lend money to an absolute monarch, since he could later cancel the debt. One of the ways around this problem was for the monarch to set up an independent fiscal authority

and demonstrate his deference to it. The most reliable fiscal authority
was one that had an indefinite lifespan, so that its decision makers
would worry about their reputations. Parliament, and republics in general, fit the bill, and so they footed the bill. Thus did the monarch
become more powerful by surrendering some of his power. (The argument was made explicitly by the sixteenth-century French political
writer Jean Bodin, as recounted by Stephen Holmes [1988, p. 215].)

Republics, however, have some of the same problems that monarchs
supposedly faced. If the people are entirely sovereign, incontestable
masters of their own current destiny, they are in the same position as
the absolute monarch. Promises they make for the future to pay back
loans to people who provide capital right now might be abridged if the
next generation is the only judge of its own case. The sovereignty of a
republic over time is reduced by its inability to tie its hands. Current
generations cannot confer benefits on later generations unless the current generation can assure investors that they will be able to reap what
they sow (Holmes 1988, p. 214).

Thus one role for independent judicial review could be to enforce
such provisions on later generations. The payoff to the nonconsenting
generations is that their adherence to the rule benefits them by increasing their capital endowment and permits them to endow generations as yet unborn. This does not solve the consent problem, but it
does make the failure to solve it more palatable to people who think
that popular sovereignty is important. Popular sovereignty may be
enhanced, not reduced, by judicially enforced constraints to keep intergenerational promises. It would be nice if every generation got a
chance to vote on that, but given the anxieties that prospect apparently
provokes at the national level, we may have to be satisfied with the
indirect evidence from the states.

This is not a bad rationale for judicial review, but it still leaves judges
with a larger license than I think is desirable. Moreover, the *Blaisdell*
decision to abandon the Contract Clause in the face of the Depression's debtor-relief legislation (see section 3.8) proves that even our
most prominent and independent court cannot be depended on to
enforce intergenerational commitments. (Recall also other nations'
inability to maintain such commitments, noted in section 3.16.) It was
for similar reasons concerning the difficulties of maintaining durable
commitments that game theorists seeking solutions to prisoners' dilemma problems agreed that it is not acceptable to impose exogenous

enforcement of a rule of promise-keeping (Ken Binmore 1989, p. 93; Thomas Schelling 1960). We must contemplate other constraints on short-sighted, opportunistic political behavior besides judicial review.

3.19   Commitment Defaults Arise More Often in Local Governments

Economists have often invoked two constraints on promise-breaking: temporal concern with reputation and the possibility that those adversely affected will leave the jurisdiction (Grossman and Noh 1994; Herb Taylor 1985). The disadvantages of a reputation for not keeping promises restrains people, and it will restrain them beyond the grave if they have some concern for the welfare of the unborn. The latter concern is greater to the extent that they realize that their own descendants will be directly disadvantaged by their own failures to keep promises. Concern for one's descendants is characterized by economists as "dynastic utility." One can argue that even dynastic utilitarians might discount the future too much, of course, but among the least promising ways to compute the proper discount rate is to leave it to judges.

Even if we agree that a self-governing people will care enough about its descendants not to cavalierly break promises made in the past, there are situations in which the reputational and dynastic restraints break down. One arises when it becomes clear that one's descendants or others one cares about will not in fact be burdened by promise-breaking. If the descendants are likely not to live in the jurisdiction, most of the costs fall on someone else. This is particularly true when the government in question is but a part of the whole that will be affected.

Small local governments are one extreme. City councils may know that rent control will reduce the housing stock in the indefinite future, but the would-be beneficiaries of future housing are mostly unrelated to the current renter-voters within the city limits, given the mobility of the population. For this reason, local and perhaps small-state regulation requires more external institutions to deal with keeping public promises.

This provides an economic-federalism rationale for judicial review. In order to run a system in which there are many governments, there must be some external control over opportunistic defaults by one unit whose costs are shifted to others or to the nation as a whole. (Other types of government that require judicial review for the same reason are the politically insulated, single-issue agencies of the federal and state governments, as described in section 9.3.) But even in the local government case, the external regulation does not always have to be the courts. If the resources subject to regulation are portable, those regulated can threaten to move them beyond the reach of the regulation. Such a threat can restrain even the most opportunistic local government. It is surely why Berkeley has stringent controls on the rent of real estate but no controls on the price of groceries.

Here is another example of mobility protecting rights, at least to some extent. Robert Margo (1991) advanced evidence that one reason that blacks were supplied with any schools at all in the Jim Crow era in the South was that employers needed to attract black workers. Black families would not move to counties that provided their children with no schooling. White county-school officials were urged by white employers to spend more on black schools because the next county's schools were attracting their workers. (I shall point out other virtues of intergovernmental competition in section 7.9.)

Reputation also constrains national governments in need of mobile capital. Economists have written much about this in the context of the periodic international debt crises. It is not the fear of gunboat diplomacy or international tribunals that keeps sovereign nations from defaulting on their debts. It is the fear that in the future they will get less favorable borrowing conditions. Sule Ozler (1993) presented evidence that countries that have had several de facto defaults pay higher interest rates. New countries, without established reputations for reliability, also pay more when borrowing.

The point of my review of these alternatives is to demonstrate that independent judicial review of legislation is just one of the protections for popular sovereignty over time. Intergenerational concern, reputation, and resource mobility are at least as reliable. (Chapter 8 explores exit and voice examples at greater length.) Courts should not automatically assume that they have to act aggressively in such cases, but in the context of local government takings, sometimes courts are the only serious constraint.

3.20 Political Process Theory Includes Economic Regulation

Unlike many other constitutional scholars, John Hart Ely did not fall into the error of making a distinction between economic and other types of regulation. One of the early cases that he invoked to support his view was Chief Justice John Marshall's opinion in McCulloch v. Maryland (1819). Maryland had imposed a bank tax that fell almost entirely on the assets of the Bank of the United States. All state-chartered banks were exempted. The U.S. Supreme Court's decision to strike down the law is usually regarded as a simple example of federal supremacy, but Ely saw another implication. Justice Marshall mentioned that Maryland's tax might not have been unconstitutional had it affected most Maryland banks as well as the U.S. chartered bank. Ely inferred that the transparent attempt by Maryland to foist fiscal burdens on unrepresented out-of-staters was an important reason for the decision in *McCulloch* (Ely 1980, p. 85).

Another example of economic rights protected under process theory is the "dormant" Commerce Clause. The U.S. Supreme Court has continued to supervise *state* regulation when it is found to burden interstate commerce excessively, unless the burdens were specifically authorized by Congress. For example, in Philadelphia v. New Jersey (1978), the Court struck down New Jersey's attempt to preserve the longevity of its garbage dumps by retarding garbage importation from other states. The Court's use of the "dormant" Commerce Clause—"dormant" because Congress has not acted—was given a positive spin by Ely (1980, p. 83), who regarded it as an example of the Court protecting the "politically powerless" out-of-state interests from in-state parochialism.

I regard Ely's insider-outsider distinction as congruent to my view of the function of a regulatory takings doctrine. Outsiders burdened by certain local land use restrictions are also voiceless, except for an immobilized and outvoted minority of landowners. However, I would allow along with Julian Eule (1982) that New Jersey landfill owners, whose interests coincided with outside waste haulers in this instance, might have more clout in the state capitol in Trenton than housing developers do at borough council meetings in Princeton.

Nonetheless, there is little in Ely's approach that appears to warrant much judicial protection for businesses, labor unions, or property owners upset by unfavorable state legislation. Those affected by the laws have access to the political process that makes the rules, and threats to move out or not move in are taken seriously, as I document in Chapter 8. This is not to say that such groups ought not to be able to challenge laws that restrict their access to the political process. Laws that attempt to prevent companies from stating their case to the public or to elected representatives deserve close judicial scrutiny.

Likewise, laws that attempt to carve out disfranchised groups who are closely associated with a particular business interest also deserve close scrutiny. The early San Francisco quasi-zoning laws that effectively prohibited certain laundries, almost all owned by Chinese, were an excellent example. The U.S. Supreme Court got it right in Yick Wo v. Hopkins (1886), which struck down the laws. But beyond such exceptions, there is nothing in process theory to give pause to congressional supporters of, say, stringent environmental regulations.

I believe that the error of the post–New Deal business jurisprudence was to neglect the differences among the types of governments and among the objects of regulation. Governments of small areas (and politically insulated state and federal government agencies) that regulate resources that cannot be removed from their jurisdiction, either because they are inherently immovable or because the web of regulation prevents their removal, are much less subject to the disciplines of politics. A reputation for uncompensated takings does such jurisdictions little harm because there is little prospect for repeat play. Unless the locality plans to annex territory whose owners could block the decision if they feared regulatory takings, the local government has no reason to forbear from gratifying the desires of current voters on this score.

It is tempting to cite in support of scrutiny of local regulation of property Ely's offhanded concession that there are at least a few substantive protections in the Constitution. With regard to private property, Ely pointed out that its mention in the Fifth Amendment does suggest its importance. He went on, however, to give a process-oriented twist to it by noting that property's protection was limited to the payment of just compensation, which also empowers the government. "Read through it thus emerges—and this account fits the historical situation like a glove—as yet another protection of the few against the many, [now quoting Laurence Tribe] 'a limit on government's power to slate particular individuals for sacrifice to the general good' " (Ely 1980, p. 97).

The trouble with this endorsement of the Takings Clause as both substance and process is that it does not tell us where the clause ends. Richard Epstein (1985) has demonstrated, much to the consternation of conventional constitutional scholarship, that virtually every government action can be said to devalue and hence "take" somebody's property interests. (Sections 4.19–4.25 address Epstein's work in detail.) We are left with a license for judicial supervision that democrats plainly want to avoid. The usual approach by the law has been to make a sharp distinction between physical invasions and regulations, a distinction that is both intellectually bankrupt and increasingly unworkable.

3.21 *"Discrete and Insular" Can Mean Economically Inelastic*

It is perhaps because of such expansive uses of the Takings Clause (or most other supposedly limitable substantive clauses) that Ely was wary of the "discrete and insular" distinction. Michael Klarman (1991b, p. 830), who is largely on Ely's side, offered among examples of wrongheaded judicial activism the regulatory takings case of Nollan v. California Coastal Commission (1987). (My view of *Nollan* in section 1.22 is more sanguine.) One way to confine the use of "discrete and insular," Ely noted, was to point out that it logically applies best to legal classifications that distinguish on the basis of immutable characteristics. One of the reasons that racial discrimination is so offensive is because race is virtually immutable. The same is true for ethnic origin. Religion is not immutable, but history teaches us that involuntary conversion is among the most strenuously resisted activities on the planet.

"Immutable" in economic terms means "perfectly inelastic." In some ways, the notion of inelasticity improves on the term, since inelasticity can come from the insensitivity of either the quantity supplied or the quantity demanded to changes in rewards and penalties. Inelasticity may be the result of facts of nature (the stock of land is fixed) or because of behavioral characteristics (the demand to maintain one's choice of religion seems highly inelastic). Inelasticity of the supply of land is half of the reason that landowners sometimes need the protection of judges in the same way that racial minorities sometimes do.

Commonly held beliefs point to the inelasticity interpretation that I believe underlies the appeal of judicial solicitude for "discrete and insular minorities." Public attitudes toward welfare entitlements are affected by perceptions of the elasticity of poverty with respect to individual effort. People who think that the poor or homeless got that way through their own fault or could undo their problems through their own efforts tend to oppose unconditional assistance to them.

Public programs for the physically disabled, however, are hardly ever opposed on such grounds. Few people think that automobile drivers fail to take precautions against spinal injuries because afterwards they will get good parking spaces.

The problem with immutability or inelasticity as a limit on objects of judicial attention is that it fits too broadly, as Ely noted. Gender fits the bill of being (genetically) immutable, but now the issue of constitutional protection is compromised by the fact that the men and women are about equal in number and that they are on more-or-less good terms with each other. Intelligence might also be regarded as inelastic in supply, but it is hard to know why Congress would write laws discriminating against the intelligent or unintelligent. (Fill in your favorite talk-show joke about legislators.) Immutability or inelasticity isn't the whole key to the "discrete and insular" puzzle, but it is nonetheless part of the solution.

3.22   Local Government Affirmative Action Needs Review

The distinction that I draw between types of political processes, particularly those that arise from majoritarian local government and those that arise from our pluralistic national government, provides a better answer to the question of when a "discrete and insular" minority needs protection. In a brilliant exposition and extension of Ely's work, Michael Klarman (1991b) made a strong case for its political process aspect. Klarman, however, attempted to discard the minority protection side, with which Ely himself was uncomfortable. Klarman argued that southern blacks would not have needed court protection of particular rights if they had had full access to the political process.

Klarman's and Ely's anxieties about the minority protection side stem from certain recent affirmative action decisions. Ely's view about affirmative action (back in 1980) was that judicial review of such laws was not necessary because there was no reason to worry that the majority would hurt itself excessively. Two recent U.S. Supreme Court cases have probed that issue.

City of Richmond v. J. A. Croson Company (1989) involved a law passed by the Richmond, Virginia, city council requiring that a certain percentage of city construction jobs be set aside for minority contractors. The Court struck this down as a violation of the Fourteenth Amendment rights of Croson, the jilted white contractor. In contrast, however, the Court in Metro Broadcasting v. FCC (1990) upheld the Federal Communication Commission's minority preference program on the grounds that Congress had at least indirectly authorized it.

The distinction that the Court drew between the two cases was that Congress deserved more respect than the states or their local governments. This position formally stems from the Fourteenth Amendment, which specifically empowered Congress to regulate the states in matters of equal protection. But Justice Sandra Day O'Connor's opinion in *Croson* also suggested that majority rule at the local level was more likely to produce unfair laws. She noted that the city of Richmond had a majority of blacks among voters and that blacks occupied five of nine seats on the city council (488 U.S. at 495). O'Connor cited John Hart Ely (1980, p. 170) in support of her position that Richmond's city council was *not* a white majority group voluntarily assuming the burden of affirmative action, but a majority of blacks distributing benefits to other blacks. (Supreme Court citations usually please authors, but Ely was a contributor to the ACLU's amicus brief that urged that Richmond's plan be upheld.)

The *Croson* Court's result was not founded solely on the principle of minority protection. The problem with Richmond's law was that the pluralistic politics that characterize congressional processes was very likely absent in the Richmond city council. The difference in behavior between local and national governments was made explicitly by Justice Antonin Scalia in his *Croson* concurrence. Scalia said that a "sound distinction between federal and state (or local) action based on race rests not only upon the substance of the Civil War Amendments, but upon social reality and governmental theory" (488 U.S. at 522).

As evidence of the "heightened danger of oppression from political factions in small, rather than large, political units," Scalia quoted from Madison's Tenth Federalist: "The smaller the number of individuals composing a majority, and the smaller the compass within which they are placed, the more easily will they concert and execute their plan of oppression" (*Croson*, 488 U.S. at 523). In *Metro Broadcasting*, in which affirmative action rules supported by Congress were upheld, Justice William Brennan, writing for the majority, read Scalia's *Croson* words back to him in support of greater judicial deference to national legislation (*Metro*, 497 U.S. at 565).

3.23   *Exit Supplements Voice*

While I think that it was appropriate to employ greater scrutiny of Richmond's law because local politics are different from national politics, the other prong of my test for judicial intervention in local economic regulation, inelastic supply or demand on the part of those suffering the burdens, is largely missing. The Croson Company, a supplier of construction materials, seemed capable of operating in many jurisdictions, so that the economic harm it suffered may have been relatively small. On the political side, if it turns out that the set-aside program results in higher local taxes or lower-quality public works because of a scarcity of black suppliers (as was apparently the case), the voters of Richmond are in a better position to remedy the situation than the federal courts.

My suggestion that Croson could seek business elsewhere will seem alarming to some. After all, one could charge, the same could have been said about southern blacks in the era of Jim Crow. Blacks could respond to discrimination by moving elsewhere. But there is a positive spin to this. Southern blacks did respond to discrimination and economic deprivation by moving to cities in the North. By doing so they not only alleviated their own burdens and imposed an economic cost on the southern states, but they built a political base in northern cities. That base contributed to the passage of the Voting Rights Act of 1965 as well as other national civil rights legislation.

The Voting Rights Act is the epitome of the "process theory" remedy for discrimination. The political voice protection of constitutional rights was thereby made possible by the economic protection of exit from unfavorable jurisdictions. John Hart Ely had briefly mentioned that Albert Hirschman's (1970) attention to exit as well as voice fits "quite snugly" in his constitutional theory (1980, p. 179). It is now a popular view. Vicki Been (1991), Saul Levmore (1990), Lowenberg and Yu (1992), and Carol Rose (1983) have likewise commended exit and voice to fend off excessive local regulation, though Levmore has pointed out that they do not help with local government land use regulations, as has Stewart Sterk (1992). A still more limited endorsement of exit is Richard Epstein (1992a).

I do not mean to say by my analysis of *Croson* that because blacks and whites are mobile, there is no need for courts to supervise race-conscious legislation. The psychological cost, the "badge of inferiority" that old-time segregation laws imposed, was not avoidable by migration. Whether a similar cost was borne by the unalterably white owners of the Croson Company, or perhaps even by those supposedly benefited by the set-aside program (Coate and Loury 1993), would seem a proper inquiry for a constitutional court.

3.24 Conclusion: Judges Must Supervise the Small Republics

Why would a free people want its economic regulations reviewed by officials who were removed from democratic disciplines? This chapter argues that judicial review of property regulation is an essential method of coordinating the intertemporal commitments of local governments. Left to their own devices, the smaller republics would discount the welfare of underrepresented outsiders. Local insiders can use regulation in a way that subverts the Constitution's clear commands not to take property without compensation. The larger republics are less subject to that temptation because the burden of regulation is more likely to fall on properly represented insiders and their progeny. Owners of property whose services are elastic in supply can protect themselves from myopic local regulation by threatening to leave the jurisdiction. The remaining category, regulation of immobile property by independent local governments and state agencies, requires most of the attention of judges in regulatory takings cases.

This chapter has established the foregoing case for judicial review of property regulation from historical, jurisprudential, and economic sources. Constitutional history indicates that local majoritarianism was an important source of anxiety for the people who framed the state and federal constitutions. The transformations of the original Constitution by the Civil War and the Great Depression indicate that judicial supervision of Congress was not viable. *Dred Scott* taught the Court not to intervene in nationally debated property issues, and the economic crisis of the 1930s overwhelmed the Court's resistance to congressional regulatory authority.

The jurisprudential theory that emerged from Footnote Four of *Carolene Products*—John Hart Ely's process theory—has been shown to be consistent with judicial review of local majoritarianism in property issues. Finally, I have argued that economic studies of commitment to price stability by central banks show the virtues of having an independent source to enforce promises. At the same time, such studies suggest that the deeper source of stability is popular desire for it. Like a central bank, an independent judiciary maintains its authority— and its independence—by enforcing intertemporal commands that are widely accepted but that would otherwise be rationally eroded by the component parts of a federal republic.

Some readers may be dissatisfied with my recommendation that courts largely avert their eyes from the regulatory excesses of Congress and, for the most part, of state legislatures. Bernard Siegan (1980) has articulately urged a return to the era of economic due process. But it is not clear that property is less secure now than it was during the *Lochner* era. In an intriguing book that uses international comparisons to show that regimes that protect property have more prosperity, the economist Gerald Scully actually ranked the United States at the top for its security of property (1992, p. 112). This is not to deny that the United States could do better, but it is not obvious that unelected judges are the ones to do the job after a half-century's vacation.

I want to emphasize that my disagreement with Siegan is not with the need for regulatory reform. Much modern environmental regulation has placed great burdens on individual property owners and imposed on the national economy costs in excess of its benefits. My disagreement is on the source of the reform. Courts of law lack both the legitimacy and the ability to undertake national reforms. Congress and the state legislatures are legitimate sources of reform, since they were the original sources of the regulatory experiments. There are now serious political debates about the fairness and efficacy of the Superfund and the Endangered Species Act, to take just two examples whose burdens are often especially acute for landowners. But such landowners seem to be making some headway when they have an opportunity to join with others. A burgeoning national property rights movement is lobbying Congress for bills to provide compensation for excessive regulation. Pluralistic politics is a problem, but it is also a solution.

4

The Economic-Utilitarian Theories of Michelman and Epstein

$\mathbf{A}$mong the most quoted words about takings are those of Justice Hugo Black in Armstrong v. United States (1960). The plaintiffs won, and the Takings Clause seemingly trumped the ancient doctrine of sovereign immunity. (The federal government had asserted that it was not liable for debts to suppliers after it had taken over a failing private shipyard.) In explaining a result that did not seem to fit previous rules, Black said, "The Fifth Amendment's guarantee . . . [is] designed to bar Government from forcing some people alone to bear public burdens which, in all fairness and justice, should be borne by the public as a whole" (364 U.S. at 49).

The sentiment is unexceptionable. Justice Antonin Scalia employed it in Nollan v. California Coastal Commission (1987, p. 835), and his usual opposite, Justice William Brennan, used it in San Diego Gas v. San Diego (1981, p. 656). In moments of reverie I imagine that land use attorneys could have the *Armstrong* quote inscribed on an inspirational poster, the kind that dentists tack on the ceiling above the chair to distract their patients. Lawyers could place the "fairness and justice" poster behind their desks to give similar comfort to their landowner clients.

To move the "fairness and justice" notion beyond the platitudinous-poster stage, this chapter explores in some detail two academic approaches to it. Frank Michelman's 1967 article, "Property, Utility, and Fairness: Comments on the Ethical Foundations of 'Just Compensation' Law," has dominated the academic discussion of the takings issue

141

for more than a quarter of a century. No other area of constitutional law has such a durable leading article.

Another major legal scholar who has employed economic reasoning to form a theory of takings is Richard Epstein. The reader may have seen Epstein's book on television during the Senate confirmation hearings of Supreme Court Justice Clarence Thomas in 1991. Senator Joseph Biden held Epstein's book aloft as he questioned the nominee about whether his judicial predisposition was favorable toward the constitutional restoration of property rights. The senator seemed alarmed that Judge Thomas might be overly sympathetic to judicial protection of property rights (*New York Times,* Sept. 11, 1991, p. A1).

4.1   Utilitarianism Is Not Loved, Just Used

The next few sections explicate Michelman's (1967) utilitarian approach to the takings issue. One of the reasons for its durable fame is that Michelman did not offer a blueprint for takings or even express much of an opinion about individual cases. (An exception was Hadacheck v. Los Angeles [1915], where the brickmaker went to jail rather than comply with the city's shutdown order and which Michelman called—and thus helped to make it—the "undying classic.") Michelman wanted to explore philosophical ways of thinking about the taking issue. Two of the ways he came up with bear a close relationship to economic analysis.

In addition to the utilitarian approach, Michelman advanced a Rawlsian fairness criterion, which I infer he prefers. I will discuss Michelman's Rawlsian criterion in the next chapter because it was the inspiration for a model that Perry Shapiro and I used to address the takings issue in a contractarian–public choice mode. For now it suffices to note that Michelman suggested that the Rawlsian and utilitarian criteria usually yield the same rules for compensation policy.

Philosophical utilitarianism was the original basis of normative economic theory, and it retains important links to modern welfare economics. Michelman acknowledged borrowing much of his analysis from Jeremy Bentham, the most famous proponent of utilitarianism and the founder of the London School of Economics. I want to mention a few points about the philosophy of utilitarianism before plowing into the analysis.

The objective of a utilitarian is to maximize happiness. It is not, of course, to obtain the greatest happiness for the greatest number, since one cannot simultaneously maximize two different things. Maximizing happiness is not much use as a personal philosophy, but as a public philosophy it has the virtue of allowing that individual notions of happiness may be taken as given. This is useful in a liberal democratic state, in which coercion, indoctrination, and paternalism are viewed with some skepticism.

Utilitarianism has fallen on hard times in philosophical circles. I overheard a jocular exchange between two philosophers a few years ago. One proposed a *Generic Journal of Philosophy*. It would have standardized titles to fit the most common submissions. The lead article would be titled, "Yet Another Argument against Utilitarianism." I won't, therefore, go into all the arguments here. The most common objections are the possibilities of moral monstrosity, in which one person's life is sacrificed so that total utility may rise, and the inability to measure directly the "happiness" that economists persist in calling "utility." (For others, see Bruce Ackerman [1977], p. 71.)

Economists have attempted to deal with the drawbacks of utility theory in several ways. Richard Posner (1980) proposed wealth maximization as an alternative, but the philosopher Jules Coleman (1980) was no more impressed with it than with ordinary utilitarianism. The time-honored response to immeasurability by economists has been to accept a given distribution of wealth, and then use the metric of voluntary exchange to infer increments in utility. (Simply calling this "revealed preference" instead of utility does not dispose of many of the philosophical difficulties.) This is obviously problematical for the takings issue, since the only reason takings are an issue is that the government forces some transactions rather than leaving them wholly voluntary, and the government in regulatory takings usually does not even offer market-value compensation.

The major excuse for using utilitarian criteria is that they seem to be the ones that command the broadest public support for economic policies. Notions of efficiency, whether they be the consensual, Pareto-superiority criterion or the potential compensation of Kaldor and Hicks (which was the basis of Posner's wealth-maximization criterion), are useful to economists only insofar as they comport with widely held democratic values. To put it bluntly, we use utilitarianism largely because the public lets us get away with it, at least for issues that fall short of life or death.

The other reason for using utilitarianism here is that philosophers have not come up with anything more helpful for the taking issue, as William Fisher's (1988) survey of the terrain indicated. It is not hard to criticize utilitarianism, but the critics are subject to the response suggested in a famous cartoon. It depicts two peevish and bedraggled soldiers in a foxhole, one saying to the other, "If you knows a better 'ole, go to it."

4.2   *Demoralization Costs Are Not Ordinary Economic Costs*

According to Michelman, a utilitarian would decide whether a government action was a taking that requires compensation by a consideration of three factors: efficiency gains, demoralization costs, and settlement costs. The terms are distinctive and often misunderstood, so I shall quote extensively from Michelman's (1967) formulation.

Efficiency gains are "the excess of benefits produced by a [government's] measure over losses inflicted by it, where benefits are measured by the total number of dollars which prospective gainers would be willing to pay to secure adoption, and losses are measured by the total number of dollars which prospective losers would insist on as the price of agreeing to adoption" (p. 1214). The beginning entitlement is that losers are asked what they need for consent, not what they would be willing to pay to avoid the loss. (The opposite possibility is explored in sections 5.16–5.21.) Note also that gainers are to do the paying; they are not asked what compensation they would require to forgo the gains. This condition presupposes the ability to identify a status quo from which the government measure proposes to move.

The efficiency gains criterion is where economists may be tempted to stop. Just compensation becomes a command for government efficiency, for, as economists such as Louis deAlessi (1969) have emphasized, without it we cannot be assured that government will truly value the resources it takes from the private sector. (This dances by the possibility that some losses may not be capable of being compensated with money, but the Constitution has sliced through that knot by asserting the power to take.) But even if we admit that actual rather than hypothetical payment is the more accurate measure of value, we face a dilemma: if we require compensation for all losses, the costs of doing so will prevent many otherwise efficient projects. Transaction costs were among the reasons given for not paying compensation in some of the cases discussed in Chapters 1 and 2. But if we do *not* pay, we risk imposing yet another type of cost.

The latter are *demoralization costs*. They are, in Michelman's words again, "the total of (1) the dollar value necessary to offset disutilities which accrue to losers and their sympathizers specifically from the realization that no compensation is offered, and (2) the present capitalized dollar value of lost future production (reflecting either impaired incentives or social unrest) caused by demoralization of uncompensated losers, their sympathizers, and other observers disturbed by the thought that they themselves may be subjected to similar treatment on some other occasion" (p. 1214). Demoralization costs, in short, are the bad (for a utilitarian) things that happen if you don't pay.

Because demoralization costs are, like all utilitarian costs, subjective, it is necessary to count the disutility of individuals who are adversely affected by government actions even if what was taken was not legally their property. For example, Abel is in adverse possession of Baker's land, but Abel has not met the generally known statutory time for vesting. Abel may nonetheless regard being ejected from the land to make way for a public highway as a taking of his property. The net effect on the aggregate demoralization cost of such "irrational" disutility is likely to be small, however. Few sympathizers or investors would register the adverse secondary effects that ordinarily swell demoralization costs.

Yet if Abel's tenure were widely regarded as ownership by most people despite the law's formal rules, the demoralization costs of ejecting Abel would be large. For example, most people regard priority in time as an important element in establishing rights, and there is some economic support for it (Donald Wittman 1980). The common-law principle that a preexisting nuisance like the brick factory in Hadacheck v. Los Angeles (the "undying classic") must yield without compensation to latecoming residents is not widely shared. This is evident in the statutory "right to farm" laws. Such laws exempt preexisting farms from nuisance suits by nonfarming newcomers. Although such laws may reflect the political power of farmers, I have found in teaching and in my zoning board experience that most people regard first-in-time as an important determinant of property rights.

4.3   Settlement Costs Are Balanced against Demoralization

More familiar to economists is Michelman's third factor, *settlement costs*. These are "the dollar value of time, effort, and resources which would be required in order to reach compensation settlements adequate to avoid demoralization costs. Included are the costs of settling not only the particular compensation claims presented, but also those of all persons not obviously distinguishable by the available settlement apparatus" (1967, p. 1214). These costs are more usually called transaction costs, though, as is pointed out below, Michelman's definition leaves room for behavioral factors not normally covered by this term and so warrants a different label.

Settlement costs should also include the deadweight loss of increased taxation to pay compensation. This may amount to a substantial fraction of the tax revenue, although the estimates vary considerably (Edgar Browning 1987). When the administrative costs of settlement and the moral hazard issue discussed in section 4.11 are also added in, settlement costs are powerful deterrents to compensation.

Michelman combines these factors into a utilitarian "filicific calculation." A government measure whose dollar benefits (B) exceed costs (C), as determined by public willingness to pay and private asking prices, respectively, should nevertheless *not* be adopted if the net benefit is exceeded by both demoralization costs (D) and settlement costs (S). Thus, a utilitarian does not do the project if $(B - C) < \min(D,S)$. Michelman did not say what course should be followed if the government decides to go ahead with an inherently inefficient project, that is, one in which $B < C$. In subsequent discussion of demoralization costs (p. 1214), however, he noted that proceeding with an inefficient project would raise demoralization costs and compel compensation. This would, as a practical matter, discourage a budget-conscious government from doing it.

If net benefits are positive and greater than *either* settlement or demoralization costs (or both), the lower of S or D should be endured by the government. If settlement costs are lower than demoralization costs, compensation should be paid in order to avoid the greater cost (demoralization). But if settlement costs are higher than demoralization costs, compensation should be denied on this utilitarian calculus. Thus the government should pay if $(B - C) > S$, and $S < D$. But the government does *not* have to pay if $(B - C) > D$, and $D < S$. (Economists will note that the foregoing rules amount to minimizing the sum of C + D + S for any given B.)

The preceding analysis is bare bones insofar as it avoids the questions that fill public finance texts about ranking various projects (we have considered the issue as if only one is proposed) and the various second-order conditions. As Daniel Farber (1992) has pointed out, there is no particular reason why Michelman's utilitarian calculus has to be a cliff of full compensation or no compensation. For example, settlement costs may increase more rapidly as full compensation is approached, while nearly all demoralization costs might be assuaged by partial compensation. Hence the foregoing rules could be put in terms of the usual economic marginal rules: increase total compensation as long as the rate of decrease of demoralization costs with respect to compensation is greater than the rate of increase of settlement costs with respect to compensation, provided that the usual second-order conditions are met. In part not to alienate the noneconomists whom I have invited to listen in, I will continue the discussion in its original bivariate choice form, since the partial compensation issue does not fundamentally change the analysis here.

4.4 Michelman Falls between Pareto and Kaldor-Hicks

Michelman's utilitarian standard is sometimes called an efficiency criterion. This can be misleading: economists evaluate public actions under two definitions of efficiency (see section 2.2), and Michelman's approach does not track either one exactly. Michelman's is not a rule that all government decisions must involve Pareto-superior moves, because it allows that in some situations [that is, when (B − C) > D, and D < S], some property owners can be left worse off if it is too costly to compensate them. It may even be possible for the government to make compensation and still carry out the project profitably (B > C + S), but still not be compelled to pay because demoralization costs are relatively low (D < S). In either case, Michelman's criterion is more permissive to the government than the Pareto-superior criterion.

Michelman's standard is, however, less permissive than the Kaldor-Hicks criterion, which says simply that the government should do projects if the gainers can compensate the losers, but does not require that it actually make the compensation. This is simply Michelman's efficiency gain, that B > C.

The Kaldor-Hicks criterion was in fact developed in response to the notion that the transaction costs of the Pareto-superiority criterion may be so large as to prohibit all projects. Nicholas Kaldor (1939) first advanced the criterion in response to claims that repeal of the English Corn Laws, which had kept grain prices high, could not be shown to be efficient, since many consumers gained but some producers lost. Under his standard, repeal of the Corn Laws was efficient. But the Kaldor-Hicks standard does not address the troubling possibility that some government actions may impose large burdens on particular individuals.

Michelman's path-breaking contribution was to define an intermediate standard. The appeal to economists of Michelman's utilitarian formulation is that it offers a coherent, efficiency-based standard (cost minimization) for choosing between the rigid Pareto-superiority criterion, which disallows consideration of settlement costs and operates only on consent, and the permissive Kaldor-Hicks criterion, which ignores the distribution of utility gains and rejects not just consent, but actual compensation.

4.5   Demoralization Costs Are Different from Ordinary Risks

Michelman's utilitarian criterion requires that demoralization costs be a distinct entity, not the same as ordinary costs. The distinctness is evident in the text quoted earlier. Demoralization costs are the "dollar value necessary to offset disutilities which accrue to losers and their sympathizers *specifically* from the realization that no compensation is offered" (my emphasis). "Specifically" means that these costs (D) do not overlap with the cost term (C) in the calculation of efficiency gains. If they did, Michelman's criterion would involve double counting or collapse into the Kaldor-Hicks criterion. Demoralization costs are not simply costs; they are costs that are imposed by the lack of compensation itself. They go away if it is known that compensation will be paid, but other costs (the cost side of benefit-cost analysis and the settlement costs) remain.

The source of the demoralization cost for Michelman was the risk of "majoritarian exploitation." He was explicit in keying demoralization costs to the distinction between this political hazard and risk owing to random events such as natural disasters. Majoritarianism is said to have greater disincentive effects because of a "perception that the force of a majority is self-determining and purposive. . . . The argument [for the existence of demoralization costs as distinct from other risks] must then proceed to the effect that even though people can adjust satisfactorily to random uncertainty, which can be dealt with through insurance, including self-insurance, they will remain on edge when contemplating the possibility of strategically determined losses" (p. 1217).

Why should people feel worse about majoritarian exploitation than about other hazards? Michelman suggests it is because majoritarian outcomes are strategically determined. People can adjust to strategic loss, but these adjustments are more costly (or involve greater disutility) than adjustments to random loss, which can be "conveniently dismissed from consciousness on the ground that, being uncontrollable, it is not worth thinking about" (p. 1217). (See also Michelman [1967, p. 1169, n. 5], differentiating his intentions from Guido Calabresi's famous treatment of compensation for accidents in tort law.)

Regardless of the source of demoralization costs, the critical point at this juncture is that they are distinct from natural hazards. It is not just ordinary risk. This is further emphasized by Michelman's introspectively derived list of causes of demoralization costs (pp. 1217–18). They include uncompensated government actions in which:

a. settlement costs are low, implying that people feel worse about not being compensated if it would have been easy to do so;
b. losers perceive that their burdens are large relative to others', so that there is disproportionate impact;
c. the efficiency gains of the project itself are so doubtful that it looks like a thin veil for unprincipled redistribution;
d. the loss is not likely to be recouped by reciprocal benefits tied in some way to the project;
e. those who lose now have little confidence that they will gain from similar projects in the future; and
f. losers lack political influence to be able to extract concessions to mitigate their burdens in the future.

An analogy of Michelman's demoralization distinction is the difference between one's feelings about a watch that is stolen and a watch that is lost. The watch is gone in both cases, but the very knowledge that it was stolen may make you feel worse. You may expend more effort in avoiding this particular kind of loss, in part because such deliberate acts may be repeated. The ability to purchase insurance against theft does not dispose of such costs, since insurance simply spreads them out over a period of time through insurance premiums. Note that the stolen watch's demoralization is net of the utility gain of the person who now has the stolen watch—and what victim has not wished that a thief's booty bring him ill fortune?

The direct disutility of the citizens whose losses are not compensated to their satisfaction is not the only demoralization cost for Michelman's utilitarians. They also count the disappointment of the losers' sympathizers, who are not necessarily losers themselves but who are made anxious (suffer disutility) as a result of the noncompensation. Added to this is the "value of lost future production (reflecting either impaired incentives or social unrest) *caused by demoralization* of uncompensated losers, their sympathizers, and other observers disturbed by the thought that they themselves may be subjected to similar treatment on some other occasion" (p. 1214, my emphasis).

The emphasis is added to indicate that Michelman considered these long-run costs to be caused specifically by demoralization; they are not merely the prudent responses to random risks. These long-run costs arise not only from "impaired incentives" but also from social unrest. Social unrest costs could include direct public and private outlays to guard against antisocial actions, but they could as well include disaffection with the entire political process.

4.6   Michelman Was Ambivalent about Government Motives

It is clear from his analysis of demoralization costs that Michelman was not exactly a Pollyanna about the workings of legislatures. Demoralization costs are said to rise if the project looks more like an unprincipled transfer of wealth. (By unprincipled, one might mean not part of a preconceived and articulated transfer program, for example, from rich to poor or from able to handicapped.) Thus there was an implicit recognition that democratic processes could go wrong. But it was not central to his analysis. The starting point for the analysis was the assumption that the government project generated efficiency gains. This was partly because Michelman wanted to plant the compensation question within the post–New Deal consensus about judicial review of business, which is to say, the courts are not to review regulations concerning property.

The problem with starting with the B > C assumption is that it overlooks the possibility that the government's choice of projects, which are means to a particular end, may depend on whether compensation must be paid or not. As I said, Michelman's analysis does allow that demoralization rises as benefits fall relative to costs, and increasing demoralization is an argument for compensation. But the unstated presumption in that case is that the government will pay if that happens. The government is not deterred by compensation; it is not induced to reevaluate the merits of the project.

This is important because of the bifurcation of compensation practice. Losses are almost always compensated when property is physically taken or when title is transferred, but hardly ever compensated when they are the result of regulation. Although most of Michelman's motivating cases involve the regulatory takings question, his presumption of B > C is most plausible in physical invasion cases. As the discussion of cases in Chapter 1 demonstrated, regulations are often rational substitutes for the physical acquisition of property. This does not automatically mean that compensation is due, but it does suggest that governments make a calculation of cost to the taxpayers when contemplating the choice of regulation versus eminent domain. As the *Lucas* outcome vividly demonstrated, governments required to pay for regulations can quickly change their minds about the need for regulation (section 1.23).

4.7 Miller v. Schoene *Raised the Problem of External Cost*

Miller v. Schoene (1928) is a famous case from Virginia that involved a biological conflict. Both red cedar trees (Juniperus Virginianus) and apple trees grow well in piedmont Virginia. Virginia apple trees were infected by a "rust"—a fungus—that destroyed the fruit and foliage. There was no ready cure for the disease (and there apparently still is not), but something was known about the life cycle of the rust.

The apple-cedar rust spends one year of its life in red cedar trees, developing spores in a fruitlike mass that is harmless to the cedar. The spores are then borne by the wind. Those that settle on apple trees cause the rust that damages the leaves and fruit of the tree. The spores of the apple rust develop and are blown back to red cedars, where the cycle continues. The close proximity of red cedars to apples is thus dangerous to the livelihood of apple growers.

The state legislature of Virginia responded to this problem by passing a law that permitted the state entomologist to order the destruction of red cedar trees within two miles of an apple orchard. There were safeguards against the abuse of this power. Ten freeholders in an area had to petition the state entomologist to discern whether the local cedar trees were infected hosts of the rust, and his decision to have the cedars destroyed was subject to appeal by the owner of the cedars. But one safeguard was not adopted: the owner of the cedars was not compensated for his losses other than by the value of cut trees, which the owner was allowed to keep.

Miller owned a stand of red cedars whose value to him was chiefly ornamental. He was required to cut down his cedars by the state entomologist, Schoene (pronounced "shay-nee" by my Pennsylvania-German forebears, but "shown" by most others). Miller appealed, but Schoene's order was upheld by the Virginia courts. The legislation was upheld by the U.S. Supreme Court as well. Justice Harlan Fiske Stone indicated that it was a close call, but his opinion dwelled on the need to make a choice. The main reason was that apple growing was a more valuable activity and hence deserved protection.

There is little doubt that the Virginia legislature did have to choose between apples and cedars when the two were in close proximity to one another. The cost of private transactions to internalize the cost seems prohibitive, insofar as there were many parties on both sides. An apple grower who paid cedar owners to cut their trees would confer a benefit upon other apple growers, who might feign indifference to the benefit when asked to contribute. (James Buchanan's [1972] comment on the case pointed out several of these problems.)

Even more likely was the possibility that one or more cedar owners would decline to cut their trees because of sincere attachment to them, strategic bargaining, or just plain spite. I found that owners of trees that blocked valuable views in Berkeley, California, usually cut them to satisfy immediate neighbors, but negotiations sometimes broke down for the three reasons cited. (I was involved in such negotiations on behalf of my landlord, and Berkeley neighbors told me about the pitfalls, which nonetheless were usually avoided.) In Virginia cedar tree negotiations, however, one bargaining failure would harm many apple growers. I know, of course, that under the conditions of the Coase theorem, these problems are magically solved, but, as Coase (1988) has repeatedly urged, analysts who wish to proceed beyond games must contemplate actual transaction costs.

4.8 High Settlement Costs Militated against Compensation

While it does seem reasonable to assume that private transactions were not feasible, this does not dispose of the question of whether the losers from Virginia's legislation should not have been compensated from public funds. If apples are more valuable than cedars, it seems, in Michelman's calculus, that the act promoted efficiency (that is, B > C). The more difficult issue is whether the cedar owners should have been paid, and here one must compare demoralization costs (D) and settlement costs (S). If D > S, the Court made a mistake. My conclusion, however, is that D < S, and D was less than efficiency gains, so that the Court's failure to order compensation was correct.

The adventitious growing habits of the red cedars, not referred to in the Court opinion but surely known to rural Virginians, are the key to the high settlement costs. Having grown up in eastern Pennsylvania, I have seen many abandoned farm fields sprout with stands of red cedars. Red cedar is one of the first woody species in forest succession (John Kricher 1988, p. 23). I always regarded red cedars as a weed of old fields. Later they are crowded out by hardwoods.

Although Miller had used the cedars for ornamental purposes, I suspect that most of the offensive cedars were growing untended in old fields. As such, the Virginia legislation might look no more onerous than a municipal ordinance that requires property owners to mow their lots to suppress ragweed. It could have been simple antinuisance legislation, and few commentators hold any brief for nuisances.

Why not compensate people for antinuisance requirements? The economic answer is that the idea of nuisance is to promote a standard of noncompensable behavior in order to save on transaction costs (Robert Ellickson 1973; Donald Wittman 1984). If we had to pay people not to commit nuisances, we would probably chose to do so in most cases. But in the process we would waste a lot of resources in making the transaction. A utilitarian looking at this as a general problem would opt for making nuisancelike activities liable to discontinuance without compensation. (This might be tempered by the priority of the nuisance in time, as mentioned in section 4.2, but priority did not seem to be an issue in the apple-cedar controversy.)

The problem in Miller v. Schoene was that the red cedar trees were not just like ragweed; red cedars had value as ornamental plants and as timber. The wood was used for cedar chests, fence posts, and pencils, and the trees' compact size and shape made them useful in ornamental

plantings and hedges (Julia Roberts 1905). A century earlier, the state
might have been prevented by federal law from cutting cedars. Forrest
McDonald (1985, p. 32) pointed out that in 1817, "the cutting of live
oaks and red cedars was prohibited by law, on the ground that they
were especially adaptable for ships' timbers."

Couldn't the legislature be required to distinguish between owners
of cedars who deliberately planted them and those who simply neglected (in an agricultural sense) their fields and fence rows? Of course
they could. But now a new evidentiary issue is raised to busy the state
while the apples are rotting. Compensating owners only for previously
planted cedars might alleviate the problem, but they are not hard to
transplant. Cedars might be transported like Birnam Wood to the
orchardists' Dunsinane, just to be paid to depart. This is reaching (as
is the simile), but so is the assumption that legislative draftsmanship
could fine-tune such problems. It is also easy to forget the previously
mentioned settlement costs that would also be required if formal compensation were voted: the excess burden of new state taxes to pay the
compensation, the costs of assessing damages, and the legal fees for
undertaking eminent domain procedures.

4.9 Demoralization Costs Were Not Trivial

For the foregoing reasons, I think the settlement costs of compensating red cedar owners for their losses would have been substantial. But
this does not end the inquiry in Michelman's framework, since we have
to ask whether demoralization costs were high, too. Demoralization
concerns the disappointment of the claimant, sympathizers, and other
people whose behavior might be adversely affected if no compensation
is forthcoming. We may assume that Miller liked his cedar trees, and if
the state wanted him to cut them down, it should have contemplated
paying for them.

The secondary components of demoralization costs are, first, the
shared sense of demoralization by other people made anxious by the
lack of compensation to Miller and, second, the inducement to inefficient behavior by others that will spread the costs of the demoralization even to people who are not bothered by the decision not to
compensate. The answer to the second is easier than the first. The
absence of compensation in this circumstance is not likely to result in
inefficient behavior. The event that gave rise to the taking (the dis-

covery of the damaging effects of the apple-cedar rust) could not have been anticipated, so almost no one's behavior is apt to be altered.

To the extent that future behavior is altered, it is most likely efficient: uncompensated destruction will discourage the growing of cedar trees or other suspected parasitic hosts near apple orchards. There is a hazard on the other side (on settlement costs), which is that apple growers might establish orchards in areas infested with cedar trees when they might otherwise easily avoid them, but this seems unlikely given the extensive husbanding that apple trees require. Orchards do not just pop up in untended fields, as red cedars do.

Sympathetic demoralization by property owners in general can only be addressed introspectively, and here Michelman's guide at least provides a vocabulary. Keep in mind that these are intended to serve not as a checklist but, rather, as a framework for deciding whether the decision not to compensate is fair: is the cedar owner bearing a cost that should be shouldered by the public as a whole? I address this question by systematically reviewing Michelman's list of sources of demoralization from section 4.5 above.

(a) Demoralization is reduced if settlement costs are high, which I have argued they are in this instance. High settlement costs make it evident to the victim and sympathizers that society might otherwise have to forgo the benefit of the ordinance. Besides this, settlement costs are apt to be high when, as here, there are numerous victims (cedar owners) who are hard to identify in advance. This fact makes it less likely that any one of them will feel as if he or she were deliberately singled out.

(b) If the losers (the cedar owners) perceive that their burdens are disproportionately large relative to others', they will feel more demoralized. This may be the case here, because Miller's use of cedars as ornamentals makes his burden larger than that of others. One might suppose that ornamental values are a small fraction of his wealth, but that by itself does not help. This is probably the best argument for demoralization cost.

(c) An efficient project, as opposed to one that is wasteful or that involves unprincipled redistribution, generates less demoralization. There is little doubt that the anticedar program is a desirable thing for the government to do. It would be hard to show that the legislation at issue involves unprincipled redistribution, especially since the cut cedars were not taken by the state or by another private party, although certainly the benefit of their cutting redounded to the apple growers.

(d) The question of reciprocity is difficult to know, but there are potentially some benefits. It is possible that owners of land with cedars on them could gain because the regulation makes their land more valuable should they want to establish an apple orchard. The legislature's commitment to promoting agriculture indicates that if these owners' crops were threatened by some as-yet-unknown parasite, help would be forthcoming. And, to reach for minor benefits, cedar owners gain as consumers by the price reduction on local apples.

Michelman's final two sources of demoralization costs are more controversial. They are that (e) those who lose now will have little confidence that they will gain from similar projects in the future, and (f) losers lack political influence to be able to extract concessions to mitigate their burdens in the future. Both criteria ask the potential claimants to look to the future, but for different reasons. In (e), the question is whether there is some probability, objectively considered, that a future legislature will do something that will benefit them. (This was analyzed by Mitchell Polinsky [1972] and adopted in part by Richard Posner [1980].) If the cedar-destruction legislation is seen as antinuisance legislation, the answer is surely yes. Society is self-insuring against nuisances, apparently, and potential nuisances can affect anyone.

The last criterion, (f), looks to the future for a different reason. It asks whether the victims *can* get something back by using their political influence sometime to obtain a cedar tree owner's compensation bill, or perhaps to get a subsidy from the state to replant fields where cedars have been removed. Note that the two criteria (e) and (f) imply different views of the legislature. In the former, the legislature follows a pattern that is predictable but not necessarily subject to the victims' influence. The cedar owners simply make a prediction about future benefits. In the latter, the cedar owners have some influence on legislation that continues beyond this particular loss.

4.10   *The Political Process Affects Demoralization Costs*

Frank Michelman in a later article (1979) changed his mind about the future benefits criterion [item (e) in section 4.5]. He argued in a slightly different context that if the legislature could provide future benefits to offset losses, it was perfectly capable of passing the compensatory legislation now, binding itself to make amends later. Since there is no objection to delaying *payment* of compensation, provided a suitable interest rate is applied, those subject to takings should not be mollified by unspoken assurances that they will get something by and by.

Just because Michelman disavows (e), should his readers? In this instance, the answer depends on whether the legislature can be thought of as having persuasive reasons for putting off a decision about whether to compensate. One can imagine reasons for putting off compensation itself—we don't have the money this year, but we'll get it to you later—but not for putting off compensation in principle. To do so is to deny that compensation is owed. To accept this argument is like saying that maybe the losers will win the lottery and feel better off.

Thus I reject the criterion that random future benefits reduce demoralization; to accept the criterion is to dismiss any taking claim. But I do not reject (nor did Michelman) the last criterion, (f), the idea that the losers might have some political power to set things right. There is a difference between a person subject to rules generated by a process in which he is, for all practical purposes, excluded or in which the outcome is a foregone conclusion, and a process in which the person has some control. As I indicated in Chapter 3, process is a linchpin of my distinction between regulatory takings by local governments and politically insulated agencies and those by state and national legislatures.

For the case of Miller v. Schoene, the difference is that rural landowners in Virginia were represented in the legislature at least as well as apple growers. Indeed, the latter were a subset of the former. If the cedar-rust legislation took away things that rural landowners were much concerned with, they might have blocked it. If cedar destruction gets out of hand, one would expect that legislative committee chairs would hear about it in the future, and remedies would be forthcoming. This is not a gamble or mere expectation; it is a description of a well-established political process. The knowledge that the cedar-destruction legislation emerged from this process ought to make cedar owners less demoralized.

Should Miller be compensated? My answer, based on the foregoing understanding, would be no, unless the impact of the destruction of his cedars was larger and hence more disproportionate than I have supposed. Miller—or at least his sympathizers—should be able to see that a policy of not compensating in instances like this is in the long-run best interests of persons like himself.

4.11 *"Moral Hazard" Is a Settlement Cost*

An additional form of settlement costs has recently been isolated by economists. This is the problem of moral hazard, the behavioral response to the foreknowledge that one will receive compensation. Moral hazard has long been a problem in eminent domain. In the early 1800s, New York City began building its Croton Reservoir system in Westchester County. Attempts by the city to acquire land by voluntary sales were mostly unsuccessful, and eminent domain creaked into motion. The historian Nelson Blake told what happened next: "The Westchester residents were eager to get all the compensation that they could from the city. Speculators bought up farm land along the aqueduct route, divided the land into village lots, and sought to convince the appraisers that each of these lots was worth as much as would have been given for several acres of farm land a short time previously" (1956, p. 149).

A formal model of takings that addressed the moral hazard problem was first published in an economics journal by Lawrence Blume, Daniel Rubinfeld, and Perry Shapiro (1984), whom I refer to below as BRS. The following parable (taken from Fischel and Shapiro 1988) is intended to capture the salient points of their article by extending one of their examples.

A family owns land in a river valley upon which they contemplate establishing a business to provide overnight accommodations. They must choose between a campground and a hotel. The campground requires investments of small amounts of capital which depreciate quickly. The hotel involves more capital, which lasts longer and provides more guest services per year. Prior to investigating the geology of the region, the family concludes that the hotel will be more profitable.

The hotel would be less profitable only if the level of the river in the valley rose to such an extent that it inundated the hotel, in which case all capital would be lost because it is "immovable" (too costly to move). In that case the campground would have been more profitable, because only a trivial amount of capital would be lost. What causes the river to rise, and what knowledge the landowners have or should have about such events, will be discussed under different scenarios. It is assumed throughout that the landowners are risk neutral, so that they act only on expected gains.

Scenario 1 involves a natural disaster. The landowners discover that there is a 20 percent probability that their land will be inundated when a natural lake is formed on account of a rock slide on government-owned land downstream from the proposed hotel. Nothing can be done to reduce the probability of this event or to mitigate the damages it will cause once it happens, and the government is known not to be responsible for the consequences of this "act of God." As a result the landowners decide to build the campground, which is assumed to be the decision that maximizes social welfare.

In *scenario 2*, suppose that prior to the landowners' decision to build the campground, the government enacted a flood compensation bill that offered to pay those affected by natural disasters for the market value of their losses. No payment in advance, other than an increase in taxes spread among all citizens, is necessary to acquire this guarantee of compensation. This bill will induce the landowners to erect the hotel rather than the campground. The outcome is inefficient because it guides capital into ventures with negative expected value. The risk to the landowner is removed by the promise of compensation, but the cost to society remains, since capital is removed from safer places to riskier ones. The incentive created by the flood compensation bill is an example of moral hazard.

Moral hazard arises from any entitlement that divorces the consequences of people's actions from their decisions. The phenomenon is pervasive in any society. Companies that provide fire insurance worry that policyholders may ignore efficient fire prevention measures; payments to victims of pollution may induce them to live too close to its source; and colleges that grant tenure to professors may find that they work relatively little thereafter. As these examples suggest, moral hazard is not confined to insurance companies or to government programs. Nor does moral hazard alone deter governments from undertaking otherwise desirable actions.

4.12 Pigovians Regard Governments as Efficiency-Minded

Scenario 3 assumes, contrary to the previous scenarios, that no natural disaster can inundate the land on which the hotel construction is planned. However, the family's land may be submerged by a dam built by a government agency granted the power of eminent domain. The government finds it socially profitable to build the dam only if some exogenous event, such as a rise in the international price of oil, makes hydropower profitable. Both the would-be hotel owners and the government dam builder know that the probability of such an event is 20 percent (the same as in the natural disaster case), and both parties know that the value of the dam if this event occurs will exceed the value of the otherwise durable hotel.

Blume, Rubinfeld, and Shapiro (1984) made an important assumption about the government's behavior in this situation. The government only undertakes projects whose benefits exceed their costs, and everyone knows that when oil prices exceed a certain level, the government will build the dam. The government cannot be swayed from this decision by any political activity or legal manipulation. Such relentless dedication to benefit/cost principles is the Pigovian assumption. It allows the landowners to regard the government's decision to build the dam as an exogenous event. The state of the world is simply that the government will seize the property if the aforementioned increase in oil prices occurs; the land is safe otherwise.

Under these conditions, BRS proved that it is inefficient to compensate the landowner for the taking. The key to their proof is that the promise of "just compensation" is a form of moral hazard. Advance knowledge of a rule that the government will pay for damages to structures is inefficient for the same reason that disaster payments are inefficient in the second scenario: durable private capital is unnecessarily put at risk of destruction. The essence of the BRS result is that government takings are analogous to these problems.

Blume, Rubinfeld, and Shapiro were not, of course, so naive as to take the Pigovian assumption literally. They also explored the "fiscal illusion" assumption, in which government underestimates costs it does not have to pay. (This will be discussed in section 5.15.) But their most provocative and widely cited result—that just compensation is inefficient—nonetheless emerges from the Pigovian assumption.

The BRS moral hazard problem could not arise if the private capital could be costlessly removed from the site. This result follows because the social cost of landowners who ignore the possible government taking of their land is not their loss of the land (the government is, after the taking, using it for a presumptively more efficient use), but the destruction of the capital they put there. It follows, then, that there is no inefficiency (on BRS grounds) entailed in paying full compensation for government takings of labor services or portable capital. Indeed, the very mobility of such resources induces rational governments to pay full compensation for their services regardless of any constitutional requirements. This observation suggests again why real estate is the focus of a disproportionate number of takings cases.

The inefficiency of compensation is not necessarily caused by strategy. The BRS result does not depend on landowners' deliberately overbuilding, which would in any event be unprofitable unless compensation for excessive structure were for more than its market value. The BRS efficiency problem is simply that the landowners rationally disregard the probability that the government may have alternative uses for their land that require the destruction or costly removal of private capital.

A way of dealing with the moral hazard problem is for the government to purchase, in advance of landowner decisions, an option to take the property without paying for lost capital. For example, the government could pay the landowner for the reduction in land value caused by the announcement that it would not pay for capital in the event of a taking (Robert Cooter 1985). If and when the taking occurs, the government pays only for the land, as if no building had been put there. Landowners in scenario 3 would then be on notice (for which they were compensated) that building the hotel would be at their own risk, and they would then efficiently take into account the probability of the dam.

Purchase of the "taking option" does not entirely dispose of BRS's moral hazard. It might be preferable to the current situation (scenario 3), depending on whether the cost of the additional transaction offsets the expected reduction in moral hazard costs. But compared with the BRS "ideal" of scenario 1 (or scenario 4 below), the moral hazard problem remains. In the time it would take for the government to adopt and implement the purchase of options, landowners might strategically build in anticipation of compensation. Only if landowners were completely surprised by the program would it avoid the moral hazard problem. Surprise, though, is something democratic agencies are usually not capable of.

4.13 Property-Rule Protection Overcomes Moral Hazard

Scenario 4 involves a private dam. (This case does not track BRS.) It involves the same facts as in scenario 3: a dam will become profitable if and only if there is a rise in oil prices, an exogenous event whose probability is 20 percent. The difference is that the prospective dam builder is a private party who cannot exercise the right of eminent domain.

The government's role in this scenario is solely to enforce contracts and protect private property from being taken by another without *consent*. Consent implies that ownership of resources is protected by a property rule, meaning that the owner can refuse to trade. The contrasting protection, under the distinctions developed by Calabresi and Melamed (1972) and described in section 2.2, is a liability rule. The typical example of liability rule protection for landowners is eminent domain, under which the government may take their property if it pays for it.

The upstream landowners must in the present scenario give their consent to the building of the dam. What will they do in this situation with regard to their business decision? They will build the campground, just as they would in the case of an uncompensated disaster. This is the efficient decision, which they will make because they can bargain with the dam builder for some of the profits of her dam in exchange for their not building the hotel. (Recall that we assumed that the dam was more profitable than the hotel, so such an exchange is feasible if transaction costs are low enough.)

It would be irrational for the upstream landowners to build the hotel to establish a better bargaining position. Property-rule protection puts them in an unimprovable position: they can refuse any offer by the dam builder regardless of the current state of their land. They are thus able to collect almost all of the surplus value of the dam, and they have no incentive to ignore the probability that a lake may be the most profitable use of their land. This example shows that Blume, Rubinfeld, and Shapiro's result depends on the nature of property rights as well as on the nature of government. (I will describe in sections 5.9–5.15 a formal model in which Shapiro and I considered characterizations of the government besides the beneficent Pigovian government.)

4.14 Andrus v. Allard *Illustrates the Moral Hazard Problem*

Andrus v. Allard (1979) is an example in which the Court's decision could be justified on the basis of the moral hazard component of settlement costs. (The Court itself only alluded to this line of reasoning.) The U.S. Eagle Protection Act of 1940 prohibited the sale, but not the possession, transport, display, or giving of eagle feathers (among other parts of eagles), even those acquired before 1940. Eagle feathers thus became financially inalienable, which greatly reduced their value to many of their owners. Owners of pre-1940 American Indian headdresses that had eagle feathers in them sought compensation for the unsalability of their inventory.

The rationale for the regulation and the lack of compensation for the lost stick of alienability from the bundle of property rights seems transparent. The government could not grant exceptions for eagle feathers that had been legally acquired prior to 1940 because, Justice Brennan's opinion noted, there was no practical way to differentiate between old and new eagle feathers.

Compensation for the regulation's devaluation of old eagle feathers would thus have run into the moral hazard problem. If the word got out that old eagle feathers were being paid for, and that the government could not distinguish old from new, the effect would have been much the same as a bounty on eagles. Eagles live in remote areas, far from most law-enforcement officers, so their illegal killing can seldom be monitored. Lack of compensation for loss of commercial value can be justified in this case on the grounds that paying compensation would almost surely have defeated the entire purpose of protecting eagles from hunting by poachers.

Justice Brennan's opinion for a unanimous Court did not rest on this rationale. Instead he emphasized the dubious proposition that loss of value for a future interest is hard to prove. But of course the same is true when a parcel of vacant land is taken for a highway. The land's value, indeed, the whole concept of present value, involves an estimate of future streams of income. Richard Epstein (1985, p. 76) properly deplored Brennan's rationale.

Susan Rose-Ackerman's (1985) analysis of *Allard* also recognized that paying compensation might induce more killing of eagles. She nonetheless believed that the Court should have required some form of compensation for holders of old eagle feathers. She suggested that the government require owners of eagle feathers to register them before the law took effect. Another possibility would have been for the government to purchase all feathers presented by a given date.

Neither of these sounds practical. Announcing a registration or purchase period would concentrate the illegal hunt for eagles into a shorter period of time. Since even poachers may have had some incentive not to take all possible eagles, and since the price of feathers would have been driven up by the announcement of the impending restrictions, drawing more poachers into action, the effect of a "window of compensation" might have been catastrophic for the endangered birds. Moreover, registration of eagle-feather inventories assumes that feathers can be monitored over a period of time. Many holders of eagle feathers live in remote areas in the West, where inventory control may be less than an exact science. In either case, the Court was in no position in 1979 to order the secretary of the interior to do something that could only have been done in 1940. (The long lag between 1940 and 1979 makes one suspect that the law may not have controlled many people's behavior.)

Another problem was raised by the actual reasoning in Andrus v. Allard. The Court said that only one aspect of ownership, the right to sell, was infringed by the federal law. The Court managed to ridicule its own reasoning by suggesting that eagle-feather owners could salvage some value by charging admission to look at displays of them. If that had been profitable, it would have encouraged more eagle hunting, and federal law would have had to forbid it, as well.

4.15   Hodel v. Irving *Exemplifies Political Process Demoralization*

In Hodel v. Irving (1987), the least-noticed of the Supreme Court's 1987 takings cases, the Court seemed to have reversed its opinion on alienability. Nineteenth-century congressional reformers were concerned that land held by individual Indians on their reservations would be sold to outsiders. In order to prevent that, Congress imposed restraints on the Indians' ability to sell or bequeath their lands. After several generations, much reservation land held by individual Indians became divided into tiny parcels. The parcels were so small and ownership was so fragmented that their use had become entirely uneconomical (Fred McChesney 1990).

The 1983 federal law at issue in Hodel v. Irving allowed the government to consolidate the highly fractionated parcels within the tribe. But the law made no provision for compensation for the smallest parcels, for the obvious reason that the transaction costs of doing so were extremely high compared with the value of each parcel. The Court nonetheless insisted that compensation be made, asserting that the right to bequeath one's property, however trivial its value, was one the Constitution protected. The Court's claim that the circumstances were different from *Allard* only underscored the inconsistency of its logic.

Hodel v. Irving was a case in which settlement costs seemed very high and the project itself had benefits in excess of costs, yet the Court seemed to act as if demoralization costs were nonetheless even higher for the Indian landowners. This position looks inconsistent with Michelman's standard, yet I think it is not. John Hart Ely's (1980) process theory explains why the uncompensated taking in Hodel may have been especially demoralizing. At issue in *Hodel* were Indian lands on reservations. Reservation Indians cannot vote in federal elections; they have no congressional representatives. The pluralistic give-and-take that modifies such decisions in other cases does not regularly include Indians. Indians do lobby, and they do have their sympathizers, of course, but that does not alter the essential disfranchisement of the group.

Indians thus meet Ely's political process criteria for Court intervention. In Michelman's terms, there is a special demoralization cost [item (f) in section 4.5] that attaches to lack of representation in the political process. Special Supreme Court solicitude for reservation Indians' property therefore seems proper. In addition, demoralization would seem to be increased by the fact that the system that resulted in the fragmentation policy was instituted for what Congress once thought was the Indians' benefit many years earlier. A party who made a gift and then withdrew it used to have a pejorative name among children.

4.16 *Moral Hazard Was Formally Encouraged in* Kirby Forest

The formal law of eminent domain recognizes the BRS moral hazard problem by resolutely marching the other way. The U.S. Supreme Court insists that there is an obligation to pay for anything that the landowner does up to the moment of a formal declaration of taking. The landowner is not forbidden to improve his property until the moment that property is transferred to the government. The U.S. Supreme Court's clearest statement of this rule is Kirby Forest Industries v. United States (1984).

Kirby Forest Industries owned forest land in Texas that was being considered for inclusion in "Big Thicket National Park" in 1967.

Kirby was by far the largest owner of the several thousand acres that were originally under study. The company agreed to a trade association's suggestion of a voluntary moratorium on timber cutting on its land as the U.S. Congress debated authorizing funds to purchase it.

Congress had at its disposal several means to take the land quickly, but it forswore them, apparently to save money (*Kirby*, p. 7, n. 9). Congress instead authorized ordinary eminent domain proceedings, which resulted in the initiation of an eminent domain trial by the government after negotiations reached an impasse on August 21, 1978. (In eminent domain trials, the government acts as the plaintiff and the property owner is the defendant.)

The U.S. District Court appointed a special commission to value the land, a common procedure in such trials. The commission arrived at the figure of $2.3 million. The federal District Court judge accepted the valuation and tacked on six percent annual interest between August 21, 1978, when the government began the trial process, and March 26, 1982, the date that the government paid the amount and acquired title. The interest was awarded, said the District Court, because Kirby had no practical use of its land after the government instituted the suit in 1978.

The trial judge thus agreed with Kirby's claim that it could not sell and could not use its property after it became known that the government would acquire it. It is easy to envision why. If Kirby had proposed to sell the property for, say, vacation home development, or if the company had announced plans to cut the timber on it, the government would have speeded up proceedings and taken the property right away. It can do this by taking title and paying an estimated amount of compensation. Two sums, the difference between the estimated and actual liability and the interest on the difference, would be determined later by a trial.

In order to induce the quicker compensation, though, Kirby would have had to taken credible, meaning costly, actions. Proposing a subdivision or planning timber cuttings involves substantial outlays by planners or foresters. And no ordinary buyer of timberland would want to endure the transaction costs of purchasing land that the government was likely to condemn. What such a purchaser would get after a costly set of negotiations and an eminent domain trial, for which legal fees are not compensable, would most likely be the price it had previously paid for it.

But instead of sustaining the (rather modest) compensation of 6 percent interest for the four years between the initiation of formal proceedings and the payment of the award, the U.S. Supreme Court struck it down entirely. The reason, the Court said, was that Kirby was legally free to do whatever it wanted with the land up to March 26, 1982, the date of payment and transfer of title. The Court reverted to bland formalities, noting that the "Government never forbade" the cutting of trees before or during the trial and that no statute authorized the government "to restrict petitioner's usage of the property prior to payment of the award" (p. 15). Formal legal issues prevailed over the obvious manipulation of the landowner by the government.

Justice Thurgood Marshall, writing for a unanimous Court in *Kirby*, mentioned the *Penn Central* criterion of "investment backed expectations." The clear implication was that if Kirby had gone to a great deal of expense preparing to cut the trees during the trial, it would have been compensated for them. This seems as clear a case of encouraging economic moral hazard as one can find. If you want to obtain even nominal damages for being held in thrall by the government during a long period of time, you had better engage in what you know will be a wasteful show of planning.

4.17 Moral Hazard in Kirby Was Offset by Government Strategy

The *rule* in *Kirby*—that the owner can do whatever he pleases up to the moment of the taking—seems to be a perfect example of BRS moral hazard. But the government's manipulative *practice*, which was upheld in *Kirby*, seems to mitigate the BRS moral hazard problem. Landowners subject to eminent domain proceedings are in fact highly restricted by the multiple means by which the government can end up with their land. If they do decide to act in a morally hazardous way and develop their land contrary to the government's interest, the government can quickly step in to stop them.

The Kirby case is not an anomaly. In a handbook that proffers advice to landowners, Theodore Novak, Brian Blaesser and Thomas Geselbracht note the traditional rule (1994, p. 243): prior to payment of compensation, "the landowner may use the property as the landowner pleases. This is true even when public acquisition seems obvious, as when the property lies along the path of a contemplated roadway." But they go on to show that the landowner may improve his property at his peril. Plans for improvements may sometimes be enjoined if the condemnor can prove they were "not undertaken in good faith" (p. 244), which hardly seems consistent with the previous quotation. Improvements begun but not completed that do not add to the property's value will not be paid for by the condemnor (p. 247). In some states, the designation of official highway corridors to be condemned in the future may have the effect of making improvements noncompensable (p. 363).

There is a considerable gap between the ringing declarations of landowner autonomy, which make one take the landowner moral hazard problem seriously, and the actual practices of condemnors, which suggest that condemning agencies can control quite a bit of the problem. This control is also evident in an article by Malcolm and Goldie Rivkin (1993). They described the mixture of regulation and appeals to self-interest by which state highway planners can get landowners to preserve proposed highway corridors from development.

The troubling part of this discovery that the government can offset BRS moral hazard is that its means of doing so seem unfair. Instead of exercising the "quick take" of Kirby's land to forestall further development, the government used that option only as a threat. The trial court's attempt at compensating Kirby for the company's loss by paying interest seems more consistent with utilitarian notions of fairness. (There may have been less manipulative reasons that the government did not act more quickly; planning a new national park may take as much time as planning to cut timber.)

This conclusion seems to set the case at odds with Michelman's criteria. But this is not necessarily so. The government's (apparently) manipulative behavior was a means of reducing one type of settlement costs, the moral hazard of overinvestment (by Kirby). If the government could not forestall some landowner investments, then settlement costs become even larger, and the utilitarian case for compensation itself is reduced.

Of course, discretionary activity by the government may not be the best way to deal with reducing the moral hazard problem. The ideal means of doing so were described by Robert Cooter (1985) in his discussion of breach-of-contract remedies. This would establish as a taking standard what an "efficient" landowner would have done absent the government's action. The approach is intended to create an exogenous standard of behavior (much like the law's "reasonable person" standard) that is not subject to manipulation by individual litigants. (The idea was also modeled by Paul Burrows [1991].)

Evidence gleaned from the *Kirby* opinion suggests that between 1967 and the end of the trial, Kirby would probably have done nothing with the land even if it were not being considered for acquisition by the government. Justice Marshall's opinion mentioned that Kirby's own representative said that the company had no plans to cut the timber in this area even in the absence of government acquisition (*Kirby,* p. 6, n. 8). It seems possible that if the government had not announced a national park, Kirby would just have let the trees grow. (The possibility of subdivision for housing was, however, allowed by the Court to be considered on remand.)

I avoid the issue of whether Cooter's ideal rule has fewer administrative problems than the approach approved in *Kirby*. Instead, I ask again, who is in the better position to implement the proper rules? My answer is that in this case, the federal government deserves more deference than a smaller unit of government. This is because the federal government rules are more likely to be subject to modification by interest groups, such as landowners, given the pluralistic nature of national politics. In this instance, the National Park Service seemed to be acting at the behest of Congress, rather than on its own, so it would not be subject to the charge that it was a politically insulated agency and hence subject to greater scrutiny.

4.18 *Anticipation Sometimes Warrants More Compensation*

The moral hazard problem as presented by BRS was one that the landowners imposed on the government. The government was the "victim" of owners who behaved inefficiently because they anticipated compensation. But anticipation can also work against the landowner.

One example is condemnation blight, ably examined by Gideon Kanner (1973). When the government contemplates a project, the public information about where it might be located affects property owners. The cloud of eminent domain hangs over properties. Unlike the opportunistic folks who are said in economic models to build in front of the bulldozers, most other owners find the prospect of a taking to be a major cost. Owners of developed property find that they cannot get tenants to sign long-term leases. Few residential or commercial tenants are eager to make location-specific investments and then be moved out, even if they are paid the market value of their tenancy.

It may be that condemnation blight is sometimes desirable from an efficiency point of view. One generally should not invest in buildings that are about to be torn down, unless, of course, the government plans to occupy the building as is. But often the government changes its mind about a project. In this case, the condemnation blight is a real cost to society. For this reason, it is desirable to compensate for condemnation blight that is ex post inefficient in order to discourage government agencies from telling too many owners that their property may be condemned.

A partial remedy for planning blight has been provided by federal legislation. According to the Uniform Relocation Assistance and Real Property Acquisition Policies Act of 1970, 42 U.S.C. §4601, if the government breaks off condemnation proceedings during a trial, it must pay the defendant property owner's legal fees. (Legal fees are not repaid to the landowner if the condemnation goes through.) This encourages the government not to walk away from trials whose outcomes seem likely not to favor it. The rule reduces planning blight by discouraging the government from instituting suits lightly.

Another example of landowner anticipation that leads to inefficient behavior came to my attention in 1987. The Educational Testing Service (ETS) is the nonprofit firm that administers the Scholastic Aptitude Test. ETS knew that it would need more office space in the next decade. It had plenty of land for expansion on its bucolic Lawrence Township (next to Princeton), New Jersey, headquarters, and it was not concerned about future construction costs. It was concerned instead about the rising antigrowth sentiment in its township. The president of ETS said in an interview with the *New York Times* (April 28, 1987, p. B3), "someday we'll be sitting here with all these fields and we won't be able to build on them" because of anticipated changes in local zoning. For this reason, ETS decided to build its new office space right away and rent the space temporarily to other tenants. (Lawrence Township opposed this, but ETS prevailed in court in a case for which I was a consultant.) Later, as the need arose, ETS would move out its tenants and consolidate its operations.

The ETS story presents the moral hazard issue in a different light. ETS anticipated an uncompensated regulation and so decided to build sooner in order to vest its rights. (This is similar to landowners who develop too soon in anticipation of a development tax, as analyzed by Daniel McMillen [1990].) One possible reform to prevent premature building would be to permit the township to require that buildings that offend future ordinances be removed without compensation. But this would violate most understandings of takings law. A more acceptable reform that would induce ETS to wait would be to guarantee that future Lawrence Township ordinances would not take its property without compensation. Imposing liability on Lawrence Township to compensate ETS for downzonings would have deterred the township from doing so and permitted ETS to wait to build, as I presume would have been more efficient in this case. In the case of regulatory takings, then, the BRS moral hazard problem can lead to the recommendation that compensation should be forthcoming more often rather than less often.

4.19 Richard Epstein's Takings *Arose from Distrust of All Politics*

It is against Michelman's post–New Deal background of deference to the government, echoed by the economists' "Pigovian" assumption (section 4.12), that Richard Epstein's work stands in greatest contrast. Epstein most emphatically does not trust the legislature to do the right thing. In Chapter 3, I endorsed a theory of constitutional adjudication described in a book by John Hart Ely entitled *Democracy and Distrust*. It is worth asking whether this distrust ought not to extend beyond self-perpetuating legislatures, as Ely recommended, to all government infringements on private property.

Exploring Epstein's larger agenda helps us to understand his *Takings*. Much of the criticism of Epstein focused on the weakest part of his book, a brief excursion into the philosophical basis for the Takings Clause, chiefly that of John Locke. This unfortunately appears in the first chapters, and many critics seem not to have gotten past that. Reference to Locke, I submit, is an invitation to fruitless debate. Locke has been cited by scholars dedicated to full compensation (Epstein) and by scholars dedicated to the nationalization of land without compensation (Nicolaus Tideman 1988, p. 1724).

A better way to understand Epstein's motivation is to read the last chapter of *Takings*, in which he defended his efforts as a response to Robert Nozick's libertarian work, *Anarchy, State, and Utopia* (1974).

Epstein admired Nozick, and he wanted to remedy one defect in the Nozickian program: there was no room for the state at all. Epstein recognized that this position is untenable, since there are numerous common-pool problems and public goods for which the state is the only realistic organizer of production. (The philosopher Ellen Paul [1987], whose libertarian book on takings had the bad luck to be published shortly after Epstein's, also found that Nozick's rules would not permit eminent domain. Unlike Epstein, she was not disturbed by this result.)

The argument for public goods as an economic basis for the state has long been recognized by economists of all political persuasions. William Baumol's *Welfare Economics and the Theory of the State* (1952) was probably the earliest lengthy exposition of the implications of the theory of public goods for politics. But Baumol's answer, like that of most economists influenced by the Pigovian tradition (that is, most economists), left an open-ended role for the government to accomplish these ends. It is surely too much to say that economists thus contributed to the rise of the welfare state, but someone who wants to shrink that state does have to address extensively developed theories of externality, public goods, and market failure.

Epstein's *Takings* tried to steer through straits bounded by statism and anarchy. His initial premise, quite plausible to modern welfare economists, was to view the state as an aggregator of individual preferences. Even the avatars of liberal-minded applied welfare economics, Richard and Peggy Musgrave (1989, p. 57), will not allow that the state is somehow more than an aggregate of its citizens' preferences. Epstein chose the Takings Clause for both liberating and restricting the state. His approach was to read it as empowering the government to take property, but only for public use and then only with just compensation. The rest of the Constitution, as well as most other institutions, was subordinated to this task.

4.20 Epstein's Jurisprudence Would Prohibit Redistribution

Unlike Michelman, Epstein offered a definite plan for how constitutional courts should address takings. Judges must ask four questions before they pass over a litigant dissatisfied with some government action (1985, p. 31).

(1) Is there a taking of property? Epstein argued that most govern-

ment actions, from local zoning to federal income taxes, take something in the sense of reducing the value of someone's assets by partial expropriation, restricting its use, limiting its transferability, or changing legal rules concerning liability for its misuse. There's nothing here to control the modern litigation explosion.

(2) If there is a taking, is it for public use? Public use for Epstein means technical public goods, common-pool problems, or external-cost issues. Judges are assumed to understand these concepts, not defer to legislative findings, as in Hawaii Housing Authority v. Midkiff (1984, discussed in section 2.5). If the answer is no, the judge orders the action to be rescinded.

(3) If the taking is for public use, is lack of compensation justified by the consent of the owner or by police-power regulations to prevent private force or fraud? Unlike modern judges, Epstein would also require that the police-power regulations in question be the most cost-effective means of achieving their ends, ends far more limited than judges in this century (including the *Lochner* Court) would have found.

(4) If cash compensation is not forthcoming, is there implicit, in-kind compensation that makes cash unnecessary? Implicit, in-kind compensation is akin to reciprocity of advantage, but Epstein required a tighter fit between the benefit and the burden than Justice Holmes (who mentioned it in *Pennsylvania Coal*).

If the answer to (3) and (4) is no, Epstein would have judges, federal or state (issues of federalism were not considered), require full compensation. Full compensation in principle would have the property owner paid the full market value of her losses. Epstein would have judges order the state to pay for consequential damages and relocation costs that are often deemed noncompensable by current constitutional law unless required by statute. In cases of actual appropriation of property, Epstein leaned toward awarding a financial premium to allow the condemnee to share in the gains to society from the public use of her property.

Epstein's premium-sharing principle explicitly requires that legitimate government programs must increase the aggregate value of national product (1985, chap. 1). There is no premium to share otherwise. Redistribution cannot do this and so was disallowed as a public purpose. Epstein did not confine the Takings Clause to its traditional boundaries of eminent domain and police powers. Welfare programs and progressive taxes are thus unconstitutional. (In a later

amendment to his work, Epstein [1992b, p. 43] allowed that *general*
federal taxes to support a *general* antipoverty scheme might be constitutional.)

An aspect of Epstein's theory that the premium reflects was that
initial shares were to be preserved when the government increases
wealth. It was not enough for the government to say to the owner of
a property taken for a highway, Here is the market value of your land
as it was prior to the project. Epstein insisted that the government
should pay some of the gains the highway creates for the public to the
owner. Such gain sharing is typically denied under most eminent domain cases. When land is taken, the government usually owes its owner
the market value of the property prior to knowing that the project was
to be undertaken (Leslie Francis 1984; United States v. Miller 1943).

4.21 Demoralization Costs Were Not an Issue for Epstein

It is tempting to try to resolve the differences between Michelman and
Epstein as a matter of emphasis. One could say that Epstein is just a
utilitarian who is a lot more skeptical that the benefits of government
programs exceed their costs. Perhaps he regarded the settlement costs
of making compensation as relatively low and demoralization costs as
usually very high. But this Procrustean exercise fails, particularly on the
last point. Demoralization costs just do not seem like a distinct cost for
Epstein.

This is most evident in Epstein's expansion of takings from few to
many: "The greater the numbers, the greater the wrong. What stamps
a government action as a taking simpliciter is what it does to the
property rights of each individual who is subject to its action: nothing
more or less is relevant, including the conduct of the government in
relation to other people" (1985, p. 94). Thus progressive income taxes
that take from millions are the same in principle as Tiburon's rezoning
that affected only Dr. Agins and a handful of other landowners. To
Michelman's utilitarian (and to me), the cost suffered by Agins is
greater than a burden of the same financial magnitude that is widely
distributed.

Epstein did allow that disproportionate impact is an important test
of whether an action's distribution of benefits is sufficient compensation to discharge the government's constitutional burden. But the size
of the group on which the disproportionate impact falls seemed not to

concern him. Moreover, Epstein seemed to dispose of demoralization cost as a separate entity when he noted that if people were risk neutral, a simple announcement by the government that it would take without compensation would "pass Constitutional muster" (1985, p. 203). As I shall argue in section 5.6 on notice and assumption of risk, economists' notion of risk neutrality does not dispose of demoralization costs or of the taking issue in general.

4.22 Epstein Analogized Public Law with Private Law

The emphasis on the government as a aggregation of individuals lead Epstein to his most consistently employed and ingenious analogy, that of public law to private law. Private law, the law governing relations between individuals, consists of common-law rules of property, tort, and contract. Public law, which is all the law that isn't private, would be limited by Epstein to permitting the state to do only those things to individuals that private law permits one individual to do to another. The only difference is that, under the Eminent Domain Clause, the state may force a transaction in situations that private law could not.

Thus a zoning law that forbade (without compensation) the erection of a structure over fifty feet in height would not be permitted, since no individual can unilaterally impose a height limitation on his neighbors. But because the height limit might provide a public good (for example, a nice view), a government-sponsored limit would be upheld if there was appropriate compensation. Epstein allowed that if the distribution of benefits of such a limitation is sufficiently even—all landowners are similarly restrained, but all are equally benefited—the compensation requirement is satisfied by implicit, in-kind compensation. This example makes Epstein's rules sound consistent with a lot of zoning regulation, so let me hasten to add that his theory would not tolerate open-space regulations, growth controls, or even the anti-industrial classification of the classic zoning case, Euclid v. Ambler (1926).

A nice illustration of Epstein's public-private analogy is the seeming paradox that arises in highway construction. An owner of commercial property has direct access to a four-lane highway. The road is converted to a limited-access highway by erecting fences and barriers. The business owner is owed compensation according to the rules of eminent domain. It may arrive in the form of alternative access to the new highway, which might meet the in-kind payment that Epstein regards as acceptable, but otherwise money compensation is available.

Consider the same business owner on the same highway prior to a different project. Rather than creating a limited-access highway by walling off the old one, the state road-builders make a brand new interstate two miles away and leave the old one as is. Most traffic is thereby diverted and the owner of commercial property sustains almost the same financial loss he would have if his access had been physically blocked. But this time no compensation is offered.

Epstein offered a simple and, I think, correct answer explaining why it is acceptable not to compensate for highway removal. When a substitute highway is built, it is like competition in the private market. An owner of a store can not enjoin the opening of a competitive store even if he can prove that it would drive him out of business. But if the new store instead erected a barrier in front of the old store or erected a sign that libeled the old store's owners, they would, of course, have legal recourse. Epstein's public-private analogy explains this otherwise puzzling difference in eminent domain law. (One could alternatively suggest that Michelman's demoralization costs are larger and settlement costs lower when an identifiable property is walled off from a highway than when the new highway siphons off the traffic from everyone near the old highway.)

4.23   Eminent Domain and the Police Power Have Different "Publics"

Another of Epstein's insights concerns the confusion over the distinction between the concept of "public use," for which property is not to be taken without just compensation, and the "public purpose" to which the police power is required to have some minimally rational relationship. Many modern courts have regarded the two as the same thing. But, as Thomas Merrill (1986a) has pointed out, the merger leads easily to an erroneous syllogism. If the public purpose (of the police power) does not require compensation, then a finding of public use (for eminent domain) does not either, if the two "publics" mean the same thing. This would indirectly read the Just Compensation Clause out of the Constitution. A highway has a public purpose and is for public use, but few would say that just compensation should not be paid to property owners who sacrifice their land for the right of way.

Epstein's public-private analogy provides an interesting answer (1985, p. 109). The "public use" of eminent domain is to the police power (justified on "public purpose") what private necessity is to self-defense. The common-law doctrine of private necessity arises when, in an emergency, a person must invade another's property. A hiker lost in the woods in a life-threatening snowstorm can break into a cabin to find shelter. He is, however, obliged to pay for any damages. There is a "just compensation" requirement for private necessity, and, as in eminent domain, it is determined by the costs imposed, not the benefits received. Self-defense, however, allows one to damage another's property (or person) to keep from being harmed. A neighbor's bull that invades your property and threatens immediate and substantial harm can be destroyed without your owing your neighbor any compensation.

On the foregoing analogy, eminent domain arises because the public is needful of the property, as when the lost hiker needed the cabin's shelter. The owner cannot resist or demand arbitrarily high compensation from the public, but compensation is nonetheless due. The owner has not done anything "wrong" to others. Under the police power, however, the state may prevent someone from using his property in a way that is harmful, as in self-defense. In these harm-prevention cases, compensation is not called for.

Epstein's analogy reveals what the term "public" (in public use and public purpose) otherwise obscures. In order for the police power and eminent domain to make sense as distinct concepts, different behavioral motivations must be assumed. The analogy he uses is simple and persuasive.

What it leaves unstated is how to draw the line between preventing harms (OK without compensation) and providing benefits (OK only if compensation provided). I will argue for a particular way of doing this in section 9.17 (essentially borrowing from Robert Ellickson), but here is Epstein's answer. The police power may respond without compensation only to prevent "force or fraud." Force means physical invasion. This is sometimes troublesome to Epstein's enterprise, and he nimbly adds some other criteria taken from the common law of nuisance (for example, noise and air pollution), but this should not obscure his emphasis on limiting the discretion of the government.

Just in case one might think that this wouldn't deter all inefficient programs, Epstein included taxation within the ambit of the Takings

Clause. Thus an inefficient rivers and harbors project, which typically compensates all owners of property but often has negligible benefits, would be held an unconstitutional and impermissible taking of the property of the general taxpayers. This illustrates another of Epstein's underappreciated contributions to takings theory. He saw both sides of the takings ledger, an accounting insight that will be employed in section 5.17 on the disparity between willingness to pay and willingness to accept.

4.24   Private Law's Evolution Is Affected by Public Law

I have used Epstein's book (among others) in undergraduate seminars on law and economics. The students have found it appealing. There is an order and symmetry about the world it creates that is attractive. Economists in general are apt to be drawn to it, and I was no exception. Thomas Grey's (1986) criticism that the world it creates would be a Malthusian society with a plutocratic state seems misplaced. To the contrary, property seems secure, transactions are not forced, and people get to order their own lives pretty much the way they want.

Provision of public goods by the government in Epstein's utopia might be more costly, but this would be mitigated by the larger total product and the encouragement to provide public goods on a private basis. Protective covenants and voluntary associations would flourish. Concern for the poor would have to be higher in Epstein's world, since the government could not undertake welfare, but private charity would undoubtedly increase. There is some evidence that charitable giving is crowded out by the government welfare programs, though I'd be unwilling to venture how much would be privately replaced if all welfare programs were eliminated. On the whole, an end to the wasteful rent-seeking, silly regulation, and oppressive taxation that holds down so much productive and creative activity seems likely to increase national welfare by all but the most equalitarian standards.

So why am I so reluctant to endorse Epstein's enterprise? The short answer is that I do not wish to be ruled by judges, and not many other people do, either. I shall sidle up to this conclusion by pursuing a seemingly technical point about Epstein's brilliant analogy between public and private law.

The baseline of private law, against which Epstein measures all public law, is not a constant standard. The common law evolves to respond to new situations and new preferences. Epstein, whose previous (and ongoing) fame has been his analysis of common law, knows this better than most, and in *Takings* he allowed public law to respond in the same direction as the private law (1985, p. 148, n. 4). The problem is that private law may have evolved the way it did in part because public law took off in the other direction.

For example, private nuisance law, whose narrow view of what is harmful informed Epstein's view of the police power, may have remained relatively static largely because police-powered zoning laws took off to supplant them. (Epstein [1985, p. 328] acknowledged this possibility without pursuing its implications.) Had zoning laws been stillborn, private nuisance law might have become more expansive so that a tall structure that obscured a view, let alone the sun, might now have become an actionable nuisance. The famous Florida court opinion in Fontainebleu Hotel v. Forty-Five Twenty-Five (1959), which denied a right of access to sunlight (on Miami Beach, of all places), pointedly mentioned that no zoning law inhibited the construction of the hotel's addition that shaded the neighbor's pool. I read the mention to mean that if zoning were not available, the court might have taken the shaded hotel's claim more seriously.

Another example is law regarding tobacco smoking. The common law might long ago have made the purveyors of cigarettes liable in tort for damages had not public regulation intervened. Indeed, one reason that public regulation of cigarette advertising was embraced by tobacco companies was to head off such private-law liability.

More speculatively, the absence of any private law for beneficence, which Epstein uses as part of his argument against redistribution (1985, p. 318), may have stayed in its nineteenth-century condition because of the rise of the welfare state in the twentieth. The law and economics argument articulated by Louis Kaplow and Steven Shavell (1994) prefers general income taxes to changes in legal rules as a means of wealth redistribution. The argument would have its legs knocked from underneath it if general income taxes and transfer programs were declared unconstitutional. This, of course, assumes the legitimacy of redistributive goals in general, which Epstein does not accept. To the extent that Kaplow and Shavell persuade judges with redistributive preferences to forgo redistributive decisions because they are taken care of by taxes and transfers, however, suppressing the taxation form of redistribution might give rise to even less efficient types.

It works the other way, too. In Boomer v. Atlantic Cement, the New York court adopted its novel, private-law remedy of damages rather than injunctions in part because it anticipated that public regulation would soon address the harms complained of (1970, discussed in section 2.7). Had the New York Court of Appeals believed that private law was the only source of regulation, the more draconian but traditional remedy of injunction might have been maintained. Epstein disapproved of *Boomer* in part because of this reason (1985, p. 165). But *Boomer* nonetheless undermines his use of private nuisance law as an independent and neutral evolutionary base point.

4.25   Judges Cannot Prevail Indefinitely

I have tried in the previous section to show that the common-law baseline can shift a great deal, making it a less than stable point from which to compare the merits of public law. The response might be, So what? It is still better for independent judges to decide what the legally enforced base should be rather than rapidly shifting, unstable legislatures and executives. The widespread support for a constitution-bound system of government surely suggests popular support for judicial review.

As I argued in Chapter 3, however, the legitimacy of judicial review in a democratic society is sufficiently limited that it needs to conserve its resources. With regard to economic issues, I proposed that the political process would normally be sufficient to protect property interests in larger jurisdictions. In large jurisdictions, economic interest groups would be able to form alliances to protect themselves from short-sighted populism. Voters and representatives in large jurisdictions also are more likely to be concerned with their reputation for fair dealings, since bad reputations are apt to harm future generations. But neither of these inhibitions on expropriation is present in small, local governments. There, the major protection of property is its mobility. Thus the residual economic category needed for judicial protection is that in inelastic supply at the local level.

Michelman (1967, p. 1246) also alluded to the possibility of structural protection for property owners. He referred to such a possibility as a "fairness machine," in which independent judicial review would seem unnecessary. When, on the one hand, the ill-effects of demoralization cost take the form of economic penalties on effectively represented members of the political body that passed the uncompensated takings, one would expect the political process to work things out. (This is much in the later spirit of John Hart Ely's process theory approach to constitutional adjudication, discussed in section 3.13.) On the other hand, a "fairness discipline" would have to be imposed by judges when such structural protections seemed absent or attenuated, as I argue is sometimes the case in local land use regulation.

Epstein was not entirely unmindful of structural protections for property. He allowed that "the need for diligent judicial supervision in land use cases derives in large measure from the persistent risk of faction in local government politics" (1985, p. 263). Continuing on land use regulation, Epstein said: "The political process is directly connected to the problem of takings" (p. 265). But the same chapter moves from local land use to price and wage regulations, activities usually undertaken by state and federal government, without missing a beat.

Epstein again threw some crumbs to political process. Truly general wage and price controls do not need judges to overturn them, since "the great reason to accept the constitutionality of the scheme is that . . . in peacetime it will crumble without constitutional invalidation, because just about everyone will work for its elimination" (1985, p. 278). Nonetheless, apparently because not everyone will work for their elimination, minimum wage and collective bargaining statutes are meat for the judges' grinder. Epstein asked rhetorically of the claim that they are outside the ambit of the Takings Clause, "But what then of a $1,000 per hour minimum wage statute, or a $10 per hour maximum wage statute . . . ?"

Well, why *don't* we have a minimum wage of $1,000, or even a measly $10? Such statutes have been thinkable for over fifty years now. I believe we lack them because the public's representatives have some notion, perhaps fortified by economic scribblings and libertarian tracts, that excessive levels might do more harm than good. It's true that we do have minimum wage statutes. One reason that economists have such difficulty finding that they do much harm, however, may be that the bodies that pass them are aware that much higher levels might yield the dire predictions that are economists' role in life to issue.

Epstein noted that federal income tax rates have steadily shrunk from a high of 90 percent in the 1950s to about 33 percent in the 1980s. He did not note that they fell because Congress cut them, not because a federal judge ordered the reduction. Epstein's reason for mentioning the decline was to suggest that the mere fact of higher marginal rates in previous years should not prevent "a responsible court from demanding that Congress not increase the levels of progressivity in future years" (1985, p. 327). What is to prevent a future court, influenced by a Rawlsian rather than a Nozickian view of the good society, from insisting that Congress must raise income tax rates to their Eisenhower-era levels? (It brings to mind John Ely's parody of a Supreme Court opinion based on philosophy: "We like Rawls, you like Nozick; we win, 6–3" [Ely 1980, p. 58].)

A more practical and final point is the inevitability of judicial imitation of the legislative and executive branches. Judicial tenure is at most for the rest of the judge's life, which is not so long for the average appellate judge. Then the legislature and executive get a chance to appoint judges who are more likely to do their bidding, or at least who will stay out of their way. This is not to say that judges just follow the will of the legislatures. They do so often enough, though, that when one proposes a system such as Epstein's that is intended to have long-term benefits, one must question its stability.

4.26   Conclusion

This chapter has built on the themes of judicial modesty developed in the previous three chapters. In Chapter 1, I pointed out that the U.S. Supreme Court had little grasp of or influence on the regulatory issue involved in *Pennsylvania Coal,* and that its modern takings decisions continue to reflect its remoteness from the facts. (To its credit, the Court seems to realize this.) Chapter 2 illustrated that democratic and economic forces have done more to shape eminent domain law than high court pronouncements. The history and theory of constitutional doctrines in Chapter 3 placed judicial review a distant third in promoting a vital economy.

Along with this nay-saying was my view that courts do have a role to play in a decentralized republic. The small republics of local governments (and, arguably, politically insulated special-purpose agencies) are apt to unfairly burden isolated minorities who cannot easily remove themselves or their assets from the jurisdiction. These assets can be seized by way of regulation without much deadweight loss, the economist's usual measure of inefficiency. I have submitted in this chapter that Frank Michelman's original framework gives a better account of why we are disturbed by this prospect, and his work likewise provides an indispensable vocabulary for analyzing the takings issue.

5

Rational Expectations
and Contractarian Conventions

In the previous chapter I described two comprehensive theories of takings by two law professors. Both theories have an economic content, but both are also concerned with questions of fair division. The main contribution by economists is the modification of Michelman's theory to account for the moral hazard issue. Here I examine what economists have recently contributed to the takings issue. Four approaches are explored, and my conclusions about them are less positive, although they do contain some useful insights.

(1) Rational expectations theory holds that landowners should have seen the taking coming and so should not expect compensation. This is shown by logic and history to be an unsatisfactory application of a good positive theory to thoroughly normative territory. The doctrine nonetheless appears in some decisions under the guises of notice, capitalization, and "moving to the taking."

(2) The insurance rationale for compensation also misses the normative point, in that it does not address why owners should have to buy insurance in the first place.

(3) A model of a constitutional convention indicates that the type of government anticipated by constitution makers makes a difference in the compensation rule they adopt. It is the anticipated behavior of the government rather than risk aversion that gives rise to just compensation. This finding shows that moral hazard issues need not defeat takings claims.

(4) The offer/ask disparity, which notes that willingness to pay for

something is often less than willingness to give up the same asset already in one's possession, has been used to justify both more and less compensation for takings. The disparity does not address which party should be in the offer or ask position, which is the essential question in takings. It also neglects the fact that actual constitution makers were probably aware of the disparity but nonetheless settled on market value as just compensation.

5.1 Do Rational Expectations Defeat the Takings Issue?

I have been writing and talking about the takings issue for more than ten years now. When I introduce the subject to a group of economists, I have found that there are two predictable responses. The most frequent is the idea that if the government is not required to pay, it will, like any other economic agent, buy more than is socially optimal. Gary Libecap (1986) was in this camp. In reviewing my claim that the takings issue was about fairness, not efficiency, Libecap wrote, "To the contrary, taking affects the incentives for selecting short- or long-term land uses and the associated patterns of investment. . . . [Uncompensated regulations] affect the substitution between land and other inputs as zoning changes relative prices. These issues are central for any evaluation of the economic impact of taking and land use restrictions and deserve more attention than provided by Fischel."

Whether the substitution promotes or reduces efficiency is not entirely clear, however. In matters of flood control, for example, Allison Dunham advanced reasonable arguments that the regulation of building construction in flood-prone areas may be an efficient substitute for the construction of dams (1959). The transaction costs of making the compensation to all potential builders might eliminate the advantages of compensated regulation over dam building and cause an excess amount of resources to be invested in dams.

When faced with the idea of transaction costs, which militate against compensation, some economists go to the opposite pole and give the second class of response: "Why pay anything at all? Why not just put owners on notice that their property may be taken? Don't we believe in rational expectations?"

Rational expectations is the theory that people forecast the future by using the best information available to them. They adjust their future-oriented behavior according to what they think will happen to them. The application of rational expectations to macroeconomics undermines the making of government stabilization policy, since people will catch on to what the government is going to do. Predictable stabilization policies will not work well. But rational expectations theory seems to simplify the government's takings policies. All the government has to do is announce the policy, and then the settlement costs will go away (Blume and Rubinfeld 1984; Louis Kaplow 1986; Susan Rose-Ackerman 1988).

The trouble with the foregoing application of rational expectations is that it moves without so much as a segue from "is" to "ought." The question in takings is normative. *Should* people be paid for their property? Yet expectations are an important part of a normative theory of property. Jeremy Bentham in fact defined property as "a basis of expectation." That is not the same as saying that property is simply an expectation, but it does raise the issue. The question that rational expectations directs us to is this: what should owners of private property expect from the government by way of compensation policies?

5.2 William Penn Reserved the Power to Take Property

A little-noticed predecessor to rational expectations is a theory of the origins of the power of eminent domain. The "reserved-power" doctrine held that the head of state was the original holder of all property as, for example, in feudal tenures. The successor state to the monarchy could thereby exercise its option to reacquire the property, which would not require compensation except as an act of grace. William Stoebuck (1972), who reviewed numerous theories of eminent domain, quickly dismissed this theory as lacking any historical support: "With one exception, to be recorded below, there is no indication that any English or American government has in fact reserved any such power" (p. 558). Stoebuck's exception might be illuminating for people who invoke notice or rational expectations.

William Penn in fact reserved 6 percent of all of the land he granted in Pennsylvania to be used for roads. Penn did this not because of great foresight, but because of lack of it. He had agreed to provide roads between towns as an inducement for settlers in Pennsylvania. When they got there, however, there was only one town, Philadelphia. Since no one knew where additional towns might crop up, Penn inserted an extra 6 percent to the acreage of all his land grants, which were apparently parceled out after the town-location problem was discovered. Stoebuck described its operation: "The understanding was that the colonial government could thereafter take back without compensation such land [whose location on the parcel was unspecified] as proved necessary for roads when their location was known. It was anticipated that some owners might subsequently lose more or less than six percent for roads, but this was agreed to as an inevitable consequence of the scheme" (pp. 558–559).

Compensation for loss of improvements and improved land taken for roads in Pennsylvania was required by a colonial statute of 1700, but lack of compensation for unimproved land continued in Pennsylvania until at least 1802. The Pennsylvania Supreme Court in M'Clenachan v. Curwin (1802) invoked the 6-percent rule in declining to compensate an owner for land used for a turnpike road between Philadelphia and Lancaster. But even in this case, the court did not simply invoke notice of the extra 6 percent. It pointed out that the turnpike would greatly increase the value of M'Clenachan's remaining property, invoking the same benefit-offset principle (which I described in section 2.10) that many other state courts had used.

By the middle of the nineteenth century, Penn's reservation clause was largely a historical curiosity. The state legislature adopted highway-building statutes that consistently provided compensation for both land and improvements (Phil Lewis 1958). The reason for the demise of the rule was its unfairness. As landholdings were distributed and became smaller, a given public road, canal, or railroad would take up a large fraction of one owner's land, none of another's. Even though Pennsylvania could credibly remind the owner that he had purchased this land with the understanding that some of it might be taken for such use, the enormous disparity in actual burdens among similarly situated owners erased the original understanding. Edward Snitzer's (1965) handbook on Pennsylvania eminent domain practice did not even mention the old rule. The learned county judge in Matter of Michael Butler (1941) invoked the 6-percent rule, but only for the principle that off-site, consequential damages were not compensable, a rule that, as will be seen, was invoked by other states as well.

5.3 Rational Expectations Were Invoked in Callender v. Marsh

With the rejection of the reserved-power doctrine by the citizens of Pennsylvania, the only historical example of a comprehensive view that compensation is defeated by notice vanished. Yet the idea has often been invoked by the courts. The most famous example was penned by the Massachusetts Supreme Judicial Court in Callender v. Marsh (1823), which disallowed compensation for consequential damage caused by road construction.

It is not widely appreciated how much the landscape of modern cities has been modified by human action. The city of Boston, founded in the 1600s, is representative. It has lopped off hills and filled in wetlands for more than three centuries. One dry, well-developed section of the city is still called the "Back Bay." Mr. Callender owned a house near the summit of Beacon Hill. The city in the early 1800s decided to reduce the grade of Beacon Street by excavating it to a lower level. In doing so, the city left Callender's house teetering high above the new, lower street level. This not only made access to his house inconvenient but threatened the integrity of the structure by removing lateral support.

In one sense, Callender's position was analogous to that which readers of Pennsylvania Coal v. Mahon (1922) have always supposed the Mahons were in when the coal company gave notice that it would mine underneath their property. *Pennsylvania Coal,* however, seemed to have turned on the explicit provision in the Mahons' deed that they lacked the right of support. No such surrender had been made to the city of Boston by Mr. Callender or his predecessors in title. His deed was free of any explicit notice that his property was at risk. His complaint noted that if a private party had so damaged his house, the private party would surely be liable. It was asserted without contradiction that Callender was obliged to undertake expensive steps to shore up his house and provide alternative access after the street work was done. Nor was state constitutional law lacking for support of Callender's claim. The Massachusetts Constitution of 1780 contained a Declaration of Rights, which was among those on which the U.S. Bill of Rights was modeled. The Declaration's tenth article provided "that whenever the public exigencies require that the property of any individual should be appropriated to public uses, he shall receive a reasonable compensation therefor."

Despite all this, the Massachusetts court in *Callender* held that no compensation was required. The street was legally acquired, and although only an easement to it was recognized, the court held that the easement implied that the city could make any modification, raising or lowering its grade for public convenience. For the consolation of Mr. Callender, the court cited the principle of rational expectations:

Those who purchase house lots bordering upon streets are supposed to calculate the change of such elevations and reductions as the increasing population of a city may require ... and as their purchase is always voluntary, they may indemnify themselves in the price of the lot which they buy, or take the chance of future improvements, as they shall see fit. The standing laws of the land giving to surveyors the power to make these improvements, every one who purchases a lot upon the summit or on the decline of a hill, is presumed to foresee the changes which public necessity or convenience may require, and may avoid or provide against a loss. (p. 431)

5.4 *The Decline of* Callender *Has Utilitarian Implications*

Callender v. Marsh was a leading case for highway departments for many years. It was used as a warrant for not paying compensation for all manner of infringements on neighboring property owners. But, like the benefit-offset doctrine discussed in Chapter 2 and Pennsylvania's reserved-power doctrine, it was gradually eroded by court decisions, legislation, and constitutional amendments. Stoebuck (1969, p. 759) regarded the strengthening of the takings clause in state constitutions, beginning with Illinois in 1870, as amounting to a reaction to the harshness of the *Callender* rule.

The puzzle of *Callender* is this: if takings law is about efficiency, and the courts early on recognized what several competent economists regard as an efficient rule, why did everyone—courts, legislatures, constitutional conventions—back away from the law of "you should have seen it coming"? The answer can be inferred from Michelman's utilitarian-fairness analysis. It seems likely that most of the projects in which the *Callender* rule was invoked passed a benefit-cost analysis. The question was whether those adversely affected but still in possession of their property should be compensated, thus triggering settlement costs, or not compensated, thereby inducing demoralization costs.

Expectations enter into both types of costs. On the one hand, if people expect to be compensated but are not, they are disappointed (demoralized). Others seeing their fate might decide to invest too little in future houses liable to be ruined by the highway department. But, on the other hand, the expectation of compensation might lead them to suboptimal uses of their land because of the moral hazard problem, an example of settlement costs. If compensation is always anticipated, too many homes might be built upon the summits of hills without regard to the probability of having to modify them. (Section 4.11 discussed this moral hazard aspect of settlement costs.)

The Michelman approach to explaining the evolution in the rules has little to do with expectations, though. The reason for the original *Callender* rule seems to have been that settlement costs would be high if consequential damages such as those endured by Mr. Callender were also included in compensation. Settlement costs included the litigation expenses, the incentive for opportunistic claims, and the high dead-weight loss of taxation in a society with crude instruments of public finance.

A rough idea of some of the settlement costs is given by Christine Rosen (1986, p. 45): "The city of Baltimore, for example, spent $6,089,074 to widen and open streets [between] 1878 and 1892. It expended less than four percent of this sum, $239,320, for paving, curbing, grading, and demolition materials and work. All the rest it spent on property damages." (The damages included the compensable value of the land, of course, but it seems unlikely that land's share would truly amount to 96 percent of the cost.)

Demoralization from the *Callender* rule was mitigated by the general benefits received from the project itself, and by the knowledge that the political authorities that authorized the project were elected or appointed by fellow property owners. Early nineteenth-century state and local politics were dominated by property owners, even in states in which property ownership was not a qualification for voting. Charges of majoritarian oppression are harder to make when the majority is composed of people like oneself.

Later in the nineteenth century settlement costs fell, in part because state fiscal systems became more efficient over time. More important, however, were the demoralization costs of not compensating, which also rose. This was partly because of the law of diminishing returns to various internal improvements, which I mentioned in section 2.15. The excess of benefits over costs became smaller for each new project, so the general benefits of the project were less likely to be regarded as compensation enough. The first road improvement was undoubtedly hailed as a universal benefit, even if some gained more than others. The third or fourth modification of the road, however, was seldom so universally welcomed, especially in an urban area in which small infringements could have disproportionately large effects.

I went through the Michelman drill on this to show that it gives a better account of actual practices than does expectations theory. Indeed, if expectations theory worked as a positive predictor, it would tell us that after years of public acquaintance with the many projects that the government undertakes, almost no property would be compensable. Included as not compensable would be not just consequential damages but physical invasion.

My criticism of the notice theory is based on its gradual rejection over time. My appeal to experience as a guide to normative policy is grounded on the normative posture that permeated the decisions to compensate more rather than less. Half of the state constitutions adopted the stronger language in response to old rules like that of Callender v. Marsh. Judges came around to the proposition that the right of access to a public way, deemed noncompensable in *Callender*, should be regarded as a compensable property right. This was the result, as Stoebuck explained, of a "more intuitive, more visceral judicial motivation. It simply would be unfair . . . that a landowner should be unprotected in reaching the adjacent public way" (1969, p. 736).

5.5   *Notice of Risk Led to the Insurance Alternative*

Lawrence Blume and Daniel Rubinfeld (1984) applied to takings law the moral hazard insight that they had derived in their earlier article with Perry Shapiro. Blume and Rubinfeld regarded the existence of moral hazard as sufficient to dismiss the traditional reasons for payment of compensation by the government. I will show in section 5.14 that this is not necessarily so, even when moral hazard is the only type of settlement cost. For now I want to examine the alternative policy that they recommended.

Blume and Rubinfeld's view was that the real reason for paying just compensation is risk aversion. The problem of not being compensated when the government takes your land is the same as not being compensated when one's car is demolished in an accident. The disutility of the concentrated burden of either action is due to risk aversion, which is why people buy insurance. Thus the payment of just compensation by the state is like the payment of an insurance claim by Allstate.

One corollary to Blume and Rubinfeld's view is that if people were either risk neutral or in a good position to insure, there would be no need for just compensation. Blume and Rubinfeld devoted most of their article to proposing a revision in just compensation practices so that the government pays only for assets taken from people who are not in a position to purchase private insurance or to self-insure.

Louis Kaplow (1986) took the insurance theme to its logical conclusion. He pointed out that the government is in almost all instances a poorer source of insurance than private firms or self-insuring individuals. Because he accepted the Blume and Rubinfeld view that just compensation can be viewed largely as an insurance scheme, he concluded that the government should never pay when it takes property, either by direct condemnation or by regulatory devaluation.

Blume and Rubinfeld and Kaplow did not explain the absence of a private, third-party insurance market for losses not covered by current eminent domain practices. It is not against the law to issue such insurance. In fact, municipal liability insurance normally covers a local government against an unanticipated monetary claim for a regulatory taking, although rates and coverage would surely respond if such awards became commonplace. There would seem to be a good market for such private insurance among property owners. Eminent domain's uncompensated costs, such as relocation, attorney's fees, and lost business goodwill, are often substantial and accrue to those who seem to be in a poor position to self-insure.

The current absence of private takings insurance might be explained more by its impracticality rather than by something more fundamental. One practical difficulty is adverse selection. A public planner, in order to reduce political opposition to his project, might tip off landowners of an impending taking and encourage them to apply for insurance. Insurance losses would mount as a result, and private insurers would withdraw. Such practical problems might, however, be overcome with legislation and experience once takings insurance was privatized. (Such a scheme would also require some means of commitment by the state not to take the assets of insurance companies without compensation.)

The more basic issue is that the private insurance argument ignores the issue of demoralization cost. Kaplow (1986) noted that Michelman (1967, p. 1217) in fact anticipated the insurance argument and specifically differentiated the problem of just compensation from it. (See also section 4.5.) Kaplow's response to what I imagine was Michelman's gently pointing this out is that the difference is "not persuasive." Although he did not say why he was not persuaded, one might, in support of Kaplow's skepticism, ask the following questions: If land-owners whose property is taken are paid, why should they care if the payment comes from private insurance rather than from the public purse? Why does a check from a private insurer not soothe demoral-ization costs as well as public compensation?

5.6   Insurance Arguments Look for Takings at the Wrong Time

The reason the check from Allstate is not the same as a check from the state is that the very need to buy insurance gives rise to demoralization costs. The private insurance proposal looks for the taking at the wrong moment in time (Fischel and Shapiro 1988). If landowners are risk averse, they can avoid the *risk* of a prospective taking by purchasing insurance or self-insuring. But demoralization costs in that setting are not all imposed at the moment the property is taken. Demoralization costs arise when landowners *realize* that their wealth is reduced, not just when the legal taking takes place. Even if they were risk neutral, so that they had no demand for insurance, landowners would be demor-alized by the uncompensated reduction in wealth, which is the value of their property prior to the risk's arising multiplied by the probability that property will be taken.

All a private insurance scheme does is to spread this loss over time and reduce variance in the insured's income stream. Risk spreading does reduce some economic costs, but private insurance does not dis-pose of the issue of uncompensated transfers of wealth. The availability of insurance is no more an argument for legalizing uncompensated takings than it is for legalizing the private theft of property.

Consider another analogy. Suppose Congress suddenly suspended all copyright laws. (Copyright is one of the few instances in which the U.S. Constitution authorized Congress to create a property right.) Authors who once relied on royalties from published works would realize that their wealth had been reduced. But because not all books might be pirated, there would be uncertainty about future incomes. Risk-averse authors might then insure. They would pay to their insur-ers premiums the capitalized value of which would be at least equal to the expected loss incurred as a result of copyright suspension. In the end, some authors would receive payments from their insurers for what used to be called copyright infringement. But few economists (and no commercial authors) would argue that such private insurance amounted to the same thing as copyright law. The fundamental change was the loss of rights previously held. Private insurance did not restore those rights.

The previous example should be qualified by pointing out that if copyright were suspended, authors would benefit as readers from the reduced price of other (existing) books, just as landowners denied compensation would benefit from lower taxes to pay for public services. Thus authors' and landowners' true complaint is that their *net* wealth is reduced by the disproportionate impact of the change. One could imagine a community made up exclusively of authors in which the abolition of copyright (within the community) might add to authors' net worth if there were costs to enforcing the copyright. In such a world, the local sacrifice of copyright protection would be compensated by the reciprocal benefits of a larger stock of literature at a lower price. This may explain the "lawlessness" of photocopying journal articles by academics noticed by Robert Ellickson (1991, p. 258). (I hasten to add that he found that academic norms frown on photocopying entire books.)

5.7　Moving to the Taking Does Not Resolve the Issue

Looking for takings at the wrong moment in time is the source of another problem that causes persistent confusion in the takings literature. This is the argument that expectations of a taking are capitalized in the value of property so that purchasers of the property pay less for it and thus should not be compensated. The story, which I have heard at zoning hearings, is that the buyer should have known that the property was at risk and should have offered a lower price. This variant on the notice rule may be called "moving to the taking." Buyers should be expected to check out the property before they purchase and should adjust the price they offer according to all its risk. The risk of a taking thus becomes capitalized into the value of property. (Recall that this was urged by the *Callender* court, quoted in section 5.3.)

Capitalization as a result of moving to the taking does not satisfy anxiety about takings because it again views the problem at the wrong moment in time. Consider landowner Abel whose property is being considered for inclusion in a scenic district. The district's regulations, if adopted, will reduce the value of his property from $300,000 to

$100,000. Before the regulations are adopted, Abel decides to sell his land to Baker. Baker (and any other buyer) would expect under a moving-to-the-taking doctrine that the reduction in the value of the land will not be compensated once Abel sells it. Baker therefore purchases it for $100,000 instead of the $300,000 it would have commanded absent the prospective taking.

It is true in these circumstances that Baker does not lose anything if the land is subsequently put in the scenic district without compensation. But Abel surely lost from the prospective taking. If he had been guaranteed compensation for takings that, like other property entitlements, ran with the land, Baker would have had to pay Abel $300,000.

To say that Baker should not be compensated because he "moved to the taking" or "purchased with notice" or "assumed the risk" or "had rational expectations" is to make one of *Abel's* property entitlements inalienable, if Abel would have received compensation by holding on to it. (If neither Abel nor Baker would have been compensated, it is simply a taking of Abel's property.) Insofar as alienability is regarded as an essential aspect of normal property rights, a rule that purchasers are not compensated is itself a taking of the seller's property.

One of the reasons for confusion about this point was the ambiguity of Michelman's treatment of it (1967, p. 1237). He offered an example in which those who purchase land they know may be taken should not be compensated. His example was a purchaser (Baker of the previous example) of land that is among parcels that are the subject of active public debate to prevent development in order to preserve the scenery along the highway. Michelman indicated that Baker should not be compensated if the regulations were subsequently adopted, because the price he paid for the land reflected the possibility of restrictions.

But it is not clear from the scenic highway example alone whether Michelman believed that the original owner (our Abel) should have been compensated had he not sold it. If, on the one hand, Abel would not have been entitled to compensation, then there is no reason to compensate Baker or any other successor in title for the same regulation, and Michelman's example is unexceptionable. If, on the other hand, Abel would have been compensated but Baker would not, Michelman made the error of looking at the taking at the wrong moment in time. The taking's demoralization occurred when Abel realized that his right to compensation was made inalienable, not when Baker was denied compensation.

Should compensation be made retroactive to Abel if a court subsequently rules that a taking has occurred? No; what Baker buys is the prospective value of the land, which includes any compensation that might be made for its regulation. The passage of time, however, might reduce either party's claim. Claims to property have always been time dependent to some extent, as in the rules about adverse possession. But it is time, not a series of sales, that soothes demoralization costs.

5.8 HFH *Invoked Notice of Risk to Justify Lack of Compensation*

Richard Epstein criticized Michelman for the scenic highway example, noting that it was invoked by the California Supreme Court in HFH v. Superior Court (1975). *HFH* is also interesting because it was part of the California Supreme Court's concerted attempt to recast the state's property law to restrict development for environmental reasons, a story that is told in Chapter 6. The court in *HFH* denied relief to a landowner whose commercial property was devalued by being rezoned to residential. The court also cited Michelman's comparison of the land purchaser to a sweepstakes-ticket purchaser to support its dictum that "the long settled state of zoning law renders the possibility of change in zoning clearly foreseeable to land speculators *and other* purchasers of property" (125 Cal. Rptr. at 374, my emphasis).

HFH is notice in spades: "Hey, all you land speculators (and anyone else who buys property), this is California. You should know that the rules are going to change, so don't come crying to us whenever it doesn't work out for you." Aside from making an unreasonable interpretation of Michelman's fuzzy example, the California Supreme Court in *HFH* misapplied his example to the facts of the case. The plaintiff, HFH, did not purchase the land while zoning changes were being considered. HFH rather sought to sell the land, which had been rezoned to its detriment six years after the company purchased it. HFH was like the seller Abel in the example, not like the buyer Baker. Thus even on the court's reading of Michelman, there was no evidence to suggest that the rezoning was foreseeable by the party who bore its financial consequences. The court declared, in effect, that all rezonings ought to have been foreseen and that foreseeability eliminates the obligation to compensate. Thus Epstein's objection to the theory that notice of a possible regulatory loss defeats all claims to compensation clearly applies to the reasoning of the California Supreme Court.

Epstein was especially critical of Michelman's comparison of Baker's purchase of land to that of a lottery ticket. A lottery is voluntarily entered into, while regulations are usually unilateral decisions by the state. But this criticism would not follow if it is assumed that Michelman would judge it fair not to grant Abel compensation, either. In this case, Baker *is* buying a lottery ticket, the same ticket Abel would have had if he had held onto the land. If it was fair for Abel to hold the ticket, it is fair for Baker. (It might not be fair for either, of course, but that is not what moving-to-the-taking arguments are about.)

Michelman was not uncritically invoking the capitalization or notice theory. Although his assumption about the seller's rights were not clear in his scenic highway example, Michelman later used an example that made it clear that mere expectation of a taking would not defeat the obligation to compensate. The case that uncharacteristically aroused Michelman's ire was an early California zoning case, Hadacheck v. Los Angeles (1915), which was discussed in section 1.2. Residential development near the burgeoning city of Los Angeles engulfed a long-established brickyard, which the city then zoned out of existence without compensation. Michelman rejected as "fantastic" the idea that Hadacheck, the brickyard owner, had no claim to compensation because he should have known what was coming: "But he is, after all a *brickmaker*" (emphasis by Michelman 1967, p. 1243).

It would seem no less fantastic for Michelman to argue (he did not) that, had Hadacheck sold his brickyard while the adverse zoning decision was being made, the purchaser would have no right to compensation. This argument would be illogical because if the hypothetical buyer had the right to be compensated that Michelman seemingly recognized in Hadacheck, then Hadacheck would lose nothing in the sale of his brickyard. He would have gotten a check that covered both the title to the property and the entitlement to be compensated for a taking.

Hadacheck is not an isolated example in Michelman's article. A fair reading of the entire section in which it appears indicates that Michelman is arguing that a necessary, utilitarian security of *most* property does not require absolute security for *all* property. Long-standing practices and unspoken understandings may, without excessive utilitarian damage, transfer some property rights to the government against private claimants. In a later exchange with Epstein, Michelman did suggest that notice would be sufficient to dispose of takings, although he alluded to the notice emerging from a larger political forum rather than from a court (1992, p. 100).

One need not agree with Michelman's handling of changing expectations to differentiate it from the idea that mere notice by the government should defeat all claims for compensation. Specifically, contrast the California Court's sweeping denial of relief for zoning changes in *HFH* with Michelman's circumspect statement that a government's declaration of preemption of ownership "with respect to 'all land' might have an intolerable effect on productivity; but it might not when limited to, say, navigable waters or liquor licenses" (1967, p. 1240).

5.9   *The Rawlsian Social Contract Can Be Applied to Takings*

One possible reason why economists neglect Michelman's distinction between random hazards and majoritarian excesses is that it seems logical to do so given their assumptions about the nature of government. The economists who have invoked the idea that compensation is inefficient have assumed a "Pigovian" model of government. As discussed in section 4.12, this model assumes that government is an unimpeachable benefit-cost machine. It does not inquire about the distribution of benefits, nor can it be manipulated by any faction of those governed. Thus losses incurred by individuals whose property is taken should be regarded as analogous to those that occur through such impersonal events as market forces or natural catastrophes. There are no majoritarian excesses possible, because government decisions do not depend on the will of anyone, let alone a self-seeking majority. Demoralization costs in such a world should be zero. Since settlement costs are high because of the moral hazard problem, the conclusion would seem to follow naturally that compensation should not be made.

This conjecture may not be enough to satisfy economists who are skeptical of the usefulness of the demoralization cost–settlement cost framework. To explore the effects of the Pigovian assumption on the takings issue without reference to demoralization costs, Perry Shapiro and I developed a contractarian model of constitutional choice (Fischel and Shapiro 1989). Modern economic theories of the social contract derive chiefly from *The Calculus of Consent,* by James Buchanan and

Gordon Tullock (1962), and *A Theory of Justice,* by John Rawls (1971). Frank Michelman applied some of Rawls's early ideas to the takings question in his 1967 article. I will follow Michelman's development rather than Buchanan and Tullock's because Michelman focused specifically on the takings issue.

Rawls's theory of "Justice as Fairness" (the title of one of his earlier articles) submitted that one way of thinking about fairness was to invoke the classical "veil of ignorance." Behind such a veil, people are ignorant of their own personal endowments, including what their position in society might be. They are, however, aware of the consequences of alternative structures of society. A society that respects property and insists on enforcing contractual obligations will produce a lot of goods, but those same rules may result in extremes of wealth and poverty. A different society that insists on egalitarian sharing by common property will avoid the latter problem but not have much to share. (I couch these societies in economic terms, but Rawls included all social positions and arrangements.)

Rawls's question was how someone in the "original position" (behind the veil) would choose among the various social arrangements. His answer featured two propositions. One was that each person would grant all others the same liberties he would choose. This implies that for the fundamental issues, everyone would choose the same arrangements.

Assumed unanimity by those in the original position gives rise to what I regard as the major flaw of this method of reasoning about social arrangements. It licenses an irrefutable egotism on the part of social thinkers. All the social philosopher has to do is assume that what he's thinking about is so fundamental that everyone else would just have to agree, and any special cause may be pleaded. The alternative approach, utilitarianism, is not much as a guide to personal morals, but it does have the virtue of recognizing that other people may have different preferences.

That problem aside, Rawls jumped into the original position with his second, more controversial proposition. He decided that social arrangements should be decided with an extreme degree of caution. There was a chance that after the veil was lifted, the thinker (and every thinker) would discover herself in the least advantageous position in society. Rawls believed that the risk was so worrisome that she would choose a society (put in place before the veil is lifted) that would maximize the prospects for the least well off in that society. This he called the "maxi-min principle": maximize the prospects for the person receiving the minimum amount of benefit from any given social arrangement.

Such a society would be highly egalitarian, but not relentlessly so. Inequality would be tolerated if the forces that gave rise to it resulted in a larger absolute share of social benefits to the person least well off. In one sense, it is like the Pareto-superiority principle, in which the proposed social measure is an entire society, and the person not to be left any worse off is the one with the smallest share. It is permissible to depart from egalitarianism only if the (unknown) person at the bottom of the slightly less egalitarian society is made better off.

5.10 Michelman Convened the "Convention of the Circumspect"

Michelman's approach was to suppose that owners of property be put in a Rawlsian original position, which Michelman called the "convention of the circumspect." At this convention, the landowners do not know their particular situation, but they do know that the government might take some of their property. The government is regarded benignly by the members of the convention, and the good things that it does redound to their benefit. The convention is also aware that if the government tries to compensate each landowner for the property it takes, its production of benefits might be eaten up by the transaction costs of doing so. Hence each conventioneer agrees to forgo compensation "as long as the disappointed claimant ought to be able to appreciate how such decisions might fit into a consistent practice which holds forth a lesser long run risk to people like him than would any consistent practice which is naturally suggested by the opposite decision" (Michelman 1967, p. 1223).

The conditions in which the landowner bites his lip and agrees that he should be able to see that noncompensation is in the interests of all people like himself turn out to be almost the same as the conditions in which settlement costs exceed demoralization costs, which were the criteria Michelman advanced from his utilitarian analysis (section 4.3). That is, the disappointed claimant ought to be able to see that compensating him for, say, a building-lot setback that reduces the value of his land would require such large settlement costs that the total product of society would be lower. Total product is reduced because of having to pay the settlement costs or because society had to forgo the efficiency gains of the land use regulation. But the latter two conditions are the same as those that reduce utilitarian demoralization costs. As if to concede their similarity, Michelman later in his article employed "unfairness costs" and "demoralization costs" interchangeably.

Michelman thought of two exceptions to the equivalence of result from utilitarian and contractarian models. One involved deceit, in which utilitarian demoralization costs are confined because the government lies to potential sympathizers about the taking. Conditions of free speech would make such schemes improbable.

The other divergence between utilitarianism and contractarianism arises when people in reality are not so rational. If losers cannot be made aware, for example, that forgoing compensation is in their long-run interest, then the utilitarian model favors compensation where the fairness model might deny it. This is because the fairness model requires for its very operation that people at a convention of the circumspect be able to take the long view and appreciate the costs of alternative arrangements. People with a reputation for reasonableness are, after all, easier to bring into a cooperative mode.

5.11 A Utilitarian Convention Might Also Be Circumspect

I introduce the contractarian system in this chapter because this is the route that Perry Shapiro and I took to build a more formal model of the takings issue. I taught economics as a visiting professor at the University of California at Santa Barbara in 1985–86. Perry Shapiro, who had coauthored with Blume and Rubinfeld the 1984 article that found that compensation for takings could be inefficient, was a colleague there. I brought my knowledge of the literature to the issue, and Shapiro applied his skills in developing formal optimization models. The result was a formal model that took its cues from Michelman's "convention of the circumspect" formulation of the problem.

The model we developed envisions allowing people to choose the rules for compensation at a heuristic constitutional convention. The conventioneers do not know the relative value of their future assets or whether their property will be taken. However, unlike Rawls and Michelman, we did not assume that people in this position are risk averse.

Instead, we adopted a utilitarian assumption about objectives that is similar to that advanced by John Harsanyi (1975) and defended in the takings context by Carol Rose (1987).

Rose asked why folks in Rawls's original position should be assumed to be risk averse at all. They may instead be, in her terms, Rational Utility Maximizers. Such people are risk neutral, meaning that they are interested in the expected value of the future activity, not in any of the moments of the distribution. Rational Utility Maximizers are willing to take their chances that they will be left at the bottom, since the chances are the same as being placed at the top. Several experimental studies, summarized by Norman Frohlich and Joe Oppenheimer (1994), have attempted to mimic the Rawlsian convention in a variety of settings. Their results suggest that people are closer to Carol Rose's conception than to John Rawls's.

Invoking the convention of the not-so-circumspect, Shapiro and I asked what rule for compensation would be chosen by the profit-maximizing, risk-neutral landowners who constitute the convention. We conceded that risk aversion, as analyzed by Blume and Rubinfeld (1984), would probably cause landowners in the original position to choose compensation, but this conclusion was then susceptible to Louis Kaplow's (1986) critique that it provides no rationale for government-sponsored insurance (section 5.5). We wanted to establish the conditions in which *government* compensation is the rule the convention would choose.

Before discussing the model's characteristics in more detail, I issue a caveat seemingly overlooked by people who have embraced similar approaches. Our model, like the previous models by economists, made no distinction between takings by physical invasion and takings by regulation. When Blume and Rubinfeld said that government should serve only as the insurer of last resort, they meant in situations involving land taken by the highway department as well as land devalued by a zoning law. Kaplow (1986) took on the insurance argument and asserted that private insurance is more efficient than public insurance, so that no compensation is required. He meant that the Tennessee Valley Authority should not have paid anyone for the land submerged by its dams, not just that owners of wetlands forbidden to develop them shouldn't get paid. I mention this to emphasize that these models assume a high degree of abstraction, and that the subtleties that supposedly divide physical and regulatory takings are not addressed.

5.12   *The Risk-Neutral Convention Is Wealth-Maximizing*

Our convention of ignorant, prospective landowners has to decide what fraction of the market value of property will be paid for government takings once the society is set in motion. We used the fraction of market value as our choice variable, rather than yes or no, to facilitate the use of calculus in the comparative statics exercise. The assumed ignorance behind the constitutional veil applies only to the relative value of what each person owns and whether the landowners will have their property taken by the government. Otherwise, these folks are hard-headed economists and political scientists. They know what the behavior of each landowner will be in response to the compensation rule, and they also know how the government will behave under each compensation rule.

The convention is interested in maximizing aggregate wealth. Wealth has both a private and a public dimension. (If it did not have a public dimension, it would both lack realism and produce the obvious rule that all government takings should simply be disallowed.) Private production is accomplished by erecting buildings and other physical capital on the landowners' land to exploit its value. Capital is borrowed from outside the economy at a constant cost.

The other form of wealth that the convention is interested in is a public good, say, roads, parks, and public safety. The public goods must be produced by the government because private transaction costs are too high to overcome the usual free-rider problems. The provision of public goods requires that the government take some private land to produce it. The reason some private wealth is lost when the public good is provided in our model is that landowners first make some private capital commitments that may be lost when the government builds its roads and parks.

Our constitutional convention will unanimously decide on a compensation rule. Unanimity results because the veil of ignorance puts everyone in the same position. All landowners have the same objectives (expected wealth maximization), the same expected (but not actual) holdings of land, the same risk preferences (risk neutrality), and the same information about all contingencies.

The foregoing assumptions allowed us to represent the constitutional choice of the compensation rule as the decision of a single representative landowner. The Rawlsian interchangeability of *we* and *I* has been criticized by Richard Epstein (1985, p. 339) and Richard Posner (1980, p. 499) as suppressing the differences among individuals that a liberal society is supposed to protect. Our demurrer was that this approach nonetheless allowed us to establish a minimum standard for paying compensation. If we find that compensation should be paid when individual differences are suppressed, we might be more confident that compensation is necessary when individuals are different and their differences are to be given respect. As I said at the outset, the Rawlsian approach has drawbacks, but in the present context it was useful for addressing the issue of whether compensation for takings results only from risk aversion.

5.13   The Expected Behavior of the Government Is Critical

The next stage in our model was to characterize the government that was to follow the convention. Our major finding was that assumptions about government behavior determine the compensation rule. We considered three forms of government. One is the inexorable government. It behaves like the 500-pound gorilla, who in jokelore sleeps wherever he wants. The second government is Pigovian, which always picks wealth-maximizing public projects. The third government is majoritarian. It is composed of democratic but cynical politicos, who do whatever is politically expedient. In this case, what they do is maximize the welfare of the majority of voters. (Recall that after the veil is lifted, people do find that they are different and thus can form voting coalitions.)

The inexorable government—the 500-pound gorilla—takes whatever it wants. For a government like this, just compensation makes no sense in our model, since just compensation's cautionary purpose is only to keep the government from doing too much taking. If the government is known to take property regardless of any rules, paying compensation can only encourage people to disregard the probability of a capital-destroying taking, much as gratuitous compensation for earthquake damage inefficiently encourages construction on fault lines. Because conventioneers are risk-neutral maximizers of expected income, they would never choose compensation as an ex ante rule if they did not expect it to deter the government.

An alternative path to the zero compensation result is that it results from a Pigovian government, in which the government unerringly maximizes social welfare. Government is a sophisticated and benign calculator of social benefits and costs. We dubbed this form of government "Pigovian" after the founder of modern welfare economics, A. C. Pigou. As such, our term had an element of libel in it. Pigou certainly did not regard government as always doing the right thing. If he had, the effort involved in writing *The Economics of Welfare* (1932) would have been wasted. Pigou's recommendations for government intervention of a particular sort would have been pointless if the government always did the right thing in the first place.

But our use of Pigou's name for an optimistic view of government is not entirely in vain, either. In formulating the reasons for which government ought to intervene in the economy, Pigou focused on the inability of private participants to get their acts together to solve their spillover problems. His unexamined assumption was that the government could do it better. Ronald Coase's famous article, "The Problem of Social Cost" (1960), was motivated by this implicit assumption, which Coase regarded as part of the "Pigovian tradition" that was prevalent among economists until his challenge. Our use of the term "Pigovian" was intended to evoke this tradition and to show that it applied to the economists who had invoked it on behalf of not compensating.

5.14 *Majoritarianism Generates a Need for Compensation*

The nature of government is thus a crucial question for models of compensation. The rationale for including the just compensation requirement in the U.S. and state constitutions was to curb the inclinations of political majorities to impose excessive burdens on politically isolated minorities (section 3.3). We represented a majoritarian government as one that selects the level of public goods that maximizes the welfare of a majority of voters, giving no weight to the welfare of the minority whose property is taken. Self-interested voters would, in the majority-rule elections that follow the lifting of the veil of ignorance, choose officials who behave as we assume. Conventioneers do not, however, know which of them will constitute a majority and which a minority once the constitution is set and the veil of ignorance is lifted.

Faced with the prospect of a majoritarian government, one might wonder why the landowners at the constitutional convention, at which unanimity must prevail, do not specify all contingencies, including the level of public output, to guard against majoritarian excesses. One reason is that the demand for the public good may be contingent on the amount of capital at given locations, a distribution that is unknown at the time of the convention. (Recall William Penn's road-building problem in section 5.2.) Decisions about the supply of public goods must be delayed until the veil of ignorance is lifted and majority rule is assumed to prevail. In any case, our model hinges on the convention's being limited to choosing the compensation rule, the fraction of the market value of property that is to be compensated.

Our primary result was that under these conditions, the constitutional convention will choose to pay more than zero but less than 100 percent of market value. This is because expected total income from private production and from the provision of public goods reaches a maximum in the optimization model somewhere between a compensation fraction of zero and 100 percent.

The intuition behind this result is that the constitutional convention balances two forms of moral hazard: (a) that the government will take too much if it is not compelled to pay, against (b) that private landowners will put too much capital at risk of destruction if they are fully compensated. The world is not "first best" in the majoritarian model, because the convention knows it cannot restrain majority rule by prior specification of the amount of property to take. It is perhaps too much to ask that an abstract model apply to actual practice, but it is interesting to note that in reality, most compensation for the taking of property does fall short of the full market value of the landowner's loss, since consequential damages, among other losses, are typically excluded from compensation.

A similar trade-off was derived by Thomas Miceli and Kathleen Segerson (1994), who modeled the regulatory takings issue as judicial promotion of efficiency rather than constitutional choice. They recognized the potential for inefficiency both by the regulator and by the landowner, and their two-sided rule of compensation attempts to reward efficient behavior and penalize inefficient behavior on both sides. This sophisticated incentive scheme is a large step forward in the economics literature, which has previously focused on the inefficient behavior of either the regulators or the owners. Miceli and Segerson's work is given no more than a brief mention here because their rule still begs the question of how judges are to decide about the efficiency of the proposed land use and the proposed regulation.

5.15   *Majoritarianism Is Similar to Fiscal Illusion*

The majoritarian model's conclusion is the same as the "fiscal illusion" case examined by Blume, Rubinfeld, and Shapiro (1984). Fiscal illusion is the systematic underestimating of costs by government decision makers when full compensation does not have to be paid. It causes the benefit-cost ratio for a given measure to be biased upwards and thus induces the otherwise Pigovian government to undertake too many projects. Blume, Rubinfeld, and Shapiro showed that if this assumption is maintained, positive compensation is optimal. Thus the Fischel-Shapiro model may be interpreted as an attempt to balance the public sector's fiscal illusion associated with less compensation against the private sector's moral hazard of placing too much capital when there is more compensation.

Our majoritarian model was different, however, from the BRS fiscal illusion cases because we invoked a public choice model, in which political authorities rationally respond to voters' desires. Fiscal "illusion" implied to us that the government means well but makes mistakes. The illusion is something an accountant could fix. In our majoritarian model, government actions that take too much property are not mistakes but deliberate policies designed to obtain votes.

Our approach thus addressed Kaplow's (1986, p. 567) criticism of the fiscal illusion assumption. He believed it equally reasonable to assume that government agencies will undervalue benefits rather than costs, perhaps because the benefits have no political constituency, while those who bear the costs are well organized. In Kaplow's alternative, then, fiscal illusion could induce too *few* takings. Our model does not fall prey to that criticism, because the overreaching of the majoritarian government is the inevitable result of maximizing behavior, not just another assumption that might be as valid as its opposite. (Kaplow's alternative also fails to track any examples I have ever heard of; the government officials I see don't want to waste their budgets paying people if they don't have to.)

The "majoritarian" political model examined in our paper assumed that majorities exploit their political position to transfer wealth to themselves at the expense of effete minorities. As I have noted elsewhere in this book, modern political economy has often focused on how less-than-majority interest groups appropriate government largess (William Niskanen 1971; George Stigler 1971). Would a constitutional convention that anticipated some "special-interest" form of government call for a different rule for compensation than that which anticipated a majoritarian government of the type we envision?

The Fischel-Shapiro model cannot resolve this issue because it assumes away voter ignorance, does not allow for legislative vote trading, and includes only a one-time provision of public goods. It also precludes straightforward redistribution of wealth because the government is constrained to take property only to produce a public good. If these assumptions were relaxed, it is not obvious what rules of compensation would be adopted. It seems reasonable to suppose that any anticipated political complications that would result in inefficient levels of government output would result in the framers' choosing to compensate for takings. The framers are, in our model, interested solely in wealth maximization. Moreover, they are not concerned with the question of how constitutional rules are to be enforced.

The reader might express some impatience at this point with a model that misses most of the nuances of the takings problem. I share that to some extent. That is why most of this book invokes history and case studies to reveal the nuances. But economic models do allow one to work through the implications of basic ideas. The major point of our model was to show that even if one ignores the demoralization (fairness) problem, and even if people are risk neutral with respect to their property, something like a just compensation rule would emerge from a constitutional setting in which the framers anticipated a majoritarian government ruled by themselves. Self-government is not contradicted by a rule imposed by prior decision makers.

5.16 The Offer/Ask Disparity Challenges Compensation Practices

This chapter's concluding sections, which draw in part from Fischel (1995), address the issue of how much compensation is enough. Economists have invoked what I call the "offer/ask" disparity to argue that more-than-market compensation should normally be the rule because property owners are being "asked" to give up something but only being paid the "offer" price that one observes in the market (Knetsch and Borcherding 1979, Knetsch 1983). This recommendation would greatly curtail the use of eminent domain. (It would also curtail the use of welfare economics, a problem that I address in Fischel [1995].)

The offer/ask disparity is well established in experimental economics. Subjects require significantly greater cash compensation to surrender a specific entitlement in their possession than they are willing to pay to gain the same entitlement if they do not currently possess it. To put it another way, the economic concept of equivalent variation (= willingness to accept or "ask") seems to be much greater than compensating variation (= willingness to pay or "offer"). This is contrary to the assumption underlying most applied welfare economics, which holds that the disparity is trivial (Robert Willig 1976).

The large size of the disparity was first empirically established in psychological experiments by the economists Jack Knetsch and J. A. Sinden (1984). The subjects, Canadian university students, were endowed with lottery tickets, which the experimenters then attempted to repurchase. Subjects in a parallel group were asked what they would be willing to pay for the same tickets, which they had not been given in the first place. The amount that the latter students were willing to pay for the tickets averaged $1.28, but the amount that the former students were willing to accept for a lottery ticket that had been given to them at the beginning of the experiment was $5.18. As the trivial dollar amounts indicate, the offer/ask disparity cannot be explained away by the traditional fallback of economists, differences in wealth or income that arise from possession or lack of possession of an entitlement.

Knetsch and Sinden's results, which seem to surprise only economists, have been replicated by a large number of experiments and surveys, which are cogently reviewed by Elizabeth Hoffman and Matthew Spitzer (1993). One response to the offer/ask disparity is that by Vernon Smith (1991). Smith conceded the existence of offer/ask and related anomalies in one- and two-shot situations, but he described experimental evidence that the disparities grow progressively narrower as subjects gain more experience. Hence for most markets the offer/ask disparity is trivial. In a similar vein, David Brookshire and Don Coursey (1987) have demonstrated that offer/ask valuations for public goods and environmental amenities, which are shown in many experiments to be quite large, are substantially reduced when the public good question is presented in a market setting. Hoffman and Spitzer noted, however, that some of these results have not been consistently replicated.

I do not pursue Smith's line of response because eminent domain typically involves episodic events. Unless a person is extremely unlucky, it is unlikely that her home will be taken to make way for a highway or a public school more than once in a lifetime, and more likely she will never have that experience. Most victims of government takings do not have repeated experiences by which they could learn to accept market valuations. For this reason, the information about preferences elicited from ordinary people in one-shot experiments seems relevant to the takings issue.

5.17   Is Money *Subject to the Offer/Ask Disparity?*

Manifestations of the offer/ask disparity have parallels in macroeconomics. My colleague Steven Venti, writing with David Wise (1990), found strong evidence that the introduction of tax-free Individual Retirement Accounts (IRAs) in the 1970s induced people to save much more. This finding was contrary to the conventional wisdom about the inelasticity of savings with respect to the net rate of interest. People could put money into IRAs to shelter it from income taxes, but they could later take the money out of the same IRA without penalty and spend it on consumer items. (The loophole has since been closed.) Thus the IRA was completely fungible; there was no reason for people to change their saving behavior. Nonetheless, Venti and Wise found that IRAs substantially increased the fraction of income saved. The puzzle is why this is so.

It is possible, of course, that the conventional Keynesian wisdom is wrong, and people really do respond to changes in the net rate of return on savings. But there is little other evidence to suggest that this is true. Richard Thaler (1990) used Venti and Wise's finding as one of several pieces of evidence that income itself is not fungible. Money itself may be subject to the offer/ask disparity. (Hoffman and Spitzer [1993, p. 84] have cautioned that experimental evidence on offer/ask for financial instruments is mixed.)

The possibility that money is subject to offer/ask disparities creates a major problem for using such disparities in analyzing eminent domain. Suppose we wanted to examine the most straightforward issue, which arises when the government acknowledges an obligation to compensate for a taking under eminent domain. The offer/ask framework has been invoked by Knetsch and Borcherding (1979) to favor substantially greater compensation for landowners than market valuation. Without challenging the (subsequent) experiments that support this conclusion, the problem I would raise is that their analysis misses the other side of the takings budget. *Taxpayers* are being asked to part with some of their income in order to pay compensation to the landowners. What if the taxpayers have some special attachment to their income that warrants a higher valuation than simply the money involved?

The reader is apt to wonder what special attachment taxpayers might have to their money. Maybe they are like the apocryphal economist who put this notice up on the bulletin board: "Lost, one wallet containing $200 and family photographs. Keep the wallet, return the cash. Sentimental value." But the foregoing discussion of Venti and Wise's findings and related work cited in Thaler (1990) suggests that there may be an offer/ask issue with respect to tax money as well as to particular commodities.

One author who has in fact invoked this proposition is Richard Epstein (1985). For Epstein, a public road-building project is both a taking from the landowners and, if compensation is paid, a taking from the taxpayers who have to finance the landowners' compensation (1985, p. 286). Either party may be thought of as being "asked" to surrender a status-quo entitlement in order to do the project. The taxpayers may, of course, get something in return for the taking of their money, such as the benefits of a public road. If so, they get "implicit, in-kind" compensation. If some taxpayers do not get such benefits in line with their share of taxes, so that there is a "disproportionate impact," the tax increase would be an unconstitutional taking by Epstein's analysis. His awareness of what might be called the "ask/ask" symmetry of the landowners' and the taxpayers' positions was especially evident when he noted that *over*compensation of the landowner amounts to an unjustified taking from the taxpayer (1985, p. 196). The government's takings ledger must be balanced on both sides.

My employment of Epstein's insight here is to show that a thorough account of forced transfers of property has to take account of both sides of the ledger. As such, Knetsch and Borcherding's (1979) invocation of the offer/ask disparity solely on behalf of landowners is undermined by their failure to consider its effect on the taxpayer.

5.18 Constitution Makers Faced the Offer/Ask Problem

One way of addressing the double-sided aspect of the offer/ask issue is to invoke a constitutional choice framework. The Rawlsian model described in sections 5.11–5.14 illustrates a theoretical means of doing this. Rather than go through that drill again, I invoke the evidence of what happened in *real* constitutional conventions discussed in section 2.9.

My purpose is to suggest that American constitution makers arrived at market value as the proper measure of just compensation by balancing the undercompensation of the market-based rule against the greater loss incurred by higher taxes and forgoing public works that full, consensual compensation would require. One cannot probe the minds of the delegates who drew up the takings clauses, let alone the voters who ratified the constitutions and their amendments. My more modest method now is to point out that framers and ratifiers were in an ideal position to see all sides of the takings issue, and their behavior reflects attempts to wrestle with the effects of compensation.

The prototypical takings clause is that of the Fifth Amendment: "nor shall private property be taken for public use, without just compensation." Although the amendment was not formally a product of the Philadelphia convention, which did not include a bill of rights, its Takings Clause and the rest of the Bill of Rights were proposed by a Congress composed of men whose wealth consisted mostly of real property.

Property was at risk of taking by eminent domain, but it was also at risk of taking by taxation. Equally important, real property, particularly land, was the repository of wealth increases created by beneficial public works. Thus property owners were in a position to realize that undercompensation for takings would be borne by themselves or by people with whom they had some natural empathy. But they were also in a position to realize that the burdens of overcompensation would be borne by themselves and their class by virtue of higher taxes or forgoing wealth-enhancing public works.

The *voters* who ratified the Bill of Rights were also mostly men of property. It seems unlikely that any voter or legislator who thought about the Takings Clause was unaware of the ancient common-law practice of determining "just compensation" by employing market valuations when they could be ascertained. British colonial practice as well as that of the states during the era of the Articles of Confederation had generally used market value as the measure of just compensation (Stoebuck 1972).

Representatives at early state constitutional conventions were also largely property owners. Most voters were, too. Thus my proposition that constitution makers must have thought about more-than-market compensation holds as well for state constitutions as for the federal document. (The states are especially important because of their ongoing amendment process.) All were as sensitive and as aware as any group is likely to be to the reluctance of property owners to surrender their land on a less than voluntary basis. Moreover, my account in sections 2.9–2.14 of the evolution of states' eminent domain clauses in the nineteenth century is consistent with an ongoing debate about the advantages and disadvantages of market value as the basis of compensation.

5.19   Constitutional Commands Are Self-Commands

The foregoing circumstantial evidence suggests to me that the equation of "just compensation" with "market value" for property taken by eminent domain was understood by American constitution writers and ratifiers. Constitution makers nonetheless chose to allow the state to pay only market value because, I believe, they were aware of the costs on the other side of the ledger that would be incurred if consent or above-market compensation of owners were required.

Given this persistent historical balancing of forgoing property on both sides of the takings ledger, I submit that latter-day critics who call for enhanced compensation under eminent domain because of the offer/ask disparity would upset the solution to the offer/ask problem that had already been struck in scores of constitutional conventions. My response does not, however, militate against intellectual efforts by Richard Epstein (1985) and Gideon Kanner (1973) to win more compensation for property owners based on arguments that present-day judges are ignoring the words or spirit of constitutional commands.

The oddity of this insight about policy is that the offer/ask experimenters have in fact discovered it themselves. John Marshall, Jack Knetsch, and J. A. Sinden (1986) described a series of experiments in which student subjects were first found to have a large disparity between offer and ask for some commodity. The results closely tracked the earlier experiments, with asking prices greatly in excess of offer prices. The subjects were subsequently asked what they would advise a friend to do in the situation to which they were exposed. The great majority of them replied that the friend should exchange the good for a price close to its market value. That is, in a neutral advisory mode, the students, who had just revealed asking prices much greater than offer prices, urged that the two prices should be about the same.

Marshall, Knetsch, and Sinden took the discovery that subjects act more rationally as advisors than they do when trading for themselves to a peculiar conclusion. They claimed that subjects acting in the advisory capacity were wrong. The authors said that subjects should have given advice based on their own behavior rather than on that which they think is better for others. Thus irrationality is to become the rule, despite the revealed preference for rationality by subjects in an advisory role.

What Marshall, Knetsch, and Sinden may have overlooked is that the advisory mode is one that people want to apply to themselves as well as others. Thomas Schelling (1984) has cogently explored the ubiquitous phenomenon of individuals writing constitutions to restrain themselves. They make New Year's resolutions; they bet each other that they will not be the first to resume smoking; they commit themselves to publishing schedules they know will be painful to maintain. The subjects' desire to behave in accordance with economic rationality is not necessarily deference to experts, as Jack Knetsch suggested it might have been in a letter to me. It is something that people seem to want to impose on themselves.

All of this is not to suggest that economists' formulation of the offer/ask problem could not contribute something to future constitutional conventions. As I will suggest in section 7.15, the nature of commonly held property has changed in the twentieth century from land held for income to land held for residence. Future constitution makers might want to offer more protection to residential landowners than is currently offered. What I want to argue in the following two sections, however, is that there are a number of pitfalls involved in applying the offer/ask formulation to regulatory takings issues.

5.20 Offer/Ask Does Not Resolve Rent-Control Issues

Some scholars have used the offer/ask disparity to analyze rent control (Russell Korobkin 1994). The conventional economic criticisms of rent control focus on the losses to future tenants of the unavailability of rental units. Binding rent control prevents would-be tenants from being able to occupy quarters for which they are willing to pay more than tenants protected by rent control. If the current tenant is willing to pay no more than $500 for her apartment, and rents are not allowed to exceed that amount, the would-be tenant who is willing to pay $800 is shut out, and conventional welfare analysis says there is a deadweight loss of $300.

In reply to this conventional wisdom, Korobkin contrasted a current tenant's willingness to *accept* removal from the unit with a future tenant's willingness to *pay* to get into the unit. The current tenant might be willing to pay only $500, but it would take $900 to get her to move. His conclusion, more or less foreordained by the framing of the question, was that rent control is most likely efficient, supply effects aside, if willingness to accept is the basis for valuation.

The problem with the focus on current versus future tenants is that the landlord was ignored entirely. In rent control, and in the takings issue generally, the essential question is what entitlements are to be recognized by the law. Once they have been recognized, one might invoke offer/ask to see how they might be protected, as Guido Cala-bresi and Douglas Melamed (1972) and scores of constitutional conventions have done. But this is an issue that is logically subsequent to a determination of who owns what.

In most landlord-tenant relations, offer/ask is simple. A tenant has a lease of three years for $500 per month. After only one year, her landlord comes up with a prospective tenant who is willing to pay $800 per month. Should he be able to break the lease and evict the tenant if he is willing to share the difference in rent with her? No, of course not. The current tenant's lease may give her much consumer surplus; the compensation she would want to vacate the apartment might be $900 per month. The law recognizes her entitlement to stay in almost all situations.

But now suppose the tenant's lease has run its three-year course. The tenant would like to stay on at $500 a month, but the landlord indi-cates that he wants $800 per month, there being prospective tenants willing to pay that amount. Should rent-control law modify the situ-ation so she can stay on at the old rent?

The reader may be surprised that my answer is, I don't know. What I do know is that statements about offer/ask disparities do not help. The real issue is whether her three-year tenancy has established a prop-erty right to continue at the same terms, prior contractual agreements notwithstanding, that trumps the property right of the *landlord* to choose another tenant at a higher rent. Which right should be chosen requires a whole raft of information about social mores, external conditions in the property market, and parallel changes in law, all of which still leave me skeptical about the merits of rent control. But the point is that offer/ask is no help at all, because the choice in this situation could be framed as ask/ask as well as offer/ask. What would the tenant have to be paid to leave, versus what would the landlord have to be paid to forgo his traditional property and contractual rights?

It might be objected that the landlord's loss is only of a prospective gain, while the tenant's loss is of actual possession (less the next best substitute). Much research done in the same vein as the offer/ask experiments establishes that people view prospective gains as less valuable than the bird in hand (Kahneman and Tversky 1979). But this, too, is an empty distinction in rent control when the landlord is properly considered. He might have mortgaged the building, capitalizing it on the basis of future income, so that there is nothing prospective about gains from higher rents. There is real money going out the door every month. The tenant might regard continued possession beyond the three-year lease as a prospective gain, as she has good reason to in most cases. I am not insisting that either of these possibilities is usually true; I am merely showing that whatever evidence we have about offer/ask valuations does not help resolve the regulatory takings issue as it applies to rent control.

5.21 Offer/Ask Would Not Help Resolve Land-Use Issues

Consider the classic regulatory takings case of Agins v. Tiburon (1980). Recall the facts from section 1.19: Tiburon residents wanted to keep Agins's five-acre ridgetop property in open space, despite the fact that many such citizens already lived on ridge-top development at even higher densities than Agins proposed. Agins was denied any compensation for a web of regulations that denied him the ability to build a new home on the ridge for more than twenty years.

Offer/ask analysis might be used to justify denial of compensation to Agins. (Discussions of offer/ask by Robert Ellickson [1989] and Herbert Hovenkamp [1991] suggest but do not endorse this.) Dr. Agins was denied the prospective gain, the story might go, not some out-of-pocket cost or the loss of a tangible object. His loss might be evaluated at an offer price rather than an asking price, contrary to Michelman's formulation (section 4.2.). The city did not build a road over his land; it merely asked him to forgo some gain. (Agins did lose money out of pocket, since he paid for the land and paid for a lawyer, but he could have recouped his money and avoided legal costs by acceding to the city's original 1973 offer to buy the land for the amount he had paid several years earlier.)

The story might then turn to Tiburon's residents. What would they have lost by allowing Agins to develop his property? Tiburon's citizens would have lost the prospect of looking at and otherwise enjoying an open ridge. It may be that their having enjoyed the view was of such duration that they should be compensated for it, and for this reason they might evaluate it at an "asking" price. Thus the offer/ask disparity might be employed to justify uncompensated regulation.

The argument does not work here, either. First of all, simply because Agins might be said to value his right to build only on an offer basis fails to give a reason why he should not be compensated at all. Simply because the value of his land rose above what he paid for it in 1968 does not prove that he would have been willing to pay only the 1968 amount. More important, the offer/ask argument again proceeds from the presumption that Tiburon has a legal entitlement to a viewscape. I would not automatically deny that Tiburon had such entitlement, although looking at its citizens' own practice of occupying high-density single-family homes on its hill certainly suggests such an entitlement should not be presumed. The point is, as it was in rent control, that the offer/ask question kicks in only after answering the question of who is entitled to what. Offer/ask might help resolve how much compensation is owed if that were an issue, but it does not help establish whether compensation should be paid.

5.22   Conclusion: Economics Helps When It Refines Experience

This chapter has been critical of several economic approaches to takings. Rational expectations, insurance, and the offer/ask disparity are largely beside the point when they are not actually misleading. The constitutional choice model gives results that are consistent with basic historical concerns about takings, but its "veil of ignorance" assumption makes it hard to apply to a world in which people often fundamentally disagree.

Why has economics not been especially helpful in resolving the takings issue? Part of the answer is that the issue involves fairness as well as efficiency. Economists are uncomfortable with fairness issues and the concept of demoralization costs, because they seem so mushy. It is not that they are subjective—all values are deemed by economic theory to be subjective—it is that we have no obvious metric for them. The same is true, however, for many other things that society puts a value on. Economists now take seriously the possibility that the mere existence of some resource is valued by people, and they have taken halting efforts to try to value it by the contingent valuation method (Helen Neill et al. 1994). Experimental economics has also addressed some fairness issues, though none as subtle as demoralization cost (Hoffman and Spitzer 1985).

The other reason for the small contribution of economics to normative theories of takings is its tendency to assume that its world view is widely shared. Economics has been most helpful in areas of the law in which it has tried to refine the experience of calculating costs and benefits, as in tort and contract law, where the parties are clearly interested in such calculation. Likewise, the economic analysis of just compensation has been helpful in refining some of the costs that go into the decision to compensate. The prospect of compensation affects people's behavior, and in some circumstances this is costly to society as a whole.

In a similar vein, economic analysis of government behavior can illuminate the instances in which compensation will have a desired result and when it may be redundant or undesirable to compensate. The public choice model has a lot to say about what the effect of takings rules might be. Governments in many instances are deterred from actions by the obligation to compensate, and removing this obligation has consequences that economic analysis can trace out better than most other disciplines.

Economic analysis becomes less persuasive, I believe, when it goes beyond the issues of costs, benefits, and consequences. To move from the conclusion that just compensation promotes efficiency (or inefficiency) to the recommendation that it ought to be paid (or not paid) is to impose the culture of economics on the culture of society at large. I am not saying that there is no interaction between the cultures, of course. We economists do teach a lot of students, and there are untutored, natural economists out there. But much of the population is indifferent to such issues, and a nontrivial minority is outright hostile to it. A self-governing people has to decide about takings and related wealth-distribution issues through the institutions that it creates.

6

Capitalizing on Land Use Regulation: Evidence from California

This chapter marks the turn away from jurisprudential issues and toward economic evidence. I concluded in the previous chapter that economists have a hard time with fairness issues because it is difficult to measure fairness. This chapter reviews evidence that legal doctrines such as regulatory takings do make a discernible difference in the use of land and its cost. This is not a direct measure of unfairness costs, but it surely is relevant to the threshold issue of whether there is anything to worry about.

The studies that I describe typically ask whether a new or different regulation has an effect on the price of real estate. The answer is that regulations are capitalized in housing and land values, although it is not immediately obvious that this is a bad thing. The evidence generally supports my view that the courts ought to devote most of their regulatory takings attention to local government property regulation and the substitution of regulation for acquisition by politically insulated agencies. Courts should usually ignore other statewide and national regulations of real property and skip lightly over local regulation of property that is elastic in supply.

The rest of the chapter presents evidence on the effect of a judicial intervention in the land market that ran in the opposite direction of what I recommend. The California Supreme Court in the late 1960s and early 1970s actively reduced the development rights of landowners. In order to inform readers of the numerous legal doctrines that affect development, I describe in some detail how the court changed the rules.

I submit that the state court's concerted war against development contributed to the remarkable increase in California housing prices that began in the 1970s, resulting in a premium over prices in other states that expanded through the 1980s (and which in the 1990s is being corrected with harsh results). The alternative explanations for this differential inflation should also give readers a sense of the factors that influence regional housing markets. My conclusion from California's negative experiment is that, although the takings issue and related protections of property are founded on fair political treatment, they also have efficiency implications for the larger economy.

6.1 Capitalization of Regulation Creates Definable Winners and Losers

It is an undergraduate exercise these days. Find a sample of single-family housing values, either individual transactions or census tract averages. Regress their value against a number of control variables—square feet of living space, number of rooms, age of structure, access to amenities or disamenities—and add a variable or two to capture the effect of some local government policy that varies within the sample. The results of this exercise show, with a regularity that makes one suspicious of the niceties of econometric technique, that local government policies do indeed make a difference (John Yinger et al. 1988).

Economists have become so used to capitalization studies that we seldom stop to think how remarkable it is that local government policies should be capitalized in individual home values. If an individual homeowner adds a garage where there was none before, it is obvious that the garage will be capitalized in the selling price because the homeowner has property rights in his dwelling. He can exclude people who might otherwise use his property, and he can transfer his rights to buyers. If he could not, then there would be no capitalization from the improvements. Strangers would use his garage to park their cars, and buyers would discount the garage's value for that reason. A necessary condition for the capitalization of any improvement is that the owners be able to exclude interlopers.

It follows that there must be some method by which interlopers are excluded from local government jurisdictions in order for local government activities to be capitalized. If there were no such method, developers would look around for communities with low tax rates and good schools and put up houses there to take advantage of the differential. A nice, double-wide house trailer would accommodate families with a taste for good schools but less-than-average means to pay for them. A lot of such development would obviously be costly to existing residents. Their taxes would have to go up or their school spending would have to go down, with the result that their houses would not command any premium over those of any other community. Since we regularly do see such a premium, it follows that there must be some way to preserve the status quo. On this line of reasoning, one can infer the existence of zoning and related land use controls without any direct evidence of their operation.

Of course, there is a great deal of direct evidence for the existence of zoning, so economists cannot claim to have equaled the feat of the astronomers who deduced from theory the existence of the planet Pluto. But, curiously enough, many economists are not convinced that zoning itself actually amounts to a constraint. Because I have devoted the larger part of my professional life to examining zoning and the issues to which it gives rise, I decided a few years ago to write a monograph summarizing the empirical work by economists on zoning (Fischel 1990). Most of it, as one would expect, was concerned with whether zoning regulations were capitalized in land and housing values.

I will not review here the studies that ask whether the activities that zoning supposedly prevents, such as the location of stores in residential neighborhoods, actually have an effect on nearby properties (Mark and Goldberg 1986). I have argued elsewhere that the studies that suggest that there is no effect draw the wrong conclusion. Evidence of lack of effect may show that zoning is working perfectly well, allowing nonconforming uses only in those cases in which the harm to the neighborhood is low or the offsetting benefits are high (Fischel 1994b). For those who doubt whether the average nonconforming store affects neighboring home values, I urge them to attend a zoning hearing at which a prospective store owner seeks a variance to locate in an otherwise residential neighborhood.

6.2 Land Use Controls Are Hard to Measure

The study of the impact of zoning and land use controls is complicated by the protean nature of the police power. There is no single variable, or single set of variables, that can be used as a consistent measure of how restrictive zoning actually is. Minimum lot size is a ubiquitous and easily measured variable, but it tells only part of the story. The developer of a project with more than a few units who meets the zoning requirements must still pass site-plan review by the planning commission and, in many states, satisfy boards that oversee historic districts, wildlife conservation, and wetlands preservation. Among the common residential zoning restraints are exclusive single-family use; one structure per lot; minimum lot size; maximum lot-coverage; minimum floor area of the house; off-street parking; front, side, and rear yard setbacks; maximum height restrictions; designation of costly-to-serve areas as agricultural, forestry, wetland, or otherwise off limits; and requirements for the provision of public infrastructure at the developer's expense. Many of these restraints are highly discretionary and site-specific in their application.

Because of the aforementioned measurement difficulties, the better studies of zoning look for major changes in zoning laws that are adopted in some places but not in others. This generates enough unanticipated variation in practices that before-and-after or cross-section comparisons can be used to make statistical inferences. (If the regulations are anticipated, land values may change in advance, greatly complicating before-and-after capitalization studies.) Most of the studies of zoning's effects that have been published in the last twenty years examine what happened to property values when some novel restriction on growth and development within a community was adopted. A disproportionately large number of such studies have emerged from California, which in the 1970s became the leader in the "growth-control" movement.

In contrast to ordinary zoning, which is nominally dedicated to the good-housekeeping rule of "a place for everything, but everything in its place," growth-control communities attempt to reduce future residential development. Allowable growth is held below the rate that was both permitted under previous zoning laws and below the rate that the community's vacant land inventory can reasonably sustain. I will describe two of the many studies done in California. (For others, see Fischel [1990] and Pogodzinski and Sass [1991].)

6.3 California Growth Controls Did Raise Housing Prices

Seymour Schwartz at the University of California at Davis was a co-author of numerous studies of growth controls in the 1970s. His first event-study was Petaluma, California, which, like Ramapo, New York, had enacted a nationally famous growth-control law in 1972. Petaluma's was enacted specifically in reaction to new residential development, which was being built to serve commuters who took Highway 101 south toward San Francisco, forty miles away. (In defense of Petaluma, much of the development that came its way was the result of the growth restrictions of Marin County, which lies between Petaluma and San Francisco.) The Petaluma plan limited building permits to a maximum of five hundred per year, well below recent and expected demand, and it rationed them with a point system that gave substantial weight to costly design features. The U.S. Court of Appeals upheld the constitutionality of such controls in Construction Industry Association v. City of Petaluma (1975).

Schwartz, David Hansen, and Richard Green (1981) found that after several years, Petaluma's standard-unit housing prices had risen 8 percent above those of nearby Santa Rosa, which had not adopted growth controls during that period and which had formerly had the same prices as Petaluma. In a follow-up study, Schwartz, Hansen, and Green (1984) found that the fraction of Petaluma's housing stock that was affordable to low- and moderate-income households had dropped significantly below that of a regional control group. The cost-increasing design points offered by the Petaluma Plan overwhelmed the few points that developers got for moderate-income housing. The latter were praised by the federal judges, who upheld the plan as constituting "inclusionary" rather than "exclusionary" zoning. The praise encouraged scores of other exclusionary communities to adopt this diversionary tactic (Ellickson 1981).

Schwartz, Peter Zorn, and David Hansen (1986) also examined the effects of the less famous but nearly as effective growth controls in Davis, California. As in Petaluma, Davis's house prices grew significantly more rapidly than those of a control sample of other Sacramento suburbs after growth controls were implemented. Their best estimate is that growth controls caused Davis's prices to be 9 percent higher in 1980 than they would have been without them.

The other group of housing price studies was done by Lawrence Katz and Kenneth Rosen at the University of California, Berkeley. A drawback of Schwartz et al. was their focus on two communities, which might be sufficiently unusual to make extrapolations unwarranted. Petaluma was a famous test case, and Davis is a university town known for its attention to environmental amenities. Notoriety itself might have sent housing prices up by signaling to house buyers the existence of an exclusive community.

Katz and Rosen (1987), following up on Rosen and Katz (1981), overcame this problem by selecting a sample of over 1,600 single-family home sales from 64 communities in the San Francisco Bay Area during 1979. Of these sales, 175 occurred in communities that had had a growth-control program (building permit moratorium or a binding rationing system) in effect for at least one year in the period 1973–1979. (Katz and Rosen conducted telephone interviews with local planners to determine which communities had adopted growth controls, a subjective approach that deals with measurement problems as well as any other.) They found that houses selling in the growth-controlled communities were 17 to 38 percent more expensive than those in other communities.

Katz and Rosen thus found a much larger price effect from growth controls than the estimates of Schwartz et al. of about 9 percent for Petaluma and Davis. Aside from econometric issues suggested by Schwartz and Zorn (1988), I would note that Davis and Petaluma are both farther from San Francisco than the communities in Katz and Rosen's sample. As George Peterson's (1974b) study of growth controls in Fairfax County, Virginia, indicated, locations farther from the center of an urban area are affected proportionately less by the imposition of identical land use controls. Tighter restrictions usually result in larger lots, which are closer to the market norm in the more distant suburbs.

6.4 Higher House Prices Reflect Both Benefits and Costs of Regulation

The inference that planners and developers have drawn from these studies is that growth controls have the undesirable effect of raising housing prices. These studies have been influential in national reports, such as that of the Advisory Commission on Regulatory Barriers to Affordable Housing (1991). But why should an increase in local housing prices be deemed undesirable? It is well established that local housing prices rise when the schools get better or the local tax rate goes down. Perhaps the adoption of growth controls should be regarded in a similarly benign fashion. Housing in well-planned communities ought to be more valuable. If growth controls contribute to good planning—a point that ought not to be automatically conceded, but that may still be valid—then it is harder to gainsay them.

The alternative and less benign economic explanation for the higher prices is the monopoly effect. By forestalling the production of new homes, existing homeowners in growth-control communities reap the benefits of higher prices. Of course, if only a handful of communities restrict growth, there will not be much effect. Developers and home-buyers will just go to the next municipality, where they will find adequate substitutes. Since almost all American metropolitan areas have a large number of local governments, the monopoly effect cannot be very large, unless all local governments suddenly shift into the growth-control mode.

Regardless of whether the higher housing prices arose from demand-stimulating "better planning" effects or supply-restricting "monopoly zoning," growth controls spread rapidly through California during the 1970s. Bernard Frieden documented California battles over growth controls in *The Environmental Protection Hustle* (1979). He found that, although growth was not stopped, new regulations resulted in fewer and more costly housing units. A similar sea change in local regulation was found by the Berkeley planning professor David Dowall in *The Suburban Squeeze* (1984). I don't mean to say that growth controls have been exclusively a California phenomenon, but every extended work on the subject that I have seen spends many pages on the policies of communities in the Golden State.

The progenitor of the idea that California housing prices were getting much out of line and that the California court decisions might be to blame was Robert Ellickson (1982b). He led his Stanford Law School students into an investigation of the operation of growth controls in the Peninsula cities of the San Francisco Bay Area. They found variation among the communities, but nonetheless a marked commitment among almost all of them to limit growth below previous norms. Ellickson noted the extraordinary growth of San Francisco metropolitan housing prices relative to those of the rest of the country, and he described several of the court decisions that I will discuss here. He did not then have access to 1980 Census data and the subsequently published national studies that I employ, so he was cautious about making the statewide generalizations that I make. Nonetheless, Ellickson's earlier work holds up remarkably well more than a decade later. (see also Case and Gale [1982].)

6.5 *California Population Growth Was Not the Cause*

I propose to address two puzzles. Why did growth controls not arise earlier, and why did they become so widespread in California? After all, growth controls are an easy method by which the net worth of home-owners can be increased. By the stroke of the municipal pen, a community can increase the value of its citizens' major assets, their homes, by at least 10 percent, and maybe much more. Why hadn't this been done in the 1950s and the 1960s? And why did the growth-control movement seem to be so virulent in California?

The facile answer is that California is where the growth is. California grew by 3.7 million people between 1970 and 1980, an increase of 18.5 percent for the decade. That was 60 percent faster than the United States as a whole. You wouldn't have growth controls if you didn't have a lot of growth to control.

But a slightly deeper probe suggests almost the opposite conclusion. The 1970s were, by any measure, the slowest-growing decade in California since the Great Depression. During the 1950s, the state's population grew by 5.1 million, an increase of 48 percent, which was 160 percent faster than the United States as a whole. In the 1960s, California grew by 4.3 million people, twice as fast as the national average. All of these numbers were lower for California in the 1970s. Moreover, immigration to California from the rest of the United States was also very low during the 1970s (Muller and Espenshade 1985). If growth itself induces growth controls, California should have adopted them decades earlier.

The other facile (but somewhat better) answer points to 1970 as marking the birth of the first "environmental decade." The National Environmental Policy Act took effect on January 1, 1970, and the states soon emulated it with acts of their own. Growth itself had gotten a bad name, as suggested by the popular success of computer-generated forecasts of environmental and economic collapse in books with titles such as *The Limits to Growth*.

This answer explains, perhaps, the greater acceptability of growth controls, but it does not explain their remarkable success in California. Why was California different from the rest of the country, and why was California of the 1970s (and 1980s) different from California during the 1950s and 1960s?

The answer is that in previous years, attempts to limit growth in

California were met by powerful adversaries: land owners, developers, and their business allies. They possessed political and, to a lesser extent, legal clout to protect their interests. This does not mean that they always won in the legislatures or in the courts, but, because they had a good chance of winning in either place, a rough balance between development and preservation of community character (that is, the status quo) was struck in most places. This compromise was similar to that in most of the rest of the country.

6.6 The California Supreme Court Changed the Rules

The difference in the 1970s can mostly be accounted for by a remarkable change in the legal status of development-minded landowners. This change was almost entirely engineered by the California Supreme Court. Led by Justices Stanley Mosk and Matthew Tobriner, the California court became the most antidevelopment in the nation.

Land use lawyers with national experience almost all regard the California courts as extreme. The political scientist Dennis Coyle (1993) has documented in detail the difference between California and other state courts by a close reading of land use opinions. Nor is it just the property-rights types who have found the California court unusual. Consider these quotes (provided by Gideon Kanner) from distinguished land-use lawyers who are generally sympathetic to zoning:

> The striking feature of California zoning law is that the courts in that state have quite consistently been far rougher on the property rights of developers than those of any other state. (Norman Williams 1974, §6.03)

> We all know the California courts won't let the landowners/ developers build anything! (David Callies 1981, p. 724)

> What can one say about the California courts other than one has to be a madman to challenge a governmental regulation in that bizarre jurisdiction? (Richard Babcock and Charles Siemon 1985, p. 257)

I used to think it was always such, so that it would be difficult to pin the rise of growth controls on the California court of the 1970s. That was until I finally read an article (Joseph DiMento et al. 1980) that I'd heard about a few years earlier but never read because of its forbidding length. The article grew out of a project in Donald Hagman's UCLA Law School land use seminar in 1977. It analyzed in great detail ninety-three land use and environmental cases from 1962 to 1980 decided by the California Supreme Court. The authors wanted to see what factors accounted for the pattern of decisions by the court in the previous fifteen years. (I will refer to the article as Hagman's, even though the eight authors are listed alphabetically, because Hagman organized it.)

Here is an overview of the Hagman seminar's findings. For the period 1962–1966, the best predictor of who would prevail in the California Supreme Court in land use cases was whichever side the government was on. If governments were on opposite sides, the regional or higher-level government would usually prevail. Developers thus could win in court against antidevelopment forces if they could get a government on their side. Given the large number of municipalities in the state, developers could often find a government that was sympathetic to them.

The later period was different. After 1967, virtually the only predictor of who would prevail in court was whichever side the antidevelopment interests were on. The government no longer always won. When the government allied itself with antidevelopment interests, it always won. When the government favored development, as by granting a special exception or variance in the face of neighborhood opposition, the court usually ruled against the government. It was almost that simple. The only complication was when government agencies were on different sides. In these instances, the more antidevelopment agency usually prevailed.

6.7 The California Court Stopped Development at Every Turn

The Hagman project revealed how thoroughly the California court worked at retarding development. It was not simply a matter of denying prodevelopment forces access to judicial relief under the due process and takings clauses. I had known that the California court had declined to engage in substantive review that might overturn local antidevelopment decisions. What was new to me were the variety of means by which any prodevelopment escape hatches were sealed. The court actively threw new roadblocks in the way of developers, the most famous being its 1972 *Friends of Mammoth* decision (discussed in section 6.20). It held that an environmental impact statement, with its accompanying opportunities for litigious delay, had to be drawn up for large *private* projects subject to a government permit. Here are some other examples:

- *Damages.* The Court made a point of steering the discussion of remedies away from damages, to the great relief of municipal officials, who would be under considerable voter pressure if they had to raise taxes to pay for regulatory takings or the higher municipal insurance premiums in the event that insurers would cover inverse condemnation judgments. HFH v. Superior Court (1975), which was discussed in section 5.8, went out of its way to deny that damages were available for a downzoning, thus confirming what had been the court's practice for nearly a decade (William Swank 1976). The court in fact was sufficiently emboldened that by 1979 it held in Agins v. Tiburon that damages were not available as a remedy for takings even in constitutional litigation. *Agins* touched off a guerrilla war between the state and the U.S. Supreme Court over the issue of damages, described in section 1.20. The U.S. Supreme Court finally resolved the issue in favor of payment of just compensation in First English v. Los Angeles in 1987. (It is not clear what the current effect of *First English* is, though Joseph Sax, who consults for environmental organizations, told me in 1992 that it has made the environmental community more cautious.)
- *Vested Rights.* Developers in most states, and in California before 1967, could assert a vested rights doctrine that protected them from adverse political and legal decisions after they had begun work on their projects. Thus developers who learned about proposals to restrict growth could take some steps to vest their projects, such as obtaining permits and producing site plans, before the laws took effect. These investments mitigated the effect of subsequent growth controls on housing production, though they may also have contributed to the boom and bust cycle in real estate development. In a series of decisions, the vested rights doctrine was narrowed nearly out of existence, so that California became "more hostile to developers than any other high court in the nation" (DiMento et al. 1980, p. 872).
- *Due Process.* Due process has historically been helpful to property owners, but the California court reversed its impact. New procedural requirements worked against development interests (p. 871). The court reined in administrative discretion when it favored developers, holding prodevelopment governments to exacting standards on agency findings. When antidevelopment governments changed the rules to the detriment of developers, however, the court re-

verted to its traditional deference to government decisions. Even the court's devotion to egalitarianism was trumped by its preservationism. In three major cases in which the issue of exclusionary zoning (which makes it more difficult for poor people to locate in a given community) arose, the California court studiously ignored the issue (p. 872).

• *Attorney Fees.* The California court did not just favor antideveloper parties; it went out of its way to subsidize them by extending the doctrine of awarding attorney's fees to those who challenged permissive governments (pp. 873–874). This was despite the U.S. Supreme Court's explicit rejection of the same argument.

• *Annexation.* Most annexations were done to promote development of lightly populated, unorganized county territories. The court realized, even before environmental organizations did, that retarding municipal annexations was an important means of retarding development (p. 905).

• *Source of Law.* The court was also creatively slippery in choosing its sources of law. If the statute seemed to favor development interests, the court would resort to common law. If the common law favored developers, the court resorted to statute (pp. 906–912).

6.8 The Court Imposed a Northern View on Southern California

The Hagman project explained two paradoxes that, as a longtime observer of California land use controls, had always puzzled me. I had noticed that the 1970s housing price explosion was statewide. Southern California prices as well as those of the San Francisco Bay Area rose considerably faster than those of the rest of the country. But most California academics who recalled the period said that this did not ring true, since antidevelopment sentiment was far more concentrated in the Bay Area than in the Southland.

The Hagman seminar provided an explanation. In reviewing how the California Courts of Appeal (the first level of appeal after trial) fared when their cases got to the California Supreme Court, the article found that the Los Angeles area's appellate courts were overturned far more frequently than the San Francisco area courts. The difference was that the Los Angeles area courts sometimes held for developers, while the Bay Area courts, true to their regional tradition, were much more antideveloper. The antidevelopment California Supreme Court (which sits in San Francisco) reversed the Southern California courts far more often.

The Hagman seminar authors, all professors or students at universities in Southern California, ruefully concluded: "the California Supreme Court kept an especially sharp eye on any tendency toward a development orientation in the 'State of Southern California' and its courts. It imposed on them a 'State of Northern California' preservationist view by calling up development-oriented court of appeal decisions and awarding victory to the preservationists" (DiMento et al. 1980, p. 870). Thus the inconsistency between my observation of similar housing price inflation but differing attitudes between north and south can be reconciled by the California Supreme Court's imposition of a uniform, antidevelopment state legal standard.

The court's antidevelopment stance cut across all aspects of development, and it accounts for another paradox. As mentioned in previous sections, the California Supreme Court during the 1970s did its best to read the just compensation remedy out of the U.S. Constitution when regulatory takings were at issue. By the 1970s, though, the court had become significantly more solicitous of landowners whose property was formally taken by eminent domain (DiMento et al. 1980, p. 874). State and local highway builders both were subject to landmark rulings that made it more costly to build roads. This solicitude for landowners affected by government building projects stands in sharp contrast to the backhanded treatment they got in regulatory issues. Nor was it a matter of different court coalitions. The same justices usually formed the majorities in both sets of cases, with Stanley Mosk or Matthew Tobriner usually writing the opinion (p. 881).

The Hagman group's explanation of this apparent inconsistency is simple and convincing. The court is perfectly consistent if one takes as its decision rule that development of any sort is to be stopped whenever it can be. New roads themselves are developments, and new roads facilitate more private development. Regulatory actions such as downzonings that retard development are upheld, while regulatory actions such as variances that allowed it were overturned. Eminent domain actions that facilitated development, such as road building, were rendered more costly, while eminent domain actions that retarded private development, such as state acquisition of beachfront property, were almost always facilitated. The Hagman group's explanation was for me like a light suddenly going on in a dark room. There is no inconsistency at all in the 1967–1977 court's pattern of decisions.

6.9   Other State Courts Were More Balanced

The Hagman project provided the detailed evidence for my view that the California court changed the state's regulatory climate in the late 1960s, setting the stage for enormous increases in housing values when general inflation began in earnest in 1974. What is less clear is that the California court's late 1960s environmental epiphany was not shared by other states. If courts in most other states also got environmental religion to the same degree that California's did, the judicial explanation that I advance does not work well. Hagman's group did not address this issue directly, but there are some indicia suggesting that, while environmentalism was going around, no other court caught the bug as severely as did the California Supreme Court.

One indicator of California's unusual position was the court's tendency to ignore "foreign precedent," that is, the decisions of its fellow state supreme courts (DiMento et al. 1980, p. 879). While the Hagman group's article suggested that this may have been the result of a certain egotism on the part of the California justices, it is equally plausible that resort to other states' antidevelopment precedents would encourage developers' attorneys to point out the more balanced views. One can, after all, find many antidevelopment decisions in New York, New Jersey, and other leading state courts. The trouble with opening up that box is that one can also find these balanced by prodevelopment decisions, couched either in landowner rights or in the rights of disadvantaged outsiders.

That other states were a mixed bag in the 1970s is borne out by the table of leading state land use cases, as established by number of citations, that the Hagman group carefully assembled (id., p. 927). The national leader at the time was Golden v. Planning Board of Ramapo, a 1972 New York case that upheld Ramapo's elaborate scheme of phased development. This decision was regarded by some as antidevelopment, but in fact it was much more balanced. Developers had to wait for infrastructure to be built before going ahead, but the town also committed itself to building the infrastructure over a period of years, a reciprocal obligation absent from any California decision regarding growth controls.

Looking down the Hagman list of leading cases, I was struck by how other states were grappling with novel environmental issues in ways that appeared to balance development with preservation at the dawn of the age of environmentalism. Their efforts were the antithesis of California's unabashed antidevelopment position. Among the mostly prodeveloper decisions in the top ten were New Jersey's *Mount Laurel* (1975), restricting local exclusion of low-income housing (discussed in section 9.8); Pennsylvania's Cheney v. Village 2 at New Hope (1968), (same); Arizona's Spur v. Del Webb (1972), balancing preexisting rural nuisances with residential development; and Pennsylvania's Appeal of Girsh (1970), overturning local exclusion of apartment houses. Had any one of these decisions been made in California, the Hagman group's characterization of the California court in the 1967–1977 period would have been seriously undermined.

I refer to this multi-author article as Hagman's product not only because he was the instigator of it, but also because I want to honor his memory (he died prematurely in 1982) for having done what few other law professors do. He followed up on most of the California cases to see what happened after the court decision. An economist's objection to the analysis might be to invoke the Coase theorem. The court decisions simply reordered property rights in California, and subsequent bargaining would presumably restore them to the party who valued them the most. There is no doubt that some of this did happen, particularly when local government sought to make developers pay exactions for permission to develop. But in a surprising (to an economist) number of cases, the result of the court decision was to prevent development permanently, at least as far as Hagman's phone calls to participants could determine (DiMento et al. 1980, p. 877).

6.10   California Housing Prices Exploded in the 1970s

It is by now common knowledge among housing experts that California has the highest housing prices in the nation. The Advisory Commission on Regulatory Barriers to Affordable Housing (1991, p. I-2) mentioned California as the state "considered to have the greatest affordability problems." Sophisticated econometric studies of housing prices across the nation found that by the mid- to late 1970s, California metropolitan areas stood out, even after other factors that might account for higher housing prices (such as population growth and climate) were statistically ironed out. Allen Goodman (1988), for example, found that California owner-occupied housing prices in 1978 were 57 percent higher than the average for the rest of country, after adjusting for quality. California apartment rents were 18 percent higher. (Similar results are in Ozanne and Thibodeau [1983].).

The California premium is such a commonplace that many people seem to assume that it has always been this way. But California housing prices exploded—there is no better word for it—during the 1970s. An easy and, it will be seen, reasonably accurate indicator of this comes from U.S. Census data on the median value of owner-occupied housing. The value of houses in California was only 27 percent higher than that of the United States as a whole in 1960 and 35 percent higher in 1970. But by 1980 the differential had more than doubled to 79 percent higher. The disparity increased in 1990 to more than 147 percent. It is actually understated by these figures, since the U.S. data include California, which had one-tenth of the nation's population in 1980.

California's Census-reported values were higher in 1960 and 1970 in part because more than 90 percent of housing in the state is in urban areas. California is the most urban state in the country, and it has been since 1970. (It ranked second to New Jersey in 1960.) Since housing of similar size is almost always more expensive in urban areas than in rural areas, the apparent 27 to 35 percent premium of 1960 and 1970 overstates the difference between California and the rest of the nation. Given that California has not become more urban relative to the rest of the country since 1970, urbanization itself cannot explain the higher premium that developed in the 1970s.

The data showing increases in median house value in the 1970s are suggestive but unsophisticated in an economic sense. No two houses are exactly alike; a house is a "bundle of characteristics." After housing prices began rising nationally in the 1970s, several economists sought to track the price rise in a sophisticated way, although none focused specifically on California. The studies that are reported below contained a sample of metropolitan housing markets within California, from which I compared their performance with the rest of the country. Taken as a whole, they indicate that California's housing prices took off rapidly around 1974 or 1975.

Thomas Thibodeau (1992) collected a large sample of metropolitan area data from the U.S. Department of Housing and Urban Development's Annual Housing Survey, which began in 1974 and lasted until 1983. Using regression techniques, Thibodeau constructed constant-quality housing price indexes for each metropolitan area in his sample in the period. Using his indexes, I calculated the inflation rates for single-family homes in the California metropolitan areas that he happened to sample and compared them with the average inflation rate for the metropolitan areas outside of California that were sampled during the same time periods.

In every case, California metropolitan areas had housing price inflation much greater than that of the rest of the country during the middle to late 1970s. The differences in inflation rates ranged from 50 percent for Sacramento when compared with other metropolitan areas outside of California during 1976–1980, to more than 100 percent for San Francisco, San Diego, and San Bernardino during the period 1975–1978. There was also remarkably little difference in the percentage increase among the California metropolitan areas during each period. For example, in 1975–1978, San Bernardino, San Diego, and San Francisco prices all grew by about 20 percent per year, give or take a point. (Similar results can be inferred from Segal and Srinivasan [1985] and Case and Shiller [1987].)

It is also notable that Thibodeau's index shows few differences in inflation rates between central cities and suburbs or between new home prices and existing home prices for any of the California metropolitan areas during the 1970s. Whatever was pushing up prices of new homes in the suburbs was doing the same to older homes in the central cities. The rising tide lifted all the boats. Perhaps a better metaphor for California would be that the same explosion blew all the boats out of the water.

6.11   California Houses Weren't Always So Expensive

What of housing price indexes before 1974? Joseph Gyourko and Richard Voith (1992) examined metropolitan-area house price appreciation between 1971 and 1989. They used median sale prices of single-family homes for fifty-six large metropolitan areas around the country. The chief advantage of their sample is that it measures a longer period of time than most others. The drawback is that they could not adjust for differences in housing quality. My previous comparison of raw Census data to sophisticated hedonic techniques suggests, however, that controlling for quality differences between regions does not affect the results much over the long term (probably because housing quality changes at about the same rate across large metropolitan areas).

Gyourko and Voith's project sought to determine the extent to which housing price appreciation was a national phenomenon as opposed to being specific to particular metropolitan areas. For the most part, Gyourko and Voith found little evidence that prices in particular areas grew consistently faster than others. Prices that grew faster than average for a few years tended to grow more slowly in the next few years. Housing price levels varied, but rates of appreciation were largely set by the national economy.

The one exception to their finding of uniformity of appreciation arose when they grouped metropolitan areas by regions of the country. They found that the Pacific region, which in their sample consisted of five California areas (Los Angeles, San Francisco, Anaheim, San Diego, and San Jose) plus Portland and Las Vegas, was significantly different from other metropolitan areas in its rate of appreciation over the two decades. No other region stood out. It is easy from their raw data to see why they were able to detect a difference. The average *annual* rate of appreciation, in *real* terms (that is, above and beyond ordinary inflation), for the five California areas was 4.53 percent, while the real appreciation rate for the other fifty-one metropolitan areas was 0.92 percent. California houses appreciated five times faster than those of the rest of the country between 1971 and 1989. The average price of a home in the California sample in 1989 was over twice that of the rest of the country ($113,100 compared with $61,100). (Portland and Las Vegas, the other two Pacific region metropolitan areas, appreciated more rapidly than the rest of the country but less rapidly than any of the five California metropolitan areas.)

With the foregoing numbers, one can compute that California housing prices were approximately the same as those of metropolitan areas in the rest of the country in 1971. Between 1971 and 1989, real prices in California increased by a factor of 2.2, while real prices elsewhere increased by a factor of only 1.2. By dividing 1989 prices by the growth factors, one arrives at what 1971 prices would be in 1989 dollars. The calculation is thus $51,400 for California and $50,900 for the rest of the United States. Remember, these are 1989 dollars; they are what average prices would be if housing had risen only by the general rate of inflation since 1971. If they look startlingly low to California eyes it is because the reader has gotten used to the facts.

This near-equality for 1971 between California and U.S. prices could be overstated, since California houses may have improved in quality more rapidly than elsewhere. But the raw data on number of rooms per home does not suggest that such a difference is large, if it exists at all. The average number of rooms for California owner-occupied housing in 1970 was 5.5, compared with 5.7 for the United States as a whole. In 1990 the parallel figures were 5.8 rooms for California and 6.0 rooms for the nation. Along with other studies that allow such comparisons, Gyourko and Voith's analysis points to an enormous and persistent divergence between California housing prices and those of the rest of the country that began in the early 1970s.

6.12 Many Events Affect Housing Prices

I have advanced the idea that the California Supreme Court's adoption of antidevelopment rules during the 1970s contributed to the persistent differential in housing prices. I do not mean to say that California prices always grew faster than every other region. Nominal prices actually dropped in California during the 1981–82 recession (Meese and Wallace 1991), though so did housing prices in most other regions. The other notable exception was the 1983–1987 inflation in housing prices in the Northeast, discussed in section 6.18 under "price bubbles." What seems unprecedented, however, is the persistence of California's differential for almost twenty years.

The other matter of timing is the relation between the beginning of the California boom and the effect of the California Supreme Court's rulings. There is some disagreement as to exactly when California housing prices took off, but two longtime academic observers (and California residents) dated it in the spring of 1975 (Grebler and Mittelbach 1979, p. 1). This makes sense. The United States in 1975 was just bottoming out of the most severe recession since the Great Depression. The 1973–1975 recession was unusual in that it was the first ever in which the rate of inflation. Demographic trends also fueled housing demand (Mankiew and Weil 1989). The earliest cohorts of the post–World War II baby boom were starting to buy houses at that time.

I mention these factors to acknowledge that the planets were in close alignment for rapid housing price inflation all across the United States in 1975. There was pent-up demand both from the recession and the baby boomers. Inflation and the housing subsidies of the U.S. federal income tax system made buying a single-family house a fine deal financially. Thus one would expect inflation in housing prices, but that would presumably happen everywhere, not just in California. These conditions also suggest why the earlier antidevelopment decisions of the California court, which Hagman's group identified as beginning in 1967, had relatively little effect at first. The low rates of inflation prior to 1973 and the severe recession of 1973–1975 suppressed much of the demand that roared out of the pen in 1975.

In sections 6.13–6.19, I briefly review alternative explanations for the California housing price differences. Several have some plausibility, but none of them accounts for the two most dramatic facts of the 1970s. California housing prices rose faster than those of the rest of the country, and faster than at any other time in the state's recent history. To explain this, one needs to find something that happened in the early 1970s that was (a) different from the rest of the country, and (b) different from California's postwar history. I submit that only the California Supreme Court's unprecedented and largely unimitated war against developers covers both conditions.

6.13 Construction Costs Were Not the Problem in the 1970s

Were construction costs higher in California? Here the evidence for the 1970s is easy. American Appraisal Associates publishes Boeckh Building Cost Index Numbers, a well-known index of construction costs that is broken down by geographic location and type of building. The index calculates materials and labor costs that go into a nationally standardized structure (frame and brick residences, brick and steel office buildings, etc.) every other month for 206 locations in the United States and Canada. The price of raw land, land development costs, and impact fees are specifically excluded.

In December 1970, Boeckh's unweighted average of the frame residence indexes for Los Angeles and San Francisco was 3 percent higher than the U.S. average for the standard frame dwelling. In December 1980, the Boeckh index for the two largest California areas was 7 percent higher than the U.S. average. Despite the huge disparity in home prices, the building trades were not getting much more money per unit.

Similar results are obtained if one uses the other California areas surveyed by the Boeckh index. Construction-cost inflation cannot have accounted for the huge housing price differential that arose in the 1970s.

The Boeckh cost index for frame homes did rise faster in California between 1980 and 1990 than in the rest of the country. In 1990, however, the price index for the noncoastal California cities grew significantly less than those of Los Angeles, San Francisco, and San Diego. This suggests intrastate rather than interstate differences in building costs, which were not present in the 1970s. In any case, the California building cost disparity would account for only some of the 1980's increased disparity. The 1970s housing price explosion, which is the focus of this chapter, is not explained at all by construction costs.

6.14 Personal Income Growth Was Slower in California

Housing prices may differ from one place to another because residents in some places are richer than in others. Family income is an important determinant of how much people spend on housing, although it must be recalled that several of the national price indexes reviewed in section 6.10 controlled for the quality of housing. Still, the suspicion remains that having rich people as buyers will bid up the prices of even standard-quality housing.

A look at the U.S. Census data shows, however, that family income does not account for the housing value disparity. In 1960 California median family incomes were 20 percent higher than those of the country as a whole, but by 1970 this disparity had been cut to 9 percent, and by 1980, it had reduced to only 2 percent higher than the national average. Things did change in the 1980s, when California's median family income rose to 15 percent higher than the national average, which, along with more rapid population growth in the 1980s, may account for the even wider disparity in housing prices by 1990. The crucial fact remains, however, that when the California housing price explosion began in the 1970s, median family incomes in California were rising *less* rapidly than those of the rest of the country.

The slower growth in California income also undermines the theory that an influx of foreign investment money drove up real estate prices. What the Japanese and others bought were commercial buildings. In order to obtain the owner-occupied homes that constitute the real estate examined in this chapter, foreign investors would have had to move to the United States and live here. If they did that, they were in the income data that the Census reports. The foreign investor argument cannot account for owner-occupied housing inflation.

A way of summarizing the income and housing price data is to divide median housing value by median family income. The resulting "affordability index" is the number of years of an average family's income it would take to purchase the average single-family house. The affordability of housing generally was improving during the 1960s for the country as a whole, while it remained steady in California:

	1960	1970	1980	1990
United States	2.1	1.7	2.2	2.2
California	2.2	2.2	3.9	4.8

In the 1970s, however, affordability worsened slightly in the United States as a whole because of real housing price increases and slower growth of family incomes. In California, however, housing became dramatically less affordable between 1970 and 1980. In the 1980s, affordability in the country as a whole leveled off, but in California, it continued to get worse. These data are reinforced by the somewhat more sophisticated data from the real estate industry that show that California metropolitan areas continue to rank among the least affordable in the country.

6.15 *Quality of Life Is High, but That's Not News*

California is a nice place to live, and we know from economic theory that nice places are usually expected to have more expensive houses than others (Blomquist, Berger, and Hoehn 1988; Jennifer Roback 1982). This observation explains why popular rankings of "best places to live" produce seemingly random rankings. Nashua, New Hampshire, ranked first on one list; Pittsburgh, Pennsylvania, and Rochester, Minnesota, on two others. To points for low crime rates, good schools, and nice weather the list makers *add* points for low housing prices. But in an efficient market, places with desirable amenities will have higher housing prices. Wages will tend to be lower in such places, too, since people will work for less to be in nice places, unless the higher housing prices consume the entire difference in amenity advantages.

Quality of life may explain why the *level* of California prices might be higher than elsewhere. It does not explain why they should have *grown* faster during the 1970s. Only if California was an even nicer place to live in 1980 than it was in 1970—a proposition I have never heard from any native Californian—would this idea hold water. I don't want to sound anti-California, so I note that Los Angeles air quality was better in 1980 than in 1970. But air cleanup was nationwide, and Los Angeles, despite having made progress, was still at the head of the list of most-polluted large urban areas in 1980.

A more sophisticated defense of the quality of life argument is that a sunny and temperate climate, such as that of coastal California, becomes more valuable to people as their incomes rise. That is, California amenities might be highly income elastic in demand; if income grows by 10 percent, the demand for amenities might grow by 15 percent. Gyourko and Voith (1992) offer this as a possible explanation for why their data showed unusually high housing appreciation in California the 1970s and 1980s.

The problems with this explanation are two. First, incomes in California were rising less rapidly than elsewhere in the 1970s, as was noted in section 6.14. If California amenities appealed more to the rich during the last two decades, many wealthy people should have headed there and pushed up average incomes along with housing prices. Second, family income growth for the nation as a whole was much slower in the 1970s than it had been in either the 1950s or 1960s. If income-elastic demand for California amenities had been driving housing prices, California prices should have risen much faster in the 1950s and 1960s.

A negative way of phrasing the same question is to ask whether other states were becoming less desirable than California in the 1970s. The energy crisis of that decade made the Sunbelt more attractive than the Snowbelt, but, as will be demonstrated in the next section, the other states of the Sunbelt did not experience housing price increases as large as those of California. Quality of life is difficult to measure, but there is little reason to suspect that it accounted for the California housing price explosion in the 1970s.

6.16 Sunbelt Growth and Proposition 13 Do Not Work

As was mentioned in section 6.5, population growth itself is not a convincing explanation for the California housing price explosion because 1970–1980 was the slowest-growing decade in the state's history. One might ask whether the growth in the number of households could account for the difference. The number of households did increase more rapidly than population in the 1970s, as the baby boomers began leaving their parents' homes, but that phenomenon occurred throughout the nation. For the 1970s, California's household growth was only 20 percent higher than that of the United States as a whole. In the 1960s, when California housing prices increased only modestly, its number of households increased 70 percent faster than did the country's as a whole.

For further evidence on the growth-causes-high-prices hypothesis, I looked at the median value of owner-occupied homes (from U.S. Census data) in three other Sunbelt states, each of which grew considerably more rapidly than California's 18 percent population increase in the 1970s. Texas had a 27 percent population increase between 1970 and 1980, Florida's population grew by 44 percent, and Arizona's by 53 percent. Yet none of these states had an increase in housing prices more rapid than that of California. It is true that all of these states had housing price increases that exceeded the national average; population growth does make a difference. But, unlike California's, the three other states' per capita income figures were growing more rapidly than in the rest of the United States, as was the average size of a house (as measured by the number of rooms).

I found no other mainland states that came close to California's inflation in housing prices in the 1970s. Growth may contribute to some housing price increases, but California's modest growth cannot account for its 1970s housing price explosion. This is in contrast to the 1980s, in which California's population did grow rapidly and housing prices rose to even higher levels relative to the country as a whole. (The apparent paradox of population growth in the face of high housing prices will be addressed in section 6.22.)

Another alternative to the growth-control explanation for the California price explosion is the impact of Proposition 13. The famous statewide voter initiative greatly reduced property taxes in 1978. Kenneth Rosen (1982) presented evidence that Proposition 13 raised housing values by about 20 percent in a single year in the San Francisco Bay Area, and Richard Meese and Nancy Wallace (1994) also found that Proposition 13 ushered in a different era in California housing price inflation. As the capitalization studies mentioned in section 6.1 indicate, housing becomes a more attractive investment with lower property taxes. Proposition 13 seems to offer at least a partial explanation for California's housing price explosion.

Although one cannot know what housing prices would have done in the absence of Proposition 13, the evidence presented in section 6.12 shows that housing prices began their extraordinary rise in California around 1975, well before the initiative. Indeed, many observers regard the rapid increase in owner-occupied housing prices and the resulting shift in property-tax assessments to homeowners as a cause of Proposition 13. The 20 percent increase that Kenneth Rosen noted for 1978 was not unusually high for California metropolitan areas after 1975. Proposition 13 can be blamed for many of California's problems, but triggering rising housing prices is not one of them.

6.17   Land Is Plentiful, and Water Has Always Been Scarce

A popular alternative to the growth-control explanation is that California reached a physical limit on development in the 1970s. Land scarcity supposedly caused by suburban sprawl, is frequently mentioned in popular publications and by advocacy groups. Evidence on California sprawl is often illustrated by aerial photographs of the San Francisco suburb Daly City, whose housing was the inspiration for Malvina Reynolds's satirical song "Little Boxes."

Facts sing a different tune. In 1980 only about 3 percent of California's land area was classified as urban or built up, about the same fraction as for the country as a whole (U.S.D.A. 1984). Land on which development could occur if it were permitted is hardly more *physically* scarce than it was in 1960 in California or almost any other state. Daly City, incidentally, had a 1970 gross density (number of residents divided by the city's land area, not just area for housing) of 16 persons per acre, equal to about two-thirds of San Francisco's density. If all Californians lived in "little boxes," only 1.3 percent of the state's 100 million acres would be occupied.

Californians at seminars on this research have pointed out that there are physical limitations in the areas in which most Californians actually live. The San Gabriel and Santa Monica Mountains and the Pacific Ocean constrain Los Angeles, and the coastal hills and the bay hem in San Francisco area development. But this does not explain why the constraints suddenly appeared in the 1970s. Many other large U.S. metropolitan areas are likewise constrained by bodies of water (New York, Boston, Chicago). The hilly terrain of the Bay Area did little to slow development in previous decades, as a casual visitor to San Francisco, Oakland, or Berkeley can readily verify with an aerobic walk. And if buildable land were running in short supply, one would think that housing prices would have escalated prior to the 1970s. Developers could read topographic maps in the 1950s and 1960s. As an explanation for why California housing prices have risen faster than those of other states, land scarcity is a canard.

A more serious limitation on California's housing development is water supply. Most California cities must pipe their water from the Sierras, which are hundreds of miles distant. Many of the 1970s building moratoriums on development took the form of refusing to accommodate more water hook-ups for developers. The statewide drought of the mid-1970s tended to support the idea that California had reached the limits of development.

But water has always been scarce in California, and droughts are frequent events. People who have not lived there, and even some who have, often do not realize that nearly all of California's population lives in a semi-desert, with heavy but irregular winter rains followed by nine or ten months of almost none at all. This makes the climate pleasant, at least along the coast, where the ocean moderates the summer heat, but it necessitates large public works to obtain water. As Norris Hundley's masterly book, *The Great Thirst* (1992), documents, obtaining water has always been an economic limitation on California's growth. There is no physical reason why it should have been more of a limitation in the 1970s than in the rapidly growing 1950s or other decades.

The water scarcity of the 1970s was often more man-made than natural. Marin County, the affluent and low-density suburban county north of San Francisco, is an example. Bernard Frieden (1979) reported that Marin's 1970s water rationing was largely caused by the county's deliberately forestalling reservoir development in order to block growth. Lloyd Mercer and Douglas Morgan (1982) noted that Santa Barbara County declined to join the California Water Project, which would have made water plentiful for urban purposes, and instead used local water rationing to prevent development in the 1970s. (It finally joined after the drought of the late 1980s.)

Assessment of water issues in California is complicated by the fact that 85 percent of the water is used in agriculture. No new water sources would need to be developed if the state could induce the farmers, who are charged only a small fraction of what urban users pay, to use slightly less of it by charging them a price that is a little closer to water's scarcity value (Delworth Gardner 1983). That such modest reallocation policies are difficult to adopt seems more the result than the cause of the antigrowth attitude, though it is hard to blame this one on the California Supreme Court.

6.18   "Price Bubbles" Do Not Work for California

Housing prices in the northeastern part of the country rose unusually rapidly during the mid-1980s. The price of housing in the Boston area, for example, grew at nearly 20 percent per year between 1983 and 1987. By 1987, some reports placed Boston housing prices ahead of the formerly undisputed mainland champion, San Francisco. One explanation was that the extraordinary growth of Boston area housing prices constituted a speculative price bubble. Karl Case (1992) and Robert Shiller (Case and Shiller 1989) became leading advocates of the bubble theory.

It is hard to persuade economists of the bubble theory because most of us regard markets as bursting speculative bubbles fairly quickly. Case's case is more persuasive than most because he forecast that the bubble would burst, and it did. Boston and other northeastern metropolitan areas have experienced significant declines in real housing prices since 1987, and the five largest California metropolitan areas were once again rated the "least affordable" in the nation, according of the Urban Land Institute's *Land Use Digest* of June 1991.

The bubble theory might seem to offer an alternative explanation to the California housing price rise. Perhaps behind the increases is just the mass psychology of speculation in a rising housing market. People see that prices "always" rise, and so they continue to buy regardless of the price. Only when budgets get too tightly strung or the economy slows down, goes this theory, will prices slow down. When they do, leveraged buyers will begin to default, and the bubble quickly bursts. Case argued that such bubbles are bad for the local economy because they exacerbate the effects of national economic cycles.

The trouble with bubble theory for California is that the state's housing price rise is much too sustained to be regarded as a speculative bubble. Bubbles are fragile. A slowdown in prices resulting from, say, a recession, causes them to burst, as Boston's did. But California's housing prices weathered a very severe, deflationary recession, that of 1982. Prices did drop in California in 1982, but they came right back to achieve even higher levels. The extraordinary California price premium has persisted for at least two decades now. Even on its own terms, the speculative bubble idea cannot explain the persistent California price premium. (Meese and Wallace [1994] used San Francisco area data to show that "economic fundamentals" explain the longer-term inflation in housing prices between 1970 and 1988, *after* they allow for a dramatic shift in Bay Area housing prices sometime around the middle 1970s. They did not compare prices outside of California, however.)

6.19   *The Voter Initiative Influences California Politics*

Many local growth controls and statewide regulatory regimes like the Coastal Zone Commission were created in the 1970s by voter initiative. Initiatives may pass laws that are different from those that emerge from legislatures. The opportunities for deliberation and study that are available, if not always exercised, by two houses of a legislature and by the governor are less obviously exercised by individual voters. The interest-group politics that characterizes legislatures also seems more attenuated in voter initiatives.

The difference that initiatives make is a cause of both celebration and dismay among scholarly observers, usually depending on the substance of the issue. Voters established the California Coastal Zone Commission in 1972 after similar bills in the legislature had been beaten back by coalitions of coastal landowners and developers. Property-rights advocates decried this outcome (Hanke and Carbonell 1978), but conservatives such as Geoffrey Brennan and James Buchanan (1979) praised the initiative process when California's Proposition 13 dramatically cut property taxes in 1978. Liberals are similarly divided. Julian Eule (1990) regarded the initiative process with skepticism because it was used to limit desegregation efforts ordered by the California courts, but Lynn Baker (1991) pointed out that many desirable reforms, such as women's suffrage in several states, had come through initiatives.

The initiative is neither unique to California—almost half of the states use it—nor was it new to California in the 1970s. The use of such measures began in California in 1911. If there was anything new about the initiative in the 1970s, it was the California Supreme Court's inclination to defer to plebescites in land use issues. Initiatives had been treated by the court like ordinary legislation, subject to the usual, loose judicial limits of due process. But as the Hagman group mentioned, the California court stopped even that loose review in the late 1960s (DiMento et al. 1980, p. 997). Thus the court gave license to the least procedurally protective device by which growth controls could be enacted at the local level, and it continues to be unusual among state courts in that respect (Callies, Neuffer, and Calibosco 1991, p. 76).

6.20 Friends of Mammoth *Was a Major Judicial Intervention*

One has to ask whether California political institutions did not make a pronounced difference in growth controls. After all, voters, politicians, and citizen activists are the ones who instigate measures that make it hard to develop new housing in California. Environmental groups may simply enjoy broader public support in California than they do in, say, Texas, Arizona, or Florida. Regardless of whether this is true, in this section I point out that the major environmental legislation that affected California land use was not solely the result of citizen politics.

The National Environmental Policy Act (NEPA) of 1970 marked the beginning of what is rightly regarded as the "environmental decade." As its main public entitlement, this act gave citizens the right to demand that a government-sponsored project have an adequate environmental impact statement. Such a declaration remains an important tool to block, delay, or modify developments sponsored in some way by the federal government. The measure was not binding on the states, however, or on owners of private property. Housing developers do not have to meet NEPA requirements or file an environmental impact statement unless their project is financed by the federal government.

California was the among the earliest of several states to adopt its own version of NEPA. The California Environmental Quality Act (CEQA) was adopted in September 1970. Like the federal NEPA, the California statute appeared to apply only to government projects. An environmental impact statement was required "on any project they intend to carry out which may have a significant effect on the environment." The legislative history of CEQA indicated that the legislature did not include under the term "project" actions by private developers that merely required regulatory review. An earlier version of a closely related bill had referred to "any project or zoning change they intended to carry out," but the words "or zoning change" were deleted (Ellickson and Tarlock 1981, p. 315).

Despite this history, which was known to the court (the lone dissenter pointed it out) the California Supreme Court decided in *Friends of Mammoth* (1972) that CEQA standards were applicable to any sizable private development that the government permitted, licensed, or subsidized. The decision effectively pulled almost all private developments of more than modest scope within CEQA review, and it became a powerful tool to block development of all kinds. As the Hagman seminar remarked, *Friends of Mammoth* "could not have been a broader charter of CEQA controversies had it been written by environmentalists" (DiMento et al. 1980, p. 977). The process and its consequences of retarding housing development and raising prices were documented by Bernard Frieden (1979) and by Fred Case and Jeffrey Gale (1982).

Friends of Mammoth was a matter of statutory interpretation, not constitutional law. The difference is that the legislature can change the law when the court interprets it under statutory canons, while it cannot when the court invokes a constitutional basis for its decision. After *Friends of Mammoth,* the state legislature did react to the decision and the chaos it caused the building industry by amending CEQA. The legislature exempted from its requirements *ongoing* private projects, but specifically included future private projects as being subject to CEQA requirements. Hence the application of CEQA to private projects has the ostensible appearance of a legislative decision.

Anyone familiar with collective decisions by representative bodies recognizes that the point from which a body starts makes a difference in the outcome of attempts to change that point. If farmers have always gotten subsidies, it is much easier to vote to continue the subsidies than if they have not. In the original CEQA bill, the starting point exempted private development from the environmental impact statement requirement. It clearly was a close call. As the legislative history suggests, environmental advocates were eager to include zoning decisions in the law. Just as obvious, the building industry and local governments were not. The compromise reached subjected some developments—projects "carried out" by the government, such as schools, municipal dumps, and the like—to the rigors of an environmental impact statement, but exempted the rest. (This has a logic, since governmental projects are typically exempt from local zoning requirements. The original NEPA and CEQA bills could be regarded as attempts to bring public review to government agencies.)

As political science has long taught, in the U.S. system of government it is easier to prevent change than to promote it. The protection of the status quo is not a constitutional accident. The multiple layers of government and the requirements of procedural due process have long been hallmarks of the constitutional system. By deliberately altering the base point for legislation, the California court manipulated the legislative agenda. *Friends of Mammoth* and the broad application of CEQA review stand as a prominent example of the court's unusually antidevelopment attitude rather than as a testimony to the environmental consciousness of the California political process.

6.21   *Growth Controls Can Spread without Regional Growth*

Several California researchers looked at growth controls around the state in the late 1980s and discovered that they had become ubiquitous. According to Madelyn Glickfeld and Ned Levine (1992), nearly all communities that responded to their survey seemed to have some sort of growth control. This conclusion is not surprising. Public officials and their planning staffs learn about growth controls. Like all professionals, planners are keen to keep up with the latest trends. If some communities are pursuing a certain course of action and it benefits local homeowners, other communities are apt to do it, too. Several researchers have remarked that after Petaluma's growth controls were validated by the courts, they quickly spread to other communities.

The other process by which growth controls become ubiquitous is market pressure. The scenario that I envision is as follows. Developers who are shut out of some communities will go to other communities nearby. Even if the substitute communities have not adopted growth controls, nearly all of them have long-standing land use ordinances. As the substitute communities become overwhelmed with building permit applications, however, they will be unable to respond within the framework of their existing regulations. Simple administrative delay will then tend to drive up housing prices. Moreover, the substitute communities will begin to perceive that growth is very rapid, even if it has not increased for the region as a whole. The substitute communities will then be more inclined to adopt growth controls, sending developers to the dwindling supply of places that welcome them and repeating the same script. Hence a change in the behavior of a relatively small number of communities can snowball into widespread effects, especially if zoning rules can be changed without much regard for procedural, let alone substantive, due process of law.

Glickfeld and Levine (1992) took the ubiquity of growth controls in California to a different conclusion, however. They constructed indexes of the stringency of growth controls in each community and statistically tested whether their indexes had any effects on housing development. It turns out that by their metric, growth controls do not have much effect.

I don't accept this result because, as I mentioned in section 6.2, it is hard to determine the effects of the protean police-power laws just by examining their text. Ira Lowry and Bruce Ferguson (1992) compared regulatory practices in three metropolitan areas (including one in California) and also concluded that looking at the regulations alone is often misleading. Aside from what I regard as the nearly insuperable problems of measuring stringency of application from laws that are highly malleable, Glickfeld and Levine's analysis did not address whether the ubiquity of growth controls affected housing prices in the state as a whole. If the major effect of California growth controls was to raise the price of housing in the entire state, it is not surprising that one should find little price effect in an in-state sample.

6.22 Growth Controls May Cause Sprawl

Glickfeld and Levine (1992) did point to an issue that requires more attention. If growth controls that were adopted in California in the 1970s were so severe, why did California's population growth increase so much during the 1980s, seemingly despite soaring housing prices? People did seem to find places to live there, even though the cost of housing was higher than elsewhere.

I have only fragmentary answers to this question. One is that most of the net migration to California has been from outside the country (Muller and Espenshade 1985). California has as many people leaving for other states as move into it from the rest of the country. Many of the emigrants are not leaving for the usual job-change and life-cycle reasons. A good number are "equity migrants," California residents who sell their bungalows and buy mansions in other states. Of course, in order to cash in on one's California bungalow, one must find a buyer, but, increasingly, the buyers are from another country. The very fact that people move specifically to take advantage of lower-priced housing elsewhere also suggests the difficulty that California businesses have in attracting executives and workers from other parts of the United States. Housing prices have long been listed as a major problem in surveys of California employers, and stories of businesses relocating to less costly areas for that reason continue to fill Los Angeles newspapers.

An obvious question is why the immigrants from abroad don't go to Cleveland or St. Louis, where the housing prices are lower. They may yet do so, but immigrants from abroad have always been initially attracted to areas in which there are other immigrants from the same country. The benefits of having, say, an established Korean community in Los Angeles apparently overwhelm the drawbacks of the extraordinary housing prices.

The other reason for California's continued growth is that the state has an immense amount of land. When the amenable, established communities become too costly to build in, developers head for the areas within the state in which costs are lower. These are the less amenable inland areas of the state. Rural areas are, for a variety of reasons, usually more disposed to accept growth than urban and suburban areas (Fischel 1985, chap. 10; Thomas Rudel 1989). The 1990 Census indicates that the fast-growing areas of California have been the inland areas of the Central Valley and the area east of Los Angeles. This pattern of settlement has its costs. Commuting is longer and the benefits of urban agglomeration are reduced, which eventually reduce productivity and income.

A third reason for California's population growth in the 1980s is that high housing prices were not as much of a deterrent when the state's economy was booming and housing prices were expected to rise even more. Workers who found jobs in the state could swallow the high level of housing prices because they could expect the prices to go even higher in a few years, thus increasing their equity. When housing prices stopped rising around 1990, however, the level itself became a more significant deterrent. Businesses that are contracting are more likely to look for cheaper sources of labor, and cheaper labor can be had where housing prices are lower. Thus the high level of prices may account for the length and depth of the early 1990s recession in California, a recession that was shorter and less severe in most of the rest of the country. (As Case [1992] noted, the Northeast also took the recession especially hard because of high housing prices, although it adjusted more rapidly than California.)

6.23 Conclusion: The California Court Created a Regulatory Commons

There are two morals to this chapter. The more obvious one is that local regulations do transfer wealth from one class of people, owners of undeveloped land, to another class of people, owners of already-existing houses. That the two are both "landowners," in that most owners of homes also own the land beneath the structure, obscures a huge disparity of interests. The absence of a coherent regulatory takings doctrine promotes this transfer of wealth in a majoritarian context.

My argument that the California Supreme Court's vigorous promotion of passive over active uses of land caused excessive housing prices has a more complex moral. It is tempting to see it as a taking writ large. Owners of undeveloped land throughout the state, whose financial interests are the only in-state representatives of housing consumers outside the local jurisdiction, lost their property rights to already-established California residents. I think this is correct, but the effect of the court's actions are more complex.

Had the court redistributed ownership from A to B, the Coase theorem holds that the efficiency effects should be nil. B can use or transfer the property as well as A. But in depriving private owners of the right to develop their property, the court did not choose any particular party to receive those rights. It redistributed development rights from A to B, C, D, and the rest of an indefinitely long alphabet.

The California court changed the legal rules so that any number of parties could stop a given development up to the moment at which it was physically improved. The court thus created a commons in the right to exclude. The problem with a pastoral commons is that potential users cannot be excluded, so that too many sheep are apt to be grazed upon it. Each shepherd knows that overgrazing is bad for future prosperity, but each also knows that if he alone conserves the grass, it will just be chewed up by another's animals. California developers, who had once been able to bargain with a local government and a finite set of state agencies, found that they had to bargain with parties whose existence they were previously unaware of.

As I argued in section 3.19, local governments are prone to the regulatory commons problem. Because the potential beneficiaries of development usually live outside the jurisdiction, and because present voters expect their children and others whose well-being they care about to live elsewhere in the future, economically myopic behavior is often rational. One purpose of judicial review is to help overcome this regulatory commons problem.

In California, however, the judiciary made the regulatory commons problem even worse. It not only encouraged local government regulation; it entitled private parties to join the feeding frenzy. Many of the newly entitled parties were in no position to perceive the costs of foregoing development, either economically or politically. A local government that excludes a housing development forgoes something, including tax revenues, land use exactions, and local jobs and business activity. State agencies that retard development may feel some political pressure for having done so, either from the local government or from the developer's organizations. But People for Open Space, an environmental organization that boasts of having preserved (mostly by regulation) millions of acres in the Bay Area, had little to lose from any of its actions. Its success in making housing more costly may disturb its members individually, but there is no way that the organization can parlay its ability to stop development into another set of goods. Even outright extortion would usually not be feasible, since the developer would realize that other organizations would then demand a payoff.

Of course it is not quite that extreme, even in California. With much time and effort, developers can assemble a group to satisfy their concerns. (The Urban Land Institute publishes how-to books for developers faced with a multitude of neighborly objectors.) But time and effort mean less housing at higher costs. What the California courts did was to create significantly higher transaction costs for development all across the state. The higher statewide housing prices that resulted have adversely affected the national economy by distorting the location decisions of firms and households.

7

Zoning, Capitalization, and the Efficiency of Local Government

This chapter reviews the Tiebout model of local government and compares it with constitutional writings about the nature of local government. Tiebout's model, amended to include more realistic assumptions about voting, taxation, and zoning, is a reasonably accurate representation of the economic role of American local governments. It is about as efficient a way of providing local public goods as one can set up in a country that spans a continent and is filled with diverse people bent on self-government.

The chapter goes on to assess the implications of the model of local government for the regulatory takings doctrine. I submit that the widespread preference for local government autonomy should give pause to judges who would strike down such regulations. The nature of the property that is protected by the Takings Clause has always been the subject of political debates. I adduce evidence that the nineteenth century's preoccupation with promoting the development of land has shifted in the present century toward protection of established uses. Most modern local land use regulation is intended to protect "land at rest," as opposed to "land at risk," to invoke the famous terms of the historian Willard Hurst (1956).

The inexorable shift in attitudes about the legitimate uses of property should be respected by modern jurists who must interpret constitutional provisions on eminent domain from the nineteenth century. I conclude, however, by differentiating local regulations that are protective of existing uses from those that unfairly exploit unrepresented

outsiders. Despite the shift in attitudes about property, the Takings
Clause is still necessary to coordinate local government regulation.

7.1 Tiebout Proposed an Efficient Model of Local Government

In Chapter 6, I noted the frequency with which economists uncover
statistical evidence that local government policies affect the values of
single-family homes. Improving local school quality, lowering local
taxes, improving air quality, tightening zoning regulations, and reducing crime rates all increase the average value of existing single-family
homes in the locality.

This is an astonishing result. Communal efforts seem to be capitalized in much the same way as private efforts to improve one's home,
such as fixing the roof or planting trees. The rate of capitalization of
communal activities is lower than that of private property, which suggests that their future benefits and burdens are of less certain durability
(John Yinger et al. 1988, p. 124), but the regularity of capitalization is
nonetheless impressive. As I showed in section 6.1, a necessary condition for this property like effect is another condition for private
property: One must be able to exclude interlopers. The method by
which one's home improvement activity is so protected is property law.
The method by which the community's investments are similarly protected is zoning law.

The touchstone of the economic analysis of local government is the
model first proposed by Charles Tiebout (1956). Tiebout was not
especially interested in local government finance. His article hardly
mentioned it. Rather, he wanted to challenge the conclusion of Paul
Samuelson and Richard Musgrave, who had proved that there exists no
realistic mechanism for solving the problem of public goods.

Tiebout argued that the free-rider and nonexclusion problems endemic to national public goods could be overcome for local public
goods. Communities could establish different mixes and levels of local
services, and people would "vote with their feet" to choose the combination that fit their budget and their preferences. Tiebout was vague
about just how "public" the local public goods were, since unlike pure
public goods, his local services were subject to congestion. (He did
title his article "A Pure Theory of Local Expenditures," not a pure
theory of local public goods.) After a certain point, the cost per capita
rose, and potential immigrants had to go to another community. That

in itself was not so bad if there were enough other communities to accommodate them.

Tiebout's model remained an intellectual curiosity for over a decade. The problem, I suspect, is that economists' reaction to it was like the first reaction of most of my students: clever model, but how many people change their residences just because they prefer the schools or the tennis courts in the next town? Wallace Oates (1969) put Tiebout on the map by offering evidence that people seem to do just that. Oates found that for a sample of communities in northern New Jersey, a state with hundreds of fiercely independent local governments, average housing values were distinctly influenced by the level and tax cost of local government services. Communities with low taxes but good local services had housing values that were higher than otherwise comparable housing in less-favored communities.

The way to reconcile Oates's findings with the commonsense idea that people seldom move just because they do not like the school principal is to consider that people move most often because they get a new job, find a spouse, or have a child. Since they have to move anyway, such households have the opportunity to compare taxes and government services in a number of different communities. Their choice of locality is especially wide if they live in metropolitan areas of more than 500,000 people (as most Americans do), which have scores if not hundreds of local governments (Fischel 1981). The potential buyers do not have to visit the schools or town halls to comparison shop. They can rely on real estate agents, friends who already live in the area, and, in larger areas, services devoted to providing such information.

The evidence supporting Oates's theory that locally provided benefits are capitalized in home values is overwhelming. Few hypotheses have been confirmed more often. The evidence that good local schools attract home buyers is especially strong (Gerald McDougal 1976; Raymond Reinhard 1981; Sonstelie and Portney 1980a).

7.2 The Median Voter Determines Local Government Decisions

While Tiebout's "voting with one's feet" system corresponded to reality in important respects, it was less realistic about how local governments decide what to provide. Tiebout's decision mechanism likened local governments to profit-making firms. This was an inspired analogy, considering the historical relationship between municipal and private corporations. Tiebout was interested in how large these "firms" would be. He proposed that competition among governments for residents would make them operate at minimum average cost for local public services. A spate of empirical articles does suggest that metropolitan areas that have many local governments have lower taxes than those whose residents have fewer alternative suppliers of public services (Eberts and Gronberg 1990; Oates 1989).

The problem with Tiebout's characterization of local governments is that it neglects voting and other political behavior (Bryan Ellickson 1971; Epple and Zelenitz 1981). One amendment is to think of communities as being just like firms that happen to respond to stockholders. In "Profit Maximizing Communities and the Theory of Local Public Expenditures," Jon Sonstelie and Paul Portney (1978) showed that competitive businesslike communities would attempt to maximize aggregate land value in their jurisdiction, and that doing so would promote efficiency.

Characterizing communities as firms controlled by stockholders is problematical, however, because in most business corporations, the rule is one dollar, one vote. This leads to the objective of maximizing profits if the usual agency problems can be overcome. But for communities, one needs an economic theory in which votes are allocated one resident, one vote. The relevant model is that of Howard Bowen (1943), who first proposed that, under certain conditions, majority-rule voting would result in efficient levels of public goods. Like Tiebout and unlike Samuelson, Bowen's public goods were not "pure" in the sense of being nonrival and nonexclusive. His chief expository example was schooling.

Bowen's insight rested chiefly on a correspondence between a voter's demand for the public goods and the individual tax burden that he faced. As a practical matter, the primary condition required for Bowen's model to give an approximation of efficient results is that the preferences of the voter with the median level of income prevail (Bergstrom and Goodman 1973). Given that this "voter" gets his way, Bowen proved that a Pareto-like equilibrium was obtained. It was not that everyone was satisfied; it was that no other level of public services could defeat this one in repeated, pairwise votes. One might call this "politically Pareto-optimal." (James Buchanan [1993] also commended the median voter model in situations in which taxes must be uniformly applied, a condition that most state constitutions require of their municipalities [Michael Bernard 1979]. Buchanan was largely addressing national issues, which might have caused him to overlook the widespread existence of state and local uniformity requirements [Lynn Baker 1994].)

Government by median voter is a testable proposition. There are, after all, alternative theories that economists have proposed. The alternatives are (a) that bureaucrats expand the level of public services to increase their own wealth and power (William Niskanen 1971), (b) that concentrated interests lobby successfully for a set of goods of little interest to the median voter (Anthony Downs 1957; George Stigler 1971), or (c) that some combination of bureaucrats and special interests set all-or-nothing voting agendas so that the median voter has to select more than she wants (Romer and Rosenthal 1979).

Thomas Borcherding and Robert Deacon (1972), closely followed by Ted Bergstrom and Robert Goodman's crisply titled "Private Demand for Public Goods" (1973), were among the first to test whether the median income voter actually got the level of public goods that Bowen hypothesized. Their results, appropriately hedged and qualified, indicated that Bowen's median voter theorem worked surprisingly well.

Both empirical studies used samples drawn from American local governments. The level of various municipal services seemed to vary among them according to the characteristics of the voters. The level of public services seems to have been set "as if" a referendum among the voters had been held on every issue. For example, William McEachern (1978) found that the level of bonded indebtedness of jurisdictions that voted directly on debt issues and those in which the city council had the final say were not significantly different. More recent studies were reviewed by Randall Holcombe (1989), who found the results sufficiently persuasive that he proposed the median voter as an appropriate benchmark for all government decisions, the analogue to perfect competition in private markets.

7.3 The Size of the Government Makes a Difference

Thomas Romer and Howard Rosenthal (1979) were not so impressed with the median voter model. They suggested that the evidence was not convincing because the level of public goods may be some multiple of what the median voter actually prefers. Thus one gets variation according to median voter characteristics, but it may be twice what the voters actually want.

Moreover, the median voter advocates have seldom addressed how the "as if" proposition actually works. Critics of the median voter note that few jurisdictions vote on public services. We have representative government in all but small New England towns. Even most town meetings are attended by only a small fraction of the eligible voters, and voters usually decide a carefully limited range of issues. In New Hampshire, for instance, the town meeting can increase or decrease the selectmen's proposed budget, but the voters may not specify which line items are to be changed.

Much of the criticism may be resolved by noting that the size of the jurisdiction seems to make a difference in whether the median voter theorem holds up. Howard Bloom and Helen Ladd (1982) asked whether budgets of Massachusetts towns and cities were opportunistically increased after property assessments were raised. The median voter model would say that an increase in property assessments would simply cause tax rates to decrease, while most of the model's competitors would say that bureaucrats or special interests would take advantage of the apparent windfall and spend more. Bloom and Ladd found evidence for both ideas. In bigger cities, councils did take some liberties with the nominally larger tax base and spend more, but in small towns, tax rates were dutifully cut. In small towns, the voters get what they want. One price of residence in a bigger city is greater slippage between want and get.

A similar result was obtained by Dennis Holtz-Eakin and Harvey Rosen (1989). Their study of capital budgeting in New Jersey municipalities found that suburban and rural jurisdictions behaved like the rational median voter, using appropriate discount rates and time horizons, while large cities did not. And even Thomas Romer, Howard Rosenthal, and Vincent Munley (1992), two of whom had cast doubt on the median voter model, found that the model worked rather well in small New York State school districts, but not (as they expected) in large, urban districts.

There are two complementary reasons for the apparent differences between small and large jurisdictions. The more obvious is that small size itself makes it more likely that voters will know what is going on in local government. The issues are fewer and political figures are accessible. More important, I believe, is that most voters in smaller jurisdictions are homeowners. They have an incentive to pay attention to politics: good decisions will increase the value of their major asset, and bad ones will reduce it. Political scientists have long been impressed by the high rate of participation by middle-class homeowners in local politics (J. M. Burns et al. 1993, p. 211).

I submit that the aforementioned evidence implies that Tiebout's neglect of local government politics requires only modest amendment in jurisdictions other than large central cities and, where they are important providers of local services, large counties. In most local governments, particularly suburban governments, one only has to replace Tiebout's managers with the median voter. The median voter will want to do most of the same things that an entrepreneurial private manager would want to do. The major difference is that the median voter cannot as easily accommodate major changes in the character of the community. Personal attachments and collective decision making will make it harder to "take the money and run" when an apparently value-increasing change in the community is in the offing.

7.4 Fiscal Zoning Makes Property Taxes Efficient

Besides his neglect of politics, which I believe is not crucial, Tiebout may be faulted for not dealing with the financing of local governments. Most local expenditures are financed through the property tax. If there are many local governments in an area, those providing high levels of public services cannot under most laws simply charge admission to the community. (They can often charge for capital expenditures such as new schools necessitated by a development, as described in section 9.11, but typically not for ongoing expenditures such as teacher salaries.) Local governments have to finance any increment to current expenditures not paid by higher governments by levying additional property taxes.

The problem this creates for Tiebout's system is that it gives an incentive for people with high demands for local public services such as schools but low demand for housing to build small houses in high-expenditure communities. They thus get much more in public services than they pay in taxes. Fine for them, but not so financially attractive for preexisting residents who live in more valuable houses. Their taxes go up to finance the newcomers, but they get no additional benefits for the services. Existing home values will fall as a result.

The Tiebout system was intellectually repaired (perhaps extended is a better word) by Bruce Hamilton (1975b), whose work has made him one of the most-cited economists in local public finance. Hamilton's path-breaking idea was simple. Suppose, like Tiebout, that there are many local governments that potentially offer different services. The initial residents vote for a certain level. In order to prevent free riding of the sort just described, the pioneers adopt zoning laws whose effect is to ensure that subsequent development will at least pay its own way. In this way, local zoning combined with uniform, ad valorum property taxation and Tiebout's voting with one's feet model ensures that the local property tax has no deadweight loss.

Lack of deadweight loss is the economists' holy grail of taxation. Even economists who scorn local government as small potatoes have to be impressed with Hamilton's result. The only other practicable system of taxation that lacked deadweight loss was the land tax of Henry George, and that never got off the ground. (Because George wanted it to apply to all land, reforms based on it met stout resistance from organized landowner groups and were defeated in several statewide initiatives during 1910–1914 [Elliot Brownlee 1979].) Moreover, Hamilton's version of the Tiebout system is even more efficient. It contains a demand-revealing mechanism—voluntary location and majority voting by a relatively homogeneous group—as well as an unavoidable tax. For the benefit of noneconomists, let me explain.

Taxes as classically regarded are compulsory payments for which there are no benefits specifically tied to the payment, other than remaining out of jail. The supply-side efficiency problem with most taxes is that they are legally avoidable. People can avoid income taxes by not making any money income; Vermonters can avoid sales taxes by crossing into New Hampshire or by bartering; and smokers can avoid cigarette taxes by cutting down or rolling their own. The economic loss entailed in avoiding the tax is the measure of the tax's deadweight loss. If it were not for deadweight loss, the amount the government received would exactly equal the private sector's loss. An efficient tax is not a painless or fair tax; indeed, it may actually be more painful because it cannot be avoided. (Witness the riotous reaction to the Thatcher government's attempt to impose something close a true head tax in Britain in 1988 [O'Sullivan, Sexton, and Sheffrin 1995].)

The property tax is often regarded as a tax on real estate. The component assessed on land cannot be avoided or passed on to anyone else, unless one finds some potential buyer foolish enough not to be aware of the tax, and fools seldom have much money for the same reason. But the part of the property tax assessed on the structure can be avoided by building a smaller one or letting the structure run down. Housing economists have traditionally not liked the property tax for that reason, although Peter Mieszkowski (1972) has pointed out that because owners of capital cannot avoid some level of property taxes, it is to some extent a progressive (but still inefficient) tax on capital.

Hamilton's fiscal zoning system cures the traditional defect of tax avoidance. Developers are not allowed to build small, cheap houses to avoid the high taxes in high-spending communities. Zoning and planning regulations can increase quality and durability with a whole range of requirements, which I will describe in section 7.6. Zoning makes the property tax a great deal harder to avoid.

Combined with the Tiebout system, fiscal zoning also makes the property tax efficient in demand. As long as there are many communities with various levels of public services, foot-voting ensures that the households will be able to find a community that satisfies their demand for services *and* permits housing that meets their demand, too. In the Tiebout-Hamilton system, the property tax becomes essentially a fee for services and so has no deadweight loss. A consequence of the sorting of households by demand for public education, which is the major local expenditure, is that there will be substantial variations in fiscal burdens and in spending per pupil among districts according to private demand.

7.5 *Homogeneity Makes for More Efficient Decisions*

A corollary of the model, and of fiscal zoning in the real world, is that local governments are apt to be more homogeneous in income and other characteristics that determine demand for local public services than they would otherwise be (Eberts and Gronberg 1981; Hamilton, Mills, and Puryear 1975). The sorting of the population that goes on in this way grates on egalitarian sensibilities and has been the object of many reform proposals. But an advantage of homogeneity is that it is more likely to meet the conditions for Bowen's median voter model.

Among the conditions for Bowen's model to work is that elections not be subject to the famous paradox of voting, in which majorities can cycle endlessly among alternatives. The voting paradox arises when voters have preferences for public goods that are extreme: they prefer a lot of x or none of x, unlike most voters, who prefer a middling amount of x as compared with a lot or none. The Tiebout model reduces the probability that such voters will be thrown together by allowing those with nonstandard preferences to sort themselves into special communities. The American utopian tradition of people migrating to underdeveloped locales and setting up their own government is a time-honored example of this sorting.

The Tiebout model in turn supplements the efficiency of Bowen's median voter. The Bowen equilibrium is efficient only insofar as the median voter's choice beats all others. When jurisdictions are filled with like-minded people, the difference between the median voter and most others is likely to be smaller. This may help explain the well-known fact that voter turnouts in local elections are smaller than in national elections. If everyone is near agreement, there is not much reason to vote.

The correspondence between demand by voters and supply by local governments at the local level is in distinct contrast to the economic literature about larger government units, namely, the states and the national government. Public choice scholars have seldom remarked on this distinction, and the avatar of public choice, James Buchanan, has argued against the Tiebout system as an efficient alternative (Buchanan and Goetz 1972). Likewise, a number of scholars have criticized the Tiebout model on technical grounds, casting doubt on the viability of the system (Mieszkowski and Zodrow 1989; Susan Rose-Ackerman 1979). Most of these criticisms have shown that the system is unstable because there is no mechanism to control immigration. The critics argue that the poor will follow the rich from community to community in search of a free ride. The criticism is telling if zoning does not in fact protect the fiscal base of the communities in the system.

7.6 Zoning Enables Communities to Internalize Fiscal Costs and Benefits

There is a remarkable amount of fiscally motivated zoning to avoid initial (or further) capital losses by resident homeowners. Some econometric evidence points to this. Barbara Sherman Rolleston's (1987) study of New Jersey municipalities found that fiscal motives are important determinants of zoning decisions, and George Peterson

(1974a) found that in Boston suburbs at least half of the benefits of minimum lot–size zoning were attributable to fiscal protection.

Most law professors who specialize in land use regard fiscal zoning as a serious constraint. Robert Ellickson and Dan Tarlock, the most economically sophisticated casebook authors, begin their chapter on urban infrastructure thus: "A municipality's land-use policies are influenced—indeed, often ultimately determined—by its fiscal situation" (1981, p. 705). All authors who address the subject agree that a zoning law whose sole purpose is to exclude low-cost housing that will not pay much in property taxes is apt to be struck down but few communities are so clumsy as to inscribe such motivation in their records.

Intention to exclude on racial grounds is necessary to get the federal courts' equal protection attention in such matters, so the Fourteenth Amendment has been a dead letter for zoning since Arlington Heights v. Metropolitan Housing (1977). The attention of the courts in New Jersey, that most suburban of states, to fiscal zoning's tendency to exclude low-income housing is evidence of its importance. In its famous *Mount Laurel* decisions (1975, 1983), the New Jersey Supreme Court acknowledged that fiscal considerations were crucial to community zoning. *Mount Laurel* attempted, without much quantifiable success, to reverse the regressive aspects of the fiscal zoning tide. (The case will be revisited in section 9.8.) Few other states have undertaken similar reforms, but most state courts have at some time acknowledged the existence of fiscal considerations in zoning decisions. Richard Briffault's lengthy article on local government law found that fiscal zoning, which he denoted by the pejorative term "exclusionary zoning," is ubiquitous and barely ruffled by the few state court decisions that attack it (1990).

A more important inroad on the Tiebout-Hamilton system is that most states provide their local governments with assistance to perform their mandated duties. This is particularly true in the case of schools. The twentieth-century trend has been for the states to pay an increasingly large fraction of local school costs. Most of the states distribute their funds in a way that tends to favor localities with fewer than average fiscal resources. There is some evidence that this slightly reduces fiscally motivated zoning (Hamilton, Mills, and Puryear 1975).

Up until 1971, when state courts began to intervene in school finance decisions with Serrano v. Priest, the decision to supplement local funds with state funds was entirely at the discretion of the legislature, unless specifically mandated by state constitutions. Such programs mitigate the pay-your-own-way consequences of the Tiebout system. To the extent that they completely offset any spending variations, of course, the efficiency of the Tiebout system is compromised. Thus the existing system is for the most part a political compromise between voters who would prefer entirely local funding and those who would prefer uniform state funding. Presumably much more than just preferences for public education goes into such decisions.

7.7   Heterogeneous Communities Do Not Disprove Tiebout

One objection to the idea that fiscal zoning is a constraint is the observation that suburbs are not homogeneous. In Hamilton's original model (1975b), zoning was characterized as rules requiring identical housing and homogeneous households. He assumed this to make the model easier to solve.

The suburban planner who advises elected officials is not so constrained. She can figure which types of housing are apt to generate which kinds of costs and adjust the land development rules accordingly. Suppose, for example, she wishes to see that new development pays its own way in school costs. For single-family houses with four bedrooms, she will demand expensive standards of construction and large lots to be sure that not too many are built. But for a developer of apartments earmarked for the elderly she can be more lenient, because they will not demand much schooling. A developer of other types of apartments may be required to pay exactions up front to cover additional public service costs. A planner can determine fiscal costs by using manuals such as *The Development Impact Assessment Handbook and Model* (Burchell, Listokin, and Dolphin 1993). (Sections 9.12–9.15 will assess the exactions issue.)

The result of such fine-tuning will be a community that is more heterogeneous than the original Hamilton model would have us believe. But effective fiscal zoning has been operating, and the local taxes plus land use exactions are largely benefit taxes. The heterogeneity of a restrictive suburb may also result from development that predated effective zoning ordinances. Early zoning of small communities is often permissive because of the continuing political influence of prodevelopment residents. As development proceeds, new residents with only their homestead at stake take over local government and enact increasingly restrictive land use ordinances. (Even if development interests foresee this, there is little they can do about it, since, as part of the police power, future zoning cannot be made subject to present contracts.)

As a result of zoning's usual ontogeny, there is no set of local governments that perfectly matches the Tiebout-Hamilton model's assumptions. The number of local governments is finite, so some preferences (for example, no schools) will not be satisfied. Zoning cannot completely discriminate by type of user, so some "free riders" as well as "free givers" (those who pay more in property taxes than they get in services) will often coexist in heterogeneous communities.

Because many apparent free givers bought their properties after the fiscal transfer was apparent, they will have paid less for their property and hence may be less generous than appearances would suggest. A 1981 Dartmouth undergraduate thesis by Jon Bain found that the value of houses in nearby Vermont, which has an income tax, could be bought for less than those in New Hampshire, which has none. (Bain used the unique sample of Hanover, N.H., and Norwich, Vt., which have a joint secondary-school system financed by a single property tax, so major service differences were controlled for.) The quantitative difference in house values was the capitalized value of the average Vermont income tax, a result also found in Pennsylvania by William Stull and Judith Stull (1991). Bain's result suggests that Dartmouth professors who live in Vermont because it is a more politically correct state in fact sacrifice little for their beliefs.

The same analysis applies to supposed free riders. If low-income people have bought into a previously established "good deal," the previous owner probably sold the house or the apartment for a higher price. Bruce Hamilton (1976) found that low-income apartments in otherwise high-income locations were priced higher, so that more than half of the fiscal "windfall" was in fact paid in higher rents or housing prices.

Because of such capitalization, limited concessions by communities to accommodate low-income housing do little harm to the efficiency of the Tiebout system. Because the price of such housing will rise owing to the associated fiscal benefits, low- and moderate-income families who decide to locate there will be those who value the local schools and other services especially highly. Hence the Tiebout sorting by demand for local services is kept largely intact.

7.8   Effective Fiscal Zoning Is Not Perfect Zoning

Fiscal zoning is routinely practiced. Local officials are acquainted with the fiscal implications of new development, and they have an array of regulatory devices to deal with it. This does not mean that the property tax and the system of zoning needed to ensure benefit taxation have no inefficiencies (Fischel 1992). Here are some qualifications:

- Fiscal zoning is most effective for new development or extensive redevelopment. Buildings deteriorate, and deterioration may lower property-tax liabilities. Minor expansions and repairs are largely outside fiscal zoning review, but not beyond the notice of the tax assessor. In both instances, the prospect of lower and higher property-tax burdens, respectively, affects owner's incentives. Thus over time, property taxes may have distorting effects. Hamilton (1975a) found that property taxes do seem like deadweight losses when one crosses from the suburbs into the central cities. In the older sections of cities the view of Peter Mieszkowski and George Zodrow (1989) seems more correct: property taxes are real taxes, not fees for service. This may explain why bigger cities have shifted away from property taxes.
- Fiscal zoning can regulate types and sizes of structures but not, for the most part, the occupants of the structures. (Housing reserved for the elderly seems to be acceptable, however, if rationalized in nonfiscal terms.) If a family wants to put four kids in a three-room apartment, there is little the local government can do about it. The fiscal zoner's major premise is that such a situation is unusual, not that it is impossible.
- Fiscal zoning is not much admired because of its apparent regressiveness (Downs 1973). The occasional judicial assaults on it may have some effect, and some local legislatures express reservations about the practice even as they undertake it. But it should be recalled that limited deviations from fiscal zoning practice are tolerable variations on the Tiebout-Hamilton theory. A rich community could salve its conscience or reduce its legal vulnerability by accepting a limited amount of "affordable" housing and then continue to employ fiscal zoning for all other developments. It would have only a one-time capital loss from the expected but limited transfer of wealth to show for it. Indeed, a limited transfer of this sort might be a source of community pride that offsets the loss in value from the fiscal transfer.

The foregoing qualifications do not subvert the basic premise of the previous sections. Local governments are capable of fending off developments that promise to be net fiscal burdens. In doing so, governments may have the support of the land market. William Wheaton (1993) demonstrated that under plausible demand and supply conditions, households will voluntarily sort themselves out in a pattern that looks like the result of fiscal zoning. I am skeptical of the idea that this shows that fiscal zoning is redundant—it's hard to believe so much effort would be devoted to attacking and defending it if it were—but Wheaton's work does help explain fiscal zoning's robustness. Few local government regulations persist in the face of one-sided opposition to market forces. The finding of Daniel McMillen and John McDonald (1991) that land values influence zoning classifications and vice versa is also consistent with my contention that fiscal zoning and market sorting are not entirely in opposition to each other.

This is not to deny that suburban zoning has many drawbacks as a mechanism for promoting efficient land use. (Robert Ellickson 1973; David Mills 1989; Robert Nelson 1977). But zoning is reasonably effective in making nonresidential land uses internalize their local spillover effects (Fischel 1975). It controls intracommunity neighborhood effects and can facilitate orderly growth in ways that are not obviously inferior to private arrangements (Fischel 1994b). Zoning is a necessary part of the Tiebout system, which allows people to choose the schools and local services that they demand. It enables service quality to be capitalized in home values, providing an incentive for voters to monitor public decisions. All this makes the local property tax tolerably efficient. The tolerance is that of the voters, who would otherwise choose a higher level of government to provide and finance many local services. To the extent that local decision making about public services is more efficient than centralized decision making, fiscal zoning promotes public sector efficiency.

7.9 *Local Governments Compete Like Private Corporations*

The American system of local government is often criticized for its apparently random development. I believe that just the opposite is closer to the truth. Local government is a deliberate and efficient product of the openness of American politics. I use "open" in both its political and its economic sense. The political sense means inclusive and participatory, while the economic sense implies the ability to come and go from one place to another (as in "open city" or "open international" models).

My chief historical source for this idea is Eric Monkkonen (1988). His book on American urban development adopts as its central hypothesis that American local governments have entrepreneurially guided their own development at least as much as they have responded to external changes. The latter belief—that cities are reactive rather than forward looking—is the conventional wisdom among economists as well as many historians, and I want to undermine it here by pointing to a few of the indicia.

Municipal corporations were in fact the dominant type of corporation in the United States until after the Civil War. As Monkkonen pointed out, the difficulties of obtaining private corporate charters prior to the general incorporation statutes of the latter half of the nineteenth century made municipalities the best outlet for the savings of strangers. Municipalities competed fiercely with one another for real estate development. Not only did they try to attract business by investing in local infrastructure; they issued bonds, backed by the power to tax, to raise money to pay railroads and factories to come their way.

Although the law of private and municipal corporations has diverged for more than a century, important parallels remain. Vicki Been (1991) has developed the modern parallels between Tiebout's model and the modern corporate model, concluding that competition among governments disciplines overregulation in both instances. In a similar vein, Daniel Fischel (1982) argued that the competition among states for granting corporate charters promotes efficiency. The winners in the so-called race to the bottom for granting corporate charters win because they offer better services and more efficient contractual arrangements, not because they sell out the stockholders in favor of the managers. I advance here a parallel argument against another allegation of a "race to the bottom" among local governments seeking to attract industry for fiscal or employment reasons.

"Race to the bottom" is a common epithet used by critics of competition among government units. It is a common criticism of market competition, as well. Who has not heard it said of competitive bidding for construction contracts that it means that the cheapest, meanest supplier will be the builder? In the political world, the claim is that by offering businesses inducements to locate in their jurisdictions, governments give away much of the fiscal benefits they want business there for in the first place, or they sacrifice other goods, like environmental quality, in their rush to get tax revenues or jobs.

The response is that they will do *some* of that, and they should (Oates and Schwab 1988). If all local governments insisted on pristine environments, there would be no place to develop factories and homes, let alone the necessary nuisances of dumps and power plants. If all governments resisted the siren song of employment, there would be few places to work. For jurisdictions to compete for jobs and taxes no more engenders a "race to the bottom" than competition for students prevents American colleges from maintaining academic standards. They dare not set undergraduate standards impossibly high, but they lose their reputations if they set them too low. (Evidence that governments worry about reputations will be reviewed in section 8.2.)

The more sober issue is not the conclusive characterization of "racing" to some extreme. It is whether local governments are more likely than some other body to make the wrong trade-off between environment and development. To the extent that their decisions affect jurisdictions whose representatives do not participate in the decisions, they might do so, and some measure of intervention by a higher level of government or by a federation of local governments might be warranted. In his survey of the literature, however, Richard Revesz (1992) concluded that the race-to-the-bottom rationale for federal (as opposed to state) environmental regulation is widely believed but not empirically supported.

The robustness of the median voter model in local government samples suggests that, within the boundaries of the community, environmental decisions about business locations reflect what a majority of people actually want (Erickson and Wollover 1987; William Fischel 1975, 1979). Moreover, the phenomenon of capitalization makes it reasonable to suppose that future generations will be taken into account. The notion that voters care only about present cash benefits and not future costs is confuted by the fact that future costs and benefits affect the present value of their major asset, their homes.

7.10 Local Government Has an Ambiguous Constitutional Status

The Constitution of the United States says nothing about the status of local governments. As a result, it is bedrock law that local governments are creatures of the state. The state creates the boundaries and can change them at will by altering the instruments that created them. Contrast this elasticity to the status of the states in the U.S. Constitution. Article IV says that no state may be divided without the consent of its legislature, and Article V puts a state's equal representation in the Senate beyond even the formal amendment process. But the stark distinction between local governments and states hides much ambivalence about local government on the part of constitutional courts. In important instances, the U.S. Supreme Court has refused to regard localities as simply deriving their power from the state (Gerald Neuman 1987).

The most dramatic example of judicial recognition of local governments as independent entities is the one-person, one-vote issue. In the 1960s, a group of U.S. Supreme Court decisions held that it was contrary to the Fourteenth Amendment for states to apportion their legislatures on any but the principle of one person, one vote. If the Court had regarded local governments as merely creatures of properly apportioned legislatures, then it would presumably not be bothered by the willingness of a state legislature to tolerate local governments that were organized on a different basis, say, one acre, one vote. The Court has not supervised the selection of members of important commissions set up by state legislatures or the governor. It makes no sense to do so if the people who appointed the commissions were themselves selected by an acceptably democratic process.

But the analogy of local governments as being subservient to the state did not work. In Avery v. Midland County (1968), the Court held that a local government could not use the subservience-to-the-state argument as an escape from the equal apportionment principle. Only in the case of specialized water districts has the Court found any exception to the one vote per capita rule, although Briffault (1993) has suggested some expansion of this exception. Thus in applying one of the most important democratic "process-oriented" reforms of the Warren Court (section 3.13), local governments were implicitly recognized as being governments that were independent of their creators, the states.

If local governments possess some independent status, might a corporate analogy work better? Although I pressed the corporate analogy in the previous section, the distinction between a government and a firm is important to understand. Several economists and lawyers have remarked on the similarities of local governments to private organizations such as condominium homeowner associations and private communal groups (Barzel and Sass 1990; Benham and Keefer 1991; Robert Ellickson 1982a). The temptation is to consider local government to be just like such associations, as Tiebout did.

The U.S. Supreme Court for a time seemed to accept the simile. In a spate of opinions in the 1970s, the Court held that in certain instances, local governments, unlike state governments, could be held liable under the Sherman Antitrust Act. This made them seem like private corporations, at least in some respects. But the business analogy was not robust. The U.S. Supreme Court cut back on local government liability a few years later (Stuart Deutsch 1984), and Congress in 1984 specifically exempted local governments from the most onerous burdens of the Sherman Antitrust Act (Mark Perry 1990). Local government monopolies are penalized only by injunctions, rather than triple damages, for most violations. Few private businesses other than major league baseball have been able to achieve such preferred status. It seems that for the most part, local governments are treated differently from businesses.

7.11 *Municipal Corporations Have Involuntary Members*

So far I have shown that local governments are regarded in the law as neither simple creatures of the state nor independent corporations. It might help to understand this ambiguous status by exploring some of the functional distinctions between private and municipal corporations. The most distinct characteristics of local governments are the lack of alternative decision-making arrangements (as opposed to jurisdictions) and the immobility of certain assets within their borders. A person who wishes not to be subject to the collective decisions of a private homeowner association, to take the closest analogy, can easily find forms of property ownership that require no collective decision making at all. One can own one's own home in fee simple. Avoidance of any but majority-rule decision making for public life, however, is impossible for the Tiebout migrants.

Although people are free to withdraw from local governments that adopt policies that they do not like, they cannot withdraw immobile assets from jurisdictions whose laws threaten to devalue those assets. It might be argued that the decision to purchase land in a majoritarian government structure implies acceptance of that risk, but such an argument supposes that there was an avoidable risk. It would be avoidable only if there were other governments that made decisions otherwise, and, under the one-person, one-vote rule, there are no such governments in the United States except a few water-supply districts.

There is some measure of protection for landowners prior to the establishment of governments. Briffault (1993) reviewed cases in which courts permitted residents in already-established governments to avoid annexation by larger governments, thus providing a measure of protection to low-density suburbs from city domination. There have also been instances of landowners who have sought to be annexed by one jurisdiction and not others. Secession by a minority of landowners from already-established governments, however, is next to impossible. There are no landowners who have avoided the consequences of one person, one vote once a general purpose, local government was established.

Not that some have not tried. My favorite example is that of Walt Disney World in Florida (*Wall Street Journal,* July 9, 1985). The Disney Corporation induced the Florida legislature to charter it as a governmental agency separate from any municipality or county. This arrangement allowed Disney to write its own rules and raise taxes for its own public infrastructure. But there was a minor detail the Disney planners had overlooked. When it came time to develop a residential community next to the theme park, it dawned on them that the first residents would be able to vote. There was no way to disfranchise them. Fearing that initial residents would vote to change the master plan and channel tax resources to themselves, the Disney Corporation changed its plan to exclude any permanent residents other than Disney personnel. The change nearly bankrupted the fledgling effort.

I have so far advanced what to some may seem like a trivial proposition, that local governments are actually governments. My purpose is to combat a nontrivial retort to my claim that local governments ought to be subject to takings law. If local governments were merely administrative units of the state, my claim that they should be subject to a different level of judicial scrutiny than the state would fail. Subsidiarity to the state would not preclude all judicial review of local zoning, but it would be along the lines of judicial review of administrative agencies, a standard of lighter burden and different purposes than the takings issue.

My argument that landowners are sometimes isolated minorities would also be difficult to sustain. I proposed in section 3.23 that landowners can generally protect their rights well enough at the state level through the usual efforts that public choice scholars condemn as rent-seeking. Why, then, can't owners of undeveloped land in Tiburon or Petaluma round up other landowners and get the state to disallow the zoning laws that so burden them?

They do try. I will describe in Chapter 8 a few instances involving rent control and other issues. But local governments are harder to beat than just any interest group because local governments are regarded as governments. They get special privileges from the legislature as well as from the courts on that account. A legislator inclined to rein in local government rent control does not simply encounter opposition from tenant organizations. She will encounter opposition from the league of cities, who will remind her that political organizations within the state are almost exclusively divided along the lines of local government boundaries. Even cities that lack rent control will be opposed in principal to an erosion of their discretionary use of the police power. Legislative electoral districts, which are divided to equalize the number of people in each district as much as possible, are nonetheless typically divided by local government boundaries. Attempts to maintain such lines are one of the few reasons that courts sometimes accede to less than numerically perfect equality between legislative districts.

7.12   Dillon's Rule Was the Touchstone of Judicial Skepticism

The previous section suggested that local governments have a functional independence from the state. It also alluded, again, to the greater vulnerability of owners of immobile property at the local level. These two conditions help explain why state courts have historically felt compelled to supervise local affairs when the same legislation adopted at the state level would not evoke judicial intervention. The classic example of such special intervention was advanced in 1871 by the distinguished judge John Dillon.

Dillon's Rule still forms the touchstone of legal treatises and courses on local government law. (I rely principally on Joan Williams [1986].) The rule holds that grants of power from the state to the municipality are to be construed narrowly. If the local government is not specifically granted the power to, say, start a business, then a judge must overturn any such attempts as being beyond the powers of the municipality. If this rule seems perfectly reasonable to the reader, consider that the judicial treatment of charters of private corporations at the time was just the opposite. Efforts by the states to restrict the scope of private corporate conduct were disfavored by the courts, but municipal corporations were by Dillon's Rule held by a much tighter leash to the instruments of their creation, state legislation.

The contemporaneous contrary opinion was held by Judge Thomas Cooley, among the most influential writers on constitutional interpretation of the Gilded Age. Cooley's *Constitutional Limitations* (1868) is regarded as laying the scholarly foundation of laissez-faire constitutionalism, whose apotheosis was Lochner v. New York (1905). The focus of Cooley's writing was not local government, and there is no "Cooley Rule" to counter Dillon's. Nonetheless, Cooley was a champion of the "inherent powers" view of local government. Although he could not avoid the fact that local government was not mentioned in the U.S. Constitution, he seems to have regarded its failure to guarantee the right of local self-governance as a regrettable oversight.

Cooley's idea that local government was a natural and necessary part of a constitutional scheme of self-government was widely shared. Local governments in most states, including those that were admitted from territorial status, predated the state government. Forrest McDonald (1985, p. 149) has pointed out that two Revolutionary War–era state constitutions, those of Massachusetts and New Hampshire, sought popular legitimacy from a vote of the towns. The two states were significant because they were the first to depart from the model of legislatures themselves drawing up and ratifying state constitutions. Popular sovereignty was initially viewed as equivalent to local government sovereignty.

Joan Williams (1986) has submitted that Dillon and Cooley were both concerned about the abuse of government power, but for different reasons. Local governments of their day were often eager to promote railroads. Dillon as a judge saw the downside risk of local governments' use of tax dollars to promote dubious railroad development projects. He was alarmed that a simple majority could plight the assets of all taxpayers in support of questionable projects, and he developed his rule of statutory construction of local government to rein in this abuse.

Cooley was also concerned about the abuse of government power, but chiefly that of the state legislature. Like modern public choice scholars, he saw the state legislature as being dominated by special interests, which led to favoritism. Cooley was a Jacksonian in outlook, skeptical of the power of state and national government not so much because it would redistribute from rich to poor as because it would redistribute from poor to rich. He viewed local governments as less inclined to that tendency and thus as an important offset to the machinations of state legislatures. Hence Cooley was willing to see local governments as independent of the state in instances in which the state tried to curb local authority in order to execute some scheme. His view was parallel to those who promoted state constitutional reforms such as home-rule charters for cities to keep legislatures from meddling in local affairs.

7.13 Modern Liberals Divide on Local Government

Cooley and Dillon would both qualify as conservatives in modern eyes. They disagreed primarily about which type of government was more dangerous to private property. Most modern conservatives regard all levels of government with more or less equal skepticism (Richard Epstein 1992a; Kmiec and Diamond 1984). The modern legal debate about the status of local governments is largely between parties who are arrayed along the leftward side of the political spectrum, but parallel issues are raised.

The traditional side of the liberal spectrum regards localism as a source of insular privilege (Briffault 1990). It urges the state government to equalize school expenditures among rich and poor communities and to rezone exclusionary suburbs to accommodate low-income housing. In its eagerness to centralize local school finance and to infringe on local zoning discretion, the modern liberal position seems to have embraced Dillon's skepticism of local majoritarianism. It is not because of Dillon's fear that municipalities oppressed owners of private property within their jurisdiction, but because of local governments' unwillingness to share their resources with outsiders. Like Dillon, modern liberals cast their lot with higher levels of government, though for obviously different purposes.

The farther-left spectrum among lawyers has taken a position similar to Cooley's. It regards local governments as important sources of the old New Left's "participatory democracy." (This has been dubbed "republican virtue" since the graying of the New Left.) Adherents of this perspective are led by the Critical Legal Studies luminary Gerald Frug (1980) and take their inspiration from Tom Hayden's transformation of Santa Monica, California, from a middle-class suburb into what a detracting local billboard proclaimed "the People's Republic of Santa Monica." These communitarian writers see virtue in what Dillon saw as a vice. There is often plenty of wealth to redistribute within a community by highly democratic processes. Santa Monica is best known for its stringent rent-control laws, but it is also famous among land use experts for its ability to extract financial exactions from local developers. It is little wonder that Frug should set up Dillon's Rule as the prevailing ethos to be disparaged.

7.14 Dillon's Rule Addressed Local Majoritarianism

Dillon's Rule as a serious constraint on local government activities in fact died a long time ago. One reason was the rise of home-rule charters for cities, which were often established by legislation and sometimes in state constitutions. Neil Littlefield (1962) explained that the home-rule movement was largely intended to insulate cities from legislative meddling, but he also noted that it undermined Dillon's Rule, which promoted judicial meddling in local affairs. Home-rule cities are usually large ones, so the main application of Dillon's Rule would be to smaller cities and towns. But even for general-incorporation (rather than home-rule) cities, the courts have long since backed off from any serious review. Euclid v. Ambler (1926) and related state decisions that upheld zoning made it clear that local governments could exercise the police power under general statutory authority. (State courts that resisted zoning were sometimes reversed by constitutional amendments, as in New Jersey and Georgia, the latter complained of by a state judge in Vulcan Material v. Griffith [1960].)

Dillon's Rule died partly because local governments were successful in persuading state legislators to delegate authority in language sufficiently broad that a narrow judicial construction was nearly impossible. The coffin was nailed shut by the 1930s judicial retreat from review of economic legislation at all levels of government. Frug's idea that local government enterprises are inhibited by the ghost of Dillon was confuted by Robert Ellickson (1982a), who uncovered evidence that it is local voters, not Dillon-inspired judges, who have rejected local government forays into banking and other types of business.

Eric Monkkonen (1988, 1990) has demonstrated that Dillon's Rule in fact never had much influence even in its supposed heyday. The constitutional manifestation of Dillon's Rule was the reformist Illinois constitution of 1870, which was influential across the nation. It set limits on local government debt and fiscal discretion for much the same reasons that Dillon did. Local governments had gotten themselves into trouble by lending money to development schemes, especially railroads, that later defaulted and left local taxpayers with the bill. This was the problem that most disturbed Dillon, too. Monkkonen's research has shown, however, that neither the Illinois limitations nor the judicial rule was much of a constraint on local governments. Municipalities continued to lend to railroads and other businesses, who seemed undeterred by the fact that the bonds were no longer as legally secure as they had been.

This is not to deny that modern judges sometimes invoke Dillon-style reasons to strike down local laws that they find offensive (Early Estates v. Housing Board 1961). But there is nothing especially compelling about their invocation of Dillon. One gets the sense that some other rationale could be found as well.

The persistence of references to Dillon's Rule by judges, despite the general ineffectiveness of the doctrine, suggests that there is an ongoing but unarticulated concern. The original problem that Dillon wanted to address was local majoritarianism, which had opportunities to exploit immobilized wealth. It is this problem that I believe the regulatory takings issue is best suited to address. Dillon's Rule provides a judicial tool that is too broad for the problem. Overbreadth of legal doctrine invites judges to intervene in political processes when no intervention is necessary as well as when it is well justified. The chief discipline on local government majoritarianism is the threat of mobility.

The difference between local government and higher governments is not simply that exit from a local jurisdiction is easier. The structure of the "voice" is substantially different. The most obvious difference, as Saul Levmore (1992) has explained, is bicameralism, which is ubiquitous at the state and national level, but nearly absent at the local level. (Smaller local governments also often lack a well-defined distinction between the executive and legislative branches of government.) Bicameralism is useful as a stopping device, a way to protect against majority tyranny of the state and national governments. Levmore explained that it is absent at the local level in large part because the threat

of exit keeps majority exploitation at bay. He mentioned two exceptions to the exit option, rent control and zoning, and noted that these
are best controlled by the takings clause. I would add that it is precisely
because of the immobility of real estate and the absence of institutions
such as bicameralism that the courts are the only means of protection
of such constitutional rights.

7.15   The Decline of "Land at Risk" Contributed to the Rise of Zoning

In the twentieth century, many local governments have shifted from
the promotion of economic activity, the excesses of which Dillon worried about, to retarding economic activity, at least that which is inconsistent with the quiet enjoyment of residential areas. The specific
excesses about which Dillon was concerned have faded, but the majoritarian problem remains. Where once local governments bound minority property owners to financial obligations that they did not want,
now local governments saddle minority property owners with regulatory burdens that similarly devalue their property.

In this section and the next, I will examine the turning point between these two excesses as an explanation for the rise of zoning in the
United States. The reason for explaining this, aside from correcting
common misconceptions, is to show why, despite much scholarly criticism, zoning is here to stay. We need to learn to live with the tension
between public and private property rights, and a regulatory takings
doctrine must be sensitive to it.

Zoning had police-power precursors in the nineteenth century, but
none of them applied their regulations to entire communities. The first
comprehensive zoning laws, which applied a plan of community development to every square inch of the community, did not appear until
after 1910. Given that I regard such zoning as a necessary condition to
capitalization of community benefits and costs, why did zoning not
appear much earlier?

I claimed in section 2.9 that constitutional protections of property
emerged from the high regard for property by democratic constitution
makers. Property's elevated status came from experience, but it was a
special kind of experience. Landownership was widespread in the pre-
Revolutionary period and through the nineteenth century (Stephen
Siegel 1986, p. 83). It was not just the "quiet enjoyment" of land that

made it attractive. Landownership was an important vehicle for creating wealth, and the ability to acquire and develop it were regarded as essential for both political and personal development (James Ely 1992a). "Land at risk," to reiterate Willard Hurst's famous phrase, was given priority in eminent domain and other legal doctrines over "land at rest" (1956).

Landownership is still widespread late in the twentieth century, but the nature of the land that is most commonly owned has drastically changed. Most people own land sometime during their lives. It is the land under their houses. Such land seldom exceeds a fraction of an acre in area. Few owners of residential parcels have plans to transform their property into something much different, or to use their property for anything besides a place of residence. The type of land owned by the vast majority of landowners today is "land at rest," though the phrase might ring off-key to weekend gardeners.

Nearly all observers who discussed zoning's short history in a 1931 symposium on zoning expressed amazement at its rapid rise between 1916, when New York City adopted zoning, and 1930 (W. L. Pollard 1931). The spread of state environmental protection statutes following the national legislation of 1970 was almost as rapid, but zoning involved decisions by thousands of local government units, not scores of state governments. The enthusiasm for zoning seemed like a mania resembling the dance crazes of the 1920s.

I submit that the shift toward a society in which most owners hold land largely for passive, residential purposes accounts for the rise of zoning at the beginning of the twentieth century. (Note this says most *owners*, not most land.) Historical accounts of the rapid rise of zoning are not satisfying. They are not so much wrong as untimely. Yes, urbanization was proceeding and urban life is complicated, requiring much coordinating regulation. But urban life has always been complicated, and there was no sudden spurt in urbanization during the early decades of the twentieth century. Progressive ideology did promote notions of scientific planning, as Robert Nelson has argued (1979), but it is not obvious why that should have taken the peculiar form of comprehensive municipal zoning. And maybe the rise of planning theories was more a result of the conditions that made zoning a ripe political movement. After all, one could say that sending Americans to the moon was the result of scientific advances, but that science was called forth and channeled into space exploration by powerful political forces.

I am skeptical of the conventional explanations of zoning's rapid expansion because several studies have shown that zoning was not a rational response to external costs in urban neighborhoods. Bernard Siegan's (1972) study of unzoned Houston showed that general land use patterns are much the same there as in cities that have long had zoning. Andrew Cappell's (1991) block-by-block study of New Haven on the eve of zoning's adoption by that city revealed that a mixture of private and public law had accomplished most of the protections promised by zoning. Daniel McMillen and John McDonald (1993) undertook an economic study of Chicago's 1925 adoption of zoning. They showed that the promises of land-value enhancement by zoning were not warranted. Sam Bass Warner's (1962) history of the suburbanization of Boston in the prezoning 1880s revealed patterns of neighborhood income-segregation that are nowadays attributed to zoning.

But if zoning did not really change things much, why was it so popular? It was popular, I submit, because by 1920 or so, most owners of land did not want things to change much. Zoning validated the desires of the passive owners of land, urban and suburban homeowners, at least when the political system offered them the opportunity to outvote development interests (James Clingemeyer 1993). That is why zoning invariably puts the single-family, owner-occupied home at the peak of its hierarchy of uses. That is why zoning is so widespread and is taken so seriously in the suburbs, where the owner-occupant is sovereign.

7.16 Suburbanization and Automobiles Also Promoted Zoning

A related trend in the early 1900s that promoted zoning was the rapid growth of the independent suburb, in which the majority of the population were not only homeowners but also worked in another jurisdiction. Independent suburbs had long been a feature of American urban form, but by the 1920s, their increasing numbers were of sufficient concern that the National Municipal League established a task force to deal with the issue. Its 1930 report, *Government of Metropolitan Areas,* expressed concern that the former method of dealing with suburban independence, annexation of the suburbs by the central city, had been retarded by many state laws requiring the consent of the suburbs to be annexed. (It is still difficult to change boundaries when the suburbs are already incorporated, according to Dennis Epple and Thomas Romer [1989].) It is evident from the league's report that most large metropolitan populations still resided in the central city in 1920. In Boston and Pittsburgh, however, the suburbs' population considerably outnumbered that of the central city, and this pattern was on the road to becoming the norm for most other large areas during the decade.

Independent suburbs behaved differently from central cities in part because they separated workplace from residence. This changed economic motives in local politics. Owners of developable property in suburbs could not as easily appeal to the economic self-interest of resident homeowners, since the economic benefits of new jobs and more goods were spread over the entire metropolitan area. As time went on, suburbs began to be created specifically to have their own zoning laws. For example, Richard Cion (1966) explained that the Lakewood plan, in which newly created suburbs of Los Angeles contracted with the county for most services, was motivated entirely by the suburbs' desire to have zoning independent of the prodevelopment city of Los Angeles.

But why didn't homeowners of the 1920s seek to maintain their land use patterns in the traditional ways, if the traditional ways had already supplied generally amenable neighborhoods? The old ways were regarded as inferior because it was becoming increasingly difficult to keep the patterns from changing. It is one thing to say that the patterns that developed looked a lot like those that zoning supposedly accomplishes, and quite another to say that those patterns would have persisted into the future under traditional legal rules. Residential neighborhoods were often subject to redevelopment for apartments. Unwelcome commercial development did spread out from its historical confines. Two contemporary, pre-*Euclid* sources that point to zoning as a solution to these problems are a municipal government text by Chester Hanford (1926) and a realtor-sponsored work by Stanley McMichael and Robert Bingham (1923).

The increasing threat to residential neighborhoods by nonresidential uses and large apartment buildings was caused by the automobile and the motor bus, which altered the routes of traffic in ways far less predictable than did traditional streetcar lines. Cappel and Warner both noted that controlling streetcar lines had been an important political means of controlling neighborhood development, a control that automobiles were not subject to. Monkkonen (1988, p. 177) likewise showed that automobile and motortruck development allowed considerably more infill development in cities and suburbs, where most suburban development had been along streetcar and railway spokes. I submit that under these conditions zoning was a rational way for the new majority of owners of "property at rest" to protect their property values.

7.17 Homeowners Have Come to Dominate Land Use Politics

Other evidence for my thesis is provided by the fact that during the early decades of zoning "passive-use" homeowners had became more numerous than owners who held property for business or speculative uses. In the latter category I include all farmers, who usually owned their homesteads, but whose wealth was chiefly defined by the commercial value of their landholdings. Owner-occupants edged up from 38 percent of all nonfarm households in 1910 to 41 percent in 1920, and then 46 percent in 1930. Contrary to the traditional tenement-house view of urban housing at the turn of the century, single-family houses constituted about two-thirds of all new urban housing units in the period 1870–1930, and the 1920s experienced an unprecedented boom in construction (Robert Barrows 1983, p. 398). By the 1920s, the majority of property owners in the United States were owners because they owned a house in which they resided, not because they owned a farm or other land whose potential for development was important to them.

The other evidence on this is from a cross-section comparison of which jurisdictions have zoning and which do not. There are a large (though declining) number of local governments that do not have zoning at all. Nearly all of the examples occur in rural areas. Rural areas dislike zoning because farmers and many other rural residents want to retain the option to develop their land (Alan Hahn 1970). A fascinating study of rural Connecticut by Thomas Rudel showed that the "unzoned" smaller towns in fact relied on an informal system of zoning based on neighborly norms that responded to spillover concerns (1989). Only after the towns became suburbanized and relational constraints were loosened did small towns adopt formal zoning.

The transformation of the ownership of land from active to passive users gradually undermined the political protections for property. With a large majority of owners of property interested in preserving the status quo, judicial review rather than politics became the fallback protection. Judges have progressively fled the scene on the mistaken idea that politics at the local level is essentially the same as politics at the state and national level.

7.18 The Property Tax Has Declined but Still Survives

American local government and its property-tax and zoning trappings represent an unusual, if not unique, government arrangement among the nations of the world. Federalism is common enough among countries. Enough federal countries exist for there to have been comparative studies of it, some noting the positive association between federalism and political freedom. But this is the federalism of the state versus nation variety. The American microfederalism of independent *local* governments is not common.

This condition has been noticed before. Many American reformers, on both the left and the right, have deplored the fragmentation of metropolitan areas and states. Commissions have at many times in the past urged the consolidation of American governments in metropolitan areas. Legislatures have experimented from the origins of the Republic with removing traditionally local functions, such as education or land use planning, to the state. The property tax has been under continuous assault by economists for at least a century, and it is widely regarded as the least popular tax.

Yet all of the indicia of localism survive. Zoning has survived attempts to adopt statewide land use controls in the 1970s. Dubbed the Quiet Revolution in a book by Fred Bosselman and David Callies (1972), the new state regulations were regarded as the wave of the future. The courts enthusiastically waved the revolution on, finding there was no constitutional objection, federal or state, to having the state take over duties that were traditionally local. Yet the Quiet Revolution is nearly silent now (Callies 1980). Some of it survives in the form of double-veto arrangements, in which local government approval of certain types of projects can be overridden by a state commission (Frank Popper 1988). But it is a mark of the political success of localism that few of these commissions can make the locals accept land uses they do not want.

Local property taxes fund a declining fraction of local expenditures, but the overall statistics mask the fact that most local governments continue to rely on property taxes. Most of the decline in the property tax has come from increased federal aid to large cities. In Mark Schneider's national sample of more than one thousand suburbs, state and federal aid accounted for only 21 percent of total suburban revenues in 1982, as compared with 51 percent for all cities and suburbs taken together (1989, p. 180). Large cities have also substituted sales and income taxes for property taxes in those same jurisdictions.

7.19   Voters Prefer the Tiebout World

The property tax has persisted despite the existence of numerous occasions on which it could be abolished by the voters. State constitutions, which authorize the types of taxes and designate the jurisdictions that can employ them, are often amended, usually by a process far simpler than that required by the U.S. Constitution. On these occasions, an unpopular tax can be changed.

The most persistent issue has been the use of the property tax to finance local schools. While state legislatures have for more than a century increased the fraction of education funding that comes from the state, sweeping reform proposals have usually been defeated when put to popular vote. School finance issues were the focus of statewide plebiscites in the early 1970s. Voters in Colorado, Michigan, Maine, Oregon, and California rejected by substantial margins proposals to reduce local property taxes and transfer the education functions they financed to the state (Campbell and Fischel 1994; Paul Carrington 1973). Studies of local referenda likewise show that voters support property taxes when they buy better schools (Hahn and Kamieniecki 1987; Sonstelie and Portney 1980b). It is a tribute to the displacement effect of judicial review that these statewide exercises in self-governance virtually ceased as soon as advocates of school finance equalization began to succeed in the courts in the 1970s.

The most dramatic apparent exception to my contention that voters prefer local taxes is the 1978 voter initiative in California, Proposition 13. There the voters really did cut property taxes and, of necessity, shifted almost all of the burden of financing schools to the state. As I have argued in two articles (1989, 1994a), Proposition 13 was a perfectly rational response by voters after the California Supreme Court had ruled in Serrano v. Priest (1976) that there could be no significant variations in local spending for schools due to differences in property-tax base. Without a connection between local property taxes and local school quality, voters have little reason to put up with property taxes. As I mentioned in the Introduction, my research into the consequences of the *Serrano* decisions has been a turning point in my view of the legitimacy of judicial review.

The property tax also survives because local officials and voters have, when not constrained by the courts, adjusted it to become a benefit tax. Examples of such adjustments are reduced taxation of farmland and other open spaces that impose few fiscal burdens, reductions for elderly taxpayers who might otherwise oppose school spending, and establishment of special-purpose taxing districts to provide services according to a geographic area that does not necessarily correspond to municipal boundaries (Inman and Rubinfeld 1979).

It is too much to suggest that the system of local government is a truly natural occurrence, as Robert Ellickson has suggested the institution of property in land is (1993). Local government seems too much of an American institution to make that claim. But as the nation that pioneered the idea of self-governance in a large republic, perhaps the better question is why other countries do not have local government to the same degree.

7.20 Conclusion: The Limits of Communitarianism

In chapter 6, I argued that newly restrictive zoning laws are capitalized in property values, making community insiders—mostly homeowners—better off and owners of undeveloped land worse off. Local land use regulations are an unusually effective means of transferring wealth from a distinct minority to a political majority and should thus be subject to special scrutiny under the Takings Clause. The present chapter has also looked at capitalization, this time from a more optimistic view of local government. Local governments that provide better services at a lower tax cost reward their citizens with higher home values. Local zoning to regulate subsequent development is necessary to enable service and tax capitalization, which provides desirable incentives for local government enterprise and efficiency. I have even gone so far as to suggest that local zoning is so durable and ubiquitous that it should be respected as a propertylike entitlement by the courts.

The findings of this chapter seem to provide some support for a communitarian view of local government (Frug 1980; Cass Sunstein 1985). In this view, democratic political action is not just an aggregation of personal preferences. Collective groups, particularly where personal participation is widespread, themselves shape preferences. (The reader's own preferences may be gauged by whether the last sentence leads him or her to think of Sunday schools or Stalinist reeducation camps.) In doing so, they help resolve commons problems within the group. Thus local collective actions are to be accorded an independent legitimacy that trumps traditional notions of private property.

Many of the differences in theories of takings arise from the view that one holds about the best way to organize human activity in small areas. Private property in land is one way of doing this. Fee ownership facilitates personal autonomy and consensual exchange. The considerable merits of private property have led Richard Epstein (1985) to deduce rules for compensation for takings from the common-law rules that govern individual relationships. His result obviously does not square with existing takings law, however, and would require a major judicial revolution to make it work (sections 4.19–4.25). Communitarians take the opposite view. They regard private transactions as destructive of community values, and they put stock in nonmarket, political resolutions (William Simon 1991). The communitarian view deplores all limitations on the regulatory authority of local governments, thus resolving the takings issue by reading it out of the Constitution.

Both views tend to undervalue local coordination problems (Ellickson 1993). The private-property approach regards local public goods as a problem easily solved, or at least not very costly to fail to solve. The communitarian view tends to overlook the coordination problem of small republics in a larger state, in which the interests of the smaller parts must be reconciled with the whole. Private property is better at the latter problem because it responds to the votes of outsiders—their willingness to pay for new homes and businesses—in a way that local communitarianism usually cannot.

The relative merits of these two views can be explored in regulatory takings decisions by imagining zoning as a substitute for private protection of communal property values. Privately planned communities mimic many of the restrictions imposed by zoning. New cities such as Reston (Virginia), Columbia (Maryland), and Foster City (California) were each developed by a single owner. Their internal land use restrictions, imposed by the developer and eventually administered by resident homeowners, are much like municipal zoning. (I discussed Foster City in Fischel [1994b].) People who buy homes in these communities formally acquire communal property rights, and I believe that such entitlements ought to be available to communities that were not lucky enough to have proprietors as farsighted as T. Jack Foster.

There is a crucial difference between the regulation of privately planned communities and municipal zoning, however. Developers of private communities have always taken pains to see to it that initial residents do not take over the land development apparatus so as to change the rules and admit new residents on less favorable terms than they themselves were admitted (Uriel Reichman 1976). Early residents of Foster City could not prevent the subsequent development of open land, unless it had been specifically reserved by the developer as a park. They could not adopt growth moratoriums or impose land use exactions whose purpose was simply to reduce fiscal burdens that they had previously agreed to pay.

The private restrictions on the regulatory powers of residential private government were not, of course, altruistically imposed by the developers. They wanted to make money by selling more lots. But it is precisely that profit motivation that made them aware of the demands of outsiders. Without similar restriction on the scope of municipal zoning laws, local insiders would be insulated from such demands. The result would be the "regulatory commons" of excessively low-density, high-cost developments described in section 6.23.

There is an alternative that would allow for very restrictive zoning but would still take into account the demand by outsiders to become insiders. This would permit communities simply to sell their zoning restrictions to the highest bidder (Fischel 1985; Nelson 1977). After downzoning all their developable space to the lowest possible densities, community authorities would then entertain financial bids from developers, accepting those whose value to the community exceeded the value of leaving the land in open space. The funds thereby raised would be redistributed to existing homeowners and other insiders in the form of property tax rebates. Developers would thus be given permits to build, and additional outsiders would be able to get into the community. (The community would have to devise some way to assure developers that they would not play the downzoning game again before they got a chance to develop.)

The foregoing scheme would promote economic efficiency in that

the community would respond to the demands of outsiders. But offering zoning for sale also shows why efficiency itself is an insufficient
rationale for just compensation under the Takings Clause. The
scheme's straightforward transfer of property rights from outvoted
owners of undeveloped land to a majority of preexisting residents is
what a regulatory takings doctrine most clearly seeks to prevent. If
there is to be any limit on regulation under the Takings Clause, some
limit on the scope of the desirable communitarian values embodied in
local government regulations must be established.

8

How Exit and Voice Discipline
Governmental Excess

It is not difficult to persuade Americans that "exit" is a good thing. Most of us are not many generations removed from ancestors who voted with their feet to try a different life in the United States. We watched for a generation as Communist countries put up fences to keep their citizens from doing the same thing. But the lesson we draw from our roots is colored by selection bias. The arrival of many of our forebears on these shores represents the failure of the threat of exit to discipline bad governments.

The problem with much writing about Albert Hirschman's exit-voice framework is that it focuses excessively on one option or the other and not enough on the interaction between the two. The threat of exit is a valuable bargaining chip that can protect economic interests that might otherwise be characterized as "discrete and insular" from excessive regulation. Focus on this threat alone, however, overlooks that the nature of the political forum in which the bargaining takes place also makes a difference. My experience in studying land use regulation suggests that larger governments (in terms of both land area and population governed) provide a more protective environment for assets that are inelastic in supply than do smaller units of government. This ties in with the theory developed in Chapter 3, which concludes that the national and most state governments should receive more judicial deference than the small republics of most cities, suburbs, and rural townships.

In this chapter I pursue evidence for this theme by describing ex-

amples of contrasting regulatory behavior among the types of governments. My examples range, in increasing order of detailed examination,
from plant-closing laws to billboard regulation, farmland preservation,
and, most extensively, rent control. Their common thread is that
interest-group politics at higher levels of government offer more protection to owners of assets that are inelastic in supply and thus more
vulnerable to regulatory takings. The proper locus of judicial attention
is local governments and state and federal agencies removed from the
give-and-take of pluralistic politics.

8.1 State Regulation Responded to the Tastes of Immigrants

Early American immigrants were attentive to the forms of property and
its regulation. James Ely (1992a, chap. 1) pointed out that early immigrants to America were often motivated by a desire to own property.
This desire seems to have shaped the behavior of colonial proprietors,
who, in yet another "race to the bottom," offered more and more
favorable terms of property tenure. Some colonial proprietors, however, did not immediately respond to the competition. New York was
initially settled by Dutch proprietors who maintained a concentrated
system of landholding and permitted only leaseholds. The lack of access to fee-simple ownership deterred immigrants eager to own land.
The fact that immigrants disdained their land system was eventually a
factor in changing New York's laws to permit fee-simple ownership
(p. 12).

Later in our history, internal immigrant groups also appeared to
respond to the regulation of property. Kansas had fitfully attempted to
reduce the consumption of alcoholic beverages. In the post–Civil War
era, the temperance movement shifted to outright prohibition. In
1880, a state constitutional amendment was passed that prohibited the
manufacture and sale of liquor in the state. The legality of this alleged
taking of the property of brewers, distillers, and bar owners was upheld
by the U.S. Supreme Court in Mugler v. Kansas (1887).

Mugler was discussed as an example of judicial deference to police
powers in section 1.2. The decision to sustain prohibition in *Mugler*
was not, however, the end of the line for alcoholic beverages in Kansas.
In his history of the state's prohibition laws, Robert Bader (1986,
p. 111) described continuing battles between the wets and the dries.
One of the points raised by the wets was that prohibition deterred

German-speaking immigrants, who were accustomed to the regular consumption of beer. Bader offered data that seem consistent with the contention. The immigrant groups more inclined to drink settled in disproportionate numbers in neighboring Missouri and Nebraska. Although some of the Kansas dries responded "good riddance" and pointed out that other religious groups more sympathetic to temperance were arriving in Kansas, deterrence of immigrants was considered a serious problem in the 1890s. Most people in Kansas and other western states were eager to attract more settlers.

Modern evidence on political sensitivity to activities in elastic supply is found in the competition among states for industrial jobs. The active manifestations of this are tax breaks to attract new industry. These are perennial, especially during hard times, and ubiquitous among the states. Collusive agreements by states not to compete with one another to attract or retain industry almost always break down. A 1992 example was the failure of New York, New Jersey, and Connecticut to maintain their formal agreement not to compete. With a close election looming and unemployment an issue, New Jersey's Governor Florio broke ranks and started hailing corporations located across the Hudson.

8.2 Plant-Closing Legislation Was Forestalled by State Reputation Concerns

The potential mobility of businesses affects states even when the state has a firm firmly in its grasp. An example is the flurry of interest in plant-closing legislation. In the oil-shock recession of 1973–1975, manufacturing plants often decided to relocate from northern states to the Sunbelt. Popular agitation in northern states induced the passage of plant-closing laws, which were designed to make it more difficult for existing firms to relocate. One such law made it to the U.S. Supreme Court in Allied Structural Steel v. Spannaus (1978). It involved a Minnesota requirement that pensions be vested for employees if an employer moved out of state, even though the preexisting labor contracts had specifically delayed vesting for several years. In a rare and subsequently circumscribed revival of the Contract Clause, the Court ruled that such a rewriting of contracts by the legislature was unconstitutional.

Most other plant-closing legislation did pass constitutional muster, but the courts seem to have been a minor player. The political process limited legislation to a few mild measures in three states that require advance notice (Ehrenberg and Jakubson 1988). The radical economists Barry Bluestone and Bennett Harrison (1982) were proponents of plant-closing legislation to stanch what they called the "deindustrialization" of the United States. They derisively quoted a Massachusetts industry lobbyist who testified in 1979, "Even serious consideration of this bill would be raising a sign on the borders of this state that investment isn't welcome here. A firm with divisions in other states would have one more incentive to expand elsewhere" (p. 240).

In a later work, however, Harrison (1987, p. 316) seemed to concede that the anxiety over the business climate was carrying the day. He noted that Wisconsin first passed, then rescinded its plant-closing laws because of such worries. Another enthusiast of plant-closing penalties, Lawrence Rothstein (1986, p. 38), ruefully noted that Rhode Island bills were defeated as legislators worried that such laws would poison the business climate and deter firms from coming into the state. Even state labor-union leaders conceded the force of what Rothstein called the "myth" of business climate. Reputation is a powerful concern for states.

8.3   Federal Law Protects Billboard Owners from Taking by Amortization

Another example supporting the behavioral distinction between local governments and the federal and state governments is billboard regulation. My discussion is drawn largely from Michael Berger's (1992) article on this subject. The Highway Beautification Act of 1965, commonly known as the Lady Bird Johnson bill, called for the elimination of billboards along highways that were financed by the federal government. This applied to the entire interstate highway system as well as many other roads. As the bill was originally proposed, states and local governments were encouraged to use their police powers to discontinue existing billboards.

The police-power means of removing billboards that Berger was concerned with were "amortization" statutes. They called for the uncompensated removal of nonconforming uses, but only after a period of years, in order to "amortize" the existing use. Amortization had been held by several state courts to satisfy the just compensation requirement for the owner where local governments had sought to eliminate nonconforming uses in newly zoned districts.

Even if a generous idea of "amortization" were subscribed to, it is doubtful that it would amount to just compensation. Amortization traditionally refers to the useful economic life of an asset. But to assume that there is no economic value left over after amortization is wrong. Many homes last much longer than their expected economic life of forty years. No one would suggest that the owners of older homes could be evicted without compensation simply because the original investments were fully amortized.

Most amortization statutes do not actually refer to useful economic life, but to a period of years during which the owner is simply assumed to be able to get an acceptable return on her investment. As the laws have been applied, however, they do not necessarily seem hostile to landowner interests. In many cases, the use to be discontinued seems to have been regarded as bordering on a nuisance. Many courts would have upheld a law requiring immediate removal of the nonconforming use. In such cases, amortization seems more like a legislative compromise in uncertain cases, in which there is some sympathy with the owner whose use has only recently become offensive.

The remarkable thing about the original proposal in Congress to use noncompensable police powers to carry out billboard removal is that it was eliminated. And not just eliminated in favor of leaving the means of discontinuing billboards unspecified. The bill, as amended and passed, required that "just compensation shall be paid upon the removal of any outdoor advertising sign." (Berger 1992, p. 19). More remarkable is that the compensation language was strengthened in 1978 in response to state and local attempts to evade its provisions. The amended act made the principle of compensation by the state or local government more important than the removal of the billboards, as the California Supreme Court ruefully noted in Metromedia v. San Diego (1980).

Berger did not discuss the politics of this event, but it can be readily inferred. The billboard companies had little influence in most local governments. Even if they did have substantial influence in the localities in which they conducted business, the sites of their signs were widely dispersed. Appeals to state government were apt to be more successful because the companies could point to employment benefits to sign painters and the like, and because they could contribute to the election campaigns of key legislators. But this was hit or miss. Some states were inclined to compensate, others not. And, as Berger noted,

most of the uncompensated billboard-removal laws had emerged from
local governments using their generally authorized police powers.

By far the better way to ensure protection of their assets was to lobby
Congress. There was justice in this, insofar as the Congress was putting
up most of the money for the highways, and uniform national standards were being imposed by the Lady Bird Act. The crucial point for
my purposes is that a tiny and unloved minority was better able to
protect its interests at the national level than at the state or local level.
This seems to have been an instance in which interest-group politics
worked most effectively in the larger republic.

8.4   Farmland Preservationists Wanted National Land Use Regulation

The story of agricultural land preservation related in this and succeed-
ing sections is another example of how the political process differs by
level of government. It shows how Congress and, to a lesser but still
important extent, the states respond to proposed economic legislation
according to the pluralistic model of politics, while the subdivisions of
the states responded with different, majoritarian legislation.

In the early 1970s, following the passage of pioneering environmental legislation, environmentalists and planners made it part of their
agenda to establish state and national land use legislation. (One of the
leaders of this movement, William Reilly [1973], became head of the
U.S. Environmental Protection Agency in 1989.) The movement
charged that local governments were making such a hash of land use
regulation that guidance from the state and federal governments was
necessary. While many local governments had adopted increasingly
restrictive zoning and planning laws, environmentalists were frustrated
that others, particularly in rural areas and cities, remained willfully
unprotected from the ravages of developers.

Hearings were held on this program, whose chief sponsor was Senator Henry Jackson (1972), but the effort never got farther than that
stage. It wasn't the constitutional lack of police power (of which zoning is an example) for the federal government that was the problem.
The problem was that senators and representatives heard rather loudly
from local government and allied interest groups that such an intrusion
on local authority was unwelcome.

Environmentalists and professional planners were disappointed by this defeat. Frank Popper (1988) recalled that the head of the American Society of Planning Officials expected a significant rise in the income of planners if Senator Jackson's bills had passed. But their efforts continued in other directions. In the late 1970s, a new proposal for federal authority over local land use was advanced. It was based on the alarming proposition that urban development was threatening the farmland base.

One threat came from an indirect source, in which suburban development was said to make it difficult for farmers who remained in the area to stay in business—the kids-in-the-cornfields syndrome. More dramatic were the direct threats to farmland. According to data gleaned from two federal studies, the absolute amount of land annually "paved over" by urban development increased from about a million acres per year in the 1950s and 1960s to two or three million acres per year in the 1970s. The National Agricultural Lands Study (1981), commissioned in 1979 by the U.S. Department of Agriculture and the President's Council on Environmental Quality, broadcast the bad news. It recommended legislation at the federal, state, and local level to halt the tide of urbanization.

8.5 *Farmland Preservation Failed in Congress*

I won't say that nothing happened as a result of the National Agricultural Lands Study, but the key federal legislation that resulted, the 1981 Farmland Protection Policy Act, was substantially watered down and has had little effect on federal policies. A House of Representatives bill that would have made protection of farmland a goal parallel to that of environmental and endangered species protection was replaced by a Senate version that eviscerated the principal enforcement mechanisms. The bill that passed (Title XV, S. 884, 1981 Farm Bill) specifically forbade legal challenges to federal agency decisions on the basis of farmland protection. Unlike laws preserving wetlands, old-growth forests, endangered species, and barrier beaches, farmland preservation nowadays generates little comment in national publications such as the prodevelopment *Urban Land*.

The reasons for the failure of farmland preservation to maintain its national profile are two. The less important is that the numbers were wrong. I undertook an examination of the data in 1980 and discovered that the studies used to generate the alleged doubling or tripling of urbanization were cut from whole cloth (Fischel 1982). The director of the National Agricultural Lands Study called me up before I published my review and threatened to sue me for libel. I took this as a sign that I was on to something, and I pressed the issue beyond the scholarly journals. My efforts, along with those of a few other skeptics like Julian Simon and Seymour Sudman (1982), may have goaded the agency that produced the suspect data to reassess them. In subsequent studies, the U.S. Department of Agriculture (1984) proved that there had been no increase in the rate of urbanization of farmland after all (Gregg Easterbrook 1986). In addition, the supposed indirect threats to agriculture caused by urbanization were shown to have little basis in fact (John Baden 1984). There is actually some evidence that farmers on balance benefit from the proximity of suburban development (William Lockeretz 1989).

Proving that the data are wrong helps undermine a misguided policy, but what really derailed federal agricultural land preservation was the opposition of powerful interest groups. Previous bills with the same intent were opposed by the American Farm Bureau Federation and the National Cattlemen's Association (Hite and Dillman 1981). The Farm Bureau and the Cattlemen are two of the most powerful agricultural lobbies in Washington. Economists and political scientists often decry the power of such groups to pick the public's pocket with special subsidies (Bruce Gardner 1992). The same organizational advantages, however, also enabled them to protect their property rights from what I would regard as unwarranted infringement by the federal government on the right to use and dispose of their property. (See also Karl Zinsmeister [1993], who decried the "Environmentalist Assault on Agriculture" while providing evidence that farmers are doing all right for themselves in Congress.)

If judges were to disable the rent-seeking activities of the farmers and the cattlemen, as Richard Epstein (1985, p. 308) would have them do, one wonders how farmers would maintain a political organization to protect what I am confident Epstein would regard as their legitimate property rights. (Epstein has informed me that he has done legal work on behalf of the Farm Bureau on these issues.) Indeed, if special-interest legislation at the national level were to provoke more judicial scrutiny, as many politically savvy legal scholars have suggested (and which Einer Elhauge [1991] critically reviewed), my story might have a different ending. Judges might regard it in the public interest to *promote* farmland preservation.

Of course, under Epstein's role for judges, courts would also strike down rent-seeking regulations such as farmland zoning. But whom would the judges rely upon in that case to tell them that it was a bad idea? Even the Illinois courts, among the most solicitous of developers and unashamed of substantive due process review, found that the agricultural zoning of a 160-acre parcel of land bordered on three sides by housing subdivisions was acceptable (Wilson v. McHenry County 1981). The equally prodevelopment Pennsylvania courts have likewise fallen in line (Cordurus Township v. Rodgers 1985), apparently influenced by the bogus government reports about running out of farmland (492 A.2d at 77). (Both of these schemes were local in origin.)

8.6 Local Governments Like Farmland Zoning

The political record of the states on farmland protection is, because there are fifty of them, more mixed. According to a law-review article that endorsed agricultural zoning, only one state, Hawaii, has adopted statewide agricultural zoning (Teri Popp 1989). Nine others specifically authorize local governments to do it, and the other forty states simply allow local governments to zone for farmland if they wish.

State legislatures in their direct actions appear to be as solicitous of farmland owners' rights as the federal government. States with specific programs to preserve farmland authorize compensation or tax breaks for farmers' agreement to forswear development for some period of time. States that authorize exclusive agricultural districts have safeguards that require that most farmers actually vote in favor of the restrictions. Many farmers do so, knowing that the tax breaks and other benefits are worth more than the remote possibility that their land will be salable for development (Henneberry and Barrows 1990; Vitaliano and Hill 1994).

Where farmland owners lose out in the agricultural preservation game is at the local level. Local governments in metropolitan areas have long been the most active progenitors of exclusive farmland zoning that is usually not desired by the landowners who are affected (Peterson and Yampolsky 1975). The question is why farmer organizations are less effective at the local level. An easy and obvious answer is that outside of truly rural areas, owners of farmland and their sympathizers are a distinct minority.

At the level of local government, the advantages of concentrated economic interest groups are greatly diminished. Small-town and suburban politicians seldom need substantial financial assistance from interest groups for their campaigns. Even if the politicians are in the developers' pockets, their constituents are apt to learn about it soon and diminish such politicians' value to owners of undeveloped land. Moreover, at the local level, it is easy for a majority to bypass elected officials entirely. Changes in zoning laws are among the items most often submitted for plebiscites, either as initiatives or as referenda. Logrolling and lobbying are useless in these elections (Callies, Neuffer, and Calibosco 1991; Julian Eule 1990).

8.7 Farmers Cannot Get State Relief from Suburban Controls

The more difficult question is why farmland owners don't appeal to the forum to which they do have good access—the state legislature—to get relief from local controls. Farmers have an enviable record of persuading state legislators to help them on other issues. Local governments supposedly derive their authority from the state, and the state legislature, where not curtailed by state constitutional home-rule provisions, can curb the enthusiasms of local government.

The disabilities of farmland owners in obtaining relief from local regulations at the state capitol are subtle but real. (See also section 7.11.) Most farmers live in areas remote from any development, and so a substantial majority of them favor local control. I find that most people do not easily grasp this point because they have an exaggerated view of how much land is taken up by urban and suburban development. Such development is about 3 percent of the U.S. land area, and it is concentrated in a few counties in any given state. Half of the population of Iowa, to take a major agricultural state, lives in sixteen of its sixty-four counties. A majority of California's fifty-four counties contain only 4 percent of the state's population. The vast majority of farmers could not care less what the zoning policies of the suburbs are. To even consider statewide preemption of local government land use controls would for most of them open a Pandora's box of regulatory legislation.

At the local level, people who favor farmland preservation for its antidevelopment purposes are much better organized. Most local governments are controlled by voters whose primary fiscal interest is in the value of owner-occupied homes (Dubin, Kiewit, and Noussair 1992).

The power of home ownership in uniting people as an interest group is greatly underestimated. Policies that protect or increase the value of existing homes receive the most solicitous concern in local government politics, as I argued in section 7.17. Homeowners thus become dyed-in-the-wool agriculturists when preservation of farmland can stop unwanted development.

Bernard Frieden (1979) discovered this in the early days of modern environmentalism. The major activities of environmental groups in the San Francisco Bay Area involved stopping housing development. The benefits of stopping local development are easily internalized by owners of already-built homes, while clean air and water cannot find well-defined constituencies. This explains what was wrong with Bruce Ackerman's (1977, p. 56) retort to Joseph Sax's (1971, p. 160) plea that environmentalists are poorly organized and so deserve the assistance of judges. Ackerman pointed out that taxpayers, who would have to foot the just compensation bill, are also poorly organized, so there was no special reason to favor environmentalists. Ackerman's point may be correct at the national level, but he overlooked that, at the local level, environmentalists are well organized when they are defending the value of the owner-occupied home.

8.8 *Inefficient State Regulations Often Have Short Lives*

In a seminar called "Economics and Constitutional Law," one of my early assignments asked students to comment on the case of Minnesota v. Clover Leaf Creamery (1981). Minnesota had passed a law banning the use of plastic milk containers. The reason offered was that plastic was not recyclable, and plastic milk containers thus constituted an environmental menace by filling up scarce space in landfills. The more credible reason was that Minnesota has a forest-products industry that is eager to promote the use of paperboard products, and banning the popular and convenient plastic containers was a way of suppressing competition for the hometown favorites.

It did not surprise me that most students wrote papers that criticized the U.S. Supreme Court's decision to reverse the Minnesota Supreme Court and hold that the law did not offend the Due Process and Commerce Clauses. (Plastic containers were mostly made by out-of-state firms.) What did surprise me in the class discussion was a student from Minnesota who remarked, almost apologetically, that milk was in fact available in plastic containers in his home state. I checked this out by calling a Minnesota friend, and a few weeks later on a visit to Minneapolis I went to a convenience store to see for myself. There they were, plastic containers without a hint of a Minnesota forest product on them.

I had a student follow up on the case, and there was no indication that the U.S. Court had changed its mind about plastic or that the Minnesota courts had found a loophole. The law was changed by the state legislature. This encouraged me to see if another famously stupid law was still around. Williamson v. Lee Optical (1955) is often cited as an example of deference by the U.S. Supreme Court to obviously special-interest legislation. The Oklahoma legislature passed a law that required (among other contortions) that before an optician can repair eyeglass lenses, the customer must obtain a prescription from a licensed optometrist or ophthalmologist. There is no credible reason for this law other than that optometrists had a more effective lobby than the opticians in the Oklahoma legislature at the time.

I undertook some Yellow Pages research to see if this irrational law of four-decades vintage was still valid. I located two opticians in Oklahoma City and called them with a pretended problem. I was traveling through and had just cracked a lens in my glasses. I needed it repaired right away. I did not have my prescription with me. Could I come in and have it done?

Sure. But the opticians told me that I had to have a prescription written by a local optometrist. One said that there was an optometrist right across the hall and his services would cost only $10, but nonetheless, the old law still stood. (One optician mentioned the law as the constraint.) To make sure it was really an Oklahoma constraint, I called two opticians in Vermont and New Hampshire with the same story. Come right in, they said. No, you don't need a prescription, and you don't need an eye exam. We can use your cracked lens to reproduce your prescription.

So some bad laws do persist, and people have to adjust to them. The main losers in Oklahoma are consumers, although one of the opticians I contacted there must have been disappointed at losing a sale, since she explained that the nearby optometrist had gone home for the day. Ten bucks additional to replace lenses with almost no gain to the consumer. ("Almost" because an optometrist might sometimes detect unnoticed eye disease, but if that's rational, we might as well require gas stations to check blood pressure with every fill-up.) The question is, is this a taking of someone's property or a violation of due-process rights? As unpleasant as the legislation looks, it is hard to see how it takes what most people would regard as property. Given the record of other states, in which opticians seem not so badly constrained, it is difficult to see how Oklahoma opticians could be said not to have been represented in the political process.

There are more famous examples of bad laws that have gotten changed. The notorious Louisiana butcher's monopoly upheld by the U.S. Supreme Court in the Slaughter-House Cases in 1873 was reversed by a new state constitution that abolished monopolies of this sort. There is a special irony here. The former monopoly sued to retain its monopoly on the grounds that the new state-constitutional provision was an unconstitutional abrogation of the previous state "contract" that granted the monopoly. The U.S. Supreme Court in Butchers Union Company v. Crescent City Company (1884) held that the new state-constitutional provision was an example of the police power, which (unlike some tax concessions) cannot be bargained away by previous legislatures. Sometimes it is a good thing that a legislature cannot be bound by the actions of its predecessors (Julian Eule 1987).

8.9 The Granger Laws Were Tempered by Elasticity of Supply

The Granger Laws provide an example of economic rationality reversing laws upheld by the courts. The Granger movement of the 1870s agitated for laws to promote farm interests. The most famous example was the Illinois law that regulated the rates that Chicago grain elevators could charge for storage. The legislation was upheld in the famous case of Munn v. Illinois (1877), in which the U.S. Supreme Court held that the Fourteenth Amendment did not bar regulation "when private property is affected with a public interest."

Granger legislation also extended to regulating the rates that railroads could charge farmers for shipping their goods (Stephen Siegel 1984). The laws did not escape the attention of a contemporary economist, Arthur Twining Hadley (1885), who favored moderate regulation of railroads. (Hadley was a founder of the American Economic Association and later was president of Yale.) He described Wisconsin's Granger legislation, which fixed "rates on different classes of road at figures which proved quite unremunerative" (1885, p. 135). The laws were upheld by the courts, but they did not last long. Hadley explained why (pp. 135–136):

> But a more powerful force than the authority of the courts was work-
> ing against the Granger system of regulation. The laws of trade could
> not be violated with impunity. The effects were most sharply felt in
> Wisconsin. The law reducing railroad rates . . . left nothing to pay
> fixed charges. In the second year of its operation, no Wisconsin road
> paid a dividend; only four paid interest on their bonds. Railroad
> construction had come to a standstill. Even the facilities on existing
> roads could not be kept up. Foreign capital refused to invest in
> Wisconsin; the men who had most favored the law found themselves
> heavy losers. These points were plain to every one. They formed the
> theme of the Governor's message at the beginning of 1876. The very
> men who passed the law in 1874, hurriedly repealed it after two years'
> trial. In other states the laws either were repealed, as in Iowa, or were
> sparingly and cautiously enforced. By the time the Supreme Court
> published the Granger decisions, the fight had been settled, not by
> constitutional limitations, but by industrial ones.

8.10   *California Rent Controls Strain the Exit-Voice Option*

The more difficult example of mobility as protection for property interests is rent control. Rent control is almost uniformly deplored by
economists, because it reduces the supply of housing. Even unabashed
liberals like Anthony Downs (1983, p. 141) have little use for it. Although rent control is hardly a ubiquitous phenomenon in the United
States, its adoption increased dramatically in California after the passage of Proposition 13 in 1978. By 1988 more than a quarter of all
rental units in California were covered by some form of rent control
(Michael Murray et al. 1991).

The California courts did not really promote rent control in the
same way that they promoted an antideveloper agenda (section 6.7).
The courts were simply permissive of local regulations. In Birkenfeld v.
Berkeley (1976), the California Supreme Court actually forbade the
city's retroactive rollback of rents, but it indicated that almost any
prospective regulation of rent was acceptable. The "emergency" criteria of Block v. Hirsh (1921), by which Justice Holmes had justified
Washington's World War I rent controls, was discarded by the California Supreme Court. (It may be unnecessary to point out the coun-
terproductiveness of even the old rationale. Suppressing prices during

a housing scarcity like the one Washington experienced during the war could only make the shortage worse.) The rent-control issue is a good test of my position that courts should usually be passive with respect to economic legislation except when the assets involved are immobile or immobilized and the protections of larger, pluralistic legislative bodies are attenuated. Rent control is worth a micro-political look.

I need to address one special condition concerning California rent controls, however. Proposition 13 in 1978 was said to have encouraged rent control because landlords did not reduce rents in response to the deep property-tax cuts (Robert Kuttner 1980). Howard Jarvis, the colorful leader of the tax revolt, had promised such a pass-through, and his credibility may have been enhanced by his day job as director of the Apartment Association of Los Angeles County. That the idea was widespread was suggested by the action of several large apartment owners, who took out ads in California newspapers prior to the vote on Proposition 13 to disclaim any promise of reduced rents (*Sacramento Bee*, May 12, 1978).

I take issue with the conventional wisdom here because my alternative explanation indicates one of the political and economic avenues by which landlords, a small and vulnerable minority in most communities, are often able to protect themselves. One argument against rent control in most jurisdictions is that homeowners end up shouldering more of the property-tax burden if apartments are devalued by rent control (Downs 1983, p. 141). This argument became less persuasive in California after Proposition 13 because homeowners' tax burdens essentially became fixed at 1 percent of 1975 or subsequent sale values (O'Sullivan, Sexton, and Sheffrin 1995). Thus few homeowners' tax burdens would rise when rent control was imposed. With substantially lower fiscal costs to homeowners, renter coalitions that had formerly been unable to succeed because of homeowner opposition were able to argue successfully for rent control. This is not to deny that Proposition 13 was a precipitating event for rent-control sentiment, but most such events do not yield durable legislation.

8.11 Rent Control Is Partly Disciplined by Capital Mobility

Another means by which apartment owners protect themselves from rent control is by leaving the jurisdiction. This is seldom literally possible, although Jeffrey Chapman (1981) reported that apartment owners demolished "hundreds" of units in anticipation of the draconian measures instituted by Santa Monica, another California city famous for stringent rent control. Apartment owners in most other instances vote against rent control by withholding new capital. When real returns on apartment housing rentals are reduced by rent control, landlords have an incentive to reduce prior investment in housing as well as to forgo future investment in rental housing. Withdrawing prior investment can be done by reducing maintenance of the unit or by converting it to alternative uses such as offices or condominiums.

Local governments that are serious about rent control are not, however, passive observers of such disinvestment (Kenneth Baar 1983). Both the state of California and local rent-control jurisdictions adopted habitability laws and other regulations designed to penalize under-maintenance, and they passed anticonversion laws intended to stem the flow of rental units to other uses. The typical diagrammatic analysis of rent control by economists, in which suppliers are assumed to be able to remove their capital in the long run, does not usually take account of such retardants. If such laws worked perfectly, the conventional economic analysis would have to be modified to differentiate between supply effects on future development and the effects on existing development.

Enforcement of maintenance and habitability laws is problematical for traditional apartments, however. For apartments, common areas are normally maintained by the owner, and remedies for an accumulation of minor infractions are hard to obtain. It is possible for tenants to get an order to fix broken plumbing but seldom one to paint the outside of the apartment, sweep the walks, or combat general dinginess. Laws that prevent the conversion of rental units to other uses can sometimes be evaded by having the owner reoccupy the unit himself or simply withdraw it from the market by demolition. Landlords can also increase their rate of return under rent control by selecting what they regard as high-quality tenants, or they can indulge in personal preferences that would be costly under normal market conditions.

Still another inefficiency remains even if the maintenance and anti-conversion police can do their job. Tenants are apt to hold onto rent-controlled apartments too long. For example, parents may stay in a spacious apartment long after their children have left home and a smaller unit would be more appropriate. (The dean of rent-control studies, Edgar Olsen [1990], said that the cost of the lock-in effect may be large.) Tenants of rent-controlled apartments may be reluctant to take jobs in other places because it would mean giving up the advantages of rent control. This is true even if the other location has rent control, since the newcomer will have higher search costs to locate a unit.

The net effect of these difficulties is that rent control is still relatively rare, even in California, where the state supreme court is highly tolerant of it. In most jurisdictions in which it does exist, rent control has relatively little effect. Studies of the experience of cities with moderate rent controls suggest that it is difficult to detect distortions from controls that adjust regularly to inflation and permit vacancy decontrol.

Vacancy decontrol means that rents are allowed to rise to market levels when a vacancy occurs, although they may be frozen again for the duration of the next tenancy. This is probably the most important loophole in rent control that reduces its adverse impacts. Michael Murray and his colleagues (1991) and Margery Turner (1990) found that such "moderate" rent control had only minor (but still adverse) impacts on the rental housing market in Los Angeles and Washington, D.C., respectively. Even New York City's rent controls, the most durable and most frequently studied in the nation, are difficult to evaluate because of the many exceptions built into the law over time (Moon and Stotsky 1993).

8.12   *Berkeley Rent Control Immobilized Apartment Capital*

But the economic-political mechanism to mitigate rent control is not foolproof. During my year in Berkeley I met Michael St. John, whose economics dissertation (1990) asked whether Berkeley's rent controls affected the sale price of larger apartment houses. Using transactions data for individual buildings, St. John found substantial reductions in value in Berkeley between 1980, when Berkeley adopted its most severe restrictions, and 1988. Berkeley apartment houses sold for about half the price of comparable units in non-rent-control communities in Alameda County. St. John also found that other Bay Area cities such as Oakland and Hayward, which had adopted rent control but allowed such adjustments as vacancy decontrol and regular inflation adjustments, did not experience reductions in the average value of apartment buildings, at least none that were statistically significant.

As St. John indicated and I confirmed by local inquiries, Berkeley's rent controls are extreme by almost any test. Between 1980 and 1988, Berkeley held nominal rents well below the rate of inflation. It did not routinely allow owners to pass through increased costs; requests to do so were processed by an independently elected rent board that was consistently hostile to owners. Tenants could not be evicted except for egregious behavior, and eviction obtained the owner little financial gain, anyway, since rents were not permitted to rise to market levels when a new tenant was found. Apartments could not be converted to other uses except in the most extenuating circumstances. Single-family homes were subject to rent control, and owners seeking to repossess their own homes could not evict a tenant if the owner had another property in which he or she could live. (Local courts did limit enforcement of this by allowing the owner to be the sole judge of whether another property was available.) The clear intent was to have the benefits of rent control accrue to seated tenants without the usual landlord supply-response.

To give an indication of the extent of the transfer of wealth afforded by Berkeley's rent controls, I offer an anecdote from my attendance at a Berkeley zoning board hearing in October 1991. One applicant was an architect who had recently purchased a two-family home. The downstairs had a tenant, which did not bother him, but he sought to expand the upstairs to provide additional living space for his family. In presenting testimony that the proposed addition would not adversely affect the neighborhood, the applicant brought in affidavits from neighboring homeowners *and* their tenants.

In New Hampshire, zoning boards don't usually ask for testimony from tenants. It is not that they are irrelevant; it is that we discount them on the assumption that their interest in the property is transitory. Therefore, I initially thought that the Berkeley zoning board's eagerness to hear from all the neighboring tenants was just a product of its ideological tilt. But as I thought about it, it occurred to me that if I were on the Berkeley zoning board, I would want to hear from tenants, too, and count their testimony at least as much as owners'. In Berkeley, tenants have almost a life-estate in their units. The prospect of low rents and perpetual leases keeps them there for a very long time. If the neighborhood is going to go bad as a result of some nearby project, the tenants have as much interest in it as most landlords.

8.13   Berkeley-Style Rent Control Warrants
Judicial Attention

Berkeley's rules did have some exceptions. The tenant-rights rules were applied most stringently to owners of larger apartment houses in that owners of smaller units could more readily convert to other uses. Many small-time owners were African-Americans who owned buildings in their own neighborhoods. Between this and other legal and illegal means of converting or withdrawing rental units, Berkeley actually lost more than 10 percent of its rental housing stock between 1980 and 1990.

St. John (1994) examined in more detail changes in Berkeley and Santa Monica in the 1980s, comparing their experience to that of other cities in their respective metropolitan areas. He found that in both cities, the groups nominally intended to be assisted by rent control—low-income people, students (in Berkeley), the elderly, and the disabled—became *smaller* fractions of each city's population between 1980 and 1990. St. John suggested that if these two cities had intended to exclude the poor, they could have come up with few policies more effective than stringent rent controls.

It seemed clear to me that the beneficiaries of Berkeley's rent controls were the middle-class professionals and the more-or-less permanent students who populate the middle ground (both in elevation and in income) of the city. One of the more entertaining *defenses* of Berkeley's rent control claimed that it helped to subsidize the major private-market success of the city, its fine selection of restaurants. The idea was seriously advanced that the lower rents of tenants allowed them to afford the likes of Chez Panisse, Lalimes, and Cafe Fanny. Alas, the argument overlooked the fact that landlords eat, too. More restaurant money for tenants means less restaurant money for landlords. (For an economic criticism of the more sober defenses of stringent rent controls, see Edgar Olsen [1991].)

I have discussed Berkeley at some length to allow that some judicial intervention on behalf of landlords is warranted. The apartment owners were clearly outnumbered and, on almost all issues up to 1988, outvoted by tenants and their allies. Support by homeowners for apartment owners largely disappeared with the passage of Proposition 13. As it happens, however, Berkeley rent controls are beginning to become more moderate. This is the result of the election of a majority of moderate members to the rent control board, who have been willing to let rents rise by something closer to the inflation rate. An uncharacteristic court decision (Searle v. Berkeley, 1990) also gave landlords a measure of relief by requiring adjustment for past inflation. That a Berkeley law professor was a co-plaintiff in *Searle* suggests that rent control had gotten so extreme that it had lost its support even in that liberal-minded faculty.

Despite such belated assistance, it still seems to me that the California courts were remiss in not providing some relief from Berkeley's draconian rent control and apartment conversion laws. St. John's capitalization results showed that apartment owners expected rent controls and related regulations to continue to depress real returns for a long time. The owners would not have sold their buildings at nearly 50 percent discounts otherwise. To my mind, the key decision was not sustaining rent control itself, but upholding each strand in the web of regulations that prevented landlords from removing their capital to more favorable jurisdictions. (I have criticized judicial approval of this web by analyzing each strand as if it stood alone as "regulation chopping" [Fischel 1991c, p. 906].) The key to Berkeley's regulations was that the city tried, with some success, to immobilize rental units. This curtailed the economic defense—elastic supply—against regulatory takings that normally keeps regulation within tolerable bounds.

8.14 Rent-Control Experience Educates Other Places

A possible reason for tolerating Berkeley's rent-control system is that it provides an example for other communities not to emulate. Only two other California jurisdictions have had rent controls as severe as Berkeley's: Santa Monica and the newly created municipality of West Hollywood. The Berkeley economist Michael Teitz, who has consulted frequently on rent control, told me in conversation that Los Angeles rent control advocates cannot convince the city council to engage in truly stringent rent control. Los Angeles council members look at the rancor of neighboring Santa Monica and step back from the abyss. In a similar vein, the *San Francisco Examiner* editorialized against an initiative that would have made San Francisco's rent-control ordinance more strict by adopting vacancy control. The editors pointed to nearby Berkeley as a bad example of what would result (Oct. 27,

1991, p. A16:1). The voters apparently agreed, and San Francisco's vacancy control initiative was defeated.

Learning about the effects of excessive regulation by experience can be costly. Aside from the usual misallocations occasioned by the actual application of the ill-founded regulation, resources are expended in trying to adopt and enforce the regulation and, on the other side, in trying to deal with it and rescind it. These costs are usually put under the rubric of "rent-seeking." Gordon Tullock (1967) invented the idea, and it has become a pervasive criticism of government regulation, particularly by social scientists who identify themselves with the public choice school of thought. One of its more powerful findings is that even if there is no allocative inefficiency from an initially inefficient regulation after all is said and done, the saying and the doing themselves involve costs as bad as the regulation itself (David Mills 1989). Serving as part of a long-run public learning experience, let alone as datum for economic research, is apt to be small compensation for Berkeley apartment owners. I am apt to agree in this case. Much of the benefit of their property was transferred to their tenants for no other reason than that their assets were immobilized by a majoritarian coalition.

I would defend most ordinary rent control from constitutional review under the Takings Clause on the left-handed grounds that judges are likely to do more harm than good in aggressively intervening in the process. In most cases, apartment owners' economic and political behavior affords an opportunity to ward off the worst regulations. In contrast to the usual case, Berkeley's regulations should have been subject to judicial review because they effectively forestalled the supply elasticity that is the landlords' last resort. In the next four sections I will describe an extreme instance in which economic and political self-help by owners subject to rent control seemed almost perfectly forestalled. Lack of judicial assistance to property owners in these cases was inexcusable (Fischel 1991c).

8.15 Mobile Home Rent Control Transferred Land Rents

Among the tenants most successful in adopting rent-control regulations in California after Proposition 13 were residents of mobile home parks. By the mid-1980s, more than a third of all mobile home units in California were in mobile home parks subject to local rent control. Mobile home rent control presents different issues than those posed by most apartment rent controls because of the unusual nature of the market (Werner Hirsch 1988; Hirsch and Hirsch 1988; Mary McAlister 1990).

Most mobile home coaches are purchased by their occupants, not rented. If the coach is brand new, it is usually transported to a rented "pad" in a mobile home park. The move to the park is the last time most coaches are moved until they are scrapped. The observed value of a used mobile home detached from its site is negligible, but this is probably because most displaced mobile homes are highly depreciated.

When the owners of a coach in a mobile home park want to relocate their household, they usually sell the coach and move themselves and their personal belongings to a different housing unit, which may, of course, be a "stick-built" home or apartment. The mobile home coach stays in place. Its new owner moves in, provided that he can obtain a lease from the park owner. The turnover in tenants of the mobile home park is referred to as a vacancy, even if the coach itself is not relocated. There are thus two transactions in most turnovers: one between coach owner and buyer, and one between park owner and buyer.

One anxiety of tenants of mobile home parks is the possibility of eviction. Eviction imposes larger than usual costs on mobile home tenants because they usually must sell their coaches, too. If the park were to go out of business, they would have to move their coaches and find another location, a substantial transaction cost. California responded to tenants' anxieties in the 1970s by adopting just-cause eviction laws that made it nearly impossible for a park owner to evict well-behaved tenants who pay their rent. (These were separate from and generally more stringent than statewide laws concerning apartment homes.)

By itself, the anti-eviction law did not seem to be a great burden on park owners. They normally had little desire to get rid of peaceable tenants who paid their rent regularly. (An important exception occurred when a park owner was using her land as a mobile home park to gain a temporary source of income while waiting for more intensive development.) The landlords' position was changed, however, under rent control with continuing controls after vacancy.

Many California communities adopted a panoply of rent-control regulations for their mobile home parks, especially during the early 1980s. But the usual inefficiencies that accompany such regulations were mitigated by the tenants' ownership of their coaches and the legislatively guaranteed inability of the park owner to evict them. As a result, it was primarily land rent, not capital returns, that was transferred from the park owner to the tenants. The park owner had provided much capital, of course, including utility connections and a road network as well as the spot for the pad itself. But these required relatively little maintenance, and some routine maintenance could be done by the coach-owner tenants themselves. The landlord responses to conventional rent control—removal of tenants, conversion to other uses, withdrawal of maintenance—were much less feasible for mobile home parks.

8.16 *Vacancy Controls Enabled Rent Control to Be Capitalized*

One potential inefficiency did remain, however. Coach owners who enjoyed rent control would lose it if they moved out of a rent-controlled park to other housing. This created an incentive to overstay. But there was a method of fixing that problem, too, which was to continue the rent control after the tenant left. If pad rents continued to be controlled after the coach was sold (recall that the coach remained on the pad), the buyer of the coach would continue to receive the benefits of rent control. Because the buyers knew this, they were willing to pay more for coaches located in mobile home parks in communities that imposed rent control and also disallowed vacancy decontrol.

Vacancy controls thus enabled sellers of coaches to capitalize the value of rent control in the sale of their coaches. For example, if the market rents for a mobile home pad would have been $3,000 per year, but regulated rents were only $2,000 per year for both the existing *and* the new tenants, the capitalized value of the $1,000 transfer (the difference between regulated and market price) would be incorporated in the price of the coach that the new tenant would pay.

Vacancy controls on ordinary apartments do not permit much capitalization because the tenant who leaves usually has no fully complementary asset that must be purchased by the incoming tenant. Of course, some capitalization is achieved by side payments or by purchasing appliances at inflated prices to induce seated tenants to leave. But I have never heard of an informal system that captured the value of future low rents as efficiently as the mobile home example.

Low rents would be as secure for future coach-owner tenants as for current occupants, since only coach owners could select buyers. Park owners could not, under yet another California law, deny occupation by any creditworthy prospective tenant. Unlike the owners of apartment buildings who could repossess rent-controlled units for their own use, an exception that is usually allowed under anti-eviction statutes, the park owners did not have the option of occupying the coaches for themselves. Park owners could, of course, purchase the coaches when they came up for sale, but they would then have to pay for the capitalized value of rent control on their own land.

Capitalization of the future benefits of rent control in coach sales would depend both on how much rents were held below market values and on buyers' estimates of how long rents would remain low under the law. Pad rents were usually permitted to increase upon sale under most ordinances, but typically by an amount considerably less than the rate of inflation.

We do not have to speculate about capitalization. A UCLA economics professor, Werner Hirsch, and his son, the attorney Joel Hirsch (1988), undertook a study of the effect of California mobile home rent controls on the price of coaches. They estimated by regression analysis that the value of coaches sold in rent-controlled communities was one-third higher than that of coaches sold in other communities. It was clear that a large fraction of the rental value of the land had been transferred to the owners of the coach by the combination of local rent control, vacancy control, and state laws that prevented park owners from selecting tenants or otherwise controlling the use of their pads.

8.17 Capitalization Made the Regulations More Efficient

Because of the transferability of rent control (by not permitting vacancy decontrol or park owner repossession), some of the major inefficiencies that plague rent control in stick-built apartments were substantially mitigated in mobile home parks. Owners of mobile home coaches had incentives to perform maintenance to make their units more salable, so the most visible and depreciable capital in the park would not become unduly run down under rent control. Coach owners did not suffer the lock-in effect that rent control imposes on tenants of most apartments. They had no incentive to remain in their units once jobs or family situations had changed, since they could take the financial benefit of rent control with them in the form of a lump-sum payment from the buyer of their coach.

I originally suspected that this was an instance in which rent control might create overmaintenance of the units. Coach-owner tenants in rent-controlled parks might overmaintain their coaches to make them last longer if, when the unit was worn out, it had to be replaced and the park owner could repossess the then literally vacant space. I had underestimated the creativeness of the mobile home tenants' lobby. State legislation prevented a park owner from interfering with tenants' ability to replace their coaches. This law, in conjunction with other tenant rights laws, effectively permits tenants to market the value of their low-rent leaseholds even if they have run-down coaches. In an instance cited in a mobile home takings case, Azul Pacifico v. Los Angeles (1991), a new tenant reported that she paid $77,000 for an old coach in a Los Angeles mobile home park. She sold that coach for $5,000 to someone who would remove it and then installed a new unit, candidly explaining that she had paid mainly for the value of the space nominally owned by the park owner.

Other inefficiencies, however, persisted under mobile home rent control. The number of new mobile home parks opened in California dropped precipitously after mobile home rent control became widespread in the early 1980s (Hirsch and Hirsch 1988, p. 463). But that drop would probably have occurred even under milder forms of rent control in which there was no capitalization. As Avinash Dixit (1991) proved, the commitment of resources into an irreversible investment (which entrance into the mobile home park business effectively became after anti-eviction statutes were passed) requires an above-average rate of return. The required rate of return increases substantially as the probability that a legal ceiling will be imposed increases. Thus any rate of return below market rates will discourage entry. According to Dixit's model, entry into the mobile home park business would have been deterred even without the capitalization of rent control in the coach market. Thus the long-run inefficiencies of rent control are not worsened by the special mobile home ordinances, and several of the short-run inefficiencies are mitigated by it.

Moreover, the lack of incentive for new parks was mitigated by California state legislation in 1980 and 1981 that limited the ability of local governments to restrict placement of mobile homes on foundations in regular residential zones. In such instances the coach owner is also the landowner, and none of the rent-control issue applies. The only obvious efficiency problem (which may be considerable) is that new owners must now pay for both land and capital costs, and the higher down payment may deter potential residents.

A state law passed in 1989 implicitly conceded the supply-retardation effects by disallowing rent control in any new mobile home parks built in California. Very few new parks have been opened, however, in part because potential park developers believe that the law will be changed to their detriment sometime in the future. (interview with Paul Deffebach of WMA, Dec. 8, 1994). Skepticism of jurisdictions that try to promise their way out of the consequences of past regulation is widespread. New York City's reneging on its promise not to impose rent control on apartments built after World War II is legendary among developers (Salins and Mildner 1992). They relate the story with an air of "fool me once, shame on you; fool me twice, shame on me."

8.18 Kozinski's Paradox Was to Find Virtue in Inefficiency

Judge Alex Kozinski's opinion in Hall v. Santa Barbara (1986) first drew mobile home rent control to my attention. *Hall* held that a mobile home rent-control regulation could be a taking of property and hence require just compensation under the Fifth Amendment, seemingly contrary to a long line of precedents that had upheld rent control. In footnote 24 of his opinion, Judge Kozinski noted, citing economists of a variety of political persuasions (conservatives Alchian and Allen and liberals Nordhaus and Samuelson), that the typical rent-control ordinance creates inefficient incentives for tenants to overstay. The Santa Barbara mobile home rent-control ordinance at issue in *Hall* cured such inefficient incentives because existing tenants could cash out future benefits when they moved, as described earlier.

In distinguishing Santa Barbara's ordinance from conventional rent control, Judge Kozinski said that "the very fact of the inefficiency—that the tenant is not given too great a stake in the property—saves most rent control schemes from potential unconstitutionality. After all, efficiency would be maximized by giving the tenant a fee simple interest in the property" (833 F.2d at 1279).

I regarded this as a sufficiently interesting statement that I wrote an article on it entitled "Exploring the Kozinski Paradox" (1991). The paradox was that a judge versed in law and economics should regard improved efficiency as a reason to strike down a regulation as a taking. The paradox was deepened because Kozinski's position went beyond what I believe most critics of law and economics would say about efficiency: that it is or should be irrelevant to judicial decisions.

The conventional anti-efficiency position has been taken most vigorously by the left-leaning Critical Legal Studies school (Duncan Kennedy 1981). Two members of the school rationalized everyday rent control on the grounds that its inefficient inalienability served the desirable goal of perpetuating a low-income community in the face of gentrification (Mark Kelman 1988; William Simon 1991). The idea, which I had heard from Berkeley rent-control advocates as well, is that cashing out rent control would be a bad idea. It would change the whole nature of the community, even if it would make each individual tenant better off.

Neither Kelman nor Simon considered mobile home rent control of the type discussed above and at issue in *Hall*. They would presumably be led to oppose it by their arguments in favor of regular, inefficient rent control, since the ability of mobile home tenants to cash out their entitlement increases the likelihood that they will leave. In this respect, Kelman and Simon seem to be on Judge Kozinski's side. (This is a little unfair to them, since both admitted in their articles that they had done no research on the rent controls they used as examples.)

Judge Kozinski's paradox was also different from Hirsch and Hirsch's (1988) criticism of capitalized rent control. They argued that the poor were not helped to buy mobile homes because prices rose after controls were imposed. Thus the ostensible purpose of the rent-control law—helping low-income people—was not served. Hirsch and Hirsch (1988, p. 462) submitted that the lack of connection between purpose and effect would render the law constitutionally vulnerable under the 1987 *Nollan* "nexus" doctrine, which I reviewed in section 1.22.

The Hirsches' position is problematic because it focuses on the beneficiaries of the program (the tenants) rather than on those who bear the burden (the park owners). The selective distribution of the benefits of rent control is no worse than many other means-tested programs for which there are queues. Government-supplied public housing does not serve all the poor, but it is hardly unconstitutional for that fact. It is the selective imposition of *costs* that the Takings Clause addresses.

8.19 Special-Interest Politics Is Criticized in Public Choice Theory

I used Judge Kozinski's dictum to explain why inefficient regulatory transfers should not usually be regarded as takings of property by judges acting under constitutional authority (Fischel 1991c). This is my position on regular rent control, at least when it is not accompanied by regulations that hog-tie the landlord's investment to its current location and use. Conversely, I argued that certain efficient regulatory transfers, those that respond to the wishes of the majority of voters and that have little deadweight loss, are stronger candidates for takings. My position is not that efficiency is bad, but that in this context, inefficiency is evidence that political and economic processes—voice and exit—are available to protect those burdened by excessive regulation, so that courts should not intervene on behalf of the aggrieved property owners. My approach finds jurisprudential virtue in two of the bugbears of economists, deadweight loss and special-interest legislation.

Finding virtue in special-interest politics has its hazards. Many in the public choice and Chicago schools of political economy derogate the results of special-interest politics. Richard Epstein's (1992c) extensive and intelligent criticism of my position assured me of the truth of this. William Riker and Barry Weingast (1988), two luminaries of public choice, have argued (not addressing me) that the role of the Supreme Court should be to protect citizens against the depredations of special-interest legislation. This is in distinct contrast to the pluralistic view of politics implicitly adopted by John Hart Ely and in Footnote Four of *Carolene Products* (see section 3.13).

Public choice theory does not, however, necessarily lead to the position that judges need to order compensation for the victims of special-interest legislation. First, not all public choice theorists regard special-interest politics as bad. Such diverse authors as Gary Becker (1983), Einer Elhauge (1991), Herbert Hovenkamp (1990), and Saul Levmore (1990) have seen as much virtue as sin in special-interest legislation. Even if one accepts that special-interest laws are generally undesirable, a public choice viewpoint does not necessarily lead to the conclusion that compensation should be made to the losers.

Glynn Lunney (1992) and Marc Poirier (1993) took the validity of public choice as a reason *not* to compensate concentrated interest groups such as landowners, who they suppose have sufficient political power to protect themselves. I think Lunney and Poirier erroneously treated local regulations of undeveloped land the same as state and national legislation of broad categories of property, but their valid point is that public choice does not necessarily call for compensation of landowners. Although the public choice viewpoint is more cynical about legislative motives than pluralism, the losers from either process have the kind of alliance-generating powers that I believe soothes demoralization costs of uncompensated devaluation of property (section 4.10).

For the sake of argument, however, let me concede the point that much, maybe most, national and state legislation is economically wasteful. My response is to ask how unelected, inherently undemocratic judges are to do better. None of the aforementioned critics of special-interest legislation has addressed the issue of judicial competence, other than implying that the authors would do it better if *they* were judges. More important, none addresses the issue of how Americans could be considered a self-governing people if they were ruled by the supposed philosopher-kings on the bench. (Antonin Scalia [1987] is persuasive on these points.)

Richard Epstein's (1992c) defense of judges was not to praise their analytical ability. To the contrary, he excoriated the reasoning and substance of most modern takings decisions. His defense of active judicial review was structural. Because Epstein regards nearly all legislation as inefficient and hence undesirable, he supports even crude judicial review as imposing at least a "second hurdle" on wasteful rent-seeking. (It isn't clear that the higher price imposed by a second hurdle would generate less total rent-seeking expenditures; it depends in part on the elasticity of demand for special-interest legislation.)

Even if one concedes Epstein's point that there is more bad legislation than good, there is nothing to prevent judges granted a wide-ranging constitutional role over legislation from turning their veto power into an affirmative action program. The California Supreme Court did just that in Serrano v. Priest and *Friends of Mammoth,* as I pointed out in sections 3.11 and 6.20, respectively. The court used its power to get what it considered desirable legislation passed, contrary to the obvious wishes of the legislature itself. Epstein's notion of having a double defensive line looks attractive until one realizes that the extra players can as easily turn around and help the offense.

8.20   *Physical Invasions Were Held Sufficient for Takings in* Loretto

The legal basis for Judge Kozinski's decision in Hall v. Santa Barbara was not what I regard as the paradoxical efficiency criterion. Instead, he argued that the combined effect of the state and local regulations was to transfer a possessory interest from park owner to coach owner. This new possessory interest constituted a permanent physical invasion of the park owner's property, which is almost always a per se taking under the test of Loretto v. Teleprompter (1982), which will be described presently.

As I indicated earlier, Kozinski's characterization of Mr. and Mrs. Hall's position in Hall v. Santa Barbara is plausible. Within California's web of state and local regulations, park owners have no reasonable expectation of ever being able to occupy the pads in their parks without the leave of their tenants. This does not mean that the park owners are bereft of any economic value from their land; they still are entitled to the controlled rent, and this stream is valuable. Hence Judge Kozinski did not base his decision on loss of value, since loss of some value as the result of regulation is usually not regarded as a compensable taking.

Loretto v. Teleprompter (1982) was a U.S. Supreme Court case that reaffirmed the physical invasion test in the context of regulatory takings. In order to facilitate access to cable television in Manhattan, New York legislation permitted cable television providers to put wires and minor equipment on private buildings. The legislation provided no compensation for such invasions, which seemed no more intrusive than telephone lines, water supply pipes, postal boxes, and other public utilities that building owners are required to provide space for without being compensated. Normally, of course, a building owner would not want to exclude services that benefited her tenants. The added benefit to the building would more than offset the damage from the physical invasion.

Mrs. Loretto, however, did object to having the cable television wires and two utility boxes (about the size of the legendary bread box) put on her roof without compensation. The U.S. Supreme Court agreed—not without some perplexed dissent—that compensation was due. New York subsequently passed a law that offered one dollar in compensation for people in Mrs. Loretto's position, and this was deemed adequate.

8.21 *Did New York Rent Controls Lead to Physical Invasion?*

I suspect that the physical invasion of the cable television box that was held a compensable taking in *Loretto* was in part occasioned by attempts to rationalize rent-control regulation. Jurisdictions that adopt rent control typically find that they must keep the landlord from collecting on the side what she cannot collect up front. One of the side-payment devices is "key money" or "finder's fees," in which new tenants pay someone to gain access to a rent-controlled apartment. Key money does not necessarily find its way to the landlord's pocket. The outgoing tenant, the neighbors, or building superintendents may get some or all of it. (For a rueful personal story about how key money works in New York City apartments, see Richard Epstein [1988, p. 741].)

An alternative to key money that would work more in the landlord's interest would be to charge above-market prices for some service connected with the building. Hence it might be in the landlord's interest to charge tenants for access to cable television, electricity, or water, knowing that the tenant will be willing to pay an extra amount rather than move to another building. This scheme has the advantage to landlords and disadvantage to tenants of collecting payments from current as well as prospective tenants. Because most buildings caught in rent control already have electricity and water, the landlord cannot use charges for them. Cable television, which arrived after most rent-controlled buildings were built, might offer a lever for the landlord to recoup some of the gap between rent-control and market rent.

In order to foil this avenue for collecting side payments, the government would want to regulate the terms by which access to cable television was permitted. Such a regulation was what gave rise to the *Loretto* case. The trivial physical invasion by the cable television company that was held to be a taking was a necessary concomitant of the regulation, which was in turn, if my speculation is correct, logically compelled by rent regulation.

The New York Court of Appeals provided evidence in support of my theory of the origins of the cable television regulation. (The New York court had ruled that no taking had occurred.) Its opinion quoted from a New York State Public Service Commission report: "In the electronic age, the landlord should not be able to preclude a tenant from obtaining CATV service (or to exact a surcharge for allowing the service) any more than he could preclude a tenant from receiving mail or telegrams direct to him." The opinion then quoted from the commission chairman's testimony, which concluded, *"Legislation is necessary, however, to prohibit gouging and arbitrary action"* (423 N.E. 2d at 327, emphasis by the court).

I do not want to oversell this proposition. There may be network externalities to having universal access to cable television that might justify some legislation. But it is interesting that the case itself arose in New York City, which has the longest-running rent controls in the country. Most landlords in cities without rent control would not feel burdened by the cable television access regulation. It simply compelled them to accept something that it was in their own financial interest to have. In a free market for apartments, only idiosyncratic or short-sighted owners would want to withhold a service that made the rent and value of their apartment houses higher.

I hope that I have at least planted a germ of doubt as to the viability of a neat separation of regulation from physical invasion by using the case in which the distinction seems so important. The lesson of *Loretto* is that there is no refuge in making a "bright-line" distinction between regulations and physical invasions. The logic of thoroughgoing regulation may lead to physical appropriation.

8.22 A Political Solution to Rent Control May Be to Shift It to the States

The U.S. Supreme Court declined to review Hall v. Santa Barbara, but in 1992 it reversed Judge Kozinski's novel argument that mobile home rent control effected a taking. In Yee v. Escondido (1992), a takings case identical to *Hall,* the plaintiffs relied heavily on Kozinski's physical invasion analogy. The U.S. Supreme Court rejected the physical invasion notion. The Court then said that the traditional regulatory taking had not been sufficiently explored by the lower courts for it to make a ruling on the merits.

The 9–0 vote to uphold mobile home rent control in Yee v. Escondido can best be understood in terms of the U.S. Supreme Court's reluctance to review state regulatory takings doctrines, as I described in section 1.24. In *Nollan* (1987) and *First English* (1987), the U.S. Supreme Court made it clear that the California courts could not ignore the concept of a regulatory taking. In *Yee* and in a previous rent-control case, Pennell v. San Jose (1988), the U.S. Supreme Court showed that it was not willing to take the next step and say just what constituted a regulatory taking.

Mobile home park owners promised to relitigate the constitutionality of mobile home rent control on the basis of regulatory takings rather than physical invasions, as Justice O'Connor suggested was proper. The more productive question is why they don't go to the California legislature for relief. This raises an important qualification to my concern with the importance of localism.

At the most general level, all local regulation can be superseded by state regulation. Although rent control was regarded by the California courts as an inherent property of local police powers (Birkenfeld v. Berkeley 1976), it is clear that the state legislature can overrule its localities. For example, shortly after the city of Berkeley adopted commercial rent control to benefit established business tenants (such as coffeehouses), the California legislature banned such regulation statewide. This was not a pure test, though, because a federal judge had previously held in Ross v. Berkeley (1987) that commercial rent control was unconstitutional, which may have deflated opposition to the law. (Judge Patel's *Ross* opinion relied in part on Judge Kozinski's now-vacated holding in Hall v. Santa Barbara.)

There are other examples of forum-shifting that have allowed developer interests to prevail at the state or national level when they could not at the local level. Many states have regularized the developer exaction process to forestall local imposition of impact fees and new requirements after projects have begun (Blaesser and Kentopp 1990). Mobile home manufacturers and coach owners have succeeded in many states in obtaining state legislation that overrides local prohibitions on siting manufactured housing in single family districts (Douglas Kmiec 1983). (This does not help park owners, because all the other requirements of single family zoning still apply.) Local laws that restrict group homes for the mentally disabled have been overridden by federal legislation.

The last example is also not a pure test, since the legislation was probably inspired by the U.S. Supreme Court's decision in City of Cleburne v. Cleburne Living Center (1985). *Cleburne* overturned a local restriction on group homes for the retarded as contrary to either the Equal Protection or the Due Process Clause, depending on which concurring opinion one reads. These examples nonetheless suggest that minority interests have a better chance in the pluralistic state and national political process. The question is whether the possibility of shifting the regulatory process from local to state or national legislatures is sufficient to protect landowner interests. The next section takes a closer look at the dynamics of local–state legislation involving mobile homes.

8.23   Tenants Prevailed Because of Local Concentration

My investigation into the politics of California mobile home rent control revealed that there are two opposing lobbying organizations. Both operate at the state and the local level. The Western Mobilehome Association (WMA) represents park owners, and the Golden State Mobilhome Owners League (GSMOL) is an organization of coach-owner tenants. (Among their differences is the way they spell mobile home.) GSMOL was instrumental in adopting the state legislation and local rent controls at issue in Hall v. Santa Barbara, and WMA has combated GSMOL consistently on these issues. Given this situation, it seems to be a closer question as to whether park owners are truly the victims of majoritarian legislation, or whether they are just the current losers in the pluralistic, logrolling politics that surely characterizes the legislature of a large state like California. If the latter characterization is more apt, my normative model would offer a weaker case for judicial intervention on behalf of park owners. (My knowledge of the politics of this issue is based largely on interviews and newspaper reading, as documented in Fischel [1991c, p. 895].)

The tenants' organization, GSMOL, has about 65,500 members; WMA has only about 2,000. But the theory of public choice tells us that counting voters does not dispose of the issue, because politicians respond to monetary support as well as votes. If WMA owners spend more than GSMOL to influence legislation (which both sides seem to concede), they should sometimes prevail even when directly opposed by GSMOL. The apparent reasons for WMA's failure to do so, however, are instructive.

Mobile home parks are not randomly distributed across the state. Some places have a large number of them, and tenants constitute a large voting bloc in such districts. One such district is Escondido, represented in the state senate by Bill Craven. Mr. Craven is a Republican whose voting record received favorable ratings by the state chamber of commerce and developer organizations. Mr. Craven was, however, the author of numerous mobile home tenant protection bills.

The reason was simple: there were more than 10,000 mobile home units in his district, and their owners made it clear to him, through GSMOL, how they thought he should vote.

That GSMOL even exists seems unusual; the free-rider problem of tenants' organizations would seem to work against it. But mobile home coach owners are easier to organize than tenants. Unlike most apartment tenants, they have a long-run financial stake in legislation, since they own their coaches. Mobile home owners are also a more homogeneous group; most are white retired people who are conservative on a majority of issues. They live in close-knit neighborhoods and meet in park community activities, and they have plenty of time to devote to local politics.

8.24   Park Owners Had No Allies

One might think that the park owners, the WMA, would have allies in other industry groups, such as apartment owners, realtors, developers, and mobile home manufacturers, to combat GSMOL on an issue as important as rent control at the state level. Yet although there is a loose political alliance in Sacramento known as the "shelter group," mobile home park owners are easily carved out of it. When the shelter group sought (unsuccessfully) statewide legislation eliminating all forms of rent control, mobile homes were quickly made an exception to the rule. The reason was that GSMOL objected and it became apparent that the legislation could not move forward unless an exception was made for mobile homes, permitting localities to adopt rent control as before. Because of the distinctiveness of the market, the usual line-drawing problems that would arise, say, between owners of small apartment houses and large units did not arise. It became easy for other members of the forces opposed to rent control to set the mobile home park owners adrift.

Realtors, apartment house owners, and developers of other housing in fact have interests slightly contrary to those of park owners. For realtors, the relative efficiency of the regulatory transfer makes them disposed toward mobile home rent control. A realtor's commission on selling a coach is enhanced if the sale price also includes the discounted value of rent control. Developers and owners of conventional apartments are perhaps more wary of the naked transfer effected by mobile home rent control, but, after all, mobile home parks are low-cost competitors for their products. They may secretly be pleased to see park expansion stymied. The tenants' organization, GSMOL, appears to have isolated its opponent at the state level in much the same way that it succeeds at the local level. The WMA amicus brief in Yee v. Escondido (1992) indicated that of the eighty-seven local jurisdictions that have mobile home rent control, only thirteen also apply rent control to apartments. None of the briefs for the park owners in *Yee* was joined by apartment owners and others usually opposed to rent control. In most takings cases, several property-oriented groups file amicus briefs.

GSMOL's success is not just the result of clever politics; it is as much the result of the nature of the mobile home park market. The subjection of park owners to majoritarian preferences at the local level is the result of their political isolation at the state level. This isolation would not amount to much if the park owners could vote with their feet or otherwise withdraw from the market, but the transfer of land rent effected by the web of regulations prevents that as well. Hence the theory of regulatory takings advanced in this book, which limits judicial intervention to instances in which the political and economic markets offer no hope of respite, supports the Ninth Circuit's *Hall* decision and Judge Kozinski's paradox of efficiency.

8.25 Conclusion: Politics Is Sometimes Not Enough

The United States has had a capitalist economy based on private property primarily because Americans prefer it to the alternatives. They have debated alternative political arrangements in the past, and their experience has led them to adopt state constitutional assurances that enable judges to look after at least some aspects of property. I have in this chapter explored the various ways by which political action, which is often disparaged as rent-seeking, is sufficient to protect property without the help of judges. It works often enough in the larger legislatures that one is tempted to leave property alone entirely. There are, however, examples that seem to indicate that the political process sometimes does not work well. They arise most often when the protections of economic exit and political voice are forestalled at the local level. When confronted with a regulatory taking claim, judges need to ask themselves whether the plaintiff has been forestalled from those options by the nature of his property and the nature of the political process.

9

Remedies for Unfair Land Use Restrictions and Exactions

Few other areas of law have been subject to as much academic criticism as regulatory takings. The first section of Andrea Peterson's (1989) article is entitled "The Chaos of Current Takings Clause Doctrine," which echoes a theme in nearly every other comprehensive article on the issue. The criticism could be turned on the scholars themselves, who have shown a tendency to change their minds about the proper approach to takings. Joseph Sax effectively renounced his well-regarded 1964 article in 1971, apparently concerned that the earlier approach would inhibit environmental activism. Even Richard Epstein has blinked. In his 1992b article (part of an interesting exchange with Michelman [1992]), Epstein conceded that a progressive income tax might not necessarily be a taking of property, as he had insisted was the case in his 1985 book. We scholars should at the least tone down our criticism of the judges if the best and the brightest among us cannot stand their ground.

Aside from some civility, the other lesson we might take is that no one is likely to discover a *Loretto* stone, so to speak, that will unlock the secrets of the takings issue. The judges and scholars who have addressed the issue in the twentieth century are as intelligent a group as is likely to address it in the twenty-first. The takings issue is muddy because it is inherently hard to deal with, not because the people who have addressed it haven't been smart enough to see the light.

The approach to "resolving" the takings issue in this chapter is to take three paths, all of which build on themes already discussed. The first approach is to see where my themes of judicial modesty, immobilized resources, and political process can be applied. Local land use regulations have been my primary focus, but other types of governments and other types of regulations might be subject to the regulatory takings question. I will also examine another doctrine under which judges might question local parochialism. The New Jersey Supreme Court's *Mount Laurel* doctrine is the most interesting experiment, and I describe some evidence that raises doubts about its effectiveness.

The second task will be to disentangle the question of land use exactions from regulatory takings. Exactions ask about fair treatment for landowners when the landowner wants to use her land more intensively and the community imposes some conditions on her. Exactions are related to, but not the same as, fair treatment of landowners when the community wants to reduce the intensity of use to the financial detriment of the owner. The U.S. Supreme Court has recently made pronouncements about exactions that offer useful guidelines.

The concluding sections describe a substantive guideline for resolving regulatory takings disputes. Robert Ellickson's "normal behavior" standard is advanced as satisfying both the efficiency and the fairness issues involved in local land use regulation. This standard has been maligned as being indeterminate, so I will conclude with an account of how it might be applied to my hometown.

9.1 "Grandfathering" Contributes to Insider-Outsider Problems

My admiration for local government's efficiency in responding to residents' desires, expressed in Chapter 7, is tempered by the flip side of that responsiveness. The reason local governments are more apt to take by regulation is that many of those affected by the regulation are not residents and so are discounted by the local political process. The demand for new housing by potential residents is represented by development-minded owners of land in the community. The would-be developers seldom live inside the community, and even when they do, they are usually a small and sometimes vilified minority.

An important source of externalizing the cost of local land use regulation is the "grandfathering" of previously existing uses. (The term seems impervious to gender leveling.) Nearly all zoning laws exempt the uses that exist at the time of the adoption of the ordinance from more stringent regulations. Grandfathering is often required by state courts, at least if the nonconforming use is not obviously noxious or dangerous.

This usually reasonable condition often creates situations in need of judicial review under John Hart Ely's "process theory." As I quoted Ely in section 3.13, one of three reasons for judicial intervention arises where "a majority enacts one regulatory regime for itself and another, less favorable one, for one or another minority" (1991, n. 4). The typical zoning ordinance is especially prone to such a hazard because of grandfathering. Existing homeowner-voters adopt stringent regulations for new development which, because of grandfathering, they are not subject to. Indeed, the term evokes the "grandfather clauses" of the post-Reconstruction era. Southern voters were exempted from literacy tests for voting by a clause that permitted them to vote if their grandfathers had voted. This seemingly neutral criterion of course disfranchised the newly emancipated African-Americans.

One current issue that I will not address is whether minority groups within local governments are singled out to bear the burdens of "LULUs," the locally unwanted land uses such as waste dumps (Vicki Been 1993). My own view is that the political process seems to be handling this problem, to the extent that it is a problem and not the result of consensual transactions in fact desired by residents of those communities. (Section 7.9 indicated that such transactions are pervasive.) Civil rights advocates in Congress and in properly apportioned state legislatures have put the issue of environmental racism on the political agenda, as John Ely's theory would predict. Given this attention, the role for the courts would seem to be slight.

9.2 Should Big Cities Get More Respect?

I have found over the years that economists' characterization of zoning can be predicted by their address. Those most apt to agree with me live in suburban areas or the exurban small towns, in which the majoritarian model of politics seems most applicable. The insider-outsider problem described in the previous section is most acute there. Economists who characterize zoning as excessively prodevelopment often live in big cities. Thus Arthur Denzau and Barry Weingast (1982), whose academic address is St. Louis, advanced a model of zoning in which development-minded landowners have disproportionate influence because of their money and their deal-making abilities. This view imports evidence from large-scale governments to the local arena. And in Chicago, the idea that zoning constrains anyone's behavior is dismissed out of hand. "The streets are for sale," a leading urban economist told me a few years after he'd moved there. (Econometric evidence for the same sentiment is provided by John McDonald [1979, p. 165].)

The distinction that I have been urging for much of this book is that the majoritarian model applies best to local government, while the pluralistic (or special-interest) model applies, for better and for worse, mainly to the federal government. I have generally assumed that the states are like the federal government. But if states receive judicial deference because of their size, what about the larger cities and counties, several of whose populations exceed that of small states?

The size of the government could be a continuous factor to be entered into the necessarily factual judicial inquiry about takings. The national government gets an almost-free pass on the issue, and most states do, too. A few small states might be subjected by especially creative courts to closer inquiry despite the U.S. Senate apportionment, which regards thirty million Californians as the political equals of half a million Vermonters. It is interesting to me that the few statewide land use restrictions that mimic suburban zoning originated and are most durable in the small states of Hawaii, Oregon, and Vermont, the largest of which (Oregon) has about the same population (2.8 million) as the nation's third-largest municipality, Chicago.

The overlap of big cities and small states is less than one might think, though. In 1990, there were eight states with fewer than one million population and eight municipalities with more than one million population. But the overlap does not seem important for most purposes. The total population of the eight smallest states is about five million, which is about 2 percent of the total population of the country. The eight biggest municipalities add up to twenty million people, however, which is a lot of people.

As the population figures for large municipalities suggest, the biggest cities are apt to have pluralistic politics because of their large population and the resulting heterogeneity of interest groups. As such, landowners should generally fare better in the politics of such locales, and judges need to be more circumspect in upsetting the results. New York City is bigger than most states, and its size encourages more internalization of opportunity costs than in smaller places.

A hint of the process is suggested by this story. The 1978 *Penn Central* decision (described in section 1.18) upheld the uncompensated preservation of air rights over the historic Grand Central Terminal. Several years after the decision, Paul Goldberger, the *New York Times* architectural critic, wrote a column on the subject of historic preservation (April 15, 1990, p. H:36). Goldberger had always favored preservationism and the *Penn Central* decision. In this column, though, he wondered whether it might have gone too far. "A city evolves over time," Goldberger wrote, "and the city that contains not enough new buildings is as robbed of the reality of time as the one that contains not enough old ones." New York's powerful building-trades unions could hardly agree more. (See also Norman Marcus [1980].)

Big cities and counties should nonetheless not get the same judicial deference to regulatory initiatives that whole states get. Geographic size counts as well as population for internalizing the benefits and costs of regulation. Most American big cities comprise less than half their metropolitan area, both in land area and population. Thus many regulatory costs and benefits that accrue to the metropolitan area as a whole will be undervalued by city regulators, who are answerable only to local voters. Econometric evidence indicates that local historic preservation schemes cause more damage to property values than the federal programs (Asabere, Huffman, and Mehdian 1994). Uncompensated landmarks designations by big-city governments still deserve judicial scrutiny.

9.3   Independent Agencies Warrant Judicial Review

In contrast to local governments, state legislatures that create general police-power laws should receive great deference by the courts on the regulatory question. This is not because property owners do not get hurt by state legislative acts. It is because, to use Michelman's terms, demoralization costs are lower and settlement costs are higher for state regulations than for local. Higher-government regulation is both more like an exogenous event—an earthquake rather than a personalized grab—and more subject to the logrolling of pluralistic politics. As I contended in section 4.10, both of these reduce the demoralization of apparently being singled out. General laws by definition involve large numbers of people, so the settlement costs of compensation are inherently high.

Administrative agencies inherit the immunity of the legislature that created them when carrying out the laws. The state environmental protection agency may seem to have its own agenda and its own constituency, but its budget and overall direction are still set by the legislature and the governor. They are subject to the usual pluralistic, interest-group pressures that make individualized burdens both less likely and easier to bear. Challenges to general laws and policies that implement them should normally be waved off the takings docket.

Some state and federal agencies require closer judicial supervision because the political leash has been deliberately slackened. In the land use area, these are usually special agencies governing geographic areas or special land uses. Examples include New York State's Adirondack Park Commission, the California Coastal Zone Commission, and New Jersey's Pine Barrens Board (Babcock and Siemon 1985; Healy and Rosenberg 1979). Isolating such areas and uses makes landowners affected by the regulations less able to form political coalitions with others similarly situated elsewhere in the state in order to mitigate their burdens. And the difficulty is often compounded by the special isolation of the commissions from ordinary state agencies and legislative oversight. There may be good administrative reasons for undertaking this kind of structure, but judges who are normally inclined to urge plaintiffs to seek political redress for their wounds should be aware of the greater difficulty in doing so. Special-agency actions bear closer scrutiny than the same actions undertaken by the legislature itself.

An example that may be used to explore this distinction is wetlands regulation. Most people who think of wetlands think of places where water is visible and cattails grow. Swamps, marshes, and bogs come to mind. Twenty-five years of environmental consciousness-raising has increased acceptance of regulations that restrict building in swampy areas. Courts of law have generally upheld wetlands preservation without much difficulty (Sibson v. State 1975).

The major problem in wetlands regulation is that the definition of wetlands has gone far beyond the laity's understanding of it. I have taken summer walks on "wetland" without getting my feet muddy, let alone wet. Aside from greatly expanding the reach of regulation, the technical definitions create unfair traps for the unwary. I dealt with a zoning case in which a retired man had filled in some apparently dry land near an intermittent stream behind his house. In this case, the state agencies gave him far more trouble than the local regulations. He was, I think, understandably upset when state agencies proposed to fine him for filling in a wetland without a permit when he had no reason to believe the land was so classified.

The problem here, I believe, is that independent state boards were granted a license by the legislature to create standards for wetlands. Thus there was less public education about what constituted a wetland and the need for caution by landowners than in the case of legislatively voted standards. This is an example in which the delegation of rule making requires some judicial oversight, though perhaps on due process grounds rather than takings. (The process that should be due is a legislative hearing concerning the definition of wetlands rather than just having the legislature delegate it.)

The reason for holding independent agencies to a higher standard than their creator, the legislature itself, is the same as for holding local governments to a higher standard. Local governments require more scrutiny in land use issues because they are not as likely to perceive the full cost of their actions. Since they have all the land they are usually going to get, and since none of it can be removed if its owners are not treated fairly, there are no mobility and few reputation disciplines. Even if there is a social cost to the taking, the cost will be borne mainly by people in other jurisdictions.

The case for the politically isolated agency is similar. It usually has a single mandate, so that adverse economic effects are of little concern to it. The heads of the agencies are often appointees who can be removed only for cause. This may be a wise idea for many purposes, but one of its consequences is a disinclination to listen when adversely affected people complain. The shared problem of the independent agencies and the local governments is their inclination to discount the voices of outsiders. This does not require that all such discounting be regarded as a taking, but it does call for a more careful weighing of settlement and demoralization costs by judges.

9.4 *Judges Should Be Subject to Takings Scrutiny*

The last group that my theory would set out for judicial supervision are judges themselves. Barton Thompson's article, "Judicial Takings" (1990), at first seemed like a sport to me. Judges are supposed to be the guardians of the Takings Clause. To subject them to similar scrutiny seemed like asking the judiciary to consume itself. But Thompson's examples are persuasive. The radical changes in state water law by the Hawaii Supreme Court were as confiscatory as any change a legislature could make. No compensation was offered to the water appropriators, who had relied for almost a century on the previous system.

The important fact (which Thompson did not dwell on) is that the judges are largely insulated from the political give-and-take. Lawyers sometimes remind me that in many states, judges are elected. I will take that seriously when someone tells me of a judge being unelected because of unpopular decisions less prominent than the death penalty. And if examples are common, why, then, have two separate elections for judges and legislators?

The problem with judicial takings is, who is to judge the judges? In the case of state courts, the natural appeal is to the federal courts. I argued in Chapter 6 that the California Supreme Court adopted doctrines that raised housing costs and adversely affected the national economy. Such interstate spillovers make it consistent with the principles of federalism for federal courts to hold that California's judicial practices are takings. This exception was invoked by Robert Ellickson, who has been otherwise assiduously dedicated to judicial federalism (1977, p. 471). As I submitted in section 1.20, the U.S. Supreme Court can be regarded as chiefly interested in disciplining the state courts that are unwilling to take takings seriously. Thompson's bold insight is not really so foreign to the actual practice of the Court.

9.5 Voter Initiatives Warrant No Less Scrutiny

Scholars debate whether voter initiatives should receive closer scrutiny by judges. Initiatives are specifically authorized by about half of the state constitutions as a check on legislatures. Questioning the nature of the process rather than the outcome itself is more consistent with the way in which "due process" is understood these days (Julian Eule 1990). Yet at the same time, initiatives are also the epitome of popular sovereignty and have been responsible for reforms that are now widely accepted (Lynn Baker 1991). The U.S. Supreme Court has generally accepted the latter view, holding that statewide initiatives should be given all of the deference that it accords legislators.

I have argued that local government land use regulations require greater scrutiny because the alternative protections of exit and voice are less available. The initiative at the local level would seem to curtail even further the voice options at the local level. Critics of initiatives believe that the ability to conduct hearings, present evidence, and refute other claims is bypassed when legislation is passed by voter initiative (Callies, Neuffer, and Calibosco 1991). (The influence of California's initiatives on the spread of growth controls was explored in section 6.19.)

The foregoing reasons would seem to militate for even greater judicial review of local regulations adopted by initiative. But it does not necessarily follow. The problem with local land use controls is not that they have been the topic of ill-considered decisions. The problem is that the decisions are perfectly rational from the resident-voter's point of view. They add to their own wealth at the expense of someone else. Thus I cannot criticize initiatives on the grounds that they do not filter the will of the people through legislative processes, because I think that, at the local level, the legislative process *does* reflect the will of the people.

What about statewide regulations adopted by initiatives? This might seem to fit my distinction, since I have argued that strongly felt preferences such as the protection of property rights have a better chance at the state level. The initiative that produced the California Coastal Zone Commission is an example. The legislature would not pass such a measure, because strongly felt preferences by coastal development interests were too influential. The 1972 initiative circumvented this protective layer and created the California Coastal Zone Commission (Hanke and Carbonell 1978).

Despite this, it seems to me that there is little justification for greater judicial scrutiny of land use regulations created by statewide vote than by the state legislature. One could simply note that there's no point in trying to tell the 500-pound gorilla—the image of "inexorable" government I used in section 5.13—where he can sleep. But I also question the patrician claim that initiative votes are insufficiently reflective. Although my home state does not have initiatives (except at the local level), I have been in California during several hotly contested statewide battles. The level of the debate at times seemed rather populist, but it also seemed to me that many voters became aware of the basic issues by this method. Moreover, research on California initiatives by James Snyder (1991) indicated that the results by assembly districts lined up fairly well with the votes by the representatives of those districts.

The rule for statewide initiatives should be simply that they are treated by the courts with no less but no more respect than legislative votes. If initiatives set up commissions that are politically insulated, then a higher level of takings scrutiny should apply to the commission's means of promoting its ends, but not to the general policies. The California Coastal Zone Commission, established by initiative, is such an example. The commission would, under my approach, get the same takings scrutiny if the state legislature had passed the legislation to establish it. The key is not the political process by which a regulatory agency is set up. The key is whether landowners have meaningful political access to alleviate concentrated burdens.

9.6   Courts Must Referee Higher-Government "Usings"

I have repeatedly drawn a political behavioral distinction between government units that are small in area and population and the larger, more heterogeneous bodies of the states and the federal government. My purpose has been to persuade the reader that judicial discipline is more necessary in the smaller than in the larger units. This leaves me open to the question of why, if my theory is valid, constitutional courts should not let the federal government and the state legislatures take land without compensation. If I intend to let the big guys off the judicial hook with respect to most regulatory issues, why not let them decide on their own whether to compensate for physical takings?

The answer lies in the virtues of tradition. If the United States did not have a tradition of judicial review to enforce compensation for physical takings, it would have been paid in almost all cases anyway, as is done in almost every other country in the world. Failure to pay would have generated so much political rancor ("demoralization," one might say) that payment would have become the norm for government acquisition. Daniel Farber (1992) and Saul Levmore (1990) have suggested that just compensation evolved for that reason, and the historical experience of the states during the Revolutionary era described in section 2.9 is consistent with it, as is the demise of William Penn's 6-percent reservation (section 5.2.). As a widely accepted norm, just compensation was safe to assign to the courts. Judicial enforcement reduced legislative transaction costs and assuaged landowner anxieties that arose from the prospect of legislative determination of compensation.

The historically designated role of the courts as referees for eminent domain proceedings warrants their continued activity. To pursue the sports metaphor, if the courts have to referee physical takings for the federal and state governments, as I believe they must, takings remains a game in which the government expects to be able to get away with unnoticed fouls. It will attempt a little opportunistic substitution of regulation for taking. Without some judicial discipline on these substitutions, the traditional referee function of the courts would be lost.

This concession sounds awfully large, so I hasten to delineate it. One test of a regulatory taking is that it is a close substitute for a physical taking. An example is the calculated sequence of adopting restrictive land use controls for the purpose of acquiring the newly regulated land at a reduced price. Even the California courts have little trouble in holding that such blatant substitution of regulation for taking cannot be permitted (Peacock v. Sacramento 1969).

Almost any general regulation should not amount to a taking at the national level provided it is not an obvious substitute for public projects normally undertaken by eminent domain. The "obvious substitute" theme is intelligently explored in Jed Rubenfeld (1993), although he does not make my local–national distinction and thus stretches the theme unnecessarily. Rubenfeld's "usings" approach has some affinity to that of Carol Rose (1983) and Joseph Sax (1964), who distinguished compensable takings by the government trading for its own account from the noncompensable arbitration of disputes among others.

To use my example from section 8.4, farmland preservation regulations get a free pass if issued by the federal government or the states, but not if issued by local governments. The distinction is that, in Rubenfeld's formulation, the federal government is not "using" the farmland for its own purposes. Downzoning land to obtain its use as a national park, by contrast, is a taking of property for which just compensation should be paid, since the normal way of acquiring national park lands is to pay the tab.

9.7 States Sometimes Take the Property of Local Governments

A related issue is whether local governments themselves should be compensated when the state government takes their property. Michael Schill (1989) considered this question thoughtfully. He concluded that, if anything, local governments should get more generous compensation for having a state road go through the local park. His major reason was that local governments are often obliged by the state to provide such facilities. Using substitute facilities as the measure of compensation (rather than market value) for governments formerly tracked the federal court rules for eminent domain. The U.S. Supreme Court reversed this rule in United States v. 50 Acres of Land (1984), however.

Schill's point about lack of substitutes for local government land was paralleled by Jack Knetsch and Thomas Borcherding's (1979) case for more-than-market compensation in general. Lack of substitute facilities that can be purchased with market-value awards means that money is not sufficient compensation for any party. My response to this argument in section 5.18 was that money is the metric that state constitution writers chose. To compensate more than this would discourage projects that people wanted and take more money from taxpayers. It is not clear to me why the lack-of-substitutes problem should be more constitutionally persuasive for local governments than for private individuals.

Schill did not devote much space to the discussion of regulatory takings of local government property. Most conventional theories of local government would dismiss the claim, since local governments are nominally creatures of the state. Political process principles would do the same thing. If anything, local governments have more effective voices in state government than most other economic interests (section 8.7). State legislators are elected from districts whose boundaries typically correspond to some set of local governments. Most legislators themselves began their political careers at the local level. It's hard to think of another interest group more likely to get a sympathetic ear in the state capitol than mayors, county councils, and school boards. For this reason, I would expect that after the *50 Acres* decision, state legislatures would be under some pressure to adopt by legislation the substitute facilities rule. Schill's analysis of their special problems seems correct, but local governments are in less need of the assistance of judges than most other owners of land.

9.8   *The* Mount Laurel *Cases Took a Different Road*

No discussion of the excesses of local land use controls can avoid adding something about the New Jersey Supreme Court's effort to combat exclusionary zoning. In 1975 the New Jersey court ruled that the township of Mount Laurel, a suburb of Philadelphia, was guilty of behaving the way I submitted in section 7.6 almost all suburban communities behave. It zoned its land with an eye to keeping fiscal costs down. This had the effect of making it difficult to develop new low-income housing. The 1975 court ordered the community, and all "developing" municipalities like it, to rezone to accommodate low-income housing. It urged the state legislature to pass laws to facilitate "Opening Up the Suburbs," as the title of Anthony Downs's 1973 book put it. The policy debate at the time between advocates of central-city redevelopment and dispersion of the poor to the suburbs was tipped by the New Jersey court in favor of decentralization.

New Jersey communities did their best not to comply with the court's order, and the state legislature was also hostile to it. Frustrated by the lack of progress, the New Jersey court in 1983 embarked on an extraordinary remedy. The *Mount Laurel II* decision held every community in New Jersey liable to an affirmative obligation to build low-income housing. It set up special judicial panels to enforce this obligation. (A good review of events with the interesting twist that the *Mount Laurel II* decision itself might have been a taking is Lawrence Berger [1991].)

The court's most aggressive technique in *Mount Laurel II* granted a "builder's remedy." A developer could exploit this by offering a deal to the court. If the court would order a community to change its zoning from, say, three-acre minimum lots to a mix of quarter-acre lots and condominiums, the developer would agree to earmark 20 percent of the new units for low-income families. The higher profits from the high-density zoning would finance the low-income units. In effect, the court required communities to sell rezonings, with the proceeds split between low-income housing and additional profits for builders from the higher-density zoning. (Rubin and Seneca [1991] noted that this plan had the potential to be welfare enhancing because of the net supply effects, but Ellickson [1981] and Fischel [1991b] regarded it a smoke screen for exclusion because compliance with inclusionary standards deflected attention from overall supply restrictions.)

Mount Laurel II generated an enormous outcry by politicians at all levels of government (Babcock and Siemon 1985). The New Jersey legislature adopted legislation that, while ostensibly intended to implement the court's decision, was subversive of it in many respects. The New Jersey Fair Housing Act of 1985 eliminated the builder's remedy in midstream, transferring the cases to a nonjudicial board with little enforcement powers of its own. The act also created a state agency, the Council on Affordable Housing, to encourage inclusionary zoning, but without its linchpin, the compulsion of the builder's remedy. The New Jersey court in Hills Development v. Township of Bernards (1986, popularly known as *Mount Laurel III*) approved this remedy, and it optimistically declared that the war was won.

The New Jersey court's decision in *Mount Laurel III* also addressed developers' objections that they had invested money relying on the court's "builder's remedy," which was now disallowed. Chief Justice Robert Wilentz took the occasion to add insult to injury: "No builder with the slightest amount of experience could have relied on the remedies provided in *Mount Laurel II* in the sense of justifiably believing that they would not be changed, or that any change would not apply to builders. If ever any doctrine and any remedy appeared susceptible to change, it was that decision and its remedy" (510 A.2d at 650).

If *Mount Laurel* worked at all, it was because developers were willing to endure the litigation costs of the builders remedy. By dismissing developers as suckers for false bait, Justice Wilentz ensured the impotence of similar remedies in the future. The Wilentz dictum should also stand as a prominent counterexample to the idea that courts are more reliable friends of developers than are legislatures.

9.9 Mount Laurel *Has Had Imperceptible Effects*

Because it has been in effect for more than a decade, it seems fair to ask whether *Mount Laurel II* actually furthered the New Jersey court's goals of opening up the suburbs. As a first pass on this, I asked students in my 1993 urban economics class to use Census data between 1980 and 1990 to compare the development of New Jersey suburbs with otherwise similar samples from nearby Pennsylvania and other northeastern states. It was clear from their reports that Mount Laurel Township itself was different from comparable suburbs in other states. It had built significantly more low-income housing and apartments. The development of most other suburbs in New Jersey, however, did not look different in these respects from development in similar suburbs in nearby Pennsylvania, Connecticut, and New York.

Armed with this insight, one of my students, Alex Giovannotto, wrote a senior honors thesis in which he marshaled more systematic evidence about the net effect of *Mount Laurel*. There are some studies that applaud *Mount Laurel*'s supply effects, but they typically only count the number of units that have been approved by the courts and by the Council on Affordable Housing (Lamar, Mallach, and Payne 1989). This is inadequate because planned units are often not built, and, more important, because it disregards the possibility that the low-income units might have been built anyway by either private or public developers. In addition, Michael Murray (1983) has shown that new public housing at least partly crowds out private housing that would have filtered down to the poor.

Giovannotto was aware of my earlier students' inability to detect *Mount Laurel* effects, so he chose a sample that was biased toward finding a positive effect. The Council on Affordable Housing identified communities with large *Mount Laurel* obligations in the early 1980s. These were presumably prime candidates for its inclusionary-zoning remedy. Giovannotto compared a suburban sample from this group with an otherwise similar sample in nearby Pennsylvania (to control for regional housing market effects). He looked for changes in the composition of the housing stock (multifamily to single family) between the 1980 and 1990 Censuses. During the decade when the *Mount Laurel* doctrine flowered, there was no statistically significant change in the proportion of the housing stock that was multifamily between the New Jersey sample and the Pennsylvania sample. Indeed, in one regression, Pennsylvania suburbs appeared to have built significantly more multifamily units than New Jersey. (Giovannotto was aware that Pennsylvania's Supreme Court was also hostile to exclusionary zoning, but that began in 1965 with National Land v. Kohn and, if anything, the Pennsylvania court's prodeveloper doctrine was softened in 1983 by Appeal of Kravitz.)

Looking at annual New Jersey building permit data, Giovannotto also showed that there was no perceptible difference between New Jersey suburbs that were identified as having high *Mount Laurel* obligations and the rest of New Jersey. The ratio of multifamily to single-family permits varied annually with national economic cycles, but not in response to the *Mount Laurel* obligation. If *Mount Laurel II* is a success on its own terms after ten years, the success is certainly subtle.

9.10 Does Mount Laurel *Pass a Political Process Test?*

In July of 1976, the New Jersey Supreme Court threatened to close the state's schools unless the legislature adopted a state income tax (New Jersey formerly had none) to fund the court's school-finance equalization decision, Robinson v. Cahill (1976). I mention this to point out that the New Jersey court was not much troubled by questions of the legitimacy of intervening in the political process (Lewis Kaden 1983). This can also be discovered from a reading of its *Mount Laurel II* opinion, in which the court refused to name the provision in the state constitution that authorized it to undertake its adventure in home building. This may be why courts in other states respectfully cite the decision, but have not followed its ambitious remedy. Nonetheless, it is worth trying to come up with a rationale for the New Jersey court's approach because it deals with local parochialism, which I have addressed as a reason for special judicial scrutiny under the Takings Clause.

In section 3.20, I applied John Hart Ely's "political process" theory of constitutional interpretation to the takings issue. A political process justification for the *Mount Laurel* decisions would start with the fact that low-income people are poorly represented in suburban municipalities. Indeed, the very reason for fiscal zoning might be said to keep them from being represented there. In this sense, the poor might be said to be analogous to owners of undeveloped land, who often do not live in the community at all, or live there in such small numbers that their weight in majoritarian politics is nil. Thus the courts have to act as their surrogates to provide them with representation. Once housing for the poor is built, the process-based argument might go, representation is complete and the courts can lay off.

Process theory is founded on the idea that judges should make democracy work better by enhancing representation. The paradigm applications of this theory are the one-person, one-vote decisions. The evidence that this theory works is that the court-imposed voting rules were rapidly embraced as a norm by the voters. Once the voters had a taste of the rule, there was little popular pressure to return to the malapportioned status quo. The same could be said, though with more qualifications, about the basic civil rights decisions. Once blacks achieved voting power formerly denied them in the state capitols and in Congress, the impetus to return to legally enforced segregation was nearly eliminated (Michael Klarman 1991b).

The same has not happened in the New Jersey legislature in response to the *Mount Laurel* decisions. The voters kept sending representatives to Trenton who clearly preferred zoning by elected local officials to zoning by unelected judges. New Jersey's constitution is not easily amended, and its judges are more insulated from politics than those of most other states. As a result, the reaction was largely one of nonco-operation and foot-dragging. The resistance of voters *at the state level* to the *Mount Laurel* policy is an important reason for other states not to imitate it.

This is not to say that blatantly exclusionary zoning ought to escape judicial notice. More modest court decisions would assist developers of such housing without embroiling the courts in the entire zoning system and generating a political reaction to subvert the doctrine. The New Hampshire Supreme Court's decision in Britton v. Town of Chester (1991) is a reasonable example. The court held for a developer of low-income housing who had been frustrated by the town for many years.

The New Hampshire court invoked some of the *Mount Laurel* rationale for its holding, but its remedy was limited to specific performance for developers who had actually conformed with reasonable zoning and planning requirements. The court did not adopt the sweeping inclusionary zoning obligations that the New Jersey court imposed on all municipalities in *Mount Laurel II*. Because of the New Hampshire court's modest case-by-case approach, there has been none of the legislative uproar that subverted the New Jersey approach. (For reasons noted in section 7.7, individualized exceptions to fiscal zoning constraints are not especially damaging to the efficiency of the Tiebout model of local government.)

9.11 Land Use Exactions Are Substitutes for Taxes

Developers in most communities pay various types of fees or provide goods in kind in order to get permission to do their projects. These payments are collectively known as "exactions." Prior to about 1970, exactions were pocket change to local governments and developers alike. Developers seldom complained about having to pay for sidewalks, parks, and sewers that directly benefited their projects. When communities wanted to expand infrastructure whose beneficiaries were widely distributed, they either paid for them out of general property taxes (spreading payments over time and future residents via the municipal bond market), or they got a grant from a state or federal agency to undertake the project.

All that has changed over the last two or three decades. Developers and redevelopers are in many communities asked to pay not just for on-site improvements but for facilities elsewhere in the community. The title of a book by Alan Altshuler and Jose Gómez-Ibáñez, *Regulation for Revenue* (1993), makes clear the real purpose of exactions. They have become a substitute for local taxes. Many of the facilities paid for with exactions have only a tenuous connection with the new development.

An extreme example cited by Altshuler and Gómez-Ibáñez is San Francisco, in which new office buildings, once regarded as fiscally beneficial, are now charged extra exactions because the projects are said to bring in more workers. San Francisco housing advocates claim that new workers bid up the price of existing housing and make existing renters worse off. Hence the office developers have been required to finance more low-income housing units. (The logical corollary of that proposition, that San Francisco should encourage businesses to leave the city in order to help low-income residents, seems never to have taken hold.)

The source of exactions, and the major reason for their growth, has been the dramatic expansion of land use regulations since 1970. The communities that collect exactions are the ones that have the most regulations. If developers could do projects "as of right," the community would have almost no leverage to exact any payment beyond property taxes. The exactions revolution followed inexorably from the regulatory revolution.

Altshuler and Gómez-Ibáñez were concerned that exactions have become unfair and inefficient alternatives to general taxation. Their reluctant conclusion, however, was that exactions, for all their faults, are better than their most likely alternative, which is growth controls. If local exactions were disallowed by courts or by state legislatures, most communities would find new ways to discourage development. This supply restriction would, the authors concluded, raise housing costs even more than exactions would. (For a more formal model reaching the same conclusion, see Joseph Gyourko [1991].)

9.12 Exactions Are Sometimes Takings

The U.S. Supreme Court has made two rulings, Nollan v. California Coastal Commission (1987) and Dolan v. Tigard (1994), which link exactions with takings. (*Nollan* was described in section 1.22, and

Dolan will be described in section 9.14.) A diagrammatic approach (adapted from Fischel [1985]) may illuminate the connection. Consider land use entitlements for a vacant parcel of land located in a partially developed suburban area. The entitlement to use this parcel can be lined up on a continuous scale, as shown in Figure 9.1. On the right side of the scale, the landowner is permitted to do nothing at all with the land. Moving to the left from this extreme point, the landowner acquires successive entitlements. First, say, she can walk on it and pitch a tent on it, which gives her some value. Next on the scale, she can plant a garden. After that, she can place a small vacation cottage; after that, a home, and so forth.

On the left side of the scale, the landowner can do anything she wants on the property, including establishing the proverbial glue factory, cattle feedlot, or toxic waste dump. She is free of the obligations of classic nuisance doctrines. Moving to the right from this extreme, she is first obligated to reduce the worst of the dangers of her property to the public, then conform to classic nuisance law, then abide by EPA standards, and so forth.

Another party's interest is implicitly represented on the diagram. The people who live near the site are affected by it, and their interests are, in most parts of the United States, represented by their local government. In many contexts, the neighbors will prefer that the landowner use her land less intensively than more intensively. Their preferences are for a use toward the right side of the diagram (less development), while the landowner will prefer a use toward the left side. (Of course, many land uses do not involve conflict between neighbors, but they generate no controversies, either.)

I shall presently use this diagram to advance a particular standard, but for now my purpose is simply to distinguish between two issues. One is the issue of where courts should divide entitlements between the owner and her neighbors. Suppose for the moment that this has been settled as point A on the diagram. The second issue is what happens when either party wants to move away from that entitlement.

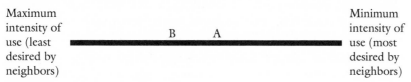

| Maximum intensity of use (least desired by neighbors) | B   A | Minimum intensity of use (most desired by neighbors) |

Figure 9.1 Land Use Entitlements

That is, if entitlement A is the status quo, under what conditions should the landowner be permitted to move to point B, which is more intensive and hence more profitable? Should she be able to do it with only the most minor conditions attached, or should the community be able to extract any amount?

This is, in its most general form, the issue of land use exactions that was raised in Nollan v. California Coastal Commission (1987). Nollan wanted to move from A, the status quo of a small beach house, to B, a somewhat larger beach house. This change supposedly was undesirable to the public because the new house would reduce the view from inland, and the coastal commission could have insisted that Nollan remain at A (small house) for that reason. Instead, the commission asked Nollan to give it an easement for public access to the beach in front of his house.

The problem with this deal, I believe, was not that it was "extortion," which means unfavorable terms of trade. The problem was that outside observers would probably not regard point B as an illegitimate entitlement. That is, Nollan's new home in fact seems perfectly consistent with the setting in which it was rebuilt. Beach houses are common in California.

To see why it is misleading to focus on the terms of trade between Nollan and the commission, envision a slightly different scenario, one favored by law and economics (Fischel 1987). Let Nollan be part of a private community, in which covenants with his neighbors govern the size of his house. He has a beach to which he has exclusive access. Now he wants to build a bigger house, and he must get the consent of all his neighbors. As the price of their consent, the neighbors demand access to Nollan's beach. Nollan weighs the value of his private beach against the value of a larger home and makes his choice. The point is that no one would be disturbed by this option, and few besides the hypothetical Mr. Nollan would call it extortion.

The difference between the hypothetical private-covenant scenario and the actual one is that Nollan and his predecessor in title would have bought into the private one with their eyes open about what they owned and could do. The problem in the actual one is that what Nollan owned had been changed without his consent. That is, the offensive part about the California Coastal Commission's action in *Nollan* is not that Mr. Nollan was asked to give up his entitlement to exclude trespassers on his beach, but that he should have had to give up much of anything to do what for years was regarded as a normal, harmless thing to do. I think that B is actually the proper "status quo" entitlement, not A, and Nollan should not have to pay (or pay very much) to have entitlement B.

One more scenario is needed to prove my point. Suppose the proposed move from A to B by Nollan was not within the range of behavior that we think of as normal for property in that situation, but instead involved effects that were seriously harmful to the neighborhood and passersby. Suppose he'd proposed a large hotel, which truly would have blocked the view and stood out like the proverbial sore thumb. In this scenario, I submit that few people would be bothered by the coastal commission's insisting that Nollan pay for the rights surrendered by the public, even if the form of the payment involved a physical invasion that bore no nexus whatsoever to the view. (One might object that there are hotels along the beach in California, but before using this as a standard of normal behavior, I would want to know the circumstances by which the developers of those hotels got permission to build there.)

9.13 The Unconstitutional Conditions Doctrine Would Not Help

Nollan was analyzed by Vicki Been (1991) as an example of an "unconstitutional condition" imposed by a government agency. An example of such a condition would be a law that prohibits free speech as a condition of government employment. Been disparaged this view because she thought that Nollan could be protected by "exit" rights. While I agreed with Been's general principle, reviewed in section 3.23, I think it does not apply to Nollan's case. While *he* was movable—he seems, indeed, to have "moved to the taking" by buying after the coastal commission's scheme was in place—the *property* itself was not. Since regulations run with the land, not with the owner, their constitutionality must also run with the land. (Section 5.7 explained why "moving to the taking" is not a satisfactory justification for withholding compensation.)

Richard Epstein, whose book on takings was discussed in Chapter 4, put a better face on *Nollan* and the unconstitutional conditions doctrine. In his 1993 book, *Bargaining with the State*, Epstein explored the doctrine with an eye to preventing the state from using its monopoly on regulation to extract economic concessions from its citizens. Among his many applications of this were land use exactions.

Epstein did not like the California Coastal Commission's regulations and would have held them to be a taking. But recognizing that his takings doctrine might not be accepted, he took a fallback position that invoked unconstitutional conditions. Epstein approved of the *Nollan* Court's use of the doctrine because he believed that it would induce the coastal commission to abandon the view-preserving regulations. He regarded the regulation as little more than a bargaining chip with which to purchase beach property. Epstein acknowledged that restricting regulatory trade might make things worse for beachfront owners, but his "empirical guess" was that the regulations would wither away after *Nollan* had ruled that they were valueless in exchange (1993, p. 183).

Epstein's "empirical guess" seems wrong. In June of 1994 I called two California eminent domain attorneys of my acquaintance and asked them whether the coastal commission had backed off from any of its restrictions since *Nollan* was decided in 1987. Gideon Kanner told me in no uncertain terms that the commission had not budged an inch on its restrictions since *Nollan,* though he blamed the lower courts for not following the U.S. Supreme Court's lead. Robert Best, who was Patrick Nollan's attorney for his U.S. Supreme Court appeal, confirmed Kanner's assessment that the coastal commission's regulations were as restrictive as ever. Best added that he'd heard some people say that *Nollan* made things worse for landowners. By making deal-making less attractive to the commission, the decision may have made it leery of initiating deals that would work to both sides' advantage. (Best said that he did not necessarily agree with this view, but he volunteered it without my reminding him that that's what I predicted would happen [Fischel 1988, p. 1588].)

Why has the coastal commission not allowed its regulations to wither away after their exchange value was reduced by *Nollan?* My experience with land use regulations is that most of them are adopted for a reason. The reasons may not always be socially desirable or efficient, but they have some value to the people who adopt them. In the case of the coastal commission, the regulations were adopted pursuant to a voter initiative whose stated purpose was to restrict coastal development more than had been done previously. Voters appear to have understood its implications (Deacon and Shapiro 1975). A clear public purpose is not, of course, a warrant for taking property without just compensation, but it does explain why making the regulations inalienable via the unconstitutional conditions doctrine is not going to make the regulations go away.

9.14 *Dolan v. Tigard Revived Proportionality in Exactions*

The most recent U.S. Supreme Court takings decision is Dolan v. Tigard (1994). Tigard, a city of thirty thousand on the metropolitan fringe of Portland, Oregon, wanted to build a bike path in its downtown area, purportedly to alleviate traffic congestion. It was also concerned that additional development near the floodplain of Fanno Creek, which runs through the downtown area, would increase the risk of flooding.

Florence Dolan owned a hardware store in downtown Tigard. Fanno Creek goes through part of her lot. She wanted to more than double the size of the building on the 1.67-acre lot and pave a larger parking lot to accommodate more business. Acting according to a previously adopted plan, the city said she could do so only if she deeded the 10 percent of the area of her lot in the floodplain to the city, to be used partly for open space and partly for a public bike path. The rationales for these require-ments were that the open space would reduce the hazard of flooding occasioned by runoff from the new parking lot, and that the bike path could reduce downtown congestion, some of which could be attributed to the expanded store's additional customers and staff.

The difference between Tigard's attempt to assume about 10 per-cent of the area of Dolan's property and the California Coastal Com-mission's attempt to allow pedestrian access to Nollan's beachfront property is that Tigard's size and lot coverage regulations *did* have something to do with the demands it made of Mrs. Dolan. The Ore-gon courts upheld the exaction, specifically finding that there was some "nexus" between the city's demand for land and Mrs. Dolan's pro-posed expansion.

Five justices of the U.S. Supreme Court nonetheless objected that the city's demand for land was too high a price to pay for what they apparently regarded as the modest inroad that Dolan's plans would make on traffic and flood risk. Chief Justice Rehnquist's majority opin-ion held that such disproportionate demands were uncompensated takings, and Mrs. Dolan prevailed. The Court distilled from some state court decisions a new standard called "rough proportionality." It in-sists that the city, not the private party, show that there is a fair ratio between the public harm that the private project might cause and the value of the asset that the private party is expected to give up.

One can sometimes end up thinking better of majority opinions by reading the dissents. Justice Stevens, joined by Justices Blackmun and Ginsburg, chided the Court for intervening in state law matters. His position would have been more persuasive if Stevens had not again revealed his long-standing hostility to the entire doctrine of regulatory takings, which stems in part from his erroneous view that *Pennsylvania Coal* was an advisory opinion. (See section 1.1 at casenote [8].)

Justice Souter's separate dissent claimed that the standard in *Dolan* did not differ from that of *Nollan*. He pointed out that the majority's major objection to Tigard's plan was that the city had not shown that the bike path *would* have offset additional congestion caused by the new construction. Tigard said only that the bike path *could* have offset increased automobile traffic.

Justice Souter was correct, but his derision of the difference between "could" and "would" served him badly. I have seen many reports dealing with the predicted effects of some project on the public. It does not take much cleverness for a planning commission to show that x "could" cause y in these contexts. Almost any event "could" contribute to some subsequent event. An applicant who denies that there is *some* chance of a connection cannot be believed. But for the government to say that x "would" cause y gives the applicant something to respond to. Frivolous predictions can be winnowed from sound ones by appeals to experience, evidence from studies, and common sense.

Chief Justice Rehnquist's demand for "rough proportionality" properly focuses the magnitudes to be compared. On the one side is the value of what the public loses from the project itself. It is not the magnitude of what the public could have exacted from the developer. Forgone revenues do not count as "harms." On the other side is the value to the owner of the property to be taken. It is what the owner loses, not what the owner gains from the rest of her property if she is allowed to develop.

9.15 Dolan *Should Dispense with* Nollan

The *Dolan* Court's insistence on proportionality between what the owner surrenders and what the public gets reflects a desirable judicial concern about unfairness by local governments. My main criticism of the decision is that it builds on the nexus doctrine of *Nollan* rather than replacing it. The only virtue of *Nollan's* nexus doctrine is that it might deter some governments from adopting regulations for the sole purpose of selling them for cash. But if the Court is willing to supervise the terms of trade for regulations with its new "rough proportionality" rule, the old nexus doctrine is unnecessary even for that task.

To see why, suppose one had a choice of doctrines in *Nollan*. If the 1994 *Dolan* doctrine had been available in 1987, the California Coastal Commission could have been asked whether the harm that Mr. Nollan was allegedly causing by building a slightly bigger building was proportional to the value of the right he was asked to give up. Since the harm to the public was trivial in his case (his new house blocked almost none of the view of the ocean), and the right he was to give up was very valuable (the right to exclude strangers from walking on his beach), the coastal commission's exaction would have been held a taking. Thus the "rough proportionality" rule would give the same result as the nexus rule.

The advantage of the *Dolan* proportionality rule is that desirable deal-making would not be as much discouraged as under the nexus rule. Suppose that Nollan's proposal really had blocked a lot of the view and that such blockage were regarded as a loss of something valuable that the public owned. In this case, the coastal commission's proposed deal would seem reasonable on a proportionality test. But under the nexus doctrine, such a reasonable deal would nonetheless be struck down, because the surrender of the view would have no logical relation to the gain in pedestrian access to the beach.

Substituting the *Dolan* proportionality rule for the *Nollan* nexus requirement would not encourage adoption of excessive regulations. A regulation worthless to the public would, on the proportionality rule, require no exaction from the landowner to get rid of it. Hence it would be valueless in a bargaining game. It is true that neither the *Dolan* proportionality rule nor the *Nollan* nexus rule compels the regulator to drop any particular regulation, but this only points to the need for an additional standard at which the Court has not yet arrived and which I will advance in section 9.17.

The other reason to replace *Nollan* is that it encourages third-party suits, which are endemic in land use law. A developer and a regulatory body may want to trade, but a third party might intervene on *Nollan's* nexus grounds. This is what happened in Municipal Art Society v. City of New York (1987). The city granted a favorable rezoning of a site that it owned in exchange for a higher price by the buyer. It would have allowed the buyer to tear down a low building, the New York Coliseum, and build a skyscraper in its stead. The Municipal Art Society, not a party to the deal, sued the city and won on grounds that are not much different from those of *Nollan* (Jerold Kayden 1991). The city's rezoning had no regulatory nexus with its desire to obtain a higher price for its land.

One might personally agree with the Municipal Art Society that the rezoning for an oversize office building in Manhattan was bad for the neighborhood. To let the society prevail on those grounds, however, is to elevate an unelected, private group above the elected officials of the city. The insistence on nexus in *Nollan* is apt to promote more undemocratic second-guessing of locally desired deals by courts. *Dolan* does not offer that leverage to third parties, and it is superior for that reason.

9.16   Dolan *Presents Administrative Problems*

To remind readers that I am an economist, I cannot let *Dolan* pass without some on-the-other-hand comments. *Dolan* poses a serious problem for judicial administration. Property and land use law are largely the province of the states, and both the majority and the dissent in *Dolan* defer to state courts. Nonetheless, by offering a federal court option for developers who are dissatisfied with local decisions, the floodgates may be hard to administer. This was certainly the problem with Norwood v. Baker (1898).

Norwood involved a special assessment whose facts are similar to those of Dolan v. Tigard, though the 1898 case was not mentioned in the 1994 opinion. The 1898 U.S. Supreme Court held that the Ohio city of Norwood had failed to give just compensation to Mrs. Baker when it took the center third of her lot for a new street. The city had found that the taken land was worth $2,000. It then turned around and assessed Mrs. Baker's remaining property (now bisected by the road) for $2,218 (the extra $218 to cover assessment costs) for the supposed benefit of creating a new street. By analogy, what the city of Tigard could have done was take the bike path by eminent domain and assess Mrs. Dolan for the entire cost. Justice Peterson's dissent in the Oregon Supreme Court in fact framed the question this way and presented evidence that the bike path provided general benefits to the city, not special benefits to Dolan (854 P.2d at 445).

The 1898 Court's decision in favor of Mrs. Baker brought a flood of similar cases into the federal docket (Ellickson and Tarlock 1981, p. 720). But the Court then closed the spigot by upholding an only slightly less arbitrary assessment in Louisville and Nashville Railroad v. Barber Asphalt Paving (1905), leaving the state courts to decide such cases on their own. *Norwood* may still have had a salutary influence on the subsequent development of state special-assessment law. It does suggest, however, that the present Court will face some difficulty administering its "rough proportionality" standard in *Dolan*.

Although I approve of some judicial supervision of exactions, it would be inconsistent with the theme of this book not to point out that there has been some political reaction to excessive exactions. Developer organizations in California have, in response to adverse decisions by the courts, lobbied for state legislation to formalize the exaction process. The result is an elaborate system of "development agreements" in which communities and developers can hammer out long-term obligations to one another (Porter and Marsh 1989). Legislation in other states adopted at the behest of developers has regularized the exaction process by adopting schedules of "impact fees" (Blaesser and Kentopp 1990). While such legislation does not guarantee fair treatment of landowners, courts should be wary of intervening where such legislation has been adopted.

9.17 The Appropriate Regulatory Base Is "Normal Behavior"

As I suggested in section 9.12, the problem of exactions is intimately connected with the reasonableness of the regulation to which an exception is sought. The more basic question that this and the following sections deal with is how to determine which initial entitlements are reasonable.

Figure 9.1 represented the range of allowable activities as a continuum. At one extreme, the owner of each individual plot is permitted to do anything he wants, regardless of its spillover consequences to his neighbors or the community at large. This extreme is, of course, an artifice of imagination. No society allows an owner blanket permission to commit nuisances and still retain the other privileges of property ownership. At the other extreme, the owner is allowed to do nothing with his land other than maintain title to it. The community can prevent any activity and compel him to satisfy any of its wishes. Again, this is artificial (though some landowners of my acquaintance would disagree), since it is hard to imagine calling such a pervasively intrusive regime one in which private property is allowed at all.

In between is the more usual mix of property rights and police-power regulations. A useful thought experiment, originally suggested by Harold Demsetz (1967) and recently explored with a wide range of examples by Robert Ellickson (1993), is to ask why this more limited, compromise range is what has evolved in most societies. Suppose a society was at the private extreme. While there are clear advantages to a private ordering, the mere description of the "entitlements" to commit mayhem suggests that all property owners would be willing to give some of them up in return for their neighbors' forbearance from the same.

Likewise at the opposite extreme, the inability to use property for productive or otherwise personally satisfying activities would make property owners willing to pay to acquire a greater range of entitlements. Because the transaction costs of moving from either extreme to the more central range are high, goes this story, it is preferable to accept some middle range between complete privatism and complete statism.

The middle range, which becomes the base point for regulatory takings, is what Ellickson described in several revealing articles (1973, 1977) as "normal behavior." The standard is more burdensome to the private landowner than the common-law injunction against nuisances. Normal behavior by a landowner involves not simply a lack of pollution or nuisances but a willingness to live up to standards exhibited by the community. A zoning requirement for all homes to be set back a uniform distance from the street is hardly prohibiting a nuisance, as that term is usually understood. But if most others in the community had generally complied with such a setback, it is certainly within the realm of normal behavior to expect other landowners to comply as well. Likewise if most single-family homes in a neighborhood were located on quarter-acre lots, a developer who sought to build ten homes per acre might reasonably be told she could not do so.

To illustrate this standard, I impose it on Figure 9.1 with the result shown in Figure 9.2. (This is discussed more fully in Fischel [1985], chaps. 8 and 9.)

As in the discussion of the *Nollan* case in section 9.12, both entitlements A and B fall within the range of normal behavior. In this case,

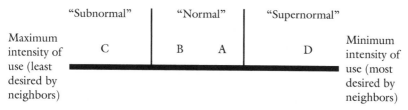

Figure 9.2 Land Use Norms

a permit to allow the existing use of the land to move from A to B should be allowed. The owner might have to pay something for this, but the transaction should be governed by the "rough proportionality" of Dolan v. Tigard to protect the landowner from unconscionable deals. But if the landowner sought point C, which is in the "subnormal" range, the zoning authority would be permitted to exact any concession or deny it altogether.

If the community were to move the entitlement from A to D, which is in the supernormal range, the landowner should be able to demand just compensation in most cases. Exceptions would occur when the community could meet the Michelman criteria (section 4.3) that settlement costs exceeded demoralization costs, and that the move was economically efficient, not just reasonably related to something the public desired. If landowners had an initial entitlement to "subnormal" point C, most communities should be able to insist on a move to "normal" point B without compensation, except when C had been specifically agreed to by previous public actions. Grandfathering subnormal nonconforming uses when standards are generally raised ought not to perpetuate uses that are genuinely harmful to the rest of the community. (The law on nonconforming uses seems consistent with this view [Curtis Berger 1983, 16.1].)

9.18 *Normal Behavior Is a Variant of the Harm/Benefit Test*

The normal-behavior standard is similar to the classic harm/benefit test. Judicial deference to the flexibility of the police power is most persuasive when the regulations prevent harmful activities. The discovery that certain kinds of waste disposal threaten drinking-water supplies surely justifies regulations—even retroactive regulations—that require costly new septic systems or sewers.

Police-power regulations that force benefits are more problematical.

As we have seen in many cases, an uncritical view of the police power encourages governments to substitute uncompensated regulation for compensable eminent domain. To quote Holmes from *Pennsylvania Coal:* "As long recognized, some values are enjoyed under an implied limitation and must yield to the police power. But obviously the implied limitation must have its limits, or the contract and due process clauses are gone." Ernst Freund's (1904) classic distinction between the noncompensable harm-prevention of the police power and the fully compensable benefit-extraction of eminent domain apparently influenced Holmes's thinking on this (Catherine Connors 1990, p. 169).

The harm/benefit rule, however, is often criticized, particularly by economists and economics-influenced lawyers. They have often pointed out that the terms harm-prevention and benefit-extraction are relative. Preventing the harm of hunger is providing the benefit of food; providing the benefit of a nice view is preventing the harm of an ugly one.

It is cleverness of this sort by which economists read themselves out of the takings debate. Few ordinary citizens would agree that displaying decorations on the side of an otherwise inoffensive building is a legal obligation because it prevents the harm of ugliness of an ordinary façade. Even fewer would say that refraining from assaulting innocent people is providing them with the benefit of safety and can be said to be praiseworthy. The question of the appropriate base point for compensation is not seriously addressed by saying that it all depends on how you phrase it. "Down" does not become "up" just because one can invert oneself on a trapeze. (For a more nuanced defense of the harm/benefit distinction, see Ellickson [1977, pp. 419–421], and Donald Wittman [1984].)

The difficulty with the rule is that standards of what is harmful change. The classic case is air pollution. Three generations ago, Pigou suggested that firms that reduced pollution should be paid subsidies (Coase 1960, p. 35). This implied that clean air was a social benefit for which compensation should be made, rather than a social cost on which taxes should be imposed. The ecological revolution is surely one in which standards of what is normal behavior have changed.

Where does this leave the normal-behavior standard, wherein judges have to decide what is normal, when normalcy is not a constant? The key to the judges' role is the level of government that adopts the new and higher standard of normal behavior. My idea is that the larger republics are more appropriate sources of declarations of what is normal behavior for property owners. This is not because I think state legislatures are unerring readers of the public pulse, but because they are no worse at it than judges. (An extraordinary example of a judge's decision to expand the scope of "harms" to include all man-made activities is Just v. Marinette County [Wisc. 1972], which is now a leading case in wetlands preservation.) Moreover, legislators are entitled to change their minds if they find out they have misjudged the public will, whereas judges interpreting the Constitution supposedly do not.

For the foregoing reasons, I am inclined to disagree with Justice Scalia's rejection of the harm-prevention standard in *Lucas,* insofar as the "harm" criterion emerged from state legislative deliberations. Scalia's skepticism of legislative language would be more telling if the declarations of "harm" were made by a local government or a special agency. The smaller republics are where the judges have to exercise independent judgment. In such cases, inquiries about what standards the voters hold themselves to are more relevant than what they say others should be held to. (In section 1.24 I submitted that Mr. Lucas was nonetheless entitled to redress when the legislature had provided no appeal mechanism to mitigate his complete economic wipeout.)

9.19 The "Conflagration Rule" Supports the Harm/Benefit Distinction

There is little need to defend the principle that regulations preventing activities that have come to be regarded as harmful do not require compensation. The only real debate about harm-prevention is over which parties—judges or legislators—should be relied on to decide what constitutes a harm. The principle of compensating for benefit-extraction, however, is not so widely understood. This section shows that the hoary "physical invasion" test of sufficiency for compensation is consistent with the benefit-extraction principle.

The purpose of eminent domain is to acquire property for projects that most people regard as providing a public benefit. New or expanded highways, airports, post offices, and schools have always been regarded as public benefits, involving a state of the world that puts the public ahead of the status quo. Consistent with this ranking is the language of the "benefit-offset" principle that I explored in section 2.10. The idea that compensation should be reduced for landowners because their remaining property was "benefited" by the new railroad was controversial, but no one said that landowners' compensation should be reduced because retention of their land without a railroad over it "harmed" the public.

There is one exception to compensation for physical invasions, though, and it proves its connection with the harm/benefit distinction. The ancient conflagration rule holds that when an urban fire threatens to burn out of control, authorities may destroy even unburned buildings to create a firebreak without compensating their owners. The idea behind the rule is to allow authorities to act without the slightest hesitation. The cautionary and legendary example of this is the Great Fire of London of 1666, which raged out of control in part because the Lord Mayor was afraid that preemptive destruction of buildings to create a firebreak would result in his being held liable for the results. (The Lord Mayor's plight was described in a Pennsylvania case, Respublica v. Sparhawk [1788], which invoked the conflagration rule to deny compensation for the loss of flour ordered removed from Philadelphia to keep it from being captured by the British during the Revolutionary War.)

A modern version of the Lord Mayor's dilemma arose after the San Francisco earthquake of 1906, in which the subsequent fire accounted for most of the property losses (Thomas and Witts 1971). San Francisco authorities actually took the trouble to consult a judge about their liability before they began dynamiting buildings to create a firebreak. The judge quickly told them of the old conflagration rule. City officials proceeded to blast away, though not always with the desired results.

The reason for the conflagration rule that Perry Shapiro and I gave is that a requirement of compensation would not deter the government from doing it anyway. Because compensation induces other types of inefficient behavior, our theory holds, it is best not to compensate when the taking is truly inevitable. (The model on which our position was based was described in section 5.11.)

The trouble with our theory, though, is that the threat of liability for taking apparently *does* make the government's agents cautious, so that takings are not inevitable even when the benefits are enormous. The stories about the London and San Francisco fires suggest that officials would hesitate to act if they had to pay. Judges' eagerness to promote quick action apparently offsets their concern about the utterly arbitrary nature of the gains and losses. One person loses his home to the fire; his neighbor's house is saved. One would think that the owners of property saved from destruction would be more than happy to pay their salvers out of increased local taxes, but this has been left as a matter of municipal and private discretion, not constitutional compulsion.

A better explanation for the conflagration rule, I believe, is that owners of flammable buildings in the path of an urban conflagration could be characterized as harboring something "harmful" to the rest of the community. Suppressing a fire has always been regarded as preventing a harm, not providing a benefit, and providing fuel for such fires adds to the harm. There is, of course, nothing blameworthy about owning a house that is unfortunately placed, but eminent domain is distinguished from tort law by the former's unwillingness to point the finger of blame. The demolished building just happens to be in the path of a raging fire, and it is therefore harmful.

The same may be said of innocent property that, because of unforeseen circumstances, becomes useful to one's enemy during war. The U.S. Supreme Court in United States v. Caltex (1952) seemed to make the harm-prevention distinction. It denied compensation for the U.S. Army's destruction of Caltex's Philippine terminal facilities, which would have otherwise fallen into the hands of the invading Japanese army. Chief Justice Vincent's opinion only hinted at the harm-prevention aspect, but Justice Douglas in dissent said that Caltex should have been compensated precisely because its facility had not become a "public nuisance."

The foregoing cases, which provide support for the harm/benefit principle, also make the physical invasion rule seem more sensible. Rather than being a formalistic fetish, judicial insistence on compensation for every physical invasion when there are no emergencies seems more consistent with overriding social norms. People believe that someone whose property is occupied as a result of government action provides a "benefit" that should be rewarded, not penalized. The physical invasion standard has been abused only because what is usually a sufficient condition for compensation has been made into a necessary condition for compensation.

9.20   Hanover, N.H., Might Flunk the "Normal Behavior" Test

Having defended the old harm/benefit rule, I might be asked why it should not be applied directly, as scholars such as Bernard Siegan (1980) and Douglas Kmiec (1988) have urged, rather than watered down to the normal-behavior standard. The answer is the virgule in "harm/benefit." It suggests a precipice between government activities that prevent harms and those that extract benefits. It overlooks the contextual subtleties of activities that should be compensable in some times and places but not in others. The virtue of a normal-behavior standard is that it admits to a range of behaviors between "subnormal" and "supernormal," and it allows that what is normal can vary by locale. This section will show some of those subtleties by applying the normal behavior standard to my hometown of Hanover, New Hampshire.

Hanover is an affluent town of about 10,000 people (including 3,500 students). Its chief industries are Dartmouth College and the U.S. Army Cold Regions Research and Engineering Laboratory. The largest area employer is a nearby regional medical center in the city of Lebanon, N.H., a small city that also happily accommodates most shopping-center and industrial development. Most of Hanover's population lives in a two-square-mile "compact area" on the southeast corner of the forty-eight-square miles (about the area of Boston) that constitute the township.

Hanover has had townwide zoning since 1961. A planning board and subdivision regulations existed before that. The current zoning ordinance, which is more restrictive than the original, was written in 1976. Annual amendments, always voted on by the entire electorate, have usually made it more restrictive still, which follows the evolution of most other zoning ordinances. I have been on the Hanover zoning board since 1987. Zoning boards are the "quasi-judicial" arbiters of disputes about the application of the laws, and they grant or withhold minor exceptions to the ordinance. Such exceptions are sometimes decisive in takings litigation.

Most of the town outside of the compact area is zoned "rural residential," which allows houses on lots of at least three acres, and "forest and recreation," which permits almost no development except seasonal dwellings. The building boom of the 1980s has filled up many of the developable three-acre lots. The result is exquisitely planned rural sprawl. The homes on the rural roads are widely spaced and mostly inconspicuous. There are few new neighborhoods in which children can assemble for an impromptu baseball game without their parents' driving them.

I suspect that if Ellickson's normal-behavior rule had been enforced for the last fifteen years, Hanover would have considerably more development than it does now. The three-acre zoning for most undeveloped residential areas does not respond to market demand. One-acre vacant lots that were subdivided before the current ordinance was in effect and that are still vacant sell for almost the same price as adjacent three-acre lots that cannot be subdivided any further. This implies that at least two of the acres on a three-acre lot are redundant as far as buyers are concerned. (A more precise study reaching a similar conclusion for Ramapo, New York, is James White [1988].)

The Hanover ordinance itself shows little evidence of imposing "growth controls." The master plan does envision the town as remaining a small college town, but there is no mention of the rate of population growth or limiting building permits. The zoning law does have some subtle features that make development difficult. One is that all rural lots must have a minimum of two hundred feet fronting on an improved public road. Many of the public roads in the outlying sections of Hanover are no longer maintained. The quaint official term for such closure is "subject to gates and bars," which once enabled farmers to pasture animals on lots that straddled the road without having their livestock wander off. The town's present policy is generally not to rededicate the roads to provide access for building lots, except to allow the owner access for a single house. Thus even though a fifteen-acre lot might be permitted by the ordinance to have five homes, it is likely to get only one if the access is a town road subject to gates and bars. The term has taken on a new connotation.

9.21 *Normal Behavior Implies a Golden Rule*

A developer would best attack Hanover's ordinance by purchasing an interest in a twelve-acre parcel of land not too far from the built-up area but in the rural residential zone. She would then propose to the planning board that the area be rezoned to permit her to subdivide the twelve acres not into *four* three-acre lots permitted by the ordinance, but into *twenty-four* half-acre lots. (I am ignoring the local street area for computational convenience.)

Her justification for proposing this is that half an acre is the median lot size on which the majority of the current single-family homes in the town were in fact built. Most of them were built prior to the adoption of the zoning ordinance. She points out that the neighborhoods with small lots are attractive and valuable and exhibit few of the classic spillover problems that zoning ostensibly deals with.

In her appeal to the planning board, the developer invokes the golden rule. If Hanover residents did not currently own property in their town but were considering moving there, what kind of zoning would they like to see? They would probably not want a place that was overrun with a jumble of poorly laid-out housing projects. But they would also not want the place to be so exclusive that they and their family and friends could not afford to buy a house there. By asking the "insiders" to think about what it might be like to be an "outsider," the developer would be invoking an ethical posture that has been admired for at least two thousand years.

But the developer can also play hardball. If the town does not rezone to suit her project within a reasonable period of time and without unreasonable subdivision-exactions demands, she threatens to sue for the difference in value for the land as currently zoned and the value as she proposed it. The interest-clock on this large amount would begin from the moment the planning board denied (as it surely would) her final appeal to them. My guess is that the initial damages would be on the order of a million dollars.

The town attorney would take this suit seriously. New Hampshire's Burrows v. Keene (1981) was one of the first state decisions to follow the regulatory takings doctrine expressed by Justice Brennan's 1980 dissent in San Diego Gas and Electric v. San Diego. (Brennan's dissent became the majority opinion in First English v. Los Angeles in 1987, as reviewed in section 1.20, but several state courts were apparently influenced by the writing on the wall.) Moreover, Hanover itself has been sued for takings damages in recent years. The case involved a change in parking requirements for a commercial building, which is a factual far cry from the present hypothetical. The town selectmen nonetheless have recent knowledge of what it is like to negotiate with a landowner who insists he's suffered a million dollars in damages and has a court that may be inclined to agree with him.

If the town attorney were faced with defending the town before a judge who was influenced by the normal-behavior standard, he might argue that a three-acre minimum lot size in a rural residential town like Hanover is perfectly consistent with normal behavior. He could show that almost all development since the 1970s has occurred at this density. No landowner has challenged the constitutionality of the ordinance on these grounds since its adoption in 1976. Many other towns in New Hampshire have similar requirements, and the state statutes that authorize zoning do not disallow any of the rules.

The town's defense attorney might also point out that just because older neighborhoods have quarter- and half-acre lots does not mean that all have to have them. He might pull in an expert witness to show that the reason that small lots in Hanover are valuable is because much of the rest of the town is zoned in such a way as to keep it a small town. He could even cite Robert Ellickson, the avatar of the damages remedy for growth controls (1977, p. 416), to the effect that preservation of "small town character" is a legitimate reason to limit growth by police-power means. The defense attorney would preemptively dismiss the idea that the high value of existing homes is the result of municipal monopoly power. He could point out that there are about a dozen other towns within twenty miles of downtown Hanover, from which a majority of the work force at the college and hospital commutes every day.

The plaintiff's attorney could respond that failure to challenge an unconstitutional condition for a long time does not moot the rights of the owners. Estoppel might be applicable to owners who actually developed, but not to those who waited. Whether the premium prices for existing homes in Hanover are due to a pleasant, small-town environment or monopoly is not the issue. What is at issue is whether one set of Hanover residents, owners of already developed homes, can maintain the parklike atmosphere of the rest of the town that enhances the value of their assets at someone else's expense. He might also point out that interstate highways and a regional airport have significantly reduced the area's isolation, so the "small rural town" defense has less merit.

9.22 Downzoning Is the More Practical Focus of Takings

It seems likely that the judge in the hypothetical Hanover case would not accept the contention that a zoning law of nearly twenty years' standing is unconstitutional. Aside from durability itself, perhaps the best reason that could be given is that Hanover is in a rural area and contains within its borders the employer of many of its residents. The college has been concerned about the effect of the cost of housing in hiring and retaining its employees, and this concern has been given a more-or-less sympathetic hearing by town officials and voters.

Thus there is some (though hardly perfect) political internalization of the costs of excessive land use regulations in Hanover, just as I found there were in Scranton, Pennsylvania, on matters concerning coal mine regulation (section 1.15). Although I sometimes joke that Hanover is the "farthest suburb of Boston," it is not a partially developed suburb trying to avoid the burdens of metropolitan location while enjoying all of the benefits. This differentiates it from the exclusive San Francisco suburb of Tiburon (of Agins v. Tiburon, 1980) and countless other tightly zoned towns around metropolitan areas.

The more likely application of the takings issue in Hanover would be a downzoning, in which land use regulations are made more restrictive and the property hence less valuable. (This was formerly the definition of "downzoning" only on the West Coast, but this meaning has now become bicoastal if not national.) Downzonings are usually done in the spirit of growth controls, which were the focus of Ellickson's 1977 *Yale Law Journal* article that developed the damages remedy that is urged here. Like growth controls, downzoning seldom arises just because professional planners think it's a good idea. Communities faced with an unwelcome development that is nonetheless consistent with the zoning ordinance often amend their laws to stop the development or at least prevent any recurrence on other land. Dick Babcock, author of *The Zoning Game,* once remarked that it should have been called *The Rezoning Game,* since that is how most controversies arise.

The truism that no one has a right to a particular zoning ordinance is one barrier to judicial review of downzoning. The California Supreme Court's 1976 dictum in HFH v. Superior Court (discussed in section 5.8) took it to its logical extreme: all landowners should expect that zoning laws will change. When it is stated that way, however, a major rationale for zoning goes up in smoke.

One important objective of any system of land use controls, including zoning, is to create order and the stable expectations that order brings. Zoning's chief advantage over private covenants is the greater ease in adopting and modifying it. To take this desirable flexibility and make it as plastic as Silly Putty is to project the modest administrative advantage of zoning (its flexibility) into a disadvantage for its basic purpose (stability of neighborhood expectations).

The capitalization evidence reviewed in section 6.1 showed that zoning does create expectations on the part of community residents that are regarded as durable enough to measurably affect the value of private homes. It seems unfair to confer this stability of expectation only upon fully enfranchised homeowners and not on owners of undeveloped land, who are often not residents and are in most suburbs a tiny minority of the electorate. If long-standing zoning regulations are immunized from the takings issue because changes would be unfair to current residents, the same argument ought to prevent radical changes that are unfair to owners of undeveloped land.

It is not necessary to claim that one has a right to a particular zoning law to invoke the Takings Clause when a rezoning is obviously aimed at a particular project or an easily exploited set of property owners. A downzoning (or other legal change to the same effect) that imposes a supernormal burden on a landowner should be regarded as a per se taking of property. This does not leave the community without any defenses. It may show that the rezoning was compelled (not simply allowed) by state or federal laws, so that the proper forum for the landowner is the state legislature, where she is apt to find more friends. For example, Hanover's floodplain regulations were prompted by federal laws requiring floodplain zoning, though I would note that my town's ordinance goes further than necessary in its outright prohibition of development in the hundred-year flood zone.

The community might also argue that standards of normal behavior have sufficiently changed, or that other factors that would raise settlement or lower demoralization costs are present. The key is that the burden of proof should be on the community to justify such actions when the new requirements are significantly more stringent than those imposed on the rest of the community. An advantage to challenging new regulatory burdens at their creation is that there is apt to be a better record of motivation for the new laws.

The approach I recommend would require that courts take more seriously charges that the new ordinance itself is unconstitutional. Most courts now require that takings claims can only be brought "as applied" to a particular property. This requires the plaintiff to exhaust all administrative remedies, which also exhausts his bank account. Aside from being an unfair burden on the plaintiff, the "as applied" doctrine creates delays during which evidence about community rationales for the rezoning goes stale.

9.23 Only the Damages Remedy Grabs Officials' Attention

"Just compensation" is the constitutional remedy for takings. Payment "in money" was added to the takings clauses of several state constitutions in reaction to the use of the benefit-offset principle and other forms of in-kind compensation. It is difficult to avoid the conclusion that monetary compensation is what constitution makers wanted when a taking occurred.

Aside from conformity with the text, a damages remedy has other advantages over injunctions or writs of mandamus that order the issuance of a building permit. A damages remedy gives the government a choice. It can continue the regulation if it values it above the market price. In this way, the court does not have to substitute its judgment for that of elected public officials.

This last statement is bound to have a hollow ring to it for many public officials. "Sure, we can keep the regulation," I hear them saying, "just pay several million dollars for it." Some communities would in fact take up that option. Palo Alto, California, bought land that it had restricted so thoroughly that a federal court held it was a taking (Arastra v. Palo Alto 1976; the city subsequently resold the land for development, just as South Carolina did in *Lucas*). In response to the claim that this would bankrupt less prosperous communities, one can only point to what the absence of compensation must be doing to the landowner and others who would benefit from his project. As Frank Michelman observed about the same claim, "What society cannot, indeed, afford is to impoverish itself" (1967, p. 1181).

Awards of large damages would, however, quickly become rare. Local governments and politically insulated agencies can easily adopt defensive rules. Almost all of them have mechanisms for granting discretionary exceptions, such as zoning variances, to forestall takings. Today's seemingly broad exposure to legal liability is largely the result of not having to think about the fair treatment of property owners. Even a mild threat of damages would stiffen the resolve of public officials who want to grant permits but are often opposed by neighborhood interests. Explaining to opponents that withholding a permit would be unfair to the applicant is less effective than explaining that it would be unfair *and* cost the taxpayers a lot of money.

The other advantage of damages, as opposed to injunctions, is that they penalize unlawful delay. The classic statement of this, which I noted in section 1.20, was cited by Justice Brennan in his dissent in San Diego Gas and Electric v. San Diego (1981, p. 656 n. 22). He quoted a California attorney who advised other city attorneys faced with defeat in court: "IF ALL ELSE FAILS, MERELY AMEND THE REGULATION AND START OVER AGAIN." His point was that communities can outwait the developers. The only cost to the community of going through the proceeding all over again is legal fees. The landowner has the same legal fees plus the opportunity cost of the land, including ongoing expenses such as interest on loans. The clear implication of the now-famous quote is that developers can be forced to accept unconstitutional conditions by making it plain that they would have to incur indefinitely large, nonrecoverable costs to vindicate their rights (Berger and Kanner 1986). The damages remedy puts municipal attorneys on notice that such delaying tactics are dangerous.

The apparent failure of the *Mount Laurel* decisions to change land use patterns in that state, described in section 9.9, is an example of how ineffective injunctions and mandates are. Even a court as devoted to an ideal as the Supreme Court of New Jersey was unable to make an appreciable dent in suburban housing patterns. The New Jersey court also erred in granting the remedy to parties with insufficient motivation. Landowners are willing to stay the course and confront regulatory roadblocks as they arise. The New Jersey court's disregard for landowners' rights in favor of the rights of a nebulous class of outsiders, most of whom were unaware of the cause of their troubles, guaranteed that state government agencies would favor the status quo. Monetary damages get the attention of local officials, and they motivate the prospective recipients, as well.

9.24 Calculating Just Compensation Is Not Easy

A few years ago, Gideon Kanner invited me to speak at an ALI-ABA (American Law Institute–American Bar Association) continuing legal education session on eminent domain. We had met at a land use conference earlier, and he was open to the possibility that a professional economist might teach lawyers something about the subject. At the first session, I tried out some of the ideas that Perry Shapiro and I had been discussing in the law and economics journals. I discussed the moral hazard issue endemic in compensation and the implications it might have for eminent domain practice.

It went over as well as a lawyer joke told by a nonlawyer. The audience was polite enough, but the post-conference reviews of my efforts were pretty negative, and I am not used to that. Gideon gave me another chance the following year. Instead of a scholarly work, I brought along a paper I had written for students in my Vermont Law School class on law and economics. It was called "Discounting in One Lesson." I used it to explain why one calculates a discount rate, how it is done, and what the difference between real and nominal interest rates was. My conference ratings went way up, and ALI-ABA asked me to publish my handout in *The Practical Litigator* (Fischel 1991a). The conference participants were practicing lawyers, not students. They had a hard time with the concept of discounting, and they appreciated having it explained to them.

The ALI-ABA experience made me more sympathetic to arguments by those who oppose takings damages on the grounds that they would not be manageable. But there is an odd asymmetry in the argument. Many state courts, including those most reluctant to undertake regulatory takings analysis, have vigorously expanded tort liability claims against local governments. Personal injury damages in particular have mushroomed, and such damages involve discounting calculations at least as complex as those for regulatory takings. If local governments can be expected to deal with discounting in personal injury cases, there is no reason they cannot deal with similar calculations in land use disputes.

Even though local governments ought to be able to calculate damages for any liability they incur, I submit that regulatory takings damages would in fact be rare because it is not hard for local agencies to avoid them. Thus the factual analogies from eminent domain litigation would be sufficient to build the doctrine of regulatory takings. Unlike eminent domain, in which governments want to take the property, inverse condemnation is something that can be avoided by a rational government. This would be my reply to the California Supreme Court in Hensler v. Glendale (1994). The court responded to this argument by inverting it. Local governments have fewer resources than the state or federal government, and so the locals need greater judicial protection, said the justices. But it is precisely because of local governments' desire to stanch fiscal hemorrhage that they will try to avoid takings.

To insulate them from takings because of their supposed poverty is like excusing thieves because of their desire to have money.

9.25 Courts Do Matter

Much of this book has dwelt upon the fallibility of the judicial process in resolving property disputes. Conscientious judges should use constitutional commands sparingly when alternative methods of property protection are realistic options. The primary candidates for judicial solicitude are owners of property that cannot be protected by the threat of economic exit and for whom political coalitions are unlikely prospects. This is especially the case for land use regulations undertaken by local governments and by special state or federal agencies that have been insulated from the give-and-take of pluralistic politics.

One might ask, however, whether local governments will in fact respond to judicial pronouncements. There are tens of thousands of local governments in the land use game, and judicial monitoring of them all would be prohibitively costly. My response is that there is an educational aspect to Supreme Court decisions that multiplies the effect of even limited decisions.

I wrote the introduction to the *Columbia Law Review* issue that published the papers of the 1988 regulatory takings conference that Richard Brooks and I organized. I summarized each paper in light of my own views, but the last article, by William Fisher, was something of a puzzle. Fisher advanced the idea that the U.S. Supreme Court acts in large part as a public educator. This function did not fit my own theories very well, so I concluded my introduction with a true story that seemed to illustrate Fisher's point (Fischel 1988, p. 1599):

> I was recently [in 1987] sitting as a member of a local zoning board listening to an applicant for a variance. After presenting his case, the applicant, who was untutored in the law and did not have an attorney, launched into a discussion of his property rights as illustrated by *First English* and *Nollan*, copies of which he presented to the board. That the facts of his case did not seem closely congruent to the facts of the two Supreme Court cases is beside the point. The cases made a strong impact on his perceptions of his property rights. (He did not get the variance, though.)

The zoning case in which this issue had arisen had the following facts. The applicant had two small lots with cottages at the edge of a town-owned nature preserve. His lots were in the area zoned "F," for "Forestry and Recreation." They did not have access to an improved road, although they are close to the settled part of town. The only permanent dwellings that are allowed in the F zone are "seasonal dwellings" (used for less than 184 days a year) on ten-acre lots. Seasonal dwellings had apparently been the prior use of the applicant's property, but he had converted one of them to year-round use for his own home and was renting out the other. He had in 1987 sought recognition of his claim for year-round use, which the zoning board denied despite his constitutional rhetoric.

The applicant is still there in 1994, using his property as before. I would say that the takings case that he submitted to the board, whose application I dismissed in 1988 as touchingly naive, have helped him considerably in his battle with town authorities, who include me. I had hoped to be able to say at this writing that the case was happily settled. The renewed attention to takings jurisprudence would have been seen as a helpful post to which reasonable compromises were hitched. But it has not happened, at least not so far.

The case involves the motivational subtleties that ultimately inform our view of takings jurisprudence. The applicant is seen by some as a lone homesteader whose use is seemingly harmless to the public. (His year-round occupation had been noticed only because of a remark he made in an unrelated controversy.) He presents himself as an ordinary citizen whose home is under attack by unreasonable public officials and whose only refuge is the Constitution. But to others, he is an opportunist who seeks to upgrade an old cottage to a use for which it was never intended and whose value has been enhanced by the public nature reserve that it adjoins. I won't say which view I take, since I expect to see him again before the zoning board. The case goes on, as does the takings issue.

Case References

General References

Index

Case References

The §§ numbers in brackets refer to sections within this book.

Agins v. City of Tiburon, 157 Cal. Rptr. 373 (1979), *affirmed* 447 U.S. 255 (1980) [§§1.18–1.22, 1.24, 2.1, 4.21, 5.21, 6.7, 9.22]

Alden Coal. See Commonwealth

Allied Structural Steel v. Spannaus, 438 U.S. 234 (1978) [§8.2]

Andrus v. Allard, 444 U.S. 51 (1979) [§§4.14, 4.15]

Appeal of Girsh, 263 A.2d 395 (Pa. 1970) [§6.9]

Appeal of Kravitz, 460 A.2d 1075 (Pa. 1983) [§9.9]

Arastra v. City of Palo Alto, 417 F.Supp. 1125 (N.D. Cal. 1976) [§9.23]

Arlington Heights v. Metropolitan Housing Development Corp., 429 U.S. 252 (1977) [§7.6]

Armstrong v. United States, 364 U.S. 40 (1960) [§4.0]

Avery v. Midland County, 390 U.S. 474 (1968) [§7.10]

Azul Pacifico v. City of Los Angeles, 948 F.2d 575 (9th Cir. 1991), *withdrawn* 1992. [§8.17]

Baker v. Carr, 369 U.S. 186 (1962) [§3.13]

Barron v. Baltimore, 32 U.S. 243 (1833) [§3.2]

Birkenfeld v. City of Berkeley, 130 Cal. Rptr. 465 (1976) [§§8.10, 8.22]

Blaisdell. See Home Building and Loan Association

Block v. Hirsh, 256 U.S. 135 (1921) [§§1.1 (n. 10), 8.10]

Bohm v. Metropolitan Elevated Railway, 29 N.E. 803 (N.Y. 1892) [§2.17]

Bookman v. New York Elevated Railway, 41 N.E. 705 (N.Y. 1895) [§2.17]

Boomer v. Atlantic Cement, 309 N.Y.S.2d 312 (1970) [§§2.7, 4.24]

Britton v. Town of Chester, 595 A.2d 492 (N.H. 1991) [§9.10]

Brown v. Board of Education, 347 U.S. 483 (1954) [§§3.6, 3.10]

Buchanan v. Warley, 245 U.S. 60 (1917) [§3.6]

Burrows v. Keene, 432 A.2d 15 (N.H. 1981) [§9.21]

Butchers Union Co. v. Crescent City Co., 111 U.S. 746 (1884) [§8.8]

Heisler v. Thomas Colliery, 118 A. 394 (Pa. 1922), *affirmed* 260 U.S. 245 (1922) [§§1.10, 1.11]

Hensler v. Glendale, 32 Cal. Rptr.2d 244 (1994) [§§1.22, 9.24]

HFH v. Superior Court of Los Angeles County, 125 Cal. Rptr. 365 (1975) [§§1.19, 5.8, 6.7, 9.22]

Hills Development Co. v. Township of Bernards, 510 A.2d 621 (N.J. 1986) *("Mount Laurel III")* [§9.8]

Hodel v. Irving, 481 U.S. 704 (1987) [§4.15]

Hodel v. Virginia Surface Mining and Reclamation Association, 452 U.S. 264 (1981) [§1.17]

Home Building and Loan Association v. Blaisdell, 290 U.S. 398 (1934) [§§3.8, 3.18]

Just v. Marinette County, 201 N.W.2d 761 (Wisc. 1972) [§9.18]

Keystone Bituminous Coal Association v. DeBenedictis, 480 U.S. 470 (1987) [§§1.1 (n. 6), 1.17, 1.23]

Kirby Forest Industries v. United States, 467 U.S. 1 (1984) [§§4.16, 4.17]

Klein v. Republic Steel, 435 F.2d 762 (1970) [§1.14]

Kohl v. United States, 91 U.S. 367 (1875) [§3.2]

Korematsu v. United States, 323 U.S. 214 (1944) [§3.15]

Lansing, City of, v. Edward Rose Realty, 502 N.W.2d 638 (Mich. 1993) [§2.6]

Lochner v. New York, 198 U.S. 45 (1905) [§§1.1, 2.17, 3.6, 3.7, 3.9, 3.11, 3.16, 4.20, 7.12]

Loretto v. Teleprompter Manhattan CATV, 423 N.E. 2d 320 (N.Y. 1981), *reversed* 458 U.S. 419 (1982) [§§1.17, 8.20, 8.21]

Louisville and Nashville Railroad v. Barber Asphalt Paving, 197 U.S. 430 (1905) [§9.16]

Lucas v. South Carolina Coastal Council, 112 S.Ct. 2886 (1992) [§§1.22–1.24, 4.6, 9.18, 9.23]

MacDonald, Sommer and Frates v. County of Yolo, 477 U.S. 340 (1986) [§1.20]

Mahon v. Pennsylvania Coal, 118 A. 491 (Pa. 1922) [§§1.9, 1.11]

Marbury v. Madison, 5 U.S. 137 (1803) [§3.2]

Matter of Michael Butler, 4 Fayette [County] Legal Journal 312 (Pa. 1941) [§5.2]

Mayor and City Council v. Baltimore Football Club, 624 F.Supp. 278 (D. Md. 1985) [§2.6]

McCulloch v. Maryland, 17 U.S. 319 (1819) [§3.20]

M'Clenachan v. Curwin, 3 Yeates 362 (Pa. 1802) [§5.2]

Metro Broadcasting v. FCC, 497 U.S. 547 (1990) [§3.22]

Metromedia v. San Diego, 164 Cal. Rptr. 510 (1980) [§8.3]

Meyer v. Nebraska, 262 U.S. 390 (1923) [§3.10]

Midkiff. *See* Hawaii Housing Authority

Miller v. Schoene, 276 U.S. 272 (1928) [§§4.7–4.10]

Minnesota v. Clover Leaf Creamery, 449 U.S. 459 (1981) [§8.8]

Mount Laurel. *See* Southern Burlington County NAACP *and* Hills Development v. Township of Bernards

Mugler v. Kansas, 123 U.S. 623 (1887) [§§1.2, 1.21, 1.23, 8.1]

Muhlker v. New York and Harlem Railroad, 197 U.S. 544 (1905) [§2.17]

Municipal Art Society v. City of New York, 522 N.Y.S.2d 800 (Sup. Ct. 1987) [§9.15]

Munn v. Illinois, 94 U.S. 113 (1877) [§8.9]

National Land and Investment v. Kohn, 215 A.2d 597 (Pa. 1965) [§9.9]

Newman v. Metropolitan Elevated Railway, 23 N.E. 901 (N.Y. 1890) [§§2.16, 2.17]

Nollan v. California Coastal Commission, 483 U.S. 825 (1987) [§§1.22, 1.24, 3.21, 4.0, 8.18, 8.22, 9.12–9.15, 9.17, 9.25]

Norwood v. Baker, 172 U.S. 269 (1898) [§9.16]

Oakland, City of, v. Oakland Raiders, 183 Cal. Rptr. 673 (1982) [§2.6]

Peacock v. County of Sacramento, 77 Cal. Rptr. 391 (Ct. App. 1969) [§9.6]

Penman v. Jones, 100 A. 1043 (Pa. 1917) [§§1.1 (n. 5), 1.9]

Penn Central Transportation Co. v. New York City, 366 N.E.2d 1271 (N.Y. 1977), *affirmed* 438 U.S. 104 (1978) [§§1.18, 1.20, 1.23, 4.16, 9.2]

Pennell v. San Jose, 42 Cal. 3d 365 (1986), *affirmed* 485 U.S. 1 (1988) [§8.22]

Pennsylvania Coal v. Mahon, 260 U.S. 393 (1922) [§§1.0, 1.1, 1.11–1.18, 1.24, 3.0, 4.20, 4.26, 5.3, 9.14, 9.18]

Petaluma. *See* Construction Industry Association

Philadelphia v. New Jersey, 437 U.S. 617 (1978) [§3.20]

Pierce v. Society of Sisters, 268 U.S. 510 (1925) [§3.10]

Plessy v. Ferguson, 163 U.S. 537 (1896) [§3.6]

Plymouth Coal v. Pennsylvania, 232 U.S. 531 (1914) [§1.1 (n. 7)]

Poletown Neighborhood Council v. City of Detroit, 304 N.W.2d 455 (Mich. 1981) [§2.6]

Prudential Insurance v. Central Nebraska Public Power and Irrigation District, 296 N.W. 752, 145 ALR 1 (Neb. 1941) [§2.12]

Respublica v. Sparhawk, 1 Dallas 352 (Pa. 1788) [§9.19]

Reynolds v. Sims, 377 U.S. 533 (1964) [§3.13]

Richmond, City of, v. J. A. Croson Co. 488 U.S. 469 (1989) [§§3.22, 3.23]

Robinson v. Cahill, 358 A.2d 457 (N.J. 1976) [§9.10]

Roe v. Wade, 410 U.S. 113 (1973) [§3.15]

Ross v. City of Berkeley, 655 F.Supp. 820 (N.D. Cal. 1987) [§8.22]

San Diego Gas and Electric v. San Diego, 450 U.S. 621 (1981) [§§1.20, 4.0, 9.21, 9.23]

Searle v. City of Berkeley Rent Stabilization Board, 271 Cal. Rptr. 437 (Ct. App. 1990) [§8.13]

Serrano v. Priest, 96 Cal. Rptr. 601 (1971) *("Serrano I")* [§§7.6, 8.19]

Serrano v. Priest, 135 Cal. Rptr. 345 (1976) *("Serrano II")* [§§3.11, 7.19]

Sibson v. State 336 A.2d 239 (N.H. 1975) [§9.3]

Slaughter-House Cases, 83 U.S. 36 (1873) [§8.8]

Southern Burlington County NAACP v. Township of Mount Laurel, 336 A.2d 713 (N.J. 1975) *(Mount Laurel I)* and 456 A.2d 390 (N.J. 1983) *(Mount Laurel II)* [§§6.9, 7.6, 9.0, 9.8–9.10, 9.23]

Spur Industries v. Del E. Webb Development Co. 494 P.2d 700 (1972) [§6.9]

United States v. Caltex, 344 U.S. 149 (1952) [§9.19]

United States v. Carolene Products, 304 U.S. 144 (1938) [§§3.9, 3.10, 3.24, 8.19]

United States v. 50 Acres of Land, 469 U.S. 24 (1984) [§9.7]

United States v. Miller, 317 U.S. 369 (1943) [§4.20]

United States v. River Rouge Improvement, 269 U.S. 411 (1926) [§2.18]

Vulcan Material v. Griffith, 114 S.E. 2d 29 (Ga. 1960) [§7.14]

Wickard v. Filburn, 317 U.S. 111 (1942) [§3.8]

Williamson v. Lee Optical, 348 U.S. 483 (1955) [§8.8]

Williamson County v. Hamilton Bank, 473 U.S. 172 (1985) [§§1.20, 2.1]

Wilson v. McHenry County, 416 N.E. 2d 426 (Ill. App. 1981) [§8.5]

Wright v. Buckeye Coal, 434 A.2d 728 (Pa. Superior 1981) [§1.14]

Yee v. City of Escondido, 274 Cal. Rptr. 551 (Ct. App. 1990), *affirmed,* 112 S. Ct. 1522 (1992) [§§8.22–8.24]

Yick Wo v. Hopkins, 118 U.S. 356 (1886) [§3.20]

General References

The §§ numbers in brackets refer to sections within this book.

Ackerman, Bruce A. 1977. *Private Property and the Constitution.* New Haven: Yale University Press. [§§2.14, 4.1, 8.7]

—— 1992. "Liberating Abstraction." *University of Chicago Law Review,* 59: 317–348. [§3.7]

Advisory Commission on Regulatory Barriers to Affordable Housing. 1991. *"Not in My Back Yard": Removing Barriers to Affordable Housing.* Washington, D.C.: U.S. Department of Housing and Urban Development. [§§6.4, 6.10]

Alpern, Andrew, and Seymour Durst. 1984. *Holdouts!* New York: McGraw-Hill. [§2.3]

[ALR Annotation] 1967. "Eminent Domain: Deduction of Benefits." *American Law Reports 3d,* 13: 1149–1219. [§2.13]

Altshuler, Alan A., and Jose A. Gómez-Ibáñez, with Arnold M. Howitt. 1993. *Regulation for Revenue: The Political Economy of Land Use Exactions.* Cambridge, Mass.: Lincoln Institute of Land Policy. [§9.11]

American Association of State Highway Officials. 1962. *Acquisition for Right-of-Way.* Washington, D.C.: Association Committee on Right of Way. [§2.18]

Aronson, Peter H. 1991. "Calhoun's Constitutional Economics." *Constitutional Political Economy,* 2: 31–52. [§3.4]

Arrow, Kenneth J. 1951. *Social Choice and Individual Values.* New York: Wiley. [§3.12]

—— 1977. *The Property Rights Doctrine and Demand Revelation under Incomplete Information.* Technical Report no. 243, Economics Series, Institute for Mathematical Studies in the Social Sciences, Stanford University, August. [§2.4]

Asabere, Paul K., Forrest E. Huffman, and Seyed Mehdian. 1994. "The Adverse Impacts of Local Historic Designation: The Case of Small Apartment Buildings in Philadelphia." *Journal of Real Estate Finance and Economics,* 8: 225–234. [§§1.18, 9.2]

Baar, Kenneth. 1983. "Guidelines for Drafting Rent Control Laws: Lessons of a Decade." *Rutgers Law Review,* 35: 725–885. [§8.11]

Babcock, Richard, and Charles Siemon. 1985. *The Zoning Game Revisited.* Cambridge, Mass.: Lincoln Institute of Land Policy. [§§6.6, 9.3, 9.8, 9.22]

Baden, John, ed. 1984. *The Vanishing Farmland Crisis: Critical Views of the Movement to Preserve Agricultural Land.* Lawrence: University Press of Kansas. [§8.5]

Bader, Robert Smith. 1986. *Prohibition in Kansas: A History.* Lawrence: University Press of Kansas. [§8.1]

Baker, Lynn A. 1991. "Direct Democracy and Discrimination: A Public Choice Perspective." *Chicago-Kent Law Review,* 67: 707–776. [§§6.19, 9.5]

——— 1994. "The Missing Equal Protection Doctrine: A Public Choice Examination of Constitutional Restrictions on Special Legislation." Manuscript, University of Arizona College of Law. [§§1.9, 7.2]

Bakken, Gordon M. 1987. *Rocky Mountain Constitution Making, 1850–1912.* New York: Greenwood Press. [§2.13]

Barrows, Robert G. 1983. "Beyond the Tenement: Patterns of American Urban Housing, 1870–1930." *Journal of Urban History,* 9: 395–420. [§7.17]

Barzel, Yoram, and Tim R. Sass. 1990. "The Allocation of Resources by Voting." *Quarterly Journal of Economics,* 105: 745–771. [§7.10]

Baumol, William J. 1952. *Welfare Economics and the Theory of the State.* Cambridge: Harvard University Press. [§4.19]

Baxter, William F., and Lillian R. Altree. 1972. "Legal Aspects of Airport Noise." *Journal of Law and Economics,* 15: 1–113. [§2.20]

Beck, John. 1986. *Never Before in History: The Story of Scranton.* Northridge, Calif.: Windsor Publications. [§1.8]

Becker, Gary S. 1983. "The Theory of Competition among Pressure Groups for Political Influence." *Quarterly Journal of Economics,* 98: 371–400. [§§3.9, 8.19]

Been, Vicki. 1991. " 'Exit' as a Constraint on Land Use Exactions: Rethinking the Unconstitutional Conditions Doctrine." *Columbia Law Review,* 91: 473–545. [§§3.23, 7.9, 9.13]

——— 1993. "What's Fairness Got to Do with It? Environmental Justice and the Siting of Locally Undesirable Land Uses." *Cornell Law Review,* 78: 1001–1085. [§9.1]

Benham, Lee, and Philip Keefer. 1991. "Voting in Firms: The Role of Agenda

Control, Size, and Voter Homogeneity." *Economic Inquiry,* 29: 706–719. [§7.10]

Berger, Curtis J. 1983. *Land Ownership and Use,* 3d ed. Boston: Little, Brown. [§9.17]

Berger, Lawrence. 1991. "Inclusionary Zoning as Takings: The Legacy of the *Mount Laurel* Cases." *Nebraska Law Review,* 70: 186–228. [§9.8]

Berger, Michael M. 1987. "Airport Noise in the 1980s: It's Time for Airport Operators to Acknowledge the Injury They Inflict on Their Neighbors." In *Proceedings of the Institute on Planning, Zoning and Eminent Domain.* New York: Matthew Bender. [§2.20]

——— 1992. "Amortization as 'Just Compensation': If It Works for Billboards, Can Office Buildings Be Far Behind?" In *Proceedings of the Institute on Planning, Zoning and Eminent Domain.* Oakland, Calif.: Matthew Bender. [§8.3]

Berger, Michael M., and Gideon Kanner. 1986. "Thoughts on the White River Junction Manifesto: A Reply to the 'Gang of Five's' Views on Just Compensation for Regulatory Taking of Property." *Loyola of Los Angeles Law Review,* 19: 685–754. [§9.23]

Berger, Raoul. 1977. *Government by Judiciary: The Transformation of the Fourteenth Amendment.* Cambridge: Harvard University Press. [§3.5]

Bergstrom, Theodore C., and Robert P. Goodman. 1973. "Private Demand for Public Goods." *American Economic Review,* 63: 280–296. [§7.2]

Bernard, Michael M. 1979. *Constitutions, Taxation, and Land Policy.* Lexington, Mass.: Lexington Books. [§7.2]

Bickel, Alexander M. 1962. *The Least Dangerous Branch: The Supreme Court at the Bar of Politics.* Indianapolis: Bobbs Merrill. [§§3.4, 3.12]

Binmore, Ken. 1989. "Social Contract I: Harsanyi and Rawls." *Economic Journal* (Supplement) 99: 84–102. [§3.18]

Blaesser, Brian W., and Christine M. Kentopp. 1990. "Impact Fees: The 'Second Generation.'" *Washington University Journal of Urban and Contemporary Law,* 38: 55–113. [§§8.22, 9.16]

Blake, Nelson M. 1956. *Water for the Cities: A History of the Urban Water Supply Problem in the United States.* Syracuse: Syracuse University Press. [§4.11]

Blomquist, Glenn C., Mark C. Berger, and John P. Hoehn. 1988. "New Estimates of Quality of Life in Urban Areas." *American Economic Review,* 78: 89–107. [§6.15]

Bloom, Howard S., and Helen F. Ladd. 1982. "Property Tax Revaluation and Tax Levy Growth." *Journal of Urban Economics,* 11: 73–84. [§7.3]

Bluestone, Barry, and Bennett Harrison. 1982. *The Deindustrialization of America: Plant Closings, Community Abandonment, and the Dismantling of Basic Industry.* New York: Basic Books. [§8.2]

Blume, Lawrence E., and Daniel L. Rubinfeld. 1984. "Compensation for Takings: An Economic Analysis." *California Law Review,* 72: 569–628. [§§5.1, 5.5, 5.11]

Blume, Lawrence E., Daniel L. Rubinfeld, and Perry Shapiro. 1984. "The Taking of Land: When Should Compensation Be Paid?" *Quarterly Journal of Economics,* 99: 71–92. [§§4.11–4.13, 4.16, 4.17, 5.11, 5.15]

Boeckh Building Cost Index Numbers. Published monthly by American Appraisal Associates, Milwaukee, Wisconsin. [§6.13]

Borcherding, Thomas, and Robert Deacon. 1972. "The Demand for the Services of Non-Federal Governments." *American Economic Review,* 62: 891–901. [§7.2]

Bork, Robert H. 1990. *The Tempting of America: The Political Seduction of the Law.* New York: Free Press. [§§2.9, 3.1]

Bosselman, Fred P., and David Callies. 1972. *The Quiet Revolution in Land Use Control.* Washington, D.C.: President's Council on Environmental Quality. [§7.18]

Bosselman, Fred P., David Callies, and John Banta. 1973. *The Taking Issue: A Study of the Constitutional Limits of Land Use Control.* Washington, D.C.: President's Council on Environmental Quality. [§§1.3, 3.2]

Bowen, Catherine Drinker. 1944. *Yankee from Olympus: Justice Holmes and His Family.* Boston: Little Brown. [§1.1]

Bowen, Howard. 1943. "The Interpretation of Voting in the Allocation of Economic Resources." *Quarterly Journal of Economics,* 58: 27–48. [§§7.2, 7.5]

Brennan, Geoffrey, and James Buchanan. 1979. "The Logic of Tax Limits: Alternative Constitutional Constraints on the Power to Tax." *National Tax Journal* (Supplement), 32: 11–22. [§6.19]

Brennan, William J., Jr. 1986. "The Bill of Rights and the States: The Revival of State Constitutions as Guardians of Individual Rights." *New York University Law Review,* 61: 535–553. [§1.20]

Brenner, Joel F. 1974. "Nuisance Law and the Industrial Revolution." *Journal of Legal Studies,* 3: 403–434. [§2.15]

Brest, Paul, and Sanford Levinson. 1983. *Processes of Constitutional Decisionmaking: Cases and Materials,* 2d ed. Boston: Little, Brown. [§§3.8, 3.10]

Briffault, Richard. 1990. "Our Localism: Part I—The Structure of Local Government Law." *Columbia Law Review,* 90: 1–115. [§§7.6, 7.13]

———— 1993. "Who Rules at Home?: One Person/One Vote and Local Governments." *University of Chicago Law Review,* 60: 339–424. [§§7.10, 7.11]

Brookshire, David S., and Don L. Coursey. 1987. "Measuring the Value of a Public Good: An Empirical Comparison of Elicitation Procedures." *American Economic Review,* 77: 554–566. [§5.16]

Brown, Wallace. 1969. *The Good Americans: The Loyalists in the American Revolution*. New York: William Morrow. [§2.9]

Browning, Edgar K. 1987. "On the Marginal Welfare Cost of Taxation." *American Economic Review*, 77: 11–23. [§§2.19, 4.3]

Brownlee, W. Elliot. 1979. "Progress and Poverty: One Hundred Years Later." *NTA-TIA Proceedings*, pp. 228–232. [§7.4]

Brunner, Karl, ed. 1981. *The Great Depression Revisited*. Boston: Martinus Nijhof. [§3.7]

Buchanan, James M. 1972. "Politics, Property, and the Law: An Alternative Interpretation of *Miller et al. v. Schoene*." *Journal of Law and Economics*, 15: 439–452. [§4.7]

——— 1991. *The Economics and Ethics of Constitutional Order*. Ann Arbor: University of Michigan Press. [§3.12]

——— 1993. "The Political Efficiency of General Taxation." *National Tax Journal*, 46: 401–410. [§7.2]

Buchanan, James M., and Charles J. Goetz. 1972. "Efficiency Limits of Fiscal Mobility: An Assessment of the Tiebout Model." *Journal of Public Economics*, 1: 25–43. [§7.5]

Buchanan, James M., and Gordon Tullock. 1962. *The Calculus of Consent: Logical Foundations of Constitutional Democracy*. Ann Arbor: University of Michigan Press. [§5.9]

Burchell, Robert W., David Listokin, and William R. Dolphin. 1993. *The Development Impact Assessment Handbook and Model*. Washington, D.C.: Urban Land Institute. [§7.7]

Burns, James M., J. W. Peltason, Thomas E. Cronin, and David B. Magleby. 1993. *State and Local Politics: Government by the People*, 7th ed. Englewood Cliffs, N.J.: Prentice-Hall. [§7.3]

Burrows, Paul. 1991. "Compensation for Compulsory Acquisition." *Land Economics*, 67: 49–63. [§4.17]

Calabresi, Guido, and A. Douglas Melamed. 1972. "Property Rules, Liability Rules, and Inalienability: One View of the Cathedral." *Harvard Law Review*, 85: 1089–1128. [§§2.2, 4.13, 5.20]

Callies, David L. 1980. "The Quiet Revolution Revisited." *APA Journal*, 46: 135–144. [§7.18]

——— 1981. "Land Use Controls: An Eclectic Summary for 1980–1981." *The Urban Lawyer*, 13: 724–763. [§6.6]

Callies, David L., Nancy C. Neuffer, and Carlito P. Calibosco. 1991. "Ballot Box Zoning: Initiative, Referendum, and the Law." *Washington University Journal of Urban and Contemporary Law*, 39: 53–98. [§§6.19, 8.6, 9.5]

Campbell, Colin D., and William A. Fischel. 1994. "Preferences for School Finance Systems: Voters versus Judges." Working Paper, Department of Economics, Dartmouth College. [§7.19]

Cappel, Andrew J. 1991. "A Walk along Willow: Patterns of Land Use Co-ordination in Pre-Zoning New Haven (1870–1926)." *Yale Law Journal,* 101: 617–642. [§7.15]

Carrington, Paul D. 1973. "Financing the American Dream: Equality and School Taxes." *Columbia Law Review,* 73: 1227–1260. [§7.19]

Case, Fred, and Jeffrey Gale. 1982. *Environmental Impact Review and Housing.* New York: Praeger. [§§6.4, 6.20]

Case, Karl E. 1992. "The Real Estate Cycle and the Economy: Consequences of the Massachusetts Boom of 1984–87." *Urban Studies,* 29: 171–183. [§§6.18, 6.22]

Case, Karl E., and Robert J. Shiller. 1987. "Prices of Single Family Homes since 1970: New Indexes for Four Cities." *New England Economic Review* (September/October): 45–56. [§6.10]

———— 1989. "The Efficiency of the Market for Single Family Homes." *American Economic Review,* 79: 125–137. [§6.18]

Chapman, Jeffrey. 1981. *Rent Controls in Los Angeles: A Response to Proposition 13.* Los Angeles: University of Southern California School of Public Affairs. [§8.11]

Cheape, Charles W. 1980. *Moving the Masses: Urban Public Transit in New York, Boston, and Philadelphia, 1880–1912.* Cambridge: Harvard University Press. [§§2.16, 2.17]

Cion, Richard M. 1966. "Accommodation Par Excellence: The Lakewood Plan." In *Metropolitan Politics: A Reader,* ed. Michael N. Danielson. Boston: Little, Brown. [§7.16]

Clingemeyer, James C. 1993. "Distributive Politics, Ward Representation, and the Spread of Zoning." *Public Choice,* 77: 725–738. [§7.15]

Coase, Ronald H. 1960. "The Problem of Social Cost." *Journal of Law and Economics,* 3: 1–44. [§§1.3, 1.16, 5.13, 9.18]

———— 1988. *The Firm, the Market, and the Law.* Chicago: University of Chicago Press. [§4.7]

Coate, Stephen, and Glenn C. Loury. 1993. "Will Affirmative-Action Policies Eliminate Negative Stereotypes?" *American Economic Review,* 83: 1220–1240. [§3.23]

Coleman, Jules L. 1980. "Efficiency, Utility, and Wealth Maximization." *Hofstra Law Review,* 8: 509–552. [§§2.2, 4.1]

Connors, Catherine A. 1990. "Back to the Future: The 'Nuisance Exception' to the Just Compensation Clause." *Capital University Law Review,* 19: 139–185. [§§1.2, 3.2, 9.18]

Cooley, Thomas M. 1868. *A Treatise on the Constitutional Limitations Which Rest upon the Legislative Power of the States of the American Union.* Boston: Little, Brown. [§7.12]

Cooter, Robert. 1985. "Unity in Tort, Contract, and Property: The Model of Precaution." *California Law Review,* 73: 1–51. [§§4.12, 4.17]

Cooter, Robert, and Thomas Ulen. 1988. *Law and Economics.* Glenview, Ill.: Scott, Foresman. [§2.7]

Cordes, Joseph J. 1979. "Compensation through Relocation Assistance." *Land Economics,* 55: 486–498. [§2.18]

Cordes, Joseph J., and Burton A. Weisbrod. 1979. "Government Behavior in Response to Compensation Requirements." *Journal of Public Economics,* 11: 47–58. [§§2.18, 2.19]

—— 1985. "When Government Programs Create Inequities: A Guide to Compensation Policies." *Journal of Policy Analysis and Management,* 4: 178–195. [§2.19]

Costonis, John J. 1974. *Space Adrift: Saving Urban Landmarks through the Chicago Plan.* Urbana: University of Illinois Press. [§1.18]

Coyle, Dennis J. 1993. *Property Rights and the Constitution: Shaping Society through Land Use Regulation.* Albany: SUNY Press. [§6.6]

Cukierman, Alex. 1992. *Central Bank Strategy, Credibility, and Independence: Theory and Evidence.* Cambridge: MIT Press. [§3.17]

Currie, David P. 1989. "*Lochner* Abroad: Substantive Due Process and Equal Protection in the Federal Republic of Germany." *Supreme Court Review,* 1989: 333–373. [§3.16]

Dahl, Robert A. 1989. *Democracy and Its Critics.* New Haven: Yale University Press. [§3.17]

Deacon, Robert, and Perry Shapiro. 1975. "Private Preference for Collective Goods Revealed through Voting on Referenda." *American Economic Review,* 65: 943–955. [§9.13]

deAlessi, Louis. 1969. "Implications of Property Rights for Government Investment Choices." *American Economic Review,* 59: 13–24. [§4.2]

Demsetz, Harold. 1967. "Toward a Theory of Property Rights." *American Economic Review,* Papers and Proceedings, 57: 347–359. [§9.17]

Denzau, Arthur T., and Barry R. Weingast. 1982. "Forward: The Political Economy of Land Use Regulation." *Urban Law Annual,* 23: 385–405. [§9.2]

Deutsch, Stuart L. 1984. "Antitrust Challenges to Local Zoning and Other Land Use Controls." *Chicago-Kent Law Review,* 60: 63–88. [§7.10]

Dillon, John F. 1871. *Treatise on the Law of Municipal Corporations.* Boston: Little, Brown. [§§7.12–7.15]

DiMento, Joseph F., Michael D. Dozier, Steven L. Emmons, Donald G. Hagman, Christopher Kim, Karen Greenfield-Sanders, Paul F. Waldau, and Jay A. Woollacott. 1980. "Land Development and Environmental Control in the California Supreme Court: The Deferential, the Preservationist, and the Preservationist-Erratic Eras." *UCLA Law Review,* 27: 859–1066. [§§6.6–6.9, 6.12, 6.19, 6.20]

Dixit, Avinash. 1991. "Irreversible Investment with Price Ceilings." *Journal of Political Economy,* 99: 541–557. [§8.17]

Dowall, David E. 1984. *The Suburban Squeeze: Land Conversion and Regulation in the San Francisco Bay Area.* Berkeley: University of California Press. [§6.4]

Downs, Anthony. 1957. *An Economic Theory of Democracy.* New York: Harper and Row. [§7.2]

———— 1973. *Opening Up the Suburbs: An Urban Strategy for America.* New Haven: Yale University Press. [§§7.8, 9.8]

———— 1983. *Rental Housing in the 1980s.* Washington, D.C.: Brookings. [§8.10]

Dubin, Jeffrey A., D. Roderick Kiewit, and Charles N. Noussair. 1992. "Voting on Growth Control Measures: Preferences and Strategies." *Economics and Politics,* 4: 191–213. [§8.7]

Dukeminier, Jesse, and James E. Krier. 1988. *Property,* 2d ed. Boston: Little, Brown. [§2.18]

Dunham, Allison. 1959. "Flood Control via the Police Power." *University of Pennsylvania Law Review,* 107: 1098–1132. [§5.1]

Dunn, L. F. 1979. "Measuring the Value of Community." *Journal of Urban Economics,* 6: 371–382. [§2.6]

Easterbrook, Gregg. 1986. "Vanishing Land Reappears." *The Atlantic,* 258: 17–20. [§8.5]

Eberts, Randall W., and Timothy J. Gronberg. 1981. "Jurisdictional Homogeneity and the Tiebout Hypothesis." *Journal of Urban Economics,* 10: 227–239. [§7.5]

———— 1990. "Structure, Conduct, and Performance in the Local Public Sector." *National Tax Journal,* 43: 165–174. [§7.2]

Ehrenberg, Ronald G., and George H. Jakubson. 1988. *Advance Notice Provisions in Plant Closing Legislation.* Kalamazoo, Mich.: W. E. Upjohn Institute for Employment Research. [§8.2]

Elhauge, Einer R. 1991. "Does Interest Group Theory Justify More Intrusive Judicial Review?" *Yale Law Journal,* 101: 31–110. [§§8.5, 8.19]

Ellickson, Bryan. 1971. "Jurisdictional Fragmentation and Residential Choice." *American Economic Review,* Papers and Proceedings, 61: 334–339. [§7.2]

Ellickson, Robert C. 1973. "Alternatives to Zoning: Covenants, Nuisance Rules, and Fines as Land Use Controls." *University of Chicago Law Review,* 40: 681–782. [§§4.8, 7.8, 9.17]

———— 1977. "Suburban Growth Controls: An Economic and Legal Analysis." *Yale Law Journal,* 86: 385–511. [§§9.4, 9.17, 9.18, 9.20–9.22]

———— 1981. "The Irony of 'Inclusionary' Zoning." *Southern California Law Review,* 54: 1167–1216. [§§6.3, 9.8]

———— 1982a. "Cities and Homeowners Associations." *University of Pennsylvania Law Review,* 130: 1519–1580. [§§7.10, 7.14]

—— 1982b. "Preface: The Effect of Growth Controls on Housing Prices on the San Francisco Peninsula." *Stanford Environmental Law Annual,* 4: 3–20. [§6.4]

—— 1986. "Of Coase and Cattle: Dispute Resolution among Neighbors in Shasta County." *Stanford Law Review,* 38: 623–687. [§§1.3, 1.15]

—— 1989. "Bringing Culture and Human Frailty to Rational Actors: A Critique of Classical Law-and-Economics." *Chicago-Kent Law Review,* 65: 23–55. [§5.21]

—— 1991. *Order without Law: How Neighbors Settle Disputes.* Cambridge: Harvard University Press. [§§1.16, 5.6]

—— 1993. "Property in Land." *Yale Law Journal,* 102: 1315–1400. [§§7.19, 7.20, 9.17]

Ellickson, Robert C., and A. Dan Tarlock. 1981. *Land Use Controls: Cases and Materials.* Boston: Little, Brown. [§§1.19, 6.20, 7.6, 9.16]

Ely, James W., Jr. 1992a. *The Guardian of Every Other Right: A Constitutional History of Property Rights.* New York: Oxford University Press. [§§2.5, 2.9, 3.2, 7.15, 8.1]

—— 1992b. " 'That Due Satisfaction May Be Made': The Fifth Amendment and the Origins of the Compensation Principle." *American Journal of Legal History,* 36: 1–18. [§2.9]

Ely, John Hart. 1973. "The Wages of Crying Wolf: A Comment on Roe v. Wade." *Yale Law Journal,* 82: 920–949. [§3.15]

—— 1980. *Democracy and Distrust: A Theory of Judicial Review.* Cambridge: Harvard University Press. [§§3.0, 3.12–3.16, 3.20–3.24, 4.15, 4.19, 4.25, 8.19, 9.10]

—— 1991. "Another Such Victory: Constitutional Theory and Practice in a World Where Courts Are No Different from Legislatures." *Virginia Law Review,* 77: 833–879. [§§3.13, 9.1]

Epple, Dennis, and Thomas Romer. 1989. "On the Flexibility of Municipal Boundaries." *Journal of Urban Economics,* 26: 307–319. [§7.16]

Epple, Dennis, and Allan Zelenitz. 1981. "The Implications of Competition among Jurisdiction: Does Tiebout Need Politics?" *Journal of Political Economy,* 89: 1197–1218. [§7.2]

Epstein, Richard A. 1985. *Takings: Private Property and the Power of Eminent Domain.* Cambridge: Harvard University Press. [§§2.6, 3.20, 4.0, 4.14, 4.19, 4.20–4.25, 5.8, 5.12, 5.17, 5.19, 7.20, 8.5]

—— 1987. "Takings: Descent and Resurrection." *Supreme Court Review,* 1987: 1–45. [§1.1 (n. 6)]

—— 1988. "Rent Control and the Theory of Efficient Regulation." *Brooklyn Law Review,* 54: 741–774. [§8.21]

—— 1992a. "Exit Rights under Federalism." *Law and Contemporary Problems,* 55:147–165. [§§3.23, 7.13]

—— 1992b. "Property, Speech, and the Politics of Distrust." *University of Chicago Law Review*, 59: 41–89. [§§4.20, 9.0]

—— 1992c. "*Yee v. City of Escondido:* The Supreme Court Strikes Out Again." *Loyola of Los Angeles Law Review*, 26: 3–22. [§8.19]

—— 1993. *Bargaining with the State*. Princeton: Princeton University Press. [§9.13]

Erickson, Rodney A., and David R. Wollover. 1987. "Local Tax Burdens and the Supply of Business Sites in Suburban Municipalities." *Journal of Regional Science*, 27: 25–37. [§7.9]

Euchner, Charles C. 1993. *Playing the Field: Why Sports Teams Move and Cities Fight to Keep Them*. Baltimore: Johns Hopkins University Press. [§2.6]

Eule, Julian N. 1982. "Laying the Dormant Commerce Clause to Rest." *Yale Law Journal*, 91: 425–485. [§3.20]

—— 1987. "Temporal Limits on the Legislative Mandate: Entrenchment and Retroactivity." *American Bar Foundation Research Journal*, 1987: 379–459. [§8.8]

—— 1990. "Judicial Review of Direct Democracy." *Yale Law Journal*, 99: 1503–1590. [§§6.19, 8.6, 9.5]

Farber, Daniel A. 1987. "Reassessing Boomer: Justice, Efficiency, and Nuisance Law." Working Paper no. 37, Stanford Law School. [§2.7]

—— 1992. "Economic Analysis and Just Compensation: An Anti-Discrimination Theory of Takings." *International Review of Law and Economics*, 12: 125–138. [§§4.3, 9.6]

Farber, Daniel A., and Philip P. Frickey. 1991. *Law and Public Choice: A Critical Introduction*. Chicago: University of Chicago Press. [§3.12]

Ferris, G. T. 1897. "Wild Animals in a New England Game-Park: The Corbin Game Preserve." *The Century Magazine*, October, pp. 924–937. [§2.3]

Finkelman, Paul. 1990. "James Madison and the Bill of Rights: A Reluctant Paternity." *Supreme Court Review*, 1990: 301–347. [§3.3]

Fischel, Daniel R. 1982. "The 'Race to the Bottom' Revisited: Reflections on Recent Developments in Delaware's Corporation Law." *Northwestern University Law Review*, 76: 913–945. [§7.9]

Fischel, William A. 1975. "Fiscal and Environmental Considerations in the Location of Firms in Suburban Communities." In *Fiscal Zoning and Land Use Controls*, ed. Edwin S. Mills and Wallace E. Oates. Lexington, Mass.: Heath-Lexington Books. [§§7.8, 7.9]

—— 1979. "Determinants of Voting on Environmental Quality: A Study of a New Hampshire Pulp Mill Referendum." *Journal of Environmental Economics and Management*, 6: 107–118. [§7.9]

—— 1981. "Is Local Government Structure in Large Urbanized Areas

Monopolistic or Competitive?" *National Tax Journal,* 34: 95–104. [§7.1]

——— 1982. "The Urbanization of Agricultural Land: A Review of the National Agricultural Lands Study." *Land Economics,* 58: 236–259. [§8.5]

——— 1985. *The Economics of Zoning Laws: A Property Rights Approach to American Land Use Controls.* Baltimore: Johns Hopkins University Press. [§§6.22, 7.20, 9.12, 9.17]

——— 1987. "The Economics of Land Use Exactions: A Property Rights Analysis." *Law and Contemporary Problems,* 50: 101–113. [§9.12]

——— 1988. "Introduction: Utilitarian Balancing and Formalism in Takings." *Columbia Law Review,* 88: 1581–1599. [§§1.22, 4.11, 9.13, 9.25]

——— 1989. "Did *Serrano* Cause Proposition 13?" *National Tax Journal,* 42: 465–474. [§§3.11, 7.19]

——— 1990. *Do Growth Controls Matter?* Cambridge, Mass.: Lincoln Institute of Land Policy. [§6.1]

——— 1991a. "Discounting in One Lesson." *The Practical Litigator,* 2: 27–36. [§9.24]

——— 1991b. "Exclusionary Zoning and Growth Controls: A Comment on the APA's Endorsement of the *Mount Laurel* Doctrine." *Washington University Journal of Urban and Contemporary Law,* 40: 65–73. [§9.8]

——— 1991c. "Exploring the Kozinski Paradox: Why Is More Efficient Regulation a Taking of Property?" *Chicago-Kent Law Review,* 67: 865–912. [§§1.23, 8.13, 8.14, 8.18, 8.19, 8.23]

——— 1992. "Property Taxation and the Tiebout Model: Evidence for the Benefit View from Zoning and Voting." *Journal of Economic Literature,* 30: 171–177. [§7.8]

——— 1994a. "How *Serrano* Caused Proposition 13." Working Paper no. 94–23, Department of Economics, Dartmouth College. [§§3.11, 7.19]

——— 1994b. "Zoning, Nonconvexities, and T. Jack Foster's City." *Journal of Urban Economics,* 35: 175–181. [§§6.1, 7.8, 7.20]

——— 1995. "The Offer/Ask Disparity and Just Compensation for Takings: A Constitutional Choice Approach." *International Review of Law and Economics* (forthcoming). [§5.16]

Fischel, William A., and Perry Shapiro. 1988. "Takings, Insurance, and Michelman: Comments on Economic Interpretations of 'Just Compensation' Law." *Journal of Legal Studies,* 17: 269–293. [§4.11]

——— 1989. "A Constitutional Choice Model of Compensation for Takings." *International Review of Law and Economics,* 9: 115–128. [§§5.9, 5.11–5.15, 9.19]

Fishback, Price V. 1992. "The Economics of Company Housing: Historical

Perspectives from the Coal Fields." *Journal of Law, Economics, and Organization*, 8: 346–365. [§1.15]

Fisher, William W. III. 1988. "The Significance of Public Perceptions of the Takings Doctrine." *Columbia Law Review*, 88: 1774–1794. [§§4.1, 9.25]

——— 1993. "The Trouble with *Lucas.*" *Stanford Law Review*, 45: 1393–1410. [§1.23]

Francis, Leslie P. 1984. "Eminent Domain Compensation in Western States." *Utah Law Review*, 1984: 429–484. [§4.20]

Freeman, A. Myrick, III. 1982. *Air and Water Pollution Control: A Benefit-Cost Assessment.* New York: Wiley. [§2.21]

Freund, Ernst. 1904. *The Police Power: Public Policy and Constitutional Rights.* Chicago: Callahan. [§9.18]

Freyer, Tony. 1981. "Reassessing the Impact of Eminent Domain in Early American Economic Development." *Wisconsin Law Review*, 1981: 1263–1286. [§2.11]

Frieden, Bernard J. 1979. *The Environmental Protection Hustle.* Cambridge: MIT Press. [§§6.4, 6.17, 6.20, 8.7]

Friedman, Lawrence M. 1986. "A Search for Seizure: *Pennsylvania Coal Co. v. Mahon* in Context." *Law and History Review*, 4: 1–22. [§§1.9, 2.11, 2.16]

——— 1988. "State Constitutions in Historical Perspective." *The Annals*, 496: 33–42. [§2.1]

Frohlich, Norman, and Joe Oppenheimer. 1994. "Preferences for Income Distribution and Distributive Justice: A Window on the Problems of Using Experimental Data in Economics and Ethics." *Eastern Economic Journal*, 20: 147–156. [§5.11]

Frug, Gerald. 1980. "The City as a Legal Concept." *Harvard Law Review*, 93: 1057–1154. [§§7.13, 7.20]

Gardner, B. Delworth. 1983. "Water Pricing and Rent Seeking in California Agriculture." In *Water Rights*, ed. Terry Anderson. San Francisco: Pacific Institute for Public Policy Research. [§6.17]

Gardner, Bruce L. 1992. "Changing Economic Perspectives on the Farm Problem." *Journal of Economic Literature*, 30: 62–101. [§8.5]

George, Henry. 1879. *Progress and Poverty.* New York: Appleton. [§2.12]

Gillman, Howard. 1993. *The Constitution Besieged: The Rise and Demise of Lochner Era Police Powers Jurisprudence.* Durham: Duke University Press. [§3.6]

Glickfeld, Madelyn, and Ned Levine. 1992. *Regional Growth–Local Reaction: The Enactment and Effects of Local Growth Control and Management Measures in California.* Cambridge, Mass.: Lincoln Institute of Land Policy. [§§6.21, 6.22]

Goodman, Allen C. 1988. "An Econometric Model of Housing Price, Permanent Income, Tenure Choice, and Housing Demand." *Journal of Urban Economics,* 23: 327–354. [§6.10]

Graglia, Lino A. 1990. "Judicial Activism of the Right: A Mistaken and Futile Hope." In *Liberty, Property, and the Future of Constitutional Development,* ed. Ellen Frankel Paul and Howard Dickman. Albany: SUNY Press. [§3.5]

Grant, J. A. C. 1931. "The 'Higher Law' Background of the Law of Eminent Domain." *Wisconsin Law Review,* 6: 67–85. [§3.2]

Grebler, Leo, and Frank G. Mittelbach. 1979. *The Inflation of House Prices: Its Extent, Causes, and Consequences.* Lexington, Mass.: Lexington Books. [§6.12]

Grey, Thomas C. 1986. "The Malthusian Constitution." *University of Miami Law Review,* 41: 21–48. [§4.24]

Grossman, Herschel I., and Suk Jae Noh. 1994. "Proprietary Public Finance and Economic Welfare." *Journal of Public Economics,* 53: 187–204. [§3.19]

Gyourko, Joseph. 1991. "Impact Fees, Exclusionary Zoning, and the Density of New Development." *Journal of Urban Economics,* 30: 242–256. [§9.11]

Gyourko, Joseph, and Richard Voith. 1992. "Local Market and National Components in House Price Appreciation." *Journal of Urban Economics,* 32: 52–69. [§§6.11, 6.15]

Haar, Charles M., and Barbara Hering. 1963. "The Determination of Benefits in Land Acquisition." *California Law Review,* 51: 833–881. [§2.18]

Hadley, Arthur Twining. 1885. *Railroad Transportation: Its History and Its Laws.* New York: Putnam's. [§8.9]

Hagman, Donald. *See* DiMento 1980

Hahn, Alan J. 1970. "Planning in Rural Areas." *AIP Journal,* 36: 40–49. [§7.17]

Hahn, Harlan, and Sheldon Kamieniecki. 1987. *Referendum Voting: Social Status and Policy Preferences.* New York: Greenwood Press. [§7.19]

Hall, Kermit L. 1993. "Of Floors and Ceilings: The New Federalism and State Bills of Rights." In *The Bill of Rights in Modern America after 200 Years,* ed. David J. Bodenhamer and James W. Ely, Jr. Bloomington: Indiana University Press. [§3.2]

Hamilton, Bruce W. 1975a. "Property Taxes and the Tiebout Hypothesis: Some Empirical Evidence." In *Fiscal Zoning and Land Use Controls,* ed. Edwin S. Mills and Wallace E. Oates. Lexington, Mass.: Lexington Books. [§7.8]

—— 1975b. "Zoning and Property Taxation in a System of Local Governments." *Urban Studies,* 12: 205–211. [§§7.4, 7.7, 7.8]

―――― 1976. "Capitalization of Intrajurisdictional Differences in Local Tax Prices." *American Economic Review,* 66: 743–753. [§7.7]

Hamilton, Bruce W., Edwin S. Mills, and David Puryear. 1975. "The Tiebout Hypothesis and Residential Income Segregation." In *Fiscal Zoning and Land Use Controls,* ed. Edwin S. Mills and Wallace E. Oates. Lexington, Mass.: Lexington Books. [§§7.5, 7.6]

Hanford, A. Chester. 1926. *Problems in Municipal Government.* Chicago: A. W. Shaw. [§7.16]

Hanke, Steve H., and Armando J. Carbonell. 1978. "Democratic Methods of Defining Property Rights: A Study of California's Coastal Zone." *Water Supply and Management,* 2: 483–487. [§§6.19, 9.5]

Harrison, Bennett. 1987. "Federal and State Legislation." In *Deindustrialization and Plant Closure,* ed. Paul D. Staudohar and Holly E. Brown. Lexington, Mass.: Lexington Books. [§8.2]

Harsanyi, John. 1975. "Can the Maximin Principle Serve as a Basis for Morality? A Critique of John Rawls' Theory." *American Political Science Review,* 69: 594–606. [§5.11]

Healy, Robert G., and John S. Rosenberg. 1979. *Land Use and the States,* 2d ed. Baltimore: Johns Hopkins University Press. [§9.3]

Henneberry, David, and Richard Barrows. 1990. "Capitalization of Exclusive Agricultural Zoning into Farmland Prices." *Land Economics,* 66: 249–258. [§8.6]

Hirsch, Werner Z. 1988. "An Inquiry into Effects of Mobile Home Park Rent Controls." *Journal of Urban Economics,* 24: 212–226. [§8.15]

Hirsch, Werner Z., and Joel G. Hirsch. 1988. "Legal-Economic Analysis of Rent Controls in a Mobile Home Context: Placement Values and Vacancy Decontrol." *UCLA Law Review,* 35: 399–466. [§§8.15–8.18]

Hirschman, Albert. 1970. *Exit, Voice, and Loyalty: Responses to Decline in Firms, Organizations, and States.* Cambridge: Harvard University Press. [§§3.23, 8.0]

Hite, J. C., and B. L. Dillman. 1981. "Protection of Agricultural Land: An Institutionalist Perspective." *Southern Journal of Agricultural Economics,* 13: 43–53. [§8.5]

Hoffman, Elizabeth, and Matthew L. Spitzer. 1985. "Entitlements, Rights, and Fairness: An Experimental Examination of Subjects' Concepts of Distributive Justice." *Journal of Legal Studies,* 14: 259–297. [§5.22]

―――― 1993. "Willingness to Pay vs. Willingness to Accept: Legal and Economic Implications." *Washington University Law Quarterly,* 71: 59–114. [§§5.16, 5.17]

Hohfeld, Wesley N. 1917. "Faulty Analysis in Easement and License Cases." *Yale Law Journal,* 27: 66–101. [§1.9]

Holcombe, Randall G. 1989. "The Median Voter Model in Public Choice Theory." *Public Choice*, 61: 115–125. [§7.2]

Holmes, Stephen. 1988. "Precommitment and the Paradox of Democracy." In *Constitutionalism and Democracy*, ed. Jon Elster and Rune Slagstad. Cambridge: Cambridge University Press. [§§3.16, 3.18]

Holtz-Eakin, Douglas, and Harvey S. Rosen. 1989. "The 'Rationality' of Municipal Capital Spending: Evidence from New Jersey." *Regional Science and Urban Economics*, 19: 517–536. [§7.3]

Horwitz, Morton J. 1977. *The Transformation of American Law, 1780–1860*. Cambridge: Harvard University Press. [§2.11]

Hovenkamp, Herbert. 1990. "Legislation, Well-Being, and Public Choice." *University of Chicago Law Review*, 57: 63–116. [§8.19]

———— 1991. "Legal Policy and the Endowment Effect." *Journal of Legal Studies*, 20: 225–248. [§5.21]

Hundley, Norris, Jr. 1992. *The Great Thirst: Californians and Water, 1770s–1990s*. Berkeley: University of California Press. [§§2.15, 6.17]

Hurst, James Willard. 1956. *Law and the Conditions of Freedom in the Nineteenth-Century United States*. Madison: University of Wisconsin Press. [§§2.15, 7.0, 7.15]

Inman, Robert P., and Daniel L. Rubinfeld. 1979. "The Judicial Pursuit of Local Fiscal Equity." *Harvard Law Review*, 92: 1662–1750. [§7.19]

Jackson, Henry M. (committee chair). 1972. *National Land Use Policy: Background Papers on Past and Pending Legislation and the Roles of the Executive Branch, Congress, and the States in Land Use Policy and Planning*. Washington, D.C.: U.S. Senate Committee on Interior and Insular Affairs. [§8.4]

Kaden, Lewis B. 1983. "Courts and Legislatures in a Federal System: The Case of School Finance." *Hofstra Law Review*, 11: 1205–1260. [§§3.11, 9.10]

Kahneman, Daniel, and Amos Tversky. 1979. "Prospect Theory: An Analysis of Decision under Risk." *Econometrica*, 47: 263–291. [§5.20]

Kahrl, William L. 1981. *Water and Power: The Controversy over Los Angeles' Water Supply in the Owens Valley*. Berkeley: University of California Press. [§ 2.3]

Kaldor, Nicholas. 1939. "Welfare Propositions of Economics and Interpersonal Comparisons of Utility." *Economic Journal*, 49: 549–552. [§4.4]

Kanner, Gideon. 1973. "Condemnation Blight: Just How Just Is Just Compensation?" *Notre Dame Lawyer*, 48: 765–810. [§§2.18, 4.18, 5.19]

———— 1980. "Inverse Condemnation Remedies in an Era of Uncertainty." In *Proceedings of the Institute on Planning, Zoning, and Eminent Domain*. Albany, N.Y.: Matthew Bender. [§2.1]

———— 1989. "Measure of Damages in Nonphysical Inverse Condemnation

392   *General References*

Cases." In *Proceedings of the Institute on Planning, Zoning, and Eminent Domain*. New York: Matthew Bender. [§2.1]

Kaplow, Louis. 1986. "An Economic Analysis of Legal Transitions." *Harvard Law Review*, 99: 509–617. [§§5.1, 5.5, 5.11, 5.15]

Kaplow, Louis, and Steven Shavell. 1994. "Why the Legal System Is Less Efficient than the Income Tax in Redistributing Income." *Journal of Legal Studies*, 23: 667–682. [§4.24]

Katz, Lawrence, and Kenneth Rosen. 1987. "The Interjurisdictional Effects of Growth Controls on Housing Prices." *Journal of Law and Economics*, 30: 149–160. [§6.3]

Kayden, Jerold S. 1991. "Zoning for Dollars: New Rules for an Old Game?" Comments on the *Municipal Art Society* and *Nollan* Cases. *Washington University Journal of Urban and Contemporary Law*, 39: 3–51. [§9.15]

Kelman, Mark. 1988. "On Democracy Bashing: A Skeptical Look at the Theoretical and 'Empirical' Practice of the Public Choice Movement." *Virginia Law Review*, 74: 199–273. [§8.18]

Kennedy, Duncan. 1981. "Cost-Benefit Analysis of Entitlement Problems: A Critique." *Stanford Law Review*, 33: 387–445. [§8.18]

Kens, Paul. 1990. *Judicial Power and Reform Politics: The Anatomy of Lochner v. New York*. Lawrence: University Press of Kansas. [§3.6]

——— 1991. "The Source of the Myth: Police Powers of the States and Laissez-Faire Constitutionalism, 1900–1937." *American Journal of Legal History*, 35: 70–98. [§3.6]

Kessler, Lauren. 1993. *Stubborn Twig: Three Generations in the Life of a Japanese American Family*. New York: Random House. [§3.15]

Klarman, Michael J. 1991a. "An Interpretive History of Modern Equal Protection." *Michigan Law Review*, 90: 213–318. [§§3.7, 3.11]

——— 1991b. "The Puzzling Resistance to Political Process Theory." *Virginia Law Review*, 77: 747–832. [§§3.12, 3.21, 3.22, 9.10]

——— 1992. "Constitutional Fact/Constitutional Fiction: A Critique of Bruce Ackerman's Theory of Constitutional Moments." *Stanford Law Review*, 44: 759–797. [§3.16]

Kmiec, Douglas W. 1981–82. "Regulatory Takings: The Court Runs Out of Gas in *San Diego*." *Indiana Law Journal*, 57: 45–81. [§§1.20, 9.20]

——— 1983. "Manufactured Home Siting: A Statutory and Judicial Overview." *Zoning and Planning Law Report*, 6: 105–110. [§8.22]

——— 1988. "The Original Understanding of the Taking Clause Is Neither Weak Nor Obtuse." *Columbia Law Review*, 88: 1630–1666. [§2.9]

Kmiec, Douglas W., and Eric L. Diamond. 1984. "The New Federalism Is Not Enough: The Privatization of Nonpublic Goods." *Harvard Journal of Law and Public Policy*, 7: 321–394. [§7.13]

Kmiec, Douglas W., and John O. McGinnis. 1987. "The Contract Clause: A

Return to the Original Understanding." *Hastings Constitutional Law Quarterly,* 14: 525–560. [§3.8]

Knetsch, Jack L. 1983. *Property Rights and Compensation: Compulsory Acquisition and Other Losses.* Toronto: Butterworths. [§§2.4, 5.16]

Knetsch, Jack L., and Thomas E. Borcherding. 1979. "Expropriation of Private Property and the Basis for Compensation." *University of Toronto Law Journal,* 29: 237–252. [§§5.16, 5.17, 9.7]

Knetsch, Jack L., and J. A. Sinden. 1984. "Willingness to Pay and Compensation Demanded: Experimental Evidence of an Unexpected Disparity in Measures of Value." *Quarterly Journal of Economics,* 99: 507–521. [§5.16]

Korobkin, Russell. 1994. "Note: Policymaking and the Offer/Asking Price Gap: Toward a Theory of Efficient Entitlement Allocation." *Stanford Law Review,* 46: 663–708. [§5.20]

Kricher, John C. 1988. *A Field Guide to Eastern Forests [of] North America.* Boston: Houghton Mifflin. [§4.8]

Kutler, Stanley. 1971. *Privilege and Creative Destruction: The Charles River Bridge Case.* New York: Norton. [§2.15]

Kuttner, Robert. 1980. *Revolt of the Haves.* New York: Simon and Schuster. [§8.10]

Kydland, Finn E., and Edward C. Prescott. 1977. "Rules Rather than Discretion: The Inconsistency of Optimal Plans." *Journal of Political Economy,* 85: 473–492. [§3.17]

LaCroix, Sumner J., and Louis A. Rose. 1995. "Public Use, Just Compensation, and Land Reform in Hawaii." *Research in Law and Economics,* 17: forthcoming. [§2.5]

Lamar, Martha, Alan Mallach, and John M. Payne. 1989. "*Mount Laurel* at Work: Affordable Housing in New Jersey, 1983–1988." *Rutgers Law Review,* 41: 1197–1277. [§9.9]

Lazarus, Richard J. 1993. "Putting the Correct 'Spin' on *Lucas.*" *Stanford Law Review,* 45: 1411–1432. [§1.22]

Levmore, Saul. 1990. "Just Compensation and Just Politics." *Connecticut Law Review,* 22: 285–322. [§§3.23, 8.19, 9.6]

——— 1992. "Bicameralism: When Are Two Decisions Better than One?" *International Review of Law and Economics,* 12: 145–162. [§7.14]

Lewis, Phil. 1958. "Eminent Domain in Pennsylvania." In *Purden's Pennsylvania Statutes Annotated.* Philadelphia: George Bisel. [§5.2]

Libecap, Gary D. 1986. Review of *The Economics of Zoning Laws,* by William Fischel. *Journal of Economic Literature,* 24: 730–732. [§5.1]

Littlefield, Neil. 1962. *Metropolitan Area Problems and Municipal Home Rule.* Ann Arbor: University of Michigan Law School Legislative Research Center. [§7.14]

Lockeretz, William. 1989. "Secondary Effects on Midwestern Agriculture of Metropolitan Development and Decreases in Farmland." *Land Economics,* 65: 205–216. [§8.5]

Lowenberg, Anton D., and Ben T. Yu. 1992. "Efficient Constitution Formation and Maintenance: The Role of 'Exit.' " *Constitutional Political Economy,* 3: 51–72. [§3.23]

Lowry, Ira S., and Bruce W. Ferguson. 1992. *Development Regulation and Housing Affordability.* Washington, D.C.: Urban Land Institute. [§6.21]

Lunney, Glynn S., Jr. 1992. "A Critical Reexamination of the Takings Jurisprudence." *Michigan Law Review,* 90: 1892–1965. [§§3.4, 8.19]

Lusky, Louis. 1982. "Footnote Redux: A *Carolene Products* Reminiscence." *Columbia Law Review,* 82: 1093–1109. [§3.10]

Manheim, Karl. 1989. "Tenant Eviction and the Takings Clause." *Wisconsin Law Review,* 1989: 925–1019. [§1.18]

Mankiew, Gregory, and David N. Weil. 1989. "The Baby Boom, the Baby Bust, and the Housing Market." *Regional Science and Urban Economics,* 19: 235–255. [§6.12]

Marcus, Norman. 1980. "A Comparative Look at TDR, Subdivision Exactions, and Zoning as Environmental Preservation Panaceas: The Search for Dr. Jekyll without Mr. Hyde." *Urban Law Annual,* 20: 3–74. [§9.2]

Margo, Robert A. 1991. "Segregated Schools and the Mobility Hypothesis: A Model of Local Government Discrimination." *Quarterly Journal of Economics,* 106: 61–73. [§3.19]

Mark, Jonathan H., and Michael A. Goldberg. 1986. "A Study of the Impacts of Zoning on Housing Values over Time." *Journal of Urban Economics,* 20: 257–273. [§6.1]

Marshall, John D., Jack L. Knetsch, and J. A. Sinden. 1986. "Agents' Evaluations and the Disparity in Measures of Economic Loss." *Journal of Economic Behavior and Organization,* 7: 115–127. [§5.19]

[Mattes brief] 1922. Brief of Argument on Behalf of City of Scranton, Mahon v. Pennsylvania Coal Co., 118 A. 491 (Pa. 1922). [§§1.5, 1.12, 1.14]

Mattes, Philip V. 1928. "The Mine-Cave Struggle." In *Jubilee History of Lackawanna County,* ed. Thomas Murphy. Topeka, Kans.: Historical Publishing Company. [§§1.8, 1.13, 1.15]

——— 1974. *Tales of Scranton.* Scranton, Pa.: published by the author, no date. (Date of publication inferred from biographical information.) [§§1.1 (n. 6), 1.13, 1.15]

McAlister, Mary E. 1990. "Hall v. City of Santa Barbara: A New Look at California Rent Controls and the Takings Clause." *Ecology Law Quarterly,* 17: 179–213. [§8.15]

McChesney, Fred S. 1990. "Government as Definer of Property Rights: Indian Lands, Ethnic Externalities, and Bureaucratic Budgets." *Journal of Legal Studies,* 19: 297–336. [§4.15]

McDonald, Forrest. 1958. *We the People: The Economic Origins of the Constitution.* Chicago: University of Chicago Press. [§3.1]

——— 1985. *Novus Ordo Seclorum: The Intellectual Origins of the Constitution.* Lawrence: University Press of Kansas. [§§2.9, 2.21, 3.3, 4.8, 7.12]

McDonald, John F. 1979. *Economic Analysis of an Urban Housing Market.* New York: Academic Press. [§9.2]

McDougal, Gerald S. 1976. "Local Public Goods and Residential Property Values: Some Insights and Extensions." *National Tax Journal,* 24: 436–447. [§7.1]

McEachern, William A. 1978. "Collective Decision Rules and Local Debt Choice: A Test of the Median-Voter Hypothesis." *National Tax Journal,* 31: 129–136. [§7.2]

McFadden, Daniel. 1976. "The Revealed Preference of a Government Bureaucracy: Empirical Evidence." *Bell Journal of Economics,* 7: 55–72. [§2.19]

McMichael, Stanley L., and Robert F. Bingham. 1923. *City Growth and Values.* Cleveland: Stanley McMichael Publishing Organization. [§7.16]

McMillen, Daniel P. 1990. "The Timing and Duration of Development Tax Rate Increases." *Journal of Urban Economics,* 28: 1–18. [§4.18]

McMillen, Daniel P., and John F. McDonald. 1991. "A Markov Chain Model of Zoning Change." *Journal of Urban Economics,* 30: 257–270. [§7.8]

——— 1993. "Could Zoning Have Increased Land Values in Chicago?" *Journal of Urban Economics,* 33: 167–188. [§7.15]

McPhee, John. 1989. *The Control of Nature.* New York: Farrar Straus Giroux. [§1.21]

Mead, Richard R. 1935. *An Analysis of the Decline of the Anthracite Industry since 1921.* Philadelphia: University of Pennsylvania. [§§1.1 (nn. 3, 11), 1.13]

Meese, Richard, and Nancy Wallace. 1991. "Nonparametric Estimation of Dynamic Hedonic Price Models and the Construction of Residential Housing Price Indexes." *AREUEA Journal,* 19: 308–331. [§6.12]

——— 1994. "Testing the Present Value Relation for Housing Prices: Should I Leave My House in San Francisco?" *Journal of Urban Economics,* 35: 245–266. [§§6.16, 6.18]

Mercer, Lloyd J., and W. Douglas Morgan. 1982. "An Estimate of Residential Growth Controls' Impact on Housing Prices." In *Resolving the Housing Crisis,* ed. M. Bruce Johnson. San Francisco: Pacific Institute for Public Policy Research. [§6.17]

Merrill, Thomas W. 1986a. "The Economics of Public Use." *Cornell Law Review,* 72: 61–116. [§§2.3, 2.6, 4.23]

—— 1986b. "Rent Seeking and the Compensation Principle." *Northwestern Law Review,* 80: 1561–1589. [§3.3]

Miceli, Thomas J., and Kathleen Segerson. 1994. "Regulatory Takings: When Should Compensation Be Paid?" *Journal of Legal Studies,* 23: 749–776. [§5.14]

Michelman, Frank I. 1967. "Property, Utility, and Fairness: Comments on the Ethical Foundations of 'Just Compensation' Law." *Harvard Law Review,* 80: 1165–1258. [§§4.0–4.10, 4.15, 4.17, 4.21, 4.22, 4.25, 4.26, 5.4, 5.5, 5.7–5.11, 9.3, 9.23]

—— 1979. "Politics and Values, or What's Really Wrong with Rationality Review?" *Creighton Law Review,* 13: 487–511. [§4.10]

—— 1988. "Takings, 1987." *Columbia Law Review,* 88: 1600–1629. [§§1.1 (n. 6), 2.21]

—— 1992. "Liberties, Fair Values, and Constitutional Method." *University of Chicago Law Review,* 59: 91–114. [§§5.8, 9.0]

Mieszkowski, Peter. 1972. "The Property Tax: An Excise Tax or a Profits Tax?" *Journal of Public Economics,* 1: 73–96. [§7.4]

Mieszkowski, Peter, and George R. Zodrow. 1989. "Taxation and the Tiebout Model: The Differential Effects of Head Taxes, Taxes on Land Rents, and Property Taxes." *Journal of Economic Literature,* 27: 1098–1146. [§§7.5, 7.8]

Miller, Donald L., and Richard E. Sharpless. 1985. *The Kingdom of Coal: Work, Enterprise, and Ethnic Communities in the Mine Fields.* Philadelphia: University of Pennsylvania Press. [§1.4]

Miller, Geoffrey P. 1987. "The True Story of *Carolene Products.*" *Supreme Court Review,* 1987: 397–428. [§3.10]

Mills, David E. 1989. "Is Zoning a Negative-Sum Game?" *Land Economics,* 65: 1–12. [§§7.8, 8.14]

Monkkonen, Eric H. 1988. *America Becomes Urban: The Development of United States Cities and Towns, 1780–1980.* Berkeley: University of California Press. [§§7.9, 7.14, 7.16]

—— 1990. "Politics, Law, and Local Debt: Illinois, 1870." Working Paper, Department of History, UCLA. Presented at Law and Society meetings, Berkeley. [§7.14]

Moon, Choon-Geol, and Janet G. Stotsky. 1993. "The Effect of Rent Control on Housing Quality Change: A Longitudinal Analysis." *Journal of Political Economy,* 101: 1114–1148. [§8.11]

Moser, Peter. 1994. "Constitutional Protection of Economic Rights: The Swiss and U.S. Experience in Comparison." *Constitutional Political Economy,* 5: 61–79. [§3.16]

Mosk, Stanley. 1988. "The Emerging Agenda in State Constitutional Rights Law." *The Annals,* 496: 54–64. [§3.11]

Muller, Thomas, and Thomas Espenshade. 1985. *The Fourth Wave: California's Newest Immigrants.* Washington, D.C.: Urban Institute Press. [§§6.5, 6.22]

Munch, Patricia. 1976. "An Economic Analysis of Eminent Domain." *Journal of Political Economy,* 84: 473–497. [§2.3]

Murray, Michael P. 1983. "Subsidized and Unsubsidized Housing Starts, 1961–1977." *Review of Economics and Statistics,* 65: 590–597. [§9.9]

Murray, Michael P., Peter Rydell, Lance Barnett, Carol E. Hillestead, and Kevin Neels. 1991. "Analyzing Rent Control: The Case of Los Angeles." *Economic Inquiry,* 29: 601–625. [§§8.10, 8.11]

Musgrave, Richard A, and Peggy B. Musgrave. 1989. *Public Finance in Theory and Practice,* 5th ed. New York: McGraw-Hill. [§4.19]

National Agricultural Lands Study. 1981. *Final Report.* Washington, D.C.: U.S. Government Printing Office. [§8.4]

National Municipal League. 1930. *The Government of Metropolitan Areas in the United States.* New York: National Municipal League. [§7.16]

———— 1963. *A Model State Constitution.* New York: National Municipal League. [§3.16]

Nedelsky, Jennifer. 1990. *Private Property and the Limits of American Constitutionalism: The Madisonian Framework and Its Legacy.* Chicago: University of Chicago Press. [§§2.21, 3.3]

Neill, Helen R., Ronald G. Cummings, Philip T. Ganderton, Glenn Harrison, and Thomas McGuckin. 1994. "Hypothetical Surveys and Real Economic Commitments." *Land Economics,* 70: 145–154. [§5.22]

Nelson, Robert H. 1977. *Zoning and Property Rights: An Analysis of the American System of Land-Use Regulation.* Cambridge: MIT Press. [§§7.8, 7.20]

———— 1979. "A Private Property Right Theory of Zoning." *The Urban Lawyer,* 11: 713–732. [§7.15]

Neuman, Gerald L. 1987. "Territorial Discrimination, Equal Protection, and Self-Determination." *University of Pennsylvania Law Review,* 135: 261–382. [§7.10]

Newton, Carl K., and Jeffrey Slattery. 1983. "The Changing Areas in Condemnation Law." *The Urban Lawyer,* 15: 791–803. [§2.18]

Niskanen, William A., Jr. 1971. *Bureaucracy and Representative Government.* Chicago: Aldine. [§§5.15, 7.2]

North, Douglas C., and Barry R. Weingast. 1989. "Constitutions and Commitment: Evolution of Institutions Governing Public Choice." *Journal of Economic History,* 49: 803–832. [§3.18]

Novak, Theodore J., Brian W. Blaesser, and Thomas F. Geselbracht. 1994. *Condemnation of Property: Practice and Strategies for Winning Just Compensation.* New York: John Wiley. [§4.17]

Novick, Sheldon M. 1989. *Honorable Justice: The Life of Oliver Wendell Holmes*. Boston: Little, Brown. [§1.1]

Nozick, Robert. 1974. *Anarchy, State, and Utopia*. New York: Basic Books. [§§4.19, 4.25]

Oates, Wallace E. 1969. "The Effects of Property Taxes and Local Public Spending on Property Values: An Empirical Study of Tax Capitalization and the Tiebout Hypothesis." *Journal of Political Economy*, 77: 957–971. [§7.1]

——— 1989. "Searching for Leviathan: A Reply and Some Further Reflections." *American Economic Review*, 79: 578–583. [§7.2]

Oates, Wallace E., and Robert M. Schwab. 1988. "Economic Competition among Jurisdictions: Efficiency Enhancing or Distortion Inducing?" *Journal of Public Economics*, 35: 333–354. [§7.9]

Ogus, Anthony. 1990. "Property Rights and Freedom of Economic Activity," In *Constitutionalism and Rights: The Influence of the United States Constitution Abroad*, ed. Louis Henkin and Albert Rosenthal. New York: Columbia University Press. [§3.16]

Ohio Constitutional Convention. 1851. *Official Reports of the Debates and Proceedings*. Reported by J. V. Smith. Columbus: Scott and Bascom. [§2.14]

Olsen, Edgar O. 1990. "Bias in Estimating the Benefits of Government Programs Due to Misapplication of Composite Commodity Theorems: Estimates for Major U.S. Housing Programs." Discussion Paper 927–90, Institute for Research on Poverty, University of Wisconsin, Madison. [§8.11]

——— 1991. "Is Rent Control Good Social Policy?" *Chicago-Kent Law Review*, 67: 931–945. [§8.13]

O'Sullivan, Arthur, Terri A. Sexton, and Steven M. Sheffrin. 1995. *Property Taxes and Tax Revolts: The Legacy of Proposition 13*. Cambridge: Cambridge University Press. [§§7.4, 8.10]

Ozanne, Larry, and Thomas Thibodeau. 1983. "Explaining Metropolitan Housing Price Differences." *Journal of Urban Economics*, 13: 51–66. [§6.10]

Ozler, Sule. 1993. "Have Commercial Banks Ignored History?" *American Economic Review*, 83: 608–620. [§3.19]

Paul, Ellen Frankel. 1987. *Property Rights and Eminent Domain*. New Brunswick, N.J.: Transaction Press. [§4.19]

Perry, Mark A. 1990. "Municipal Supervision and State Action Antitrust Immunity." *University of Chicago Law Review*, 57: 1413–1445. [§7.10]

Peterson, Andrea L. 1989. "The Takings Clause: In Search of Underlying Principles." *California Law Review*, 77: 1299–1363 and 78: 53–162. [§§1.18, 9.0]

Peterson, George E. 1974a. "The Influence of Zoning Regulations on Land and Housing Prices." Working Paper 1207–24, Urban Institute, Washington, D.C. [§7.6]

——— 1974b. "Land Prices and Factor Substitution in the Metropolitan Housing Market." Working Paper, Urban Institute, Washington, D.C. [§6.3]

Peterson, George E., and Harvey Yampolsky. 1975. *Urban Development and the Protection of Metropolitan Farmland.* Washington, D.C.: Urban Institute Press. [§8.6]

Pigou, A. C. 1932. *The Economics of Welfare,* 4th ed. London: Macmillan. [§§5.13, 9.18]

Pogodzinski, J. Michael, and Tim R. Sass. 1991. "Measuring the Effects of Municipal Zoning Regulations: A Survey." *Urban Studies,* 28: 597–621. [§6.2]

Poirier, Marc R. 1993. "Takings and Natural Hazards Policy: Public Choice on the Beachfront." *Rutgers Law Review,* 46: 243–347. [§§1.23, 8.19]

Polinsky, A. Mitchell. 1972. "Probabilistic Compensation Criteria." *Quarterly Journal of Economics,* 86: 407–425. [§4.9]

——— 1979. "Controlling Externalities and Protecting Entitlements: Property Right, Liability Rule, and Tax-Subsidy Approaches." *Journal of Legal Studies,* 8: 1–48. [§2.3]

Pollard, W. L., ed. 1931. "Zoning in the United States" (symposium title). *The Annals,* 155–Part II: 1–227. [§7.15]

Popp, Terri E. 1989. "A Survey of Governmental Response to the Farmland Crisis: States' Application of Agricultural Zoning." *University of Arkansas at Little Rock Law Journal,* 11: 515–556. [§8.6]

Popper, Frank. 1988. "Understanding American Land Use Regulation since 1970." *APA Journal,* 54: 291–301. [§§7.18, 8.4]

Porter, Douglas R., and Lindell L. Marsh, eds. 1989. *Development Agreements: Practice, Policy, and Prospects.* Washington, D.C.: Urban Land Institute. [§9.16]

Posner, Richard A. 1980. "The Ethical and Political Basis of the Efficiency Norm in Common Law Adjudication." *Hofstra Law Review,* 8: 487–507. [§§4.1, 4.9, 5.12]

——— 1991. "Democracy and Distrust Revisited." *Virginia Law Review,* 77: 641–652. [§3.13]

——— 1993. "What Do Judges and Justices Maximize? (The Same Thing Everybody Else Does)." *Supreme Court Economic Review,* 3: 1–42. [§3.14]

Power, Garrett. 1983. "Apartheid Baltimore Style: The Residential Segregation Ordinances of 1910–1913." *Maryland Law Review,* 42: 289–328. [§3.6]

Pulliam, Mark S. 1983. "Brandeis Brief for Decontrol of Land Use: A Plea for Constitutional Reform." *Southwestern University Law Review,* 13: 435–476. [§3.2]

Rasmusen, Eric. 1992. "Judicial Legitimacy as a Repeated Game." Working Paper 93–017, Department of Economics, Indiana University (forthcoming in *Journal of Law, Economics, and Organization*). [§3.14]

Raushenbush, Hilmer S. 1924. *The Anthracite Question.* New York: Wilson. [§1.4]

Rawls, John. 1971. *A Theory of Justice.* Cambridge: Harvard University Press. [§§4.25, 5.9, 5.11]

Reichman, Uriel. 1976. "Residential Private Governments: An Introductory Survey." *University of Chicago Law Review,* 43: 253–306. [§7.20]

Reilly, William K., ed. 1973. *The Use of Land: A Citizens' Policy Guide to Urban Growth.* New York: Thomas Crowell. [§8.4]

Reinhard, Raymond M. 1981. "Estimating Property Tax Capitalization: A Further Comment." *Journal of Political Economy,* 89: 1251–1260. [§7.1]

Revesz, Richard L. 1992. "Rehabilitating Interstate Competition: Rethinking the 'Race to the Bottom' Rationale for Federal Environmental Regulation." *NYU Law Review,* 67: 1210–1255. [§7.9]

Riker, William H., and Barry R. Weingast. 1988. "Constitutional Regulation of Legislative Choice: The Political Consequences of Judicial Deference to Legislatures." *Virginia Law Review,* 74: 373–402. [§8.19]

Riva, Enrico. 1984. "Regulatory Takings in American Law and 'Material Expropriation' in Swiss Law—A Comparison of Applicable Standards." *The Urban Lawyer,* 16: 425–458. [§3.16]

Rivkin, Malcom D., and Goldie W. Rivkin. 1993. "Transportation Corridor Preservation." *Urban Land,* November, pp. 24–28. [§4.17]

Roback, Jennifer. 1982. "Wages, Rents, and the Quality of Life." *Journal of Political Economy,* 90: 1257–1278. [§6.15]

Roberts, E. F. 1986. "Mining with Mr. Justice Holmes." *Vanderbilt Law Review,* 39: 287–304. [§1.16]

Roberts, Julia E. 1905. *The Tree Book: A Popular Guide to a Knowledge of the Trees of North America and to Their Uses and Cultivation.* Garden City, N.Y.: Doubleday, Page. [§4.8]

Roberts, Peter. 1901. *The Anthracite Coal Industry.* New York: Macmillan. [§§1.1 (n. 11), 1.5]

——— 1904. *Anthracite Coal Communities.* New York: Macmillan. [§1.15]

Rolleston, Barbara Sherman. 1987. "Determinants of Restrictive Suburban Zoning: An Empirical Analysis." *Journal of Urban Economics,* 21: 1–21. [§7.6]

Romer, Thomas, and Howard Rosenthal. 1979. "The Elusive Median Voter." *Journal of Public Economics,* 12: 143–170. [§§7.2, 7.3]

Romer, Thomas, Howard Rosenthal, and Vincent G. Munley. 1992. "Economic Incentives and Political Institutions: Spending and Voting in School Budget Referenda." *Journal of Public Economics,* 49: 1–33. [§7.3]

Rose, Carol M. 1983. "Planning and Dealing: Piecemeal Land Controls as a Problem of Local Legitimacy." *California Law Review,* 71: 837–912. [§§3.23, 9.6]

—— 1984. "*Mahon* Reconstructed: Why the Takings Issue Is Still a Muddle." *Southern California Law Review,* 57: 561–599. [§§1.1 (n. 11), 1.2]

—— 1987. " 'Enough and as Good' of What?" *Northwestern University Law Review,* 81: 417–442. [§5.11]

—— 1989. "The Ancient Constitution vs. the Federalist Empire: Anti-Federalism from the Attack on 'Monarchism' to Modern Localism." *Northwestern University Law Review,* 84: 74–105. [§3.4]

Rose, Joseph B. 1984. "Landmarks Preservation in New York." *The Public Interest,* 74: 132–145. [§1.18]

Rose-Ackerman, Susan. 1979. "Market Models of Local Government: Exit, Voting, and the Land Market." *Journal of Urban Economics,* 6: 319–337. [§7.5]

—— 1985. "Inalienability and the Theory of Property Rights." *Columbia Law Review,* 85: 931–969. [§4.14]

—— 1988. "Against Ad Hocery: A Comment on Michelman." *Columbia Law Review,* 88: 1697–1711. [§5.1]

Rosen, Christine Meisner. 1986. *The Limits of Power: Great Fires and the Process of City Growth in America.* Cambridge: Cambridge University Press. [§5.4]

Rosen, Kenneth T. 1982. "The Impact of Proposition 13 on House Prices in Northern California: A Test of the Interjurisdictional Capitalization Hypothesis." *Journal of Political Economy,* 90: 191–200. [§6.16]

Rosen, Kenneth T., and Lawrence F. Katz. 1981. "Growth Management and Land Use Controls: The San Francisco Bay Area Experience." *AREUEA Journal* 9: 321–344. [§6.3]

Ross, William G. 1994. *A Muted Fury: Populists, Progressives, and Labor Unions Confront the Courts, 1890–1937.* Princeton: Princeton University Press. [§3.14]

Rossiter, Clinton, ed. 1961. *The Federalist Papers.* New York: Mentor Books. [§3.4]

Rothstein, Lawrence E. 1986. *Plant Closings: Power, Politics, and Workers.* Dover, Mass.: Auburn House. [§8.2]

Rothstein, Paul. 1992. "The Demand for Education with 'Power Equalizing' Aid." *Journal of Public Economics,* 49: 135–162. [§3.11]

Rubenfeld, Jed. 1993. "Usings." *Yale Law Journal,* 102: 1077–1163. [§§2.7, 9.6]

Rubin, Jeffrey I., and Joseph J. Seneca. 1991. "Density Bonuses, Exactions, and the Supply of Affordable Housing." *Journal of Urban Economics,* 30: 208–223. [§9.8]

Rudel, Thomas K. 1989. *Situations and Strategies in American Land-Use Planning.* Cambridge: Cambridge University Press. [§§6.22, 7.17]

St. John, Michael. 1990. "The Impact of Rent Controls on Property Value." Working Paper 90–178, Institute of Business and Economic Research, Haas School of Business, University of California, Berkeley. [§§8.12, 8.13]

——— 1994. "The Distributional Impact of Restrictive Rent Control Programs in Berkeley and Santa Monica, California." Paper presented at Western Economic Association meetings, Vancouver, British Columbia. [§8.13]

Salins, Peter D., and Gerard C. S. Mildner. 1992. *Scarcity by Design: The Legacy of New York City's Housing Policies.* Cambridge: Harvard University Press. [§8.17]

Sax, Joseph. 1964. "Takings and the Police Power." *Yale Law Journal,* 74: 36–76. [§§9.0, 9.6]

——— 1971. "Takings, Private Property, and Public Rights." *Yale Law Journal,* 81: 149–186. [§§8.7, 9.0]

Scalia, Antonin. 1987. "Economic Affairs as Human Affairs." In *Economic Liberties and the Judiciary,* ed. James A. Dorn and Henry G. Manne. Fairfax, Va.: George Mason University Press. [§8.19]

Scheiber, Harry N. 1971. "The Road to *Munn:* Eminent Domain and the Concept of Public Purpose in the State Courts." *Perspectives in American History,* 5: 329–402. [§2.11]

——— 1973. "Property Law, Expropriation, and Resource Allocation by Government, 1789–1910." *Journal of Economic History,* 33: 232–251. [§§2.10, 2.11, 2.13]

——— 1989. "The Jurisprudence—and Mythology—of Eminent Domain in American Legal History." In *Liberty, Property, and Government: Constitutional Interpretation before the New Deal,* ed. Ellen F. Paul and Howard Dickman. Albany: SUNY Press. [§§2.5, 2.13]

Schelling, Thomas. 1960. *The Strategy of Conflict.* Cambridge: Harvard University Press. [§3.18]

——— 1984. "Self-Command in Practice, in Policy, and in a Theory of Rational Choice." *American Economic Review,* Papers and Proceedings, 74: 1–11. [§5.19]

Schill, Michael H. 1989. "Intergovernmental Takings and Just Compensation: A Question of Federalism." *University of Pennsylvania Law Review,* 137: 829–901. [§9.7]

Schneider, Mark. 1989. *The Competitive City: The Political Economy of Suburbia.* Pittsburgh: University of Pittsburgh Press. [§7.18]

Schultz, David A. 1992. *Property, Power, and American Democracy.* New Brunswick, N.J.: Transaction Publishers. [§2.6]

Schwartz, Seymour I., David E. Hansen, and Richard Green. 1981. "Suburban Growth Controls and the Price of New Housing." *Journal of Environmental Economics and Management,* 8: 303–320. [§6.3]

——— 1984. "The Effect of Growth Control on the Production of Moderate-Priced Housing." *Land Economics,* 60: 110–114. [§6.3]

Schwartz, Seymour I., and Peter M. Zorn. 1988. "A Critique of Quasiexperimental and Statistical Controls for Measuring Program Effects: Application to Urban Growth Control." *Journal of Policy Analysis and Management,* 7: 491–505. [§6.3]

Schwartz, Seymour I., Peter M. Zorn, and David E. Hansen. 1986. "Research Design Issues and Pitfalls in Growth Control Studies." *Land Economics,* 62: 223–233. [§6.3]

Scully, Gerald W. 1992. *Constitutional Environments and Economic Growth.* Princeton: Princeton University Press. [§3.24]

Segal, David, and Philip Srinivasan. 1985. "The Impact of Suburban Growth Restrictions on U.S. Housing Price Inflation, 1975–1978." *Urban Geography,* 6: 14–26. [§6.10]

Siegan, Bernard H. 1972. *Land Use without Zoning.* Lexington, Mass.: Lexington Books. [§7.15]

——— 1980. *Economic Liberties and the Constitution.* Chicago: University of Chicago Press. [§§3.6, 3.24, 9.20]

Siegel, Stephen A. 1984. "Understanding the *Lochner* Era: Lessons from the Controversy over Railroad and Utility Rate Regulation." *Virginia Law Review,* 70: 187–263. [§8.9]

——— 1986. "Understanding the Nineteenth-Century Contract Clause: The Role of the Property-Privilege Distinction and 'Takings' Clause Jurisprudence." *Southern California Law Review,* 60: 1–108. [§§2.10, 3.2, 7.15]

Simon, Julian L., and Seymour Sudman. 1982. "How Much Farmland Is Being Converted to Urban Use?" *International Regional Science Review,* 7: 257–272. [§8.5]

Simon, William H. 1991. "Social-Republican Property." *UCLA Law Review,* 38: 1335–1413. [§§7.20, 8.18]

Smith, Vernon L. 1991. "Rational Choice: The Contrast between Economics and Psychology." *Journal of Political Economy,* 99: 877–897. [§5.16]

Snitzer, Edward L. 1965. *Pennsylvania Eminent Domain.* Philadelphia: George Bisel. [§5.2]

Snyder, James M., Jr. 1991. "The Dimensions of Constituency Preferences: Voting on California Ballot Propositions, 1974–1990." Working Paper, Department of Economics, University of Chicago. [§9.5]

Sonstelie, Jon C., and Paul R. Portney. 1978. "Profit Maximizing Communities and the Theory of Local Public Expenditures." *Journal of Urban Economics,* 5: 263–277. [§7.2]

———— 1980a. "Gross Rents and Market Values: Testing the Implications of Tiebout's Hypothesis." *Journal of Urban Economics,* 7: 102–118. [§7.1]

———— 1980b. "Take the Money and Run: A Theory of Voting in Local Referenda." *Journal of Urban Economics,* 8: 187–195. [§7.19]

Sterk, Stewart E. 1992. "Competition among Municipalities as a Constraint on Land Use Exactions." *Vanderbilt Law Review,* 45: 831–867. [§3.23]

Stevenson, George E. 1931. *Reflections of an Anthracite Engineer.* New York: private printing. [§§1.5–1.7, 1.16]

Stewart, Richard B. 1990. "Madison's Nightmare." *University of Chicago Law Review,* 57: 335–356. [§3.4]

Stigler, George J. 1971. "The Theory of Economic Regulation." *Bell Journal of Economics,* 2: 3–21. [§5.15]

Stoebuck, William B. 1969. "The Property Right of Access versus the Power of Eminent Domain." *Texas Law Review,* 47: 733–765. [§§2.14, 2.18, 5.4]

———— 1972. "A General Theory of Eminent Domain." *Washington Law Review,* 47: 553–608. [§§2.1, 2.8, 5.2, 5.18]

Stull, William J., and Judith C. Stull. 1991. "Capitalization of Local Income Taxes." *Journal of Urban Economics,* 29: 182–190. [§7.7]

Sunstein, Cass R. 1985. "Interest Groups in American Public Law." *Stanford Law Review,* 38: 29–87. [§7.20]

Swank, William K. 1976. "Note. Inverse Condemnation: The Case for Diminution in Property Values as Compensable Damage." *Stanford Law Review,* 28: 779–804. [§6.7]

Taylor, Herb. 1985. "Time Inconsistency: A Potential Problem for Policymakers." *Business Review of the Federal Reserve Bank of Philadelphia,* March–April, pp. 3–12. [§3.19]

Thaler, Richard. 1990. "Anomalies: Saving, Fungibility, and Mental Accounts." *Journal of Economic Perspectives,* 4: 193–205. [§5.17]

Theobald, Neil D., and Lawrence O. Picus. 1991. "Living with Equal Amounts of Less: Experiences of States with Primarily State-Funded School Systems." *Journal of Education Finance,* 17: 1–6. [§3.11]

Thibodeau, Thomas. 1992. *Residential Real Estate Prices, 1974–1983: From the Standard Metropolitan Statistical Area Annual Housing Surveys.* Mount Pleasant, Mich.: Blackstone. [§6.10]

Thomas, Gordon, and Max Morgan Witts. 1971. *The San Francisco Earthquake.* New York: Stein and Day. [§9.19]

Thompson, Barton H., Jr. 1990. "Judicial Takings." *Virginia Law Review,* 76: 1449–1544. [§9.4]

Tideman, T. Nicolaus. 1982. "A Tax on Land Value *Is* Neutral." *National Tax Journal,* 35: 109–112. [§2.12]

—— 1988. "Takings, Moral Evolution, and Justice." *Columbia Law Review,* 88: 1714–1730. [§4.19]

Tideman, T. Nicolaus, and Gordon Tullock. 1976. "A New and Superior Process for Making Social Choices." *Journal of Political Economy,* 84: 1145–1160. [§2.3]

Tiebout, Charles M. 1956. "A Pure Theory of Local Expenditures." *Journal of Political Economy,* 64: 416–424. [§§7.1–7.8, 7.19]

Treanor, William M. 1985. "The Origins and Original Significance of the Just Compensation Clause of the Fifth Amendment." *Yale Law Journal,* 94: 694–716. [§2.9]

Tribe, Laurence H. 1980. "The Puzzling Persistence of Process-Based Constitutional Theories." *Yale Law Journal,* 89: 1063–1080. [§3.13]

—— 1988. *American Constitutional Law,* 2d ed. Mineola, N.Y.: Foundation Press. [§2.9]

Tullock, Gordon. 1967. "The Welfare Costs of Tariffs, Monopolies, and Theft." *Western Economic Journal* 5: 224–322. [§8.14]

Turner, Margery A. 1990. "Impacts of Rent Control on the Washington, D.C., Housing Market: An Empirical Case Study." *Research in Urban Economics* 8: 135–159. [§8.11]

Tyack, David B. 1968. "The Perils of Pluralism: The Background of the *Pierce* Case." *American Historical Review,* 74: 74–98. [§3.10]

Underkuffler, Laura S. 1990. "On Property: An Essay." *Yale Law Journal,* 100: 127–148. [§3.3]

U.S. Bureau of Mines. 1912. *Mining Conditions under the City of Scranton.* Bulletin no. 25. Washington, D.C.: U.S. Government Printing Office. [§1.5]

U.S. Coal Commission. 1925. *Report of the U.S. Coal Commission, Part II: Anthracite—Detailed Studies.* Washington, D.C.: U.S. Government Printing Office. [§§1.7, 1.15]

U.S. Department of Agriculture, Soil Conservation Service. 1984. *1982 National Resources Inventory.* Washington, D.C.: U.S.D.A. [§§6.17, 8.5]

Venti, Steven F., and David A. Wise. 1990. "Have IRA's Increased U.S. Saving?: Evidence from Consumer Expenditure Surveys." *Quarterly Journal of Economics,* 105: 661–698. [§5.17]

Vitaliano, Donald F., and Constance Hill. 1994. "Agricultural Districts and Farmland Prices." *Journal of Real Estate Finance and Economics,* 8: 213–223. [§8.6]

Warner, Sam Bass. 1962. *Streetcar Suburbs: The Process of Growth in Boston, 1870–1900.* New York: Atheneum. [§§2.17, 7.15]

Weinstein, Michael M. 1981. "Some Macroeconomic Impacts of the National

Industrial Recovery Act, 1933–35." In *The Great Depression Revisited,* ed. Karl Brunner. Boston: Martinus Nijhof. [§3.7]

Wheaton, William C. 1993. "Land Capitalization, Tiebout Mobility, and the Role of Zoning Regulations." *Journal of Urban Economics,* 34: 102–117. [§7.8]

White, James R. 1988. "Large Lot Zoning and Subdivision Costs: A Test." *Journal of Urban Economics* 23: 370–384. [§9.20]

Williams, Joan C. 1986. "The Constitutional Vulnerability of American Local Government: The Politics of City Status in American Law." *Wisconsin Law Review,* 1986: 83–153. [§7.12]

Williams, Norman. 1974. *American Planning Law.* Chicago: Callaghan. [§6.6]

Williams, Norman, Marlin Smith, Charles Siemon, Daniel Mandelker, and Richard Babcock. 1984. "The White River Junction Manifesto." *Vermont Law Review,* 9: 193–245. [§1.20]

Williams, Robert F. 1988. "Evolving State Legislative and Executive Power in the Founding Decade." *The Annals,* 496: 43–53. [§3.4]

Willig, Robert D. 1976. "Consumer's Surplus without Apology." *American Economic Review,* 66: 589–597. [§5.16]

Winter, Ralph K., Jr. 1972. "Poverty, Economic Inequality, and the Equal Protection Clause." *Supreme Court Review,* 1972: 41–102. [§3.11]

Wittman, Donald. 1980. "First Come, First Served: An Economic Analysis of 'Coming to the Nuisance.'" *Journal of Legal Studies,* 9: 557–568. [§§4.2, 4.8]

——— 1984. "Liability for Harm or Restitution for Benefit?" *Journal of Legal Studies,* 13: 57–80. [§9.18]

Wright, Helen S. 1924. *Coal's Worst Year.* Boston: Gorham Press. [§1.4]

Wylie, Jeanie. 1989. *Poletown: Community Betrayed.* Urbana: University of Illinois Press. [§2.6]

Yinger, John, Howard S. Bloom, Axel Borsch-Supan, and Helen F. Ladd. 1988. *Property Taxes and House Values: The Theory and Estimation of Intrajurisdictional Property Tax Capitalization.* Boston: Academic Press. [§§6.1, 7.1]

Zinsmeister, Karl. 1993. "The Environmentalist Assault on Agriculture." *The Public Interest,* 112: 90–98. [§8.5]

Index